MOON HANDBOOKS

CABO

CAPE REGION

MAP SYMBOLS

- ● LODGING
- ■ OTHER LOCATIONS
- ▶ RESTAURANT/BAR
- ★ POINT OF INTEREST
- ▲ Mountain
- ✕ AIRFIELD/AIRSTRIP
- ⛳ GOLF COURSE
- 🏠 PEMEX GAS STATION

Creeks
Lakes
Swamps
Seasonal Lake

- ▬▬▬ · ▬▬▬ NATIONAL BORDER
- ▬▬▬▬▬ LIMITED ACCESS HWY
- ▬▬▬▬▬ MAIN HWY
- ▬▬▬▬▬ OTHER HWY
- ▬ ▬ ▬ DIRT ROAD
- ○ CITIES
- ○ TOWNS/VILLAGES
- ⬒ US HIGHWAYS
- ⬒ MEXICAN FEDERAL HWYS
- ▬▬▬ RAIL ROAD
- ▨ *Public Lands*

Sea of Cortez

Isla Partida
Isla Espíritu Santo

Punta Norte

Isla Cerralvo

Canal de Cerralvo

Punta Arenas de la Ventana
Punta Perico
Ensenada de los Muertos
Bahía de Los Muertos

Bahía de La Ventana

El Sargento
La Ventana

Punta Coyote
Playa Tecolote
Pichilingue

La Paz

11

Bahía de La Paz

San Juan de la Costa

Aguajito

El Porvenir

El Centenario

LA PAZ INTERNATIONAL AIRPORT ✕

Llano de la Paz

Sierra Novillo

San Juan de Los Planes

286

1
19

San Pedro

El Triunfo

1

San Antonio

San Agustín

San Agustin

Punta Conejo
Punta Conejo

Punta Marquez

Aguja

El Chivato

El Tomate

El Rosario

Los Inocentes

Santa Marta

Meliton Albanez

Ejido la Matanza

El Carrizal

La Playita

19

Cardonal
San Bartolo
Punta Pescadero
Los Barriles
Buena Vista
Bahía de Palmas
Punta Colorada
Punta Arena
La Rivera
El Rincón
Cabo Pulmo
Cabo Pulmo
Morro Los Frailes
Bahía de Los Frailes
Punta Boca del Tule

1

Rancho San Dionisio
Santiago
Agua Caliente
Miraflores
Caduaño
Sierra La Trinidad
Los Frailes
Rancho la Vinorama
Río San José
Santa Anita
Río San José
Punta Gorda
La Fortuna
Pueblo la Playa

Picacho de la Laguna ▲

Sierra de la Laguna

Todos Santos
El Pescadero
El Aguaje
Sierra de la Laguna
Santa Rosa
LOS CABOS INTERNATIONAL AIRPORT ✈
San José Viejo
San José del Cabo
Punta Palmilla

Punta Lobos
Playa San Pedro
Playa San Pedrito
Playa Los Cerritos
Playa Gaspareño
Colonia Elias Calles
La Candelaria
Río Candelaria
Bahía Chileno

19

Playa Migriño
Cabo Falso
Cabo San Lucas
Bahía San Lucas
Cabo San Lucas

Bahía San Lucas

PACIFIC   *OCEAN*

10 mi
10 km

0
0

MOON HANDBOOKS

CABO
LA PAZ TO CABO SAN LUCAS
THIRD EDITION

JOE CUMMINGS

**AVALON
TRAVEL**
publishing

MOON HANDBOOKS: CABO
THIRD EDITION

Published by
Avalon Travel Publishing, Inc.
5855 Beaudry St.
Emeryville, CA 94608, USA

Printed by Colorcraft, Ltd.

Please send all comments,
corrections, additions,
amendments, and critiques to:

**MOON HANDBOOKS: CABO
AVALON TRAVEL PUBLISHING, INC.
5855 BEAUDRY ST.
EMERYVILLE, CA 94608, USA**
e-mail: info@travelmatters.com
www.travelmatters.com

Printing History
1st edition—1995
3rd edition—September 2000
5 4 3 2 1 0

ISBN: 1-56691-207-5
ISSN: 1082-5169

Editors: Karen Gaynor Bleske, Valerie Sellers Blanton, Deana Corbitt Shields
Map Editor: Mike Ferguson
Production & Design: Carey Wilson
Cartography: Mark Stroud/Moon Street Cartography
Index: Sondra Nation

Front cover photo: Hotel Hacienda del Mar, by Greg Vaughn/www.GregVaughn.com © 2000

All photos by Joe Cummings unless otherwise noted.
All illustrations by Bob Race unless otherwise noted.

Distributed in the United States and Canada by Publishers Group West
Printed in China

CONTENTS

INTRODUCTION . . . . **1~32**
The Land 1
  Birth of a Peninsula; Geography; The Sea of Cortez
Climate 5
  Hot and Cold; Wet and Dry; Travel Seasons
Flora 8
  Cacti; Agaves; Trees; Herbs
Fauna 12
  Land Mammals; Marine Mammals; Fish; Birds; Reptiles and Amphibians
History 20
  Pre-Cortesian History; The Spanish Conquest of Baja California; The
  Mission Period; Independence from Spain; The 20th Century and
  Beyond
The People 30
  Origins; Language

SPECIAL TOPICS
Baja Island-Hopping . . . . *4*   *Endangered Sea* *15*
Love Herb . . . . *11*   *What's a Gringo?* *32*

ON THE ROAD . . . . **33~98**
  Travel Highlights
Sports and Recreation 34
  Hiking and Backpacking; Fishing; Boating; Sea Kayaking; Windsurfing;
  Surfing; Snorkeling and Scuba Diving
Accommodations 46
  Hotels and Motels; *Casas de Huéspedes* and *Pensiones*; Camping
Food and Drink 50
  Where to Eat; What to Eat; Buying Groceries; Nonalcoholic Beverages;
  Alcoholic Beverages; Cantinas and Bars
Health and Safety 61
  Food and Water; Sunburn and Dehydration; Motion Sickness; Bites and
  Stings; Medical Assistance; Safety
Immigration and Customs 66
  Entry Regulations; Border Crossings; Customs; Legal Matters
Money, Measurements, and Communications 73
  Currency; Changing Money; Money Management; Measurements and
  Standards; Telephone Services; Postal Service
Services and Information 81
  Business Hours; Travel Services; Maps
Getting There 82
  By Air; By Land; By Ferry from Mainland Mexico
Getting Around 88
  By Air; By Bus; Taxi; Cycling; Driving in the Cape Region

SPECIAL TOPICS

World Fishing Records
  Set in Baja 36
Fish Translator 38
Antojitos 52
Cooking Methods 53
The Liquid Heart of Mexico 58-59
Bar Lingo 60

Let's NAFTA 69
Buying or Leasing Property
  in the Cape Region 70-71
Roadside Religion 93
Road Signs 94
Words and Phrases to Know 96

LA PAZ AND VICINITY . . . . 99~133

History; Sights; Hotels; Bed and Breakfast Inns; Apartments, Condos, and Long-Term Rentals; Camping and RV Parks; Food; Entertainment; Events; Shopping; Beaches; Islands; Sports and Recreation; Information and Services; Getting There; Getting Around; Southeast of La Paz

SPECIAL TOPICS

English Pirates on the
  Sea of Cortez 101
The Pearls of La Paz 102

Diving and Snorkeling
  around La Paz 127

CENTRAL CAPE . . . . 134~143

San Pedro to San Bartolo; Santiago; Miraflores; Sierra de La Laguna

EAST CAPE . . . . 144~154

Bahía de Palmas; Punta Pescadero and El Cardonal; Los Barriles; Buena Vista; La Ribera; Around Punta Colorada; El Camino Rural Costero; Cabo Pulmo; Bahía de Los Frailes; South to San José del Cabo

SAN JOSÉ DEL CABO . . . . 155~182

Climate; History; Sights; Accommodations; Food; Entertainment and Events; Shopping; Sports and Recreation; Information and Services; Transportation

The Corridor 174

Beaches and Activities; Hotels; Golf Courses

SPECIAL TOPICS

Legend of the Flame 157   *Beaches along the Corridor* 174

CABO SAN LUCAS . . . . 183~211

Climate; History; Land's End; Beaches; Accommodations; Food; Entertainment and Events; Shopping; Fishing; Diving and Snorkeling; Other Sports and Recreation; Information and Services; Getting There; Getting Around

WEST CAPE . . . . **212~235**
    Cabo Falso to Playa Migriño; La Candelaria; El Pescadero and Vicinity
Todos Santos 220
    Climate; History; Sights; Beaches; Accommodations; Food;
    Entertainment and Events; Sports and Recreation; Shopping; Information
    and Services

SPECIAL TOPIC
    Clayware of Candelaria *214*

RESOURCES . . . . **236~240**
    Booklist 236
    On the Internet 239

GLOSSARY . . . . **241~242**

SPANISH PHRASEBOOK . . . . **243~247**

INDEX . . . . **248~258**
    Accommodations 248
    Restaurants 249
    General Index 251

MAPS

COLOR SUPPLEMENT

Cape Region . . . . ii-iii

INTRODUCTION

Amerindians of Baja California 20
Sebastián Vizcaíno Expeditions 24
Cape Missions. 25

LA PAZ AND VICINITY

La Paz 104
Downtown La Paz 105
Beaches and Islands near La Paz 119
Isla Espíritu, Isla Partida,
    and Los Islotes 121
Isla San José. 123

CENTRAL CAPE

Santiago to Miraflores 137
Sierra de La Laguna Hiking Trails 141

CABO SAN LUCAS

San José del Cabo 156
Downtown San José. 158
La Playita/Pueblo La Playa 159
The Corridor 176
Cabo San Lucas 185

WEST CAPE

El Pescadero to Todos Santos 218
Todos Santos 223

ABBREVIATIONS

a/c—air-conditioned, air
    conditioning
ATV—all-terrain vehicle
Av.—Avenida
Blvd.—Boulevard
C—Celsius
cm—centimeter(s)
Col.—*Colonia* (neighborhood)
COTP—Captain of the Port
d—double occupancy
F—Fahrenheit
4WD—four-wheel drive
IDD—international direct dial

kg—kilogram(s)
km—kilometer(s)
kph—kilometers per hour
mph—miles per hour
nte.—*norte* (north)
ote.—*oriente* (east)
PADI—Professional
    Association of Dive
    Instructors
pte.—*poniente* (west)
q—quadruple occupancy
RV—recreational vehicle
s—single occupancy

s/n—*sin número* ("without
    number," used for street
    addresses without building
    numbers)
t—triple occupancy
tel.—telephone number
WW II—World War II

(Also see the Glossary for
    definitions of Mexican
    acronyms such as
    CONASUPO and FONATUR.)

ACKNOWLEDGMENTS

THE AUTHOR WISHES TO THANK the following people for their assistance in updating this guide: Arlaine Cervantes, Lynne Cummings, Jennifer Deaville, Howard Ekman, Uguet Hidalgo, Janet Howey, Tim Means, Elena Moreno, Martín Verdugo, and Rosamaría Zaragoza.

KEEPING CURRENT

Since this book went to press, hotels have opened and closed, restaurants have changed hands, and roads have been repaired or fallen into disrepair. Also, prices have probably increased; therefore, all prices herein should be regarded as approximations and are not guaranteed by the publisher or author.

We want to keep this book as accurate and up to date as possible and would appreciate hearing about any errors or omissions you encounter while using *Cabo Handbook*.

If you have any noteworthy experiences (good or bad) with establishments listed in this book, please pass them along to us. If something is out of place on a map, tell us; if the best restaurant in town is not included, we'd like to know. Found a new route across the sierra? Share it with other Cape Region travelers. All contributions will be deeply appreciated and properly acknowledged. Address your letters to:

Joe Cummings
Moon Handbooks: Cabo
Avalon Travel Publishing
5855 Beaudry St.
Emeryville, CA 94608
USA
e-mail: info@travelmatters.com
　　　(Please put Moon Handbooks: Cabo in subject line.)

ACCOMMODATIONS PRICE KEY

Shoestring	under US$15
Budget	US$15-35
Inexpensive	US$36-55
Moderate	US$56-80
Expensive	US$81-120
Premium	US$120+

INTRODUCTION

With its crystalline shores embracing verdant mountains, the Cape Region of Baja California Sur resembles a diamond-and-emerald pendant floating on azure seas. This once-remote corner of the Mexican republic offers striking tropical-desert scenery, uncommon wildlife, pristine beaches, friendly residents, and some of the world's best sportfishing. Add a highly favorable year-round climate and you've got one of Mexico's most reliable yet relatively little-known travel experiences.

Los Cabos—the area extending from San José del Cabo to Cabo San Lucas—is currently the seventh most popular tourist destination in Mexico and the second fastest-growing resort area in the country. Elsewhere in the Cape Region, historic mining and farming towns, the colorful waterfront state capital of La Paz, the interior sierras, and many miles of undeveloped beach on both sides of the peninsula receive but a trickle of visitors, many of them annual returnees for whom Cape explorations have become a pleasurable obsession.

THE LAND

BIRTH OF A PENINSULA

Baja California's Cape Region lies at the tip of the world's fourth-longest peninsula (after the Kamchatka, Malay, and Antarctic). Today the peninsula is separated from mainland Mexico by roughly 250 km of ocean at the widest gap, but it wasn't always so. At one time Baja's entire length was attached to a broad tropical plain along Mexico's Pacific coast. The 23-ton duck-billed hadrosaur roamed the region (its fossilized bones have been found near El Rosario), as did mammoth, bison, hyracotherium (a fox-sized primitive horse), and camel. The peninsula's eventual divergence from the mainland came about as a result of the continual shifting of massive sections of the earth's surface, a process known as plate tectonics.

Like much of coastal California to the north, Baja California is part of the North Pacific Plate, while the rest of the North American continent belongs to the North American Plate. The boundary line between these two plates is the San Andreas Fault, which extends northwest through the center of Mexico's Sea of Cortez and into California, where it parallels the coast on a southeast-northwest axis before veering off into the Pacific Ocean near San Francisco. The North Pacific and North American plates have shifted along this gap for millions of years, with the Pacific plate moving in a northwesterly direction at a current rate of about one to two inches a year.

This movement eventually tore basins in the earth's crust, which allowed the Sea of Cortez to form, thus separating the land area west of the fault zone from land to the east. At one time the Sea of Cortez extended as far north as Palm Springs, California; the sea would have continued moving northward at a gradual pace had it not met with the Colorado River. Silting in the Colorado River delta reversed the northward movement of the basins, holding the northern limit of the Sea of Cortez at a point well below what is now the U.S.-Mexican border. Cut off by delta sedimentation, California's Salton Sea is a remnant of the northernmost extension of the Sea of Cortez.

As the peninsula moved slowly northwestward (257 km from the mainland by the time the Sea of Cortez became a stable feature—about five million years ago), the coastal plains tipped toward the west, creating a series of fault-block mountain ranges that include one of the Cape Region's most outstanding topographic features, the Sierra de La Laguna.

GEOGRAPHY

In many ways, Baja California's Cape Region boasts the peninsula's most distinctive geography. The area receives substantially more rainfall than any other part of Baja, save the Californian Region in the northeast. The Sierra de La Laguna—a topographic anomaly among Baja's mountain ranges (see Mountains, below)—catches most of this rainfall, so the highlands here are more lushly vegetated than in the sierras to the north, while the coastal lowlands remain fairly dry for beachgoing tourists. And unlike the rest of the peninsula, about a fourth of the Cape Region falls below the Tropic of Cancer. The combination of tropical latitude with moist uplands and dry coastal areas has created two unique biomes in the region—the Cape Oak-Piñon Woodlands and the Cape Arid Tropical Forest—both of which are discussed below.

Mountains

Baja California's mountain ranges, or sierras, run down the center of the peninsula from northwest to southeast—a continuation of a mountain system that stretches southward from Alaska's Aleutian Islands to the spectacular rock formations at Cabo San Lucas. Because of the way the underground fault blocks tipped to create these sierras, the mountains tend to slope gradually toward the west and fall off more dramatically toward the east. The Cape Region's Sierra de La Laguna is an exception; it tips eastward so that its steepest slopes face west. It's also the only granitic fault-block range on the southern half of the peninsula—the others are volcanic.

The Sierra de La Laguna has been called an "island in the sky" because of its remarkable isolation from the Central Desert to the north and the Gulf Coast Desert to the east. Up to 100 cm (40 inches) of rain falls annually on the peaks

Estero San José

here, helping to support a unique ecosystem—the **Cape Oak-Piñon Woodlands.** These high-altitude woodlands harbor extensive stands of **Mexican piñon pine, madroño,** and *palmita.* Lower down, abundant runoff sustains communities on either side of the range. Substantial underground springs supply water for orchards near the pueblos of Todos Santos, El Triunfo, and San Antonio. The western escarpment, facing the Pacific Ocean, is dissected by stream-eroded canyons and *arroyos* (streambeds) that are dry most of the year. But the arroyos on the eastern slopes are filled with water much of the year, enabling the areas around Miraflores, Santiago, and San Bartolo to support fruit and vegetable farming.

Deserts

About 25% of the Cape Region's land area can be classified as desert, averaging less than 25 cm (10 inches) of rain per year. The Cape's desertlands belong to the Sonoran Desert, which extends across northwestern Mexico into parts of southeastern California and southern Arizona. But any visitor who has previously traveled in other parts of the Sonoran Desert will note many subtle differences on the Cape. Because of the Cape's mountainous interior and the marine environment that surrounds it on three sides, the aridity of any given area can vary considerably. As a result, the Cape's desertlands belong to a subclassification of the Sonoran Desert known as the **Gulf Coast Desert.** This narrow subregion stretches along the Sea of Cortez from just below Bahía de los Angeles to the tip of the peninsula near San José del Cabo.

On average, the elevation is substantially higher here (with peaks up to 1,500 meters) than in the deserts to the north, and the terrain is marked by several broken sierras of granitic and volcanic rock. These sierras contain numerous arroyos and a few perennial streams that allow for sustainable farming.

The southern reaches of the Gulf Coast Desert receive a bit of extra precipitation from the occasional tropical storm that blows in from the south. As a result of the added moisture and elevation, many more trees and flowering cacti are found here than in other Baja deserts. Sea of Cortez islands feature similar terrain, although the endemic vegetation varies from island to island.

Cape Arid Tropical Forest

The coastal areas of the Cape Region as well as the lower slopes of the Laguna and Giganta mountain ranges share characteristics typical of both tropical and arid biomes, hence the seemingly oxymoronic term "arid tropical forest." Like tropical forests worldwide, the lower Cape forests produce trees, shrubs, and undergrowth of varying heights that create a canopied effect. Mixed with this tangled growth are a profusion of succulents more associated with arid climes, including the **cardón-barbón,** a shorter cousin of the towering cardón found throughout Baja's deserts.

Much of the vegetation in the Cape Arid Tropical Forest is normally associated with the tropical thorn forests of coastal Colima and Guerrero on the Mexican mainland. Prominent marker plants unique to the Cape subregion include the **Tlaco palm, wild fig** *(zalate),* **wild plum** *(ciruelo),* *mauto,* and the alleged aphrodisiac herb **damiana.**

Coastal Wetlands Region

Wetland pockets lie in shallow areas along bays and lagoons in numerous spots along the Cape coast. They usually consist of **saltmarshes,** which contain high concentrations of salt-tolerant plants such as cordgrass, eelgrass, saltwort, and salt cedar; or **mangrove forests,** containing

red mangrove

one or more of the five species of mangrove *(mangle)* common in Baja. Within any given wetland, the water level, salinity, and temperature can vary considerably; hence, an extensive variety of plants and animals can adapt to wetland areas. Because of this environmental variation, saltmarshes and mangrove wetlands support the highest biomass concentrations on the planet. For most visitors, the main attraction of the wetlands is the abundance of waterfowl.

Areas with substantial wetlands in the Cape Region include Bahía de La Paz (mangrove forests), Todos Santos (mixed saltwater/freshwater estuarine marshes), and Estero San José (mixed saltwater/freshwater estuarine marshes).

Islands

Most of the islands and islets surrounding the Baja California peninsula are found on the Sea of Cortez side; among the largest are Isla Espíritu Santo and Isla Cerralvo near La Paz. Many of these islands were created as the peninsula broke away from mainland Mexico and hence are "land-bridge" or "continental" islands rather than true oceanic islands. The islands are arid—their low elevation doesn't allow them to snag much of the rain that moves up from the south in summer. But because of their isolation, the Cortez islands feature a high number of endemic plant and animal species; at least half of the 120 cactus varieties found on the islands are endemic.

THE SEA OF CORTEZ

The Sea of Cortez was apparently named by Spanish sea captain Francisco de Ulloa, who sailed its entire perimeter 1539-40 at the command of the most infamous of all Spanish conquistadors, Hernán Cortés. Four years previ-

BAJA ISLAND-HOPPING

Visitors intent on setting foot on the delicate islands of the Sea of Cortez should heed the recommendations proffered by Conservation International Mexico, as follows:

- Check your equipment and provisions thoroughly before landing to avoid the introduction of rats, mice, insects, or seeds from other islands or from the mainland. Check your shoes and cuffs.

- Don't bring cats, dogs, or any other animals to the islands.

- Don't take plants, flowers, shells, rocks, or animals from the island.

- The animals and plants that live on the islands are not used to human presence. Keep this in mind during your visit.

- Keep a minimum distance of 45 meters (150 feet) from all sea bird and sea lion colonies, and keep at least 300 meters away from pelicans during their nesting period (April-May).

- Don't cut cacti or shrubs. Don't gather wood; plants take a long time to grow on these arid islands. Dry trunks are the home of many small animals. If you need to cook, take your own stove, and avoid making fires.

- Don't make new walking paths. Don't remove stones or dig holes; you will be causing erosion.

- Human waste and toilet paper take a long time to decompose on the islands. Go to the bathroom in the water and burn your toilet paper very carefully, or use smooth stones . . . be creative.

- Don't camp on the island unless you know low impact techniques. Conservation International Mexico can provide you with that information.

- Help keep the islands clean. Don't throw or leave garbage on the islands or in the sea. Help even more by bringing back any garbage you find.

- To camp or even land for any activity on the islands of the Sea of Cortez you need a permit from the Secretaría del Medio Ambiente, Recursos Naturales y Pesca (SEMARNAP). To obtain a permit, contact Instituto Nacional de Ecología, Dirección de Aprovechamiento Ecológico, Av. Revolución 1425, Tlacopac, San Angel, México D.F. 01049, México.

For more information, contact Conservation International Mexico, Calle Miramar 59-A, Col. Miramar, Guaymas, Son. 85450, México, tel. (6) 221-0194, fax (6) 221-2030, e-mail CI-Guaymas@conservation.org.

ously Cortés had himself sailed the sea in an aborted attempt to colonize the peninsula. After de Ulloa's voyage, the name Mar de Cortés appeared intermittently on maps of the region, alternating with Mar Vermejo ("Vermillion Sea," in reference to the color reflected from huge numbers of pelagic crabs). The Mexican government officially renamed it the Gulf of California (Golfo de California) early in the 20th century. Sailors, writers, and other assorted romantics, however, have continued to call it by its older name.

The sea is roughly 1,125 km (700 miles) long, with an average width of 150 km (93 miles). Its sea-bottom profile is one of the sheerest in the world; underwater valleys and canyons run its entire length, forming abysses that reach depths of up to 3.4 km (2.1 miles). This abrupt relief causes some of the world's largest tidal margins, particularly in the north near the mouth of the Colorado River.

Oceanographers have divided the Sea of Cortez into four regions based on the prominent characteristics—depth, bottom contours, and marine productivity—of each zone. The northern quarter of the gulf, between the Colorado River delta and the Midriff Islands, is shallow in relation to the zones farther south because of silt deposited by the Colorado River. The silt has also rounded the bottom contours. The tidal range in this zone is up to 10 vertical meters (33 vertical feet), and the seawater's saline content is very high due to evaporation. Before the damming of the Colorado River, the bore created when the seaward river currents met the incoming tide was powerful enough to sink ships.

The next zone farther south encompasses the Midriff Islands, where basins reach depths of 820 meters (2,700 feet). Strong currents here bring nutrients up from the bottom while aerating the water. This leads to an unusually high level of biological productivity, otherwise known as "good fishin'."

From the Midriff Islands to La Paz, basin depth doubles, silting is minimal, and water temperatures begin decreasing dramatically. The final sea zone below La Paz is oceanic, with trenches and submarine canyons over 3,650 meters (12,000 feet) deep. Around the tip of the cape, the Sea of Cortez meets the Pacific Ocean and their respective currents battle, producing some wicked riptides. This means that although the tip of the cape is the warmest area on the peninsula during the winter months, beach swimming can be treacherous.

The Sea of Cortez is biologically the richest body of water on the planet, supporting over 900 species of marine vertebrates and over 2,000 invertebrates at last count. The reported number rises with the publication of each new marine study. Scripps Institution of Oceanography in San Diego, California, has pronounced the Cortez "one of the most productive and diverse marine nurseries on Earth," while at the same time recognizing that greedy commercial interests may be devastating the natural balance in the Cortez through overfishing.

CLIMATE

In satellite photographs of the North American continent snapped a hundred miles above the earth, Baja's Cape Region invariably jumps off the plate. The rest of the continent north and east may be obscured by whorls of clouds while the shores, plains, and mountains of the Cape are carved into the photographic image, remarkably clear. The chances of a day without rain in the winter are 95% in Baja, beating out Hawaii's 84% and Florida's 87%.

How does the Cape Region get so much sunshine? The simple answer is that it's positioned almost out of reach of the major weather systems that influence climate in western North America. Northwesterly storms from Eurasia and the Arctic bring rain and snow to the American Northwest and Midwest all winter long, while tropical storms roll across the South Pacific from Asia, dumping loads of rainfall along the lower Mexican coast and Central America in summer.

The Cape is only slightly affected by the outer edges of these systems. Anchored between the warm, fish-filled waters of the Sea of Cortez and the heaving Pacific Ocean, bisected by plains and mountains, the Cape's isolated ecosystems range in climate from Mediterranean to desert to tropical. In some areas, overlapping microclimates defy classification, combining elements of semiarid, arid, subtropical, and tropical climes.

HOT AND COLD

Three variables influence temperatures at any given Cape location: elevation, latitude, and longitude. In plain talk, that means the higher you climb, the cooler it gets; the farther south you go, the warmer it gets; and it's always cooler on the Pacific side of the peninsula and warmer on the Sea of Cortez side. The Tropic of Cancer (approximate latitude 23.5° N) slices across the Cape Region from Todos Santos on the west coast, through Santiago in the interior, to the East Cape south of Bahía de Palmas. Tropical temperatures are thus the norm throughout the Cape except in the high sierra.

Pacific Coast

Because of prevailing ocean currents, the Pacific coast of the Cape shows the least overall variation in temperatures, staying relatively balmy year-round. From March to July, the California Current flows southward along the coast, bringing cooler temperatures from the north that moderate seasonal atmospheric warming, while in December and January the coast is warmed by the northward movement of the Davidson Current. These seasonal currents stabilize the air tem-

peratures so that Cabo San Lucas, for example, averages 18° C (64° F) in January and 29° C (84° F) in August, a range of only 11° C (20° F).

In winter, the West Cape and Cabo San Lucas usually enjoy the warmest temperatures of any coastal area in the Cape Region because of their relative protection from cool northern winds.

Sea of Cortez

The Sea of Cortez has its own set of currents—sometimes lumped together as the Gulf Current—that are fed by tropical waters of the South Pacific. The waters travel in a counterclockwise direction north along the mainland's upper Pacific coast and then south along the peninsular coast. As a result, the Sea of Cortez enjoys an average annual surface temperature of 24° C (75° F), significantly warmer than the Pacific's 18° C (64° F). The high rate of evaporation at the north end of the sea also contributes to warmer air temperatures; this combination of warm air and water temperatures means the Sea of Cortez can be classified as "tropical" over its entire length.

The weather along the East Cape is warm and sunny all winter long with average January temperatures around 23° C (74° F). In August, temperatures average 31° C (88° F) in San José del Cabo, although daily high figures in summer can easily reach 38° C (100° F) or more.

Winters on the Sea of Cortez coast can be cooler than you might suspect, due to the coastline's relatively open exposure to northeastern

Playa Sirenita,
East Cape

winds. In La Paz and the East Cape, for example, it's not unusual for nighttime temperatures in January and February to drop as low as 14° C (57° F). At the same time, the Pacific coastline directly opposite may be as much as 5° C (10° F) warmer, especially along the West Cape. Cabo San Lucas has the warmest overall winter temperatures of any coastal location in the region.

The Corridor

What's the weather like in between? Geographers officially place the boundary between the Pacific Ocean and the Sea of Cortez at Land's End, the rock formation near the entrance of Bahía San Lucas, Cabo San Lucas. But the area stretching along the tip of the Cape from Cabo San Lucas to San José del Cabo—known in the tourist industry as the "Corridor" (*Corredor Náutico* or "nautical corridor" in local Spanish)—mingles both Pacific and Cortez influences to create a microclimate that's warmer than Pacific locations yet cooler than Cortez areas. Overall, however, temperatures along the Corridor tend to be more in line with southern Sea of Cortez zones.

Chubascos, Coromuels, Cordonazos

Monthly average wind velocities for Baja California as a whole are moderate. From mid-May to mid-November, however, tropical storms from the south or east, known as *chubascos,* can bring high winds and rain to the coasts of the Cape Region. Although they usually blow over quickly, local mythology has it that if a *chubasco* lasts more than three hours, it will last a day; if it lasts more than a day, it will last three days; and if more than three days, it'll be a five-day blow.

Occasionally these storms will escalate into hurricanes, which are much less frequent here than in the Gulf of Mexico and Caribbean. In 1997 two such storms passed near the west coast of Baja, neither doing much damage; that same year the Gulf of Mexico saw around a dozen hurricanes. Back in 1993, however, a *chubasco* caused major damage and loss of life along the Sea of Cortez coast between Cabo San Lucas and San José del Cabo (the area of the Cape Region most exposed to tropical storms).

Another Sea of Cortez weather pattern is the *cordonazo,* a small but fierce summer storm that originates locally and is usually spent within a few hours. A more welcome weather phenomenon is

the *coromuel* of Bahía de La Paz, a stiff afternoon breeze that blows from offshore during the hot summer and early fall months. This wind was named for English Lord Protector Oliver Cromwell, identified with English pirates who took advantage of the wind's regular occurrence for the plunder of ships trapped in the bay.

WET AND DRY

The "Land of Little Rain," as Baja has been called, isn't unique in its aridity, since most of the earth's desert areas are found at latitudes between 15° and 30° either north or south of the equator; Baja is positioned roughly between 23° N and 31° N. Global convection currents in the atmosphere create a more or less permanent high-pressure shield over these zones, insulating them from the low-pressure fronts that bring rain clouds.

Rainfall in the Cape Region varies from under 25 cm (10 inches) per year in the driest areas east of the Sierra de La Laguna (from San José del Cabo north to La Paz) to upwards of 100 cm (40 inches) in the interior of the Sierra de La Laguna.

Variation in rainfall also occurs on a seasonal basis. In the Cape Region, rain usually arrives Aug.-Nov., peaking at an average of 5.8 cm in September for Cabo San Lucas and La Paz. Since mountain peaks trap rain clouds, the Cape's higher elevations invariably receive more rain than the low-lying coastal zones.

TRAVEL SEASONS

The flat end of the peninsula from San José del Cabo to Cabo San Lucas is warm year-round. Pacific influences generally moderate the heat July-Sept., while the tropic waters of the Gulf Current make this stretch the warmest coastal zone on the peninsula during winter months. Except for the occasional *chubasco* in late summer, the climate seems nearly perfect here, which is why "Los Cabos" has become such a popular vacation destination. Cabo San Lucas receives about 45% of its measurable annual rainfall—a total of 15-18 cm a year—in September, so if there's a month to avoid for weather reasons, that's the one.

August and September may also be uncomfortably warm for visitors from Northern California, the northwestern U.S. states, or Canada, though for most U.S. residents it's no worse than summers back home. Todos Santos over on the West Cape's Pacific coastline is considerably cooler than Cabo San Lucas in the summer, and Cabo San Lucas is usually cooler than San José del Cabo or La Paz.

The two months when you're least likely to have Los Cabos beaches to yourself are December and January, when large numbers of gringos come here seeking respite from rainstorms and blizzards.

FLORA

A thorough examination of all the plants and creatures of interest in the Cape Region might take volumes. The following sections cover some of either the most remarkable or most common forms of Cape plantlife. The complex interconnecting ecosystems of the peninsula and its islands hold a high number of unique species and remain relatively unexplored by biologists. Several botanists, marine biologists, zoologists, and paleontologists have undertaken solo research in the area, but only in the last five years has the first interdisciplinary team, sponsored by a Canadian university, begun studying the region.

CACTI

Cardón

One of the most common cacti throughout Baja, including the Cape Region, is the towering cardón *(Pachycereus pringlei),* the world's tallest cactus. Individuals can reach as high as 18 meters (60 feet) or more and weigh 12 tons, not counting the root system, which can spread up to 50 meters (150 feet) in diameter. More commonly they top out at seven to nine meters. The giant, pale green trunks feature 11-17 vertical ribs and may measure one meter thick. Some cardón live over 400 years.

The cardón is often confused with the smaller saguaro cactus of Sonora and Arizona; one major difference is that the branches of the cardón tend to be more vertical than those of the saguaro. The hardwood cores of cardón columns have been used by *bajacalifornianos* for centuries as building beams and fence posts. Among Mexicans, a cardón forest is called a *cardonal.*

Biznaga

Another extremely common and highly visible cactus is the *biznaga* or barrel cactus (genus *Ferocactus).* At least a dozen species—most of them endemic—grow in the Cape Region. The cactus's English name refers to its shape, which is short and squat like a barrel. Most common varieties reach about waist-high. One variety, however, *Ferocactus diguettii,* easily reaches four meters (13 feet) in height and a meter (3.28 feet) in diameter. It grows only on a few Sea of Cortez islands and sports red-tinged spines and, in spring, gorgeous yellow to red flowers.

The Amerindians of Baja California Sur reportedly used hollowed-out *biznagas* as Dutch ovens, inserting food into the cavity along with heated stones, then sealing the cactus off till the

barrel cactus

food was cooked. The sturdy, curved spines also served as fishhooks on native fishing expeditions.

Pitahaya

Among Baja's original populations, another important cactus was the *pitahaya dulce,* known among Anglos as organ pipe cactus. It has slender, vertical ribs that grow in clusters, and its spiny, orange-size fruit contains a sweet, juicy, pleasant-tasting pulp the color of red watermelon. According to accounts of Spanish missionaries, the Pericú Amerindians based their yearly calendar on the ripening of the fruit in late summer and early fall. During this season, the Amerindians engaged in a veritable fruit orgy, gorging themselves on the pulp until they fell asleep, then waking to begin eating again. The early Spanish explorers took the fruit along on long sea journeys—its vitamin C content helped to prevent scurvy.

The *pitahaya dulce* is commonly found in Baja California south of the Sierra de San Borja and on several Sea of Cortez islands. A similar species, *pitahaya agria* (*agria* means sour in Spanish; *dulce* is sweet), branches more densely and lower to the ground, hence its English name **galloping cactus.** It grows throughout the peninsula and on most Sea of Cortez islands. The fruit of the *pitahaya agria* is similar in appearance to that of the *pitahaya dulce* but, as implied by the Spanish name, it's less sweet, more acidic. Both types of pitahaya fruit remain popular among Cape residents and travelers; the sweet ones ripen in July.

Opuntia

Another cactus variety well represented throughout Baja is the genus *Opuntia,* which includes all types known as **cholla,** as well as the **nopal,** or **prickly pear.** Chollas are a bane to hikers because they're so prolific and densely covered with spines. A typical branch looks somewhat like braided or twisted rope. The cholla historically has had few domestic uses, although a tea made from the roots of the fuzzy-looking **teddy-bear cholla** (also called "jumping cholla" for its propensity to cling to the lower legs of hikers) is reportedly used by the Seri Amerindians as a diuretic.

In contrast, the much-loved prickly pear has broad, flat stems and branches and a sparser distribution of spines. In Northern Mexico and Baja its fleshy pads are a dietary staple. The most highly prized parts of the nopal are the young stem shoots, called *nopalitos,* and the ripe fruits, dubbed *tuna.* The flavor of the pads is a bit bland, like a cross between bell pepper and okra. The fruit, on the other hand, is juicy and sweet, and available in season in many Baja markets. If you want to taste it in the wild, remove the *tunas* carefully, cut them lengthwise with a sharp knife, and scoop out the insides with a spoon.

AGAVES

Several species of the sizable agave family are native to the Cape Region. All have long, spine-edged leaves, as well as flowers that bloom on tall stalks.

Yucca

One of the most common and striking desert plants is the yucca, which appears in several varieties throughout the Cape Region. The **tree**

yucca

yucca, called *datilillo* or "little date" for its resemblance to a date palm, is the largest of the agaves. *Datilillos* grow in clusters three to seven meters tall, their daggerlike blades supported by long woody trunks. This endemic is found throughout the plains and chaparral subregions on the peninsula's Pacific side—just about anywhere except in the mountains.

Yuccas are extremely useful plants for rural *bajacalifornianos.* The fruit and flowers are edible (a candy called *colache* is made from the cooked flower buds), the roots can be boiled to make soap or leather softener, and the tough leaf fibers are used to make cordage, sandals, baskets, and mats.

Maguey

Also common are the many varieties of maguey, or century plant. The maguey has broad, closely clustered leaves that grow at ground level without a visible trunk. In most species, the plant flowers only once in its lifetime, sending up a tall, slender stalk after maturation—typically at 5-20 years, depending on variety and locale. Early Anglo settlers in the southwestern U.S. spread the myth that magueys bloomed only once in a hundred years, hence the fanciful name "century plant."

The maguey was an important food source for certain aboriginal populations, who harvested the plant just before it bloomed (when it's full of concentrated nutrients). Trimmed of its leaves, the heart of the plant was baked in an underground pit for one to three days, then eaten or stored. Some ranchers still prepare it in this manner today. As with *datilillo,* the leaf fibers are used as cordage for weaving various household goods.

Sotol

Sotol is similar to yucca, but its leaves are narrower and softer. Some sotols produce long flower stalks like those of the century plant, though the flower buds occur along the stalk's entire length instead of only at the top.

One spectacular variety of sotol native to the Cape Region's higher elevations is the endemic *Nolina beldingii,* sometimes

Tlaco palm

called *palmita* because of its resemblance to a small palm tree. *Palmitas,* whose flower stalks can reach seven meters in height, grow clusters of thick leaves branching from their short, woody trunks.

TREES

Palms

Five varieties of palm grow wild in the Cape Region; three are native, while two are introduced species. Palms are important to the local economy of the peninsula's southern half, where they're most common. The long, straight trunks are used as roof beams, the leaves are used in basketry and for *palapa* roof and wall thatching, and the fruits provide a source of nutrition.

Among the most handsome Baja palm trees is the endemic **Tlaco palm** (also called "taco palm," *palma palmía,* and *palma colorado*), common in the canyons and arroyos of the Cape Region mountains. The smooth, slender trunks, crowned by fan-shaped leaves, stand up to 20 meters (65 feet) tall. Its durable trunk has long been valued for house construction. A closely related species, the aptly named **Guadalupe Island palm,** is native to Isla Guadalupe; its self-shedding trunk leaves little or no shag, which has made the tree popular as a cultivated palm.

Baja's tallest palm variety is the endemic **Mexican fan palm** (also called Baja California fan palm, skyduster, or *palma blanca*), which reaches heights of 27-30 meters (90-100 feet). As the name implies, its leaves are fan-shaped. Although it's not as durable as the Tlaco palm, the long trunk makes the tree useful for local construction. The fan palm's native habitats are north of the Cape Region in the Sierra de la Giganta and on Isla Ángel de la Guarda, but it is used as an ornamental throughout Baja.

Two palm varieties were imported to Baja for their fruit value. The **date palm** was introduced to Baja by Jesuit missionaries and is now common near former mission sites, including San José del Cabo. The tree typically reaches 15-20 meters tall at maturity; its oblong fruit grows beneath feather-shaped leaves in large clusters, turning from pale yellow to dark brown as it ripens. Baja dates are eaten locally and shipped to mainland Mexico but are generally not considered of high enough quality for export. The 30-meter, feather-leafed **coconut palm** commonly grows along coastal areas of the Cape Region and is an important local food source.

Oaks and Pines

Tens of thousands of visitors drape themselves along Cape Region beaches every year without any inkling that in the Sierra de La Laguna mountains rising behind the coastal plains stands one of Mexico's most remarkable relic piñon–live oak woodlands. Two endemic species of oak *(encino)* found in the sierra include the **cape oak,** usually seen growing in higher canyons and arroyos, and the **black oak,** confined to the Cape Region's lower slopes.

The **Mexican piñon pine** (known as *pino piñonero* in Mexico) grows profusely at higher elevations in the Sierra de La Laguna, where the wood is a commonly used building material and the nuts are sometimes gathered for food.

Mimosas

This subfamily of the Leguminosae or pea family includes dozens of genera common to arid and semiarid zones worldwide. Characterized by linear seedpods and double rows of tiny leaves, common varieties in the Cape Region include the **mesquite** and various endemic kinds of **acacia.**

Amerindians have long used the trunk, roots, leaves, beans, and bark of the mesquite tree for a variety of purposes, from lumber to medicine. Ground mesquite leaves mixed with water form a balm for sore eyes, a remedy still used by *curanderos* (healers) in rural Mexico today. Chewing the leaves relieves toothache. And mesquite gum has been used as a balm for wounds, a ceramic glue, dye, and digestive.

Mesquite beans are a good source of nutrition—a ripe bean pod, growing as long as nine inches, contains roughly 30% glucose and is high in protein. Many animals and birds savor the beans; horses will eat them until they're sick. Rural Mexicans grind the dried pods into a flour, with which they make bread and a kind of beer. The Seri Amerindians, who live along the Sono-

LOVE HERB

Probably the most well-known herb native to Baja's Cape Region is **damiana** *(Turnera diffusa),* a small shrub with bright, five-petaled yellow or golden flowers. The plant's aphrodisiac properties are its main claim to fame; these are often derided as nonsense by self-appointed Baja analysts. But according to botanist Norman C. Roberts, damiana "stimulates the genito-urinary tract and is used in the treatment of sexual problems such as impotence, frigidity, sterility, and sexual exhaustion." The herb is also used as a sedative and diuretic.

Damiana grows most commonly in rocky areas of the Cape Region but is also found as far away as Sonora, Texas, and the West Indies. The herb is most commonly ingested in sweetened tea made from the leaves or in a liqueur containing damiana extract. In resort areas a "Baja margarita" substitutes damiana liqueur for triple sec.

KAREN McKINLEY

ran coast of the Sea of Cortez, have separate names for eight different stages of the bean pod's development.

One of the prettiest endemic mimosas is the **palo blanco,** which has a tall, slender trunk with silver-white bark and a feathery crown that produces small, white, fragrant blossoms March-May. *Bajacalifornianos* use the bark of the palo blanco to tan leather; at the end of the 19th century the main industry at Cabo San Lucas was the shipping of palo blanco bark to San Francisco tanneries.

Wild Figs
Three types of wild fig trees *(zalates),* one endemic, are common in the Cape Region's rocky areas. In the village of Pueblo La Playa, east of San José del Cabo, stands a vintage collection of *zalates* of impressive stature.

Cottonwoods and Willows
Various cottonwoods *(alamos)* and willows *(sauces)* grow at higher elevations throughout the Cape Region. The *huerivo* or *güeribo (Populus brandegeei)* is a beautiful endemic cottonwood found in sierran canyons and arroyos. Its tall, straight trunk reaches heights of 30 meters and is a highly valued source of lumber for building construction and furniture-making.

HERBS

Baja's most famous herb is the reputed aphrodisiac **damiana** (see the special topic Love Herb).

Another psychoactive plant found in Baja is **datura** or **jimsonweed** *(toloache).* A member of the potato family—a group that also includes nightshade and tobacco—jimsonweed produces large, fragrant, trumpet-shaped flowers that open in the evening and close by noon the following day. According to one folk remedy, the flowers will relieve insomnia if placed beside the pillow at night. All parts of the plant are considered toxic; in certain Yaqui Indian ceremonies, the seeds are eaten for their hallucinatory effect. Datura grows in abundance on rocky and sandy soils below 800 meters (2,600 feet) throughout the peninsula and on some Sea of Cortez islands.

FAUNA

LAND MAMMALS

One of the most widespread carnivores on the peninsula as well as on some Sea of Cortez islands is the **coyote,** which seems to be able to adapt itself equally well to mountain, desert, and coastal terrains. Anyone venturing into the interior of the peninsula is virtually guaranteed to spot at least one. In some areas they don't seem particularly afraid of humans, although they always maintain a distance of at least 15 meters between themselves and larger mammals. A coyote will sometimes fish for crab, placing a furry tail in the water, waiting for a crab to grab on, and then, with a flick of the tail, tossing the crab onto the beach. Before the crustacean can recover from the shock, the coyote is enjoying a fine crab feast.

Rarely sighted in the Sierra de La Laguna is the **mountain lion**—also called cougar, panther, or puma—which, like all cats, is mostly nocturnal. These beautiful creatures occasionally attack humans, so those hiking in the sierras should avoid hiking at night. If you do meet up with a lion, wildlife experts suggest you convince the beast you are not prey and may be dangerous yourself. Don't run from the animal, as this is an invitation to chase. Instead, shout, wave your hands, and, if the lion acts aggressively, throw stones at it. If you're carrying a backpack, raise it above your shoulders so that you appear larger. One or more of these actions is virtually guaranteed to frighten the lion away. If not, grab the biggest, heaviest stick you can find and fight it out to avoid becoming cat food.

Smaller, less intimidating carnivores commonly encountered in the Cape Region include the **gray fox, ringtail, bobcat, lynx, skunk, raccoon,** and **badger.**

One of the largest mammals still roaming wild in Baja is the **mule deer,** of which there is an endemic peninsular variety. Mule deer are most commonly seen on mountain slopes below 1,500 meters. Lesser numbers of **white-tailed deer** inhabit higher elevations. Deer are a popular source of meat for ranchers living in the sierras; the ranchers also use deerskin to make soft, homemade boots called *teguas.*

At least four varieties of rabbit hop around the Cape Region: the **brush rabbit, desert cottontail, black-tailed jackrabbit,** and the rare, endemic **black jackrabbit.** Each is especially adapted to its particular habitat. The long, upright ears of the black-tailed jackrabbit, for example, enable it to hear sounds from a long distance, a necessity for an animal that is prey for practically every larger animal in the Cape Region. The more delicate ears of the desert cottontail act as radiators on hot desert days, allowing the rabbit to release excess body heat into the air. The black jackrabbit *(Lepus insularis)* is found only on Isla Espíritu Santo. Zoologists haven't yet been able to explain why the fur of this rabbit is mostly black, or why a cinnamon-red coloring appears along the ears and underparts.

The Cape supports a wide variety of common and not-so-common rodents—the **white-tailed antelope squirrel, marsh rice rat, Botta's pocket gopher,** and **piñon mouse,** to name a few. What may surprise some travelers is how many varieties manage to survive in the Gulf Desert. Among these are the **desert pocket mouse, cactus mouse, desert wood rat,** and five endemic species of **kangaroo rat.**

MARINE MAMMALS

The protected lagoons of Baja's Pacific coast and the warm waters of the Sea of Cortez are practically made for whales and dolphins. All told, 25 species of cetaceans frequent Baja waters, from the **blue whale,** the largest mammal on earth, to the **common dolphin** *(Delphinus delphis),* which is sometimes seen in the Sea of Cortez in pods as large as 10,000. Other whale species known to either visit the Cape Region

or make it their year-round home include **minke, fin, Sei, Bryde's, humpback, gray (see below), goose-beaked, sperm, dwarf sperm, false killer, killer,** and **pilot.** Other commonly seen dolphins include **Pacific white-sided, bottlenosed, spotted, Risso's, spinner,** and **striped.**

California sea lions, or *lobos marinos,* are also plentiful; most live around the Sea of Cortez islands of San Esteban, San Jorge, Angel de la Guarda, San Pedro Mártir, and Espíritu Santo.

Gray Whales
The marine mammal usually of most interest to Cape whalewatchers is the **Pacific or California gray whale,** which migrates some 19,300 km (12,000 miles) a year between its feeding grounds above the Arctic Circle and its calving grounds in the Pacific lagoons of southern Baja. The gray whale is the easiest to view since it frequents shallow coastal waters. Although the lagoons used by the grays for calving are found north of the Cape Region in south-central Baja, the whales can sometimes be seen from shore as they make their way around the tip of the Cape to "exercise" the newly born calves.

Whalewatching Tours: Like many two-legged mammals, gray whales prefer to spend their winters south of the border. During the Dec.-April calving season, whalewatching tours to the nearest calving lagoon (Bahía Magdalena, around 200 km/120 miles northwest of La Paz) can be arranged through hotels and travel agencies in La Paz, San José del Cabo, or Cabo San Lucas.

close encounters of the barnacled kind

COURTESY OF SPECIAL EXPEDITIONS

FISH

The seas surrounding Baja California contain an amazing variety of marinelife. In the Sea of Cortez alone, around 900 varieties of fish have been identified. Marine biologists estimate a total of around 3,000 species, including invertebrates, between the Golfo de Santa Clara at the north end of the sea and the southern tip of Cabo San Lucas. This would make the area the richest sea, or gulf, in the world—a marine cornucopia that has inspired the nickname "God's Fishtank." The wide spectrum of aquatic environments along both coasts is largely responsible for this abundance and has led to Baja's reputation as a mecca for seafood aficionados as well as fishing and diving enthusiasts.

About 90% of all known Baja fish varieties are found close to the shores of the peninsula or its satellite islands. The Midriff Islands area in the center of the Sea of Cortez is especially rich in life—tidal surges aerate the water and stir up nutrients, supporting a thick food chain from plankton to fish to birds and sea lions. The Cortez, in fact, has acted as a giant fish trap, collecting an assortment of marine species over thousands of years from the nearby Pacific, the more distant equatorial zones of South America, and even the Caribbean, through a now-extinct water link that once existed between the two seas.

A brief guide to Baja's fish is provided below. Habitats are described as being onshore, inshore, or offshore. Onshore fish frequent the edge of the tidal zone and can be caught by casting from shore; inshore fish inhabit shallow waters accessible by small boat; and offshore fish lurk in the deep waters of the open Pacific or the southern Sea of Cortez. (Also see Sports and Recreation.)

Billfish

The Cape Region is the undisputed world billfishing capital; serious saltwater anglers from across the globe make the pilgrimage to La Paz or Cabo San Lucas in hopes of landing a **swordfish, sailfish,** or **striped, blue,** or **black marlin.** The sailfish and striped marlin are generally the most acrobatic, but all billfish are strong fighters. They inhabit a wide range of offshore waters in the Pacific and in the Sea of Cortez south of

Bahía Magdalena and the Midriff Islands; the swordfish is found mostly on the Pacific side.

Corvinas and Croakers

About 30 species in Baja belong to this group of small- to medium-size fish that make croaking sounds. Varieties found inshore to onshore include **white seabass, Gulf corvina, orangemouth corvina, California corvina, yellowfin croaker,** and **spotfin croaker.**

Jack

Popular jacks include **yellowtail** (one of the most popular fish used in *tacos de pescado*), **Pacific amberjack,** various **pompanos, jack crevalle,** and the strong-fighting **roosterfish,** named for its tall dorsal comb. These fish are most prevalent in inshore to onshore areas in the Sea of Cortez and in the Pacific south of Magdalena.

Dorado, Mackerel, and Tuna

Among the more sought-after food fish, found offshore to inshore throughout parts of both seas, are: **dorado,** sometimes called dolphinfish

yellowfin tuna

MARIO BAÑAGA JR./PISCES FLEET

ENDANGERED SEA

Novelist John Steinbeck, in his 1941 account of a scientific marine expedition into the Sea of Cortez accompanying marine biologist Ed Ricketts, described how he watched six Japanese shrimpers—weighing at least 600 tons each—purse-dredge the sea bottom, killing hundreds of tons of fish that were merely discarded after each dredging. One of his reactions: "Why the Mexican government should have permitted the complete destruction of a valuable food supply is one of those mysteries which have their ramifications possibly back in pockets it is not well to look into."

In 1996 the *Sacramento Bee* published a multi-page report by Pulitzer-winning writer Tom Knudson, exposing corruption among fishing interests and the state governments on all sides of the Cortez. The evidence presented in the report is clear: overfishing by greedy commercial interests is devastating the natural balance in the Sea of Cortez. Reading this report is virtually guaranteed to put you off eating any seafood for a while.

According to the report, primary culprits include gillnetters, purse seiners, spear-fishermen, and shrimp trawlers. The trawlers drag huge cone-shaped, fixed nets over the ocean bottom, ripping up the seafloor; for every pound of shrimp harvested they destroy 10 pounds of other sealife. Asian long-liners were a problem in the 1960s through the '80s, but their presence in the Sea of Cortez has diminished drastically; in fact long-liners hardly ever enter the Sea of Cortez anymore, instead staying just outside international limits in the Pacific.

Two species native to the northern Sea of Cortez, **totuava** and **vaquita dolphin,** are of particular concern. Gillnetting for the totuava (yielding 70 to 100 tons annually) has severely threatened the vaquita, which is now thought to be the world's most endangered marine mammal. The current vaquita population is estimated at only 200-500 individuals. Mexican laws passed in 1993 included a ban on the use of gillnets in the upper Sea of Cortez, yet their current use is not uncommon.

Most of the species taken commercially from the Sea of Cortez are sold primarily in the U.S., Canada, Korea, and Japan. In addition to the vaquita and totuava, those disappearing fast include the sea cucumber, bay scallop, sardine, shrimp, turtle, marlin, grouper, yellowfin tuna, yellowtail, manta and other rays, and sharks. The Pacific manta has been virtually wiped out by gillnetting, while porpoises, dolphins, and sea lions face a similar fate. An estimated 17 major species have declined 60-90% over the last decade alone.

Sportfishing is not a problem except when anglers go over their limits, which isn't uncommon. The federal limit on taking dorado, for example, is three per angler, but it's not unusual to see Americans and Canadians coming back from a day's fishing with catches of over 10 times the limit—and bragging about it. Many foreigners practice spearfishing in Baja, which is a federal crime in Mexico if done in conjunction with scuba gear. There's no sport to scuba spearfishing, which can only be likened to shooting ducks in a barrel.

In order to protect the Cortez ecosystem from coastal industries and overfishing, the Mexican government has asked the United Nations to bestow International Biosphere Reserve status upon the northern Sea of Cortez and its surrounding shores. With such status, the area would become eligible for various kinds of U.N. and international conservation funds.

Whether or not the request is granted, the government is taking further steps to upgrade protection for the sea, which is finally being recognized as one of Mexico's greatest natural assets. A 3,700-square-mile Mexican biosphere reserve has been established in the northern Sea of Cortez; within a core zone of 636 square miles, reaching from San Felipe to Golfo de Santa Clara, all sportfishing, commercial fishing, and oil drilling are banned. The remaining area is a buffer zone in which "sanitary fishing" (meaning no shrimp trawling) is permitted under strict regulations.

Unfortunately, Mexican government resources for enforcing the country's many fine-sounding laws are hopelessly inadequate. The PESCA inspector in Loreto, for example, is paid only US$50 a week—less than half the wage of an average Mexican factory worker—and isn't even supplied with a boat or car, nor telephone, paper, electric lights, or even gas money to use with his own car.

The only way the situation will improve is with international, e.g., U.N., involvement. One can only hope that intervention is soon enough and strong enough to preserve Mexico's great marine resources.

(though it isn't related to mammalian dolphins or porpoises) or mahimahi (its Hawaiian name); **sierra,** especially good in ceviche; the knife-shaped **wahoo,** one of the fastest of all fish, reaching speeds of 50 knots; **Pacific bonito;** and three kinds of tuna—the **bluefin, albacore,** and highly prized **yellowfin.** Yellowfins can weigh up to 180 kg (400 pounds) and are among the best tasting of all tunas.

Bass

Seabass are inshore fishes; different species dominate different Baja waters and all commonly find their way into Mexican seafood restaurants. The larger bass are *garropa* (groupers), the smaller *cabrilla.*

Flatfish

These include flounder and halibut, usually called *lenguado* in Spanish. The most common variety on the Pacific side is **California halibut;** on the gulf side it's **Cortez halibut.** Both make good eating and are often used in tourist areas for *tacos de pescado.*

Snapper

Generally found south of Magdalena and round the Cape as far north as the upper Sea of Cortez, locally popular snappers include **red snapper, yellow snapper, barred pargo,** and **dog snapper.** All snappers are called *pargo* in Spanish, except for the red snapper, which is *huachinango.* All are common food fish.

Sharks, Rays, and Squid

Of the more than 60 species of sharks found in Baja waters, some are rare and most stay clear of humans. The more common species are found offshore to inshore from Magdalena to the Midriff, and include the **smooth hammerhead, common thresher, bonito (mako), sand, blue, blacktip,** and the **whale shark,** the world's largest fish, which reaches 18 meters and 3,600 kg (almost four tons). Shark-fishing is an important activity in Baja, supplying much of the seafood eaten locally. Hammerhead, thresher, bonito, and leopard shark fillets are all very tasty.

Rays are common in warmer offshore-to-inshore waters throughout Baja. Many varieties have barbed tailspines that can inflict a painful wound. Contrary to myth, the barb is not actually venomous, although a ray "sting" can be extremely painful and easily becomes infected. Experienced beachgoers perform the "stingray shuffle" when walking on sandy bottoms; if you bump into a ray resting on the bottom, it will usually swim away; if you step on one, it's likely to give you a flick of the barb.

Common smaller rays found inshore include the **butterfly ray** and the aptly named **shovelnose guitarfish,** a ray with a thick tail and a flat head. Two species of ray—the **mobula** and the huge **Pacific manta ray**—are sometimes called "devilfish" because of their horn-like pectoral fins. The Pacific manta possesses a "wingspan" of up to seven meters (23 feet) and can weigh nearly two tons. Pacific Mantas have become rare due to overfishing. Another fairly large ray, the **bat ray,** is sometimes confused with the manta, though it doesn't have the manta's characteristic pectoral fins. A friendly manta will allow scuba divers to hitch rides by hanging on to the base of the pectorals; most divemasters now discourage such activity.

manta ray

Squids of various species and sizes—most under 30 cm (one foot) in length—are found throughout the Pacific Ocean and Sea of Cortez. In deeper Pacific waters off the west coast glides the enormous **Humboldt squid,** which reaches lengths of four and a half meters (15 feet) and may weigh as much as 150 kg (330 pounds). In the Cape Region, squid (*calamar* in Spanish) is popularly eaten in *cocteles* or used as sportfishing bait.

Elongated Fish

These varieties share the characteristics of long, slender bodies and beak-like jaws. The sharp-toothed **California barracuda** swims in the Pacific from the border down to Cabo San Lucas, while a smaller, more edible variety is found in

KAREN McKINLEY

the Sea of Cortez. In spite of their somewhat frightful appearance, barracudas rarely attack humans.

The silvery **flying fish** can be seen leaping above offshore waters throughout the Pacific and lower Sea of Cortez. It is not generally considered a food fish. The most edible of the elongated fish is probably the acrobatic **Mexican needlefish,** or *agujón,* which reaches two meters in length and has green bones.

Shellfish

Baja's shores abound with deep-water and shallow-water shellfish species, including multiple varieties of **clams, oysters, mussels, scallops,** and **shrimp,** many of which have disappeared from coastal California, U.S.A. Baja's most famous shellfish is undoubtedly the **spiny lobster,** which appears on virtually every *mariscos* menu on the peninsula.

BIRDS

Hosting around 300 known species of birdlife—one of the highest concentrations in North America—the peninsula and islands of Baja California provide undisturbed avian habitat par excellence. Ornithological research focusing on the Cape Region, however, is incomplete, and reference materials are difficult to come by; one of the most up-to-date works available is Peterson and Chalif's *A Field Guide to Mexican Birds,* last published in 1973 (see Booklist).

Coastal and Pelagic Species

The vast majority of the Cape's native and migrating species are either coastal or open-sea (pelagic) birds. The Sea of Cortez islands are particularly rich in birdlife; the Mexican government has designated 49 of the islands as wildlife refuges to protect the many rare and endangered species there. Among the more notable island birds are the rare and clownish **blue-footed booby** and its more common cousins, the **brown booby** and the **masked booby.**

Common throughout the coastal areas of southern Baja is the **magnificent frigate,** called *tijera* (scissors) in Mexico because of its scissors-shaped tail. In spite of their seafood diet, frigates can't swim or even submerge their heads to catch fish—instead they glide high in the air on boomerang-shaped wings, swooping down to steal fish from other birds, especially slow-witted boobies.

Among the more commonly seen birds along the Sea of Cortez coast is the **brown pelican,** which in global terms is not so common. As a species, pelicans go back 30 million years; paleontologists use the modern pelican as a model for creating visual representations of the pteranodon, an extinct flying reptile with an eight-meter wingspan. Brown pelicans, the only truly marine species among the world's seven pelican species, dive 10-30 meters (30-100 feet) under water to catch fish. Other pelicans only dip their beaks beneath the surface and tend to frequent inland waterways rather than marine habitats. Browns have almost entirely disappeared from the U.S. shores of the Gulf of Mexico, and they are declining in the coastal islands of California apparently due to the pesticide content of the Pacific Ocean. Baja's Cortez and Pacific coasts are among the last habitats where the brown pelican thrives.

Another noteworthy bird along the coast is the **fisher eagle,** which, as its name implies, catches and eats fish. The fisher eagle is also occasionally seen along freshwater rivers and around the Pacific lagoons.

Other coastal birds of Baja include two species of **cormorant,** the **long-billed curlew,** four species of **egret,** four species of **grebe,** 10 species of **gull,** three species of **heron,** the **belted kingbird,** two species of **ibis,** three species of **loon,** the **osprey,** the **American oystercatcher,** six species of **plover,** six species of **sandpiper,** the **tundra swan,** and seven species of **tern.**

Certain fish-eating birds are usually seen only by boaters since they tend to fly over open ocean. These pelagics include two species of **albatross,** the **black-legged kittiwake,** the **red phalarope,** three species of **shearwater,** the **surf scoter,** the **south polar skua,** five species of **storm petrel,** the **black tern,** and the **red-billed tropic bird.**

Estuarine and Inland Species

Another group of waterfowl in southern Baja frequents only freshwater ponds, *tinajas* (springs), lakes, streams, and marshes. These birds include two species of **bittern,** the **American coot,** two species of **duck,** the **snow goose,** the **northern** harrier, six species of heron, the white-faced ibis, the common moorhen, two species of rail, five species of sandpiper, the lesser scaup, the shoveler, the common snipe, the sora, the roseate spoonbill, the wood stork, three species of teal, the northern waterthrush, and the American wigeon. Some of these birds are native, others winter here. One of the best and most convenient places to view such birdlife is the estuary in San José del Cabo.

In the sierras dwell the golden eagle, the western flycatcher, the lesser goldfinch, the black-headed grosbeak, the red-tailed hawk, two species of hummingbird, the pheasant, the yellow-eyed junco, the white-breasted nuthatch, the mountain plover, four species of vireo, eight species of warbler, the acorn woodpecker, and the canyon wren.

Common in the desert and other open country are three species of falcon (peregrine, prairie, and Cooper's), three species of flycatcher, six species of hawk, the black-fronted hummingbird, the American kestrel, the merlin, two species of owl, the greater roadrunner, eight species of sparrow, two species of thrasher, the vernon, the turkey vulture, the ladder-backed woodpecker, and the cactus wren.

REPTILES AND AMPHIBIANS

Among the slippery, slimy, scaly, crawly things that live in the Cape Region are around two dozen species of lizards, frogs, toads, turtles, and snakes.

Lizards

One four-legged reptilian of note is the chuckwalla, which is found on certain islands in the Sea of Cortez; it sometimes grows to nearly a meter in length. The chuckwalla drinks fresh water when available, storing it in sacs that gurgle when it walks; when a freshwater source is not available, the lizard imbibes saltwater,

which it processes in a sort of internal desalinator. Another good-sized lizard is the desert iguana, found throughout the Gulf Coast Desert and possibly farther north. Larger iguanas are sometimes eaten in ranchero stews and are said to taste better than chicken. The coast horned lizard, similar to the horny toad of the American Southwest, is another endemic.

great blue heron

Turtles

Of the six turtle varieties present, five are sea turtles: the leatherback, green, hawksbill, western ridley, and loggerhead. The loggerhead migrates back and forth between the Japanese island of Kyushu and the Sea of Cortez, a distance of 10,460 km. Because their eggs, meat, and shells are highly valued among coastal Mexican populations, all are on the endangered species list. The Mexican government has declared turtle hunting and turtle egg collecting illegal; the devastation of the turtle population has slowed considerably but hasn't yet stopped. *Bajacalifornianos* say they're upholding the laws while anglers along the mainland coast of the Sea of Cortez still take sea turtles.

The main culprit has apparently been Japan, formerly the world's largest importer of sea turtles—including the endangered ridley and hawksbill. The Japanese use the turtles for meat, turtle leather, and turtle-shell fashion accessories. In 1991 the Japanese government announced a ban on the importation of sea turtles, so perhaps the Sea of Cortez populations will make a comeback.

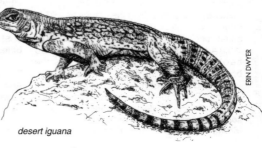

desert iguana

ERIN DWYER

Snakes

The rocky lowlands and chaparrals make perfect snake country. The bad news is that about half the known species are venomous; the good news is they rarely come into contact with humans. Scorpion stings far outnumber snakebites in Baja.

Harmless species include the **western blind snake, rosy boa, Baja California rat snake, spotted leaf-nosed snake, western patchnosed snake, bull snake, coachwhip, king snake, Baja sand snake,** and **California lyre snake.**

The venomous kinds fall into two categories, one of which contains only a single snake species, the **yellow-bellied sea snake.** Sea snakes usually flee the vicinity when they sense human presence, but as a general precaution don't grab anything in the water that looks like a floating stick—that's how sea snakes deceive their prey.

The other venomous category comprises the rattlesnakes; there are supposedly 18 species stretched out along Baja California. The most common is the Baja California rattler, whose range includes the lower three-fourths of the peninsula. Look for scaly mounds over the eyes if you care to make an identification. The most dangerous of Baja rattlers is the Western diamondback; it's the largest and therefore has the greatest potential to deliver fatal or near-fatal doses of venom. Fortunately the diamondback is mostly confined to the canyons of the northern sierras; I've never heard of a sighting in the Cape Region.

The general Spanish term for snake is *serpiente;* a nonvenomous snake is referred to as *culebra,* the venomous sort *víbora.* A rattlesnake is *un serpiente de cascabel* or simply *un cascabel.* An encouraging factoid: according to Spanish records, no missionary ever died of a snakebite during the 300-year period of Spanish colonization of the New World.

HISTORY

PRE-CORTESIAN HISTORY

Because the Cape lacks spectacular archaeological remains, such as the Mayan and Aztec ruins in the southern reaches of mainland Mexico, it has largely been ignored by archaeologists. It is highly likely, however, that the area was inhabited by human populations well before the rest of Mexico. Baja California Sur was the logical termination for the coastal migration route followed by Asian groups who crossed the Bering Strait land bridge between Asia and North America beginning around 50,000 B.C.

The Cochimís and Guaycuras

Amerindian groups living in the central and southern reaches of the peninsula when the Spanish arrived were apparently much less advanced technologically than the Yumanos of northern Baja, not to mention Amerindian groups found in central and southern mainland Mexico. Because of the lack of archaeological research in these areas, the only record we have of these cultures consists of Spanish accounts, which were undoubtedly biased in light of their mission to subordinate the peoples of the New World. Mission histories are full of lurid tales of Amerindian customs, many probably written to convince the Spanish crown of the desperate need to missionize the natives. Nevertheless, the Amerindians of central and southern Baja appeared to have been among the more "primitive" of the tribes encountered by the Spanish in Mexico or Mesoamerica. In modern archaeological terms, they hadn't progressed beyond the Paleolithic epoch (the early Stone Age).

According to these accounts, the Guaycuras, divided into the Pericú, Huchiti, and Guaicura tribes, occupied the Cape Region. One fringe anthropological view has suggested a portion of the Guaycura tribes may have descended from Tahitian seafarers blown off course on their way to Hawaii. Whatever their place of origin, the Guaycuras spent most of their daylight hours searching for food; the men hunted small game or gathered shellfish while the women gathered fruit, seeds,

and roots. If game was scarce, the people subsisted on a variety of insects and would even eat dried animal skins, including, according to reports, the leather boots of the conquistadors.

The southern Amerindians generally lived in the open and sought shelter only in the severest weather. Men wore little or no clothing, while women wore leather or yucca-fiber thongs around the waist with woven grasses or twigs suspended from the front and animal skins in the back. These garments were sometimes painted with bright colors. The tips of arrows and spears were generally of sharpened hardwood only, though chipped stone points were

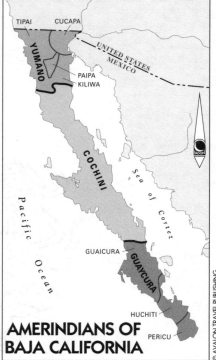

AMERINDIANS OF BAJA CALIFORNIA

occasionally used. The Guaycuras also used reed blowguns. The most important time of year for these Amerindians was when the fruit of the pitahaya cactus ripened; the fruit was then so abundant the Amerindians allegedly abandoned all activities save sleeping and eating.

None of the Guaycuras apparently left behind any artwork. This has been attributed to their harsh living environment; they may have had little time or energy for artistic pursuits. However, in the inland areas of the south-central peninsula once inhabited by Cochimí and Guaycura tribes, numerous spectacular rock-art sites have been discovered. The Cochimís told the Spanish this rock art was created by a race of giants who'd preceded them. Almost nothing is known about this lost Amerindian culture, a people Baja rock-art expert Harry Crosby has dubbed "The Painters." Because rock-art sites in the Cape Region are less numerous than those found farther north in the Sierra de la Giganta and Sierra de San Francisco, modern researchers have almost totally neglected them.

THE SPANISH CONQUEST OF BAJA CALIFORNIA

Following 700 years of conflict with the Moors over control of the Iberian Peninsula, Spain in the 15th century emerged as the most powerful nation in Europe. Convinced that a Roman Catholic God was destined to rule the world with Spain as His emissary, the Spanish monarchy sent Christopher Columbus in search of a new route to the Far East. His mission was to establish contact with a mythical "Great Khan" in order to develop an alternate trade route with the Orient, since Arabs controlled the overland route through the Middle East. Along the way as many pagans as possible would be converted to Christianity. Once the Arab trade monopoly was broken, the Holy Land would be returned to Christian control.

Columbus's landing in the West Indies in 1492 was followed by Pope Alexander VI's historic 1493 decree giving the Spanish rights to any new land discovered west of the Azores, as long as the Spanish made "God's name known there." Hence, the Spanish conquest of the New World started as a roundabout extension of the Holy Crusades.

A succession of Spanish expeditions into the Caribbean and Gulf of Mexico rapidly achieved the conquest of Mexico and Central America. Conquistador Hernán Cortés subdued the Valley of Mexico Aztecs in three years (1519-21), and the allegiance—or decimation—of other Aztecs and Mayans followed quickly.

Early California Explorations

When the Spanish conquistadors came to the western edge of mainland Mexico and looked beyond toward the landforms they could see above the sea, they concluded that Baja California was a huge island and the as-yet-unnamed Sea of Cortez led to the Atlantic. The idea of a "northwest passage" to the Atlantic persisted for years, even among seasoned explorers like Cabrillo, Drake, and Vizcaíno. Cortés himself directed four voyages from the mainland to the island of La California, although he actually accompanied only the third. The history of these early expeditions exposes the enmity and extreme sense of competition among those conquistadors supposedly working toward a common cause.

The first voyage, launched in 1532, never made it to the peninsula. The ships were captured in the Sea of Cortez by Nuño de Guzmán, an arch-rival of Cortés operating farther north in Mexico. The next year a second expedition,

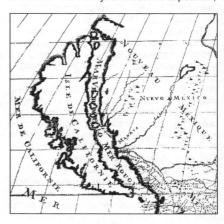

A 1694 French map depicted California as an island.

under Capt. Diego Becerra of the *Concepción,* suffered a mutiny in which the captain was killed. Basque pilot Fortún Jiménez took charge and the ship landed in Bahía de La Paz in early 1534. Thus the first European visitors to reach Baja California, a group of mutineers, arrived there just 42 years after Columbus touched down in the West Indies and nearly a century before the Pilgrims landed at Plymouth Rock.

Before they had much of a chance to explore, Jiménez and 22 of his crew were killed by Amerindians while filling their water casks at a spring. The survivors managed to sail the *Concepción* back to the mainland, where most were promptly captured by Guzmán. One of the escapees managed to reach Cortés with tales of rich caches of black pearls on a huge island with "cliffs and headlands and rocky coasts," as in the California of popular myth.

Cortés, inspired by these stories, organized and led a third expedition, partially financed by his own personal wealth. His party consisted of three ships and a group of 500 Spanish colonists that included women and children. They landed at the northeast end of Bahía de La Paz—which Cortés named Santa Cruz—in May of 1535, the same year New Spain was officially established. Although Cortés apparently found pearls in abundance, his attempt to colonize the peninsula lasted only two years, by which time disease, hostile Amerindians, and *chubascos* had driven the colonists back to the mainland.

The fourth attempt by Cortés to establish a Spanish foothold on California soil was led by the highly competent Capt. Francisco de Ulloa, who'd accompanied Cortés on the failed Santa Cruz expedition. Cortés stayed behind on this one, hoping Ulloa's expedition would be able to find a more hospitable California beachhead. Ulloa set sail from Acapulco with two ships in July 1539, and over the next eight months he managed to explore the entire perimeter of the Sea of Cortez, reaching the mouth of the Río Colorado and rounding the Cape along the Pacific coast as far north as Isla Cedros.

Upon reaching Isla Cedros, Ulloa reportedly sent one ship back to Acapulco for supplies; it isn't known for certain what happened to the other vessel. According to some historical accounts, Ulloa found his way back to the mainland and was murdered by one of his own crew near

Guadalajara; other accounts say he disappeared north of Isla Cedros. At any rate, his written report of the voyage—which indicated Baja was not an island but a peninsula—didn't surface until a hundred years later. His biggest contribution to the geography of the times was the naming of the Mar de Cortés, now the Sea of Cortez or Gulf of California.

After squandering most of his wealth in futile attempts to explore Baja, Cortés was recalled to Spain in 1541, never to return to Mexican shores. In his place, Spain dispatched experienced Portuguese navigator Juan Rodríguez Cabrillo in 1542 with orders to explore the Pacific coast. Starting from the southern tip of the peninsula, his expedition made it as far north as the Oregon coast and mapped several major bays along the way, including those of San Diego and Monterey. Cabrillo himself never made it past California's Santa Barbara Islands; he died there following a mysterious fall.

Manila Galleons and Privateers

On the other side of the globe, events were unfolding that would influence Baja California's history for the next 250 years. Although Portuguese navigator Ferdinand Magellan reached the Philippines in 1521, it wasn't until 1565 that López de Legaspi defeated the archipelago's native defenders. Immediately thereafter, Esteban Rodríguez and Padre Andrés de Urdaneta pioneered a ship route from Manila to the New World that took advantage of the 14,500-km (9,000-mile) Japanese Current across the northern Pacific, thus establishing a trade connection between the Orient and New Spain.

The ships making the annual roundtrip voyages between Manila and Acapulco beginning in 1566 came to be called "Manila galleons." The lengthy sea journey was very difficult, however, because of the lack of fresh water during the final weeks of the five- to seven-month eastward crossing. This provided further impetus for establishing some sort of settlement in lower California where ships could put in for water and supplies.

A California landfall became even more desirable when in 1572 the Manila galleons started carrying shipments of gold, silks, and spices to New Spain. The ships were so heavy they became easy prey for faster pirate vessels. By 1580, England's Sir Francis Drake had entered

Manila galleon

the Pacific via the Straits of Magellan and circumnavigated the globe, thus ending Spanish dominion over the seas. Drake plundered Spanish ships with regularity, and as news of the treasure-laden ships spread, other English as well as Dutch privateers were lured into the Pacific.

Their raids on Spanish ships became an embarrassment to the crown and a drain on Spanish wealth, so the Spaniards were forced to seek out harbors in Baja's Cape Region where they could hide. Since the first land sighting on the east Pacific leg of the Manila-Acapulco voyage was below the peninsula's midpoint, the Cape Region was the logical choice for a landing. Following much experimentation, Bahía San Lucas and Bahía de La Paz became the two harbors most frequently used.

Eventually, however, the keen privateers figured out how to trap Spanish ships in the very bays their crews sought for protection. Thomas Cavendish plundered the Manila galleon *Santa Ana* at Cabo San Lucas in 1587, and so many ships were captured in Bahía de La Paz that the landfall there, originally called Santa Cruz by Cortés, eventually earned the name Pichilingue, a Spanish mispronunciation of Vlissingen, the provenance of most of the Dutch pirates.

Pirating continued off the Baja coast throughout the entire 250-year history of the Manila-Acapulco voyages. One of the more celebrated English privateers in later years was Woodes Rogers, who arrived in the Pacific in 1709 and captured the Manila galleon *Encarnación* off Cabo San Lucas. On his way to Baja California that same year Rogers rescued Alexander Selkirk, a sailor marooned on an island off the coast of Chile for four years. Selkirk served as shipmaster on Rogers's vessel and later became the inspiration for Daniel Defoe's 1719 novel *Robinson Crusoe*.

Further Exploration and Colonization Attempts

As the Spaniards' need for a permanent settlement in California grew more dire, coastal explorations were resumed after a hiatus of over 50 years. Cabrillo was succeeded by merchant-turned-admiral Sebastián Vizcaíno, who in 1596 landed at the same bay on the southeast coast chosen by his predecessors, Jiménez and Cortés. This time, however, the natives were friendly—perhaps because it was pitahaya fruit season when they arrived—and Vizcaíno named the site La Paz (Peace). After loading up on pitahaya fruit—effective for preventing scurvy—and pearls, Vizcaíno continued north along the Sea of Cortez coast, stopping to gather more pearls before returning to the mainland.

In 1602 Vizcaíno commanded a second, more ambitious expedition that sailed along the Pacific coast to near present-day Mendocino in California. His names for various points and bays along the coasts of both Californias superseded most of those bestowed by Cabrillo and Cortés.

Upon his return Vizcaíno told his superiors that the Monterey Bay area of California was well suited to colonization. However, because he was no longer in favor with New Spain's fickle viceroys, no one paid much attention to his findings and he was reassigned to an obscure Sinaloa port. The cartographer for the voyage, Gerónimo Martínez, was beheaded for forgery, although his maps of the Californias remained the best available for over 200 years.

This neglect of California's potential enabled an Englishman to put first claim to the territory. Sir Francis Drake, who landed at what is now Drake's Bay in northern California during his

1578-80 voyage, christened the land New Albion on behalf of the English crown. Like the Spanish maps of the time, his maps depicted California as an island.

For a time Spain left both Californias unexplored. In 1615 Capt. Juan de Iturbi obtained the first official concession for peninsular pearl diving, but no land settlement was established. After two of his ships were captured by Dutch privateers off Cabo San Lucas, de Iturbi sailed his remaining vessel northward in the Sea of Cortez as far as the 28th parallel, harvesting pearls along the way. Because of dwindling provisions, the expedition was forced to return to the mainland after only a few months.

The peninsula remained unconquered by the Spanish for another 80 years. In 1683 Spain's Royal Council for the Indies authorized an expedition under Adm. Isidor Atondo y Antillón and Padre Eusebio Francisco Kino that managed to occupy an area of La Paz for three and one half months before dwindling provisions and hostile

SEBASTIÁN VIZCAÍNO EXPEDITIONS

—— Expedition of 1596
······· Expedition of 1602-03

Monterey

San Diego

PACIFIC OCEAN

Mazatlán

Cabo San Lucas

Navidad

0   300 mi
0   300 km

Acapulco

© AVALON TRAVEL PUBLISHING

natives drove it back to the mainland. After two months of rest and provisioning on the mainland, they crossed the Sea of Cortez again, this time establishing a mission and presidio just above the 26th parallel at a place they named San Bruno. Supported by a friendly Amerindian population, the mission lasted 19 months. Lack of water and food—they had to rely on supply ships from the mainland—forced Kino and Atondo back to the mainland.

Kino never returned to Baja California but later became famous for his missionary efforts in northwestern Mexico and Arizona, where he is said to have converted thousands of Amerindians to Roman Catholicism. In 1701 he accompanied an expedition from the northwest of Sonora to the mouth of the Río Colorado that confirmed Ulloa's claim that Baja California was a peninsula. Kino died in Sonora in 1711.

THE MISSION PERIOD

The Founding of the Jesuit Missions

Padre Juan María Salvatierra finally succeeded in giving Spain and the Church what they wanted—a permanent Spanish settlement on the Baja California peninsula. Backed by the mainland missionary system, a 30,000-peso annual subsidy from the Royal Council of the Indies, and a contingent of Spanish soldiers, Salvatierra landed in San Bruno in October 1697, located a better water source 24 km south of the original presidio, and proceeded to establish the mother of all California missions, Nuestra Señora de Loreto.

The founding of the Loreto mission initiated what Baja historians usually call "the Jesuit missionary period," lasting 1697-1767. During this interval, the Jesuits established 20 missions, stretching from the southern tip of the peninsula to near present-day Cataviña in central Baja. That wasn't a spectacular accomplishment compared with the progress of mainland colonization, but lower California was a much more difficult area to colonize. It had taken 167 years from the time the first Spaniard had set foot on her shores until the first successful settlement was established on Baja California soil.

The Spanish mission system basically worked like this: the padres, always in the company of

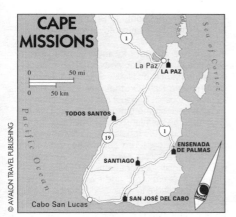

armed escorts, approached groups of natives and offered them the protection of the Church and the Spanish crown in return for a willingness to undergo religious instruction. Those natives who agreed were congregated at a suitable spot and directed to build a mission. The mission in turn became a refuge for the Amerindians and a place for them to learn European farming techniques and other trades, as well as Catholic ways. Once pacification was complete, the mission became a secularized church community (pueblo) and the missionaries moved on to new areas.

The system worked well with the docile Amerindians of Central Mexico but was often unsuccessful among the nomadic, fiercely independent Amerindians of Northern Mexico and Baja. Elsewhere in Mexico and Latin America, the norm was to secularize after 10 years; in Baja, the Spanish Church never voluntarily secularized its missions.

Amerindian Revolts, Disease, and the Decline of the Jesuits

Several times during the Jesuit period, groups of Amerindians revolted against missionization. The most significant rebellion occurred in 1734-36 among the Pericú of the southern peninsula. Apparently the revolt was triggered by Padre Nicolás Tamaral's injunction against polygamy—long a practice among the Pericú and Guaicura, tribes in which women outnumbered men. The punishment of a Pericú shaman under the injunction doubled the perceived assault on native culture, and a group of disaffected Amerindians organized themselves against the entire mission structure.

In October 1734, the Pericú attacked and burned the missions at Santiago and San José del Cabo, killing Padre Tamaral and his counterpart at Santiago. They also set fire to the mission in Loreto, although the padre there escaped unharmed and was able to send to the mainland for assistance. In Todos Santos, the rebels killed 49 Amerindian inhabitants who tried to defend their pueblo. The provincial governor of Sinaloa, after receiving letters from Loreto describing the uprising, dispatched a ship from the mainland with 60 Yaqui warriors and a number of Spanish soldiers. The troops marched from mission to mission, meeting little resistance from the poorly equipped Pericú.

Unrest among the Pericú continued for another two years, a situation that led to the founding of a large garrison at San José del Cabo. As a further precaution, the garrisons at every mission in the south were expanded by 10 soldiers each. Besides reinforcing the missions, this increased military presence encouraged Manila galleons to make Cabo San Lucas a regular stop on their return voyages from the Orient.

In the years to follow, epidemics of smallpox, syphilis, and measles—diseases borne by Europeans for which Amerindians had no natural immunity—devastated the Amerindian population. In 1738 Padre Jacobo Baegert of Misión San Luis Gonzaga estimated the Baja Amerindian population at about 50,000. In three outbreaks of smallpox in 1742, 1744, and 1748, an estimated 42,000 Amerindians—84% of the native population—perished. Gathering the Amerindians into mission settlements only hastened their demise, intensifying the spread of contagions. A significant number of Amerindians also lost their lives in continued rebellions against the padres. The La Paz mission was abandoned in 1748; by 1767 only one member of the entire Huchiti branch of the Guaycura nation survived.

As the southern Amerindians died out, the missionaries moved quickly northward, seeking new sheep for their flocks. The last four missions established by the Jesuits, Santa Gertrudis (1752), San Borja (1762), Calamajué (1766), and Santa María (1767), were scattered widely in northern Baja in an obvious push toward California.

In 1767 King Charles III ordered the expulsion of the Jesuit Order from all Spanish dominions, including Baja California. Accounts of the expulsion disagree as to the reasons behind his action. According to crown representatives, the Jesuits were too power-hungry and would no longer be held accountable for their actions. The Jesuits themselves claimed persecution because they'd dared criticize corruption among the nobility and royalty of Europe. Whatever the reason, in 1768 the 16 Jesuit padres of Baja found themselves herded onto a ship bound for the mainland port of San Blas, where the same ship received a contingent of Franciscan padres sent to replace them.

Franciscan and Dominican padres succeeded the Jesuits, but by the end of the 18th century it was clear that Spain and the Church could no longer afford to support the Baja missions. The peninsula's Amerindian population had dwindled to less than 5,000 by 1800, and without an abundance of free native labor, maintaining a colony wasn't an easy task. The California missions to the north seemed much more promising—water was more readily available and the Amerindian labor force was more docile and plentiful. The growing unrest in Mexico placed the peninsula even lower on Spain's list of priorities.

INDEPENDENCE FROM SPAIN

The Catholic Church in Mexico had amassed huge amounts of wealth by the beginning of the 19th century and had become a lender to the colony's growing entrepreneurial class. At the other end of the economic spectrum, the increasing numbers of mestizos—Mexican-born residents of mixed Spanish and Amerindian ancestry—were denied land ownership and other rights and were generally treated as second-class citizens.

Fearing the Church was becoming too powerful, King Charles III of Spain decreed in 1804 that all church funds be turned over to the royal coffers. To comply with the decree, padres all over Mexico were forced to call back large sums of money lent out to entrepreneurs, and economic chaos ensued. Mexicans blamed their economic and social problems on Spain's remote rule; when Napoleon invaded Spain in 1808, limiting authority to Spanish loyalists in Mexico City, the disaffected clergy began planning a revolt.

Mexico's struggle for independence from Spain began on 16 September 1810, a date celebrated annually as Diez y Seis or Mexican Independence Day. On that day, Padre Miguel Hidalgo y Costilla issued a call for independence today known as the Grito de Dolores (Dolores Cry) from the mainland city of Dolores, Guanajuato. Although the rebels who gathered around Hidalgo soon captured Zacatecas, Valladolid, and San Luis Potosí, Mexico wasn't completely free of Spanish rule for another 11 years. When Hidalgo was captured and executed by loyalists, another padre took his place and the fighting continued until Mexico City acceded to the demands of the rebels in 1821.

The 1821 Plan de Iguala treaty between Spain and Mexico guaranteed three political underpinnings of the new regime: the religious dominance of the Catholic Church, a constitutional monarchy, and equal rights for mestizos. Former Viceroy Agustín de Iturbide was appointed emperor of the new republic, but his reign only lasted two years before he was overthrown by another junta that established a short-lived federal republic called Los Estados Unidos de México—the United States of Mexico—in 1824.

Over the next six years the Mexican republic endured two more coups; it wasn't until 1829 that all Spanish troops were expelled from Mexico. In 1832 all non-Dominican missions in Baja were secularized and converted to parish churches. The Dominican missions of the northern peninsula were allowed to remain because they were considered the only outposts of civilization north of La Paz and Loreto, and as such were important links with prospering Alta California. Another change in policy involved the encouragement of Anglo-American immigration to the northeastern Mexican state of Coahuila y Texas—a policy that would have profound implications later on.

The Mexican-American War

In 1833 Antonio López de Santa Anna, a megalomaniacal general in charge of enforcing the expulsion of Spanish troops, seized power and revoked the Constitution of 1824, thus initiating a series of events that eventually led to a war with the U.S. and the resultant loss of huge amounts of territory. During the first 30 years of Mexican independence, Mexico changed governments 50 times; Santa Anna—who called himself the "Napoleon of the West"—headed 11 of these regimes.

Mexican citizens everywhere were angry at the revocation of their republican constitution by a self-appointed dictator. But none were more frustrated than the Anglo-American immigrants who had voluntarily abandoned their U.S. citizenship in order to take Mexican citizenship under the Constitution of 1824 and live in the northern half of Coahuila y Texas. In 1836 the "Texicans" declared an independent Republic of Texas, fought and lost San Antonio's famous Battle of the Alamo, then routed Santa Anna's troops at San Jacinto, Texas.

Defeated and captured, Santa Anna signed the Velasco Agreement, which guaranteed Texas independence and recognized the Rio Grande as the border between Mexico and the new Texan republic. There matters lay until the U.S. granted statehood to the near-bankrupt republic in 1845. Santa Anna's government refused to recognize the Velasco Agreement, claiming Texas only extended as far south as the Nueces River, about 160 km north of the Rio Grande at the widest gap. When the U.S. Army moved into the area south of the Nueces, Santa Anna retaliated by sending troops across the Rio Grande, thus initiating the Mexican-American War.

After a series of skirmishes along the Rio Grande, U.S. president James Polk ordered the army to invade Mexico. In Baja California, Mexican and American forces engaged at Santo Tomás, Mulegé, La Paz, and San José del Cabo. Mexico City finally fell to U.S. troops in March 1847, and Santa Anna signed the Treaty of Guadalupe Hidalgo in 1848. In the treaty, Mexico conceded not only the Rio Grande area of Texas but part of New Mexico and all of California for a payment of US$25 million and the cancellation of all Mexican debt.

In retrospect, it is likely the annexation of Texas was part of a U.S. plan to provoke Mexico into declaring war so the U.S. could gain more of the Southwest. The war so damaged Mexico's already weakened economy that in 1853 Santa Anna sold Arizona and southern New Mexico

to the U.S. for another US$10 million. During that same year, American freebooter William Walker sailed to La Paz and declared himself "President of Lower California." He and his mercenary troops fled upon hearing that Mexican forces were on the way. He was later tried—and acquitted—in the U.S. for violation of neutrality laws. Walker was executed after a similar escapade in Nicaragua two years later.

For the Mexican population, already strongly dissatisfied with Santa Anna, these losses of territory became the final straw; in 1855 Santa Anna was overthrown by populist Benito Juárez.

Depopulation of the Peninsula, Civil War, and Reform

The second half of the 19th century was even more turbulent for Mexico than the first. At the end of the Mexican-American War, the California Gold Rush of 1849 lured many Mexicans and Amerindians away from the peninsula to seek their fortunes in California, further reducing Baja's already scant population and transforming it into

Benito Juárez

a haven for bandits, pirates, and an assortment of other outlaws and misfits. Only six Dominican padres remained on the peninsula by the 1880s.

Meanwhile, back on the mainland, a civil war (called the "War of Reform" in Mexico) erupted in 1858 following the removal of Santa Anna; self-appointed governments in Mexico City and Veracruz vied for national authority. Once again, Church wealth was the principal issue. The liberals, under Zapotec Amerindian lawyer Benito Juárez, had promulgated a new constitution in 1857 and passed a law further restricting the financial powers of the Church; all Church property save for the church buildings themselves had to be sold or otherwise relinquished. A reactionary opposition group took control of Mexico City and fighting continued until 1861, when the liberals won and Juárez was elected president.

Juárez immediately had to deal with the 1862 French invasion of Mexico, which came in response to Mexico's nonpayment of debts to France. Napoleon's first invading force was defeated at Puebla on the Gulf of Mexico coast, but the following year the French captured the port and continued onward to take Mexico City, where they installed Austrian Ferdinand Maximilian as emperor of Mexico. Under U.S. pressure, the French gradually withdrew from Mexico and Juárez was back in power by 1867.

Over the next four years Juárez initiated many economic and educational reforms. Upon his death in 1872, political opponent Porfirio Díaz took over and continued reforms begun by Juárez, albeit in a more authoritarian manner. Díaz and/or his cronies ruled for the next 28 years, suspending political freedoms but modernizing the country's education and transportation systems.

Foreign Investment in Baja California

In Baja, Díaz and the "Porfiriato" encouraged foreign investment on a large scale, and in the 1880s vast land tracts were sold to American or European mining, farming, manufacturing, and railway concessions. All but the mining concessions met failure within a few years, mainly because the investors weren't prepared to deal with the peninsula's demanding climate and lack of transportation.

Mineral excavation in late 19th-century Baja enjoyed a boom—gold, silver, copper, and gyp-sum were the main finds, along with graphite, mercury, nickel, and sulfur. One of the most successful mining endeavors was that of Compañía del Boleo, a French mining syndicate in Santa Rosalía that for many years was the largest copper-mining and smelting operation in Mexico.

THE 20TH CENTURY AND BEYOND

The Mexican Revolution

By the early 20th century, it was obvious that the gap between rich and poor was increasing, caused by the extreme procapitalist policies of the Díaz regime and the lack of a political voice for workers and peasants. In response to the situation, a liberal opposition group, using Texas as a base, formed in exile, organizing strikes throughout the country. This forced Díaz to announce an election in 1910; his opponent was Francisco Madero, a liberal from Coahuila. As it became clear that Madero was garnering mass support, Díaz imprisoned him on trumped-up charges.

Upon his release, Madero fled to Texas and began organizing the overthrow of the Díaz government. The rebels, with the assistance of the colorful bandit-turned-revolutionary Pancho Villa and peasant-hero Emiliano Zapata, managed to gain control of the Northern Mexican states of Sonora and Chihuahua. Unable to contain the revolution, Díaz resigned in May 1910 and Madero was elected president. His one-time allies, however, broke into several factions—the Zapatistas, Reyistas, Vasquistas, and Felicistas, named for the leaders of each movement—and Madero was executed in 1913. Baja California had its own faction, the Magonistas, who briefly held Tijuana in 1911.

For the next six years the various factions played musical chairs with national leadership; Mexico remained extremely unstable until revolutionary leader Venustiano Carranza emerged as president. Carranza held a historic convention that resulted in the Constitution of 1917, the current Mexican constitution. This document established the *ejido* program to return lands traditionally cultivated by the Amerindian peasantry, but taken away by rich ranch and plantation owners under Díaz, to local communities throughout Mexico. Three years later opponent Álvaro Obregón and his supporters overthrew Carranza.

Obregón managed to hang onto the office for four years, establishing important educational reforms; he was followed in 1924 by Plutarco Elías Calles. Calles instituted wide-reaching agrarian reforms, including the redistribution of three million hectares of land. He also participated in the establishment of the National Revolutionary Party (PNR), the forerunner of the Institutional Revolutionary Party (PRI), Mexico's dominant party today.

U.S. Prohibition

In the same year that Obregón took power in Mexico City, the U.S. government amended its own constitution to make the consumption, manufacture, and sale of alcoholic beverages a federal offense. This proved to be a disastrous experiment for the U.S., ushering in an era of organized crime, but was a boon to Baja California development. Americans began rushing across the border to buy booze from the restaurants, cantinas, and liquor stores of Northern Mexico.

Border towns added casinos and brothels to the assortment of liquor venues and became so prosperous that the municipal leadership was able to lobby successfully for the division of Baja California into northern and southern territories. On the negative side, the border towns became renowned as world sleaze capitals. Their reputations persisted long after Prohibition ended in 1933, and the Mexican government outlawed gambling—prostitution remained legal—in 1938.

Nationalist Reforms and World War II

The year 1938 proved a turning point in modern Mexican history as PNR candidate Lázaro Cárdenas ascended to the presidency. Cárdenas, a mestizo with Tarascan Amerindian heritage, instituted the most sweeping social reforms of any national leader to date, effecting significant changes in education, labor, agriculture, and commerce.

His land reforms included the redistribution of 18.6 million hectares (46 million acres) among newly created *ejidos*—a legacy that is as hot a topic for debate today as it was then. Foreign-owned oil interests were expropriated and a national oil company, Petróleos Mexicanos (Pemex), was established. Even though foreign investors were compensated for expropriations at fair market value (under a treaty signed by both the U.S. and Mexico), these reforms frightened off foreign investors for many years and it has been only very recently that Mexico has reattracted foreign capital. Cárdenas also reorganized the PNR as the Mexican Revolution Party (PRM—Partido de la Revolución Mexicana), which soon changed its name to the Institutional Revolutionary Party (PRI—Partido Revolucionario Institucional).

Baja Statehood and the Transpeninsular Highway

After the war Mexico continued to industrialize, and the economy remained relatively stable under one PRI president after another. In 1952 the Territory of (Northern) Baja California was declared Mexico's 29th state as its population moved past the 80,000 required for statehood. Northern Baja was, in fact, better off economically than most of the rest of the country. The boomtowns of Tijuana and Mexicali were servicing a fast-growing border economy and Valle de Mexicali farming competed well with California's Imperial Valley. In 1958 it was determined that Baja was second only to Mexico City in the number of automobiles per capita.

Meanwhile wealthy Americans had been flying to La Paz and Cabo San Lucas since the late 1940s to fish the teeming waters of the Sea of Cortez. In 1948 several Hollywood celebrities (including Bing Crosby, John Wayne, and Desi Arnaz) built a resort known as Las Cruces on the Cortez coast east of La Paz, and in 1958 a lone American investor constructed the Hotel Palmilla at Punta Palmilla on the Corridor. Others quickly followed, including the Hotel Cabo San Lucas, Hotel Hacienda, and Hotel Finisterra in Cabo San Lucas, and the Rancho Buena Vista on Bahía de Palmas.

Throughout the 1960s most of Baja south of Ensenada remained benevolently neglected, which led travel writers of the time to employ the famous catchphrase, "the forgotten peninsula." The Cape Region was a little-known beach and sportfishing destination limited to pilots, diehard anglers, and celebrities. The overall population of the Territory of Southern Baja California was stagnating, perhaps even decreasing; except for La Paz, it was limited to tiny collections of hardy souls here and there who scratched for cash as rancheros or *pescadores* (fishermen). Even La Paz was just a step above a sleepy backwater port, although its status as a duty-free port was beginning to attract a steady trickle of mainland Mexicans.

By the 1970s it was obvious that southern Baja wasn't going to catch up with northern Baja unless transportation between the south, north, and mainland improved. Travel between Tijuana and La Paz took up to 10 days via rough dirt tracks. Construction of the Transpeninsular Highway (Mexico 1) was finally completed in 1973, connecting Tijuana with Cabo San Lucas for the first time. In less than a year, the population of Baja California Sur passed the 80,000 mark and the territory became Mexico's 30th state.

The 1,700-km-long Transpeninsular Highway has greatly contributed to the modernization of one of Mexico's last frontiers. Fishing and agri-

cultural cooperatives can now transport their products to the border or to the ports of Santa Rosalía, Guerrero Negro, and La Paz. The highway has brought Americans, Canadians, and Europeans deep into the peninsula in greater numbers than ever before, and the revenue from their visits provides another means of livelihood for the people of Baja.

Like the border visitors of the Prohibition years, the foreigners who come to the Cape Region today are seeking something that's scarce in their own countries. For some it may be the unfenced desert solitude, for others the pristine beaches or historic mission towns. The challenge of the future for the Cape's burgeoning tourist industry is how to develop and maintain an adequate infrastructure without sacrificing those qualities that make Baja California Sur unique.

THE PEOPLE

Baja California Sur occupies a place in the Mexican psyche somewhat analogous to that of Hawaii for many Americans. It's seen as a place that's part of the nation yet almost out of reach—an exotic destination most of the population will never have an opportunity to see. Hence, mainlanders typically regard the *bajacalifornianos* of the southern peninsula as somehow "different" from themselves. And it's true, the people of Baja California Sur are in many ways a breed apart from their mainland compatriots. As Mexico's last frontier, El Sur continues to attract residents seeking a rugged, independent lifestyle they haven't been able to find in mainland Mexico.

The enticements of a highly favorable climate, bounteous sea, and wide-open spaces have drawn a mix of Baja natives, transplanted mainlanders, and gringos to the Cape Region. The region as a whole—from La Paz to Cabo San Lucas and everywhere in between—receives less than 350,000 tourists a year (roughly one-tenth the number that visit the city of San Francisco in a year). About 40% of these visitors hail from elsewhere in Mexico while the other 60% come from the U.S., Canada, Europe, Asia, and Latin America.

Approximately 370,500 people live in Baja California Sur, most of them in La Paz, San José del Cabo, or Cabo San Lucas. Obviously, most

of the Cape Region is sparsely populated—the average density is only 1.5 persons per square km (about four persons per square mile). Outside the three most populated cities it's less than one person per 26 square km (one body per 10 square miles).

Mexico's population growth rate is currently estimated at 1.9% per annum, relatively low for a developing country. The average for the Cape Region is probably higher than the national average because of immigration. Yet Baja California Sur remains the country's least populated state.

ORIGINS

Bajacalifornianos (sometimes called *bajacalifornios*) are an unusually varied lot. Elsewhere in Mexico, the average citizen is a mix of Spanish and Amerindian bloodlines. In the Cape Region the mix is typically more complicated, mainly because southern Baja remained a frontier much longer than the rest of the country, attracting people who arrived in the New World long after the Spanish colonized the Mexican mainland. It was 167 years after the conquest of Mexico before the Spanish were able to maintain a permanent settlement on the peninsula; by this time, tales of the Californias were on the tongues of adven-

enjoying the bounteous sea

turers throughout the world. The first paved highway between the Cape Region and the U.S. border was completed only about two decades ago.

By the end of the 19th century the Cape had become a favorite spot for sea-weary sailors to jump ship. The eastern shores of the peninsula were placid, and there was little chance deserters would be rounded up and incarcerated by local militia, who were scarce then and remain so today. Most of the ex-sailors who retired in this manner were English, but during WW I a few Germans and other Europeans came ashore. Their ship captains might have considered them cowardly deserters, but survival in southern Baja in the 19th and early 20th centuries was possible only for the brave, hardy, and resourceful.

Since in a very real sense much of Baja is still a frontier area—with more immigrants wandering in year by year—Baja's demographics have yet to solidify into recognizable pie-graph proportions. About two percent of the residents aren't even Mexican citizens; many are American, Canadian, or European retirees, and a lesser number are gringos who've simply dropped out of the rat race. With the recent relaxation of investment and trade laws, a growing number of foreigners are also setting up businesses on the Cape.

LANGUAGE

As in the rest of Mexico, Spanish is the primary language in Baja California Sur. English is wide-ly spoken by merchants, hotel staff, and travel agents in La Paz, San José del Cabo, and Cabo San Lucas. Even in these cities, however, you can't count on finding English-speaking Mexicans outside the tourist districts.

If you restrict your daily schedule to hotel, beach, restaurant, and nightclub visits, you'll get by fine using English. But if you don't speak Spanish and you hope to do the Cape circuit or to explore the interior, you'd be wise to learn at least enough of the language to cope with everyday transactions. Knowing a little Spanish will not only mitigate communication problems, it will also bring you more respect among the local Mexicans, who quite naturally resent foreign visitors who expect Mexicans to abandon their mother tongue whenever a gringo approaches. A popular sign seen in tourist restaurants reads "We promise not to laugh at your broken Spanish if you won't laugh at our broken English."

Dictionaries and Phrasebooks

The Glossary and Spanish Phrasebook at the back of this book will get you started on a basic vocabulary in *español.* For further study, you'll want a dictionary and a larger phrasebook. One of the best portable dictionaries for the Spanish student is the paperback *University of Chicago Spanish-English, English-Spanish Dictionary,* which emphasizes New World usages and contains useful sections on grammar and pronunciation. If even this small volume is too large for your backpack, the *Collins Gem Dictionary:*

WHAT'S A GRINGO?

The Latin-American Spanish word "gringo," reportedly a corruption of the Spanish word *greigo* or "Greek," has different meanings in different parts of Latin America. In Argentina and Uruguay, for example, it is used to refer to anyone of Italian descent. In Mexico and Central America, it's almost always reserved for persons of northern European descent, especially Canadians and Americans. In Cabo Pulmo, I once heard a naive, newly arrived white Canadian archaeologist comment that it would be easy for him to carry out his research in Baja because he wasn't a gringo. (Sorry, pal, but you're a gringo, too.) In spite of everyday linguistic evidence to the contrary, many non-Spanish speakers insist that only Americans are gringos. The Mexicans, however, have a more precise epithet for Americans: *yanquis* or "Yankees."

Is "gringo" a derogatory term? It can certainly be used that way. Most of the time, however, it's simply an unconscious racial identification of neutral value. Educated Mexicans tend not to use it; instead they would typically say *norteamericano* or *americano* for Americans. Some Mexicans insist on the former even though the term is a slight to Canadians and Mexicans, who, after all, are North Americans, too. *Canadiense* is used for Canadians, *alemán* for Germans, and so forth. A more precise term for U.S. citizens is *estadounidense*.

Spanish-English, English-Spanish comes in a tiny 4-by-3.5-by-1-inch edition with a sturdy plastic cover and over 40,000 entries.

Berlitz's *Latin-American Spanish For Travellers* is a small phrasebook divided by topics and situations (e.g., grammar, hotel, eating out, post office). Not all the phrases and terms it contains are used in Baja, but it's better than nothing.

One of the best references for off-the-road adventurers is Burleson and Riskind's *Backcountry Mexico: A Traveler's Guide and Phrase Book* (University of Texas Press). Although it's rather bulky for carrying in a backpack and is oriented toward travel in northern mainland Mexico, it contains many words and phrases of value to sierra hikers and campers.

ON THE ROAD

TRAVEL HIGHLIGHTS

Time, money, and personal inclinations will compel most visitors to make advance decisions as to which parts of the Cape Region they'll see and which they'll have to leave out. The following list, organized by theme rather than geographic area, contains what we consider the best of what the Cape Region has to offer.

Beaches: Playa del Amor, Cabo San Lucas; Playa Balandra, La Paz; Playa San Pedrito, West Cape; Playa Santa María, The Corridor
Desert Environments: La Candelaria; Todos Santos to Rancho Los Inocentes
Fishing: Bahía de Palmas, East Cape; Bancos Gorda, near San José del Cabo; Banco San Jaime, near Cabo San Lucas; Punta Pescadero to Punta Perico, East Cape
Hiking and Backpacking: Cañon San Dionísio; Sierra de La Laguna
Islands: Isla Cerralvo; Isla Espíritu Santo
Kayaking: Bahía de La Paz; Isla Espíritu Santo
Nightlife: Cabo San Lucas; San José del Cabo
Off-Highway Cycling: El Camino Rural Costero, San José del Cabo to Cabo Pulmo; Los Barriles–Bahía de los Muertos; foothills behind Pescadero, West Cape
Sierra Towns: San Bartolo; Santiago

Snorkeling and Diving: Cabo Pulmo, East Cape; El Bajo, near La Paz; Los Islotes, near La Paz
Surfing: Playa Costa Azul, San José del Cabo; "Monuments," The Corridor; La Pastora, West Cape
Windsurfing: Bahía de la Ventana, near La Paz; Bahía de Palmas, East Cape

The Cape Loop

Those with enough time and money to rent a car in La Paz, San José del Cabo, or Cabo San Lucas can make a rewarding circular route around the Cape Region via paved highways Mexico 1 and Mexico 19. Extending a total distance of approximately 564 km (350 miles), this route will take visitors along the lower slopes of the Sierra de La Laguna, through the sierra's former mining towns, across the Plains of La Paz, and along the coastlines of the East and West Capes as well as the "Corredor Náutico" between San José del Cabo and Cabo San Lucas.

This loop can be comfortably driven in two or three days (see the Cape Distances chart for distances and driving times), but visitors with additional time will be able to stop more frequently and see more of the region. The more adventurous can widen the loop by taking the sandy Camino Rural Costero (Rural Coastal Road)—see La Ribera to San José del Cabo for details.

SPORTS AND RECREATION

The Cape Region's major attractions largely fall under this heading—from trekking in the Sierra de La Laguna to scuba diving off Cabo Pulmo. An added bonus is that, for the most part, you can enjoy outdoor recreation at little or no cost. User demand is low, and when fees are involved they're usually quite reasonable.

HIKING AND BACKPACKING

Trails

Hiking trails, from wide, 150-year-old paths created by Indians or shepherds to smaller, more recent trails worn by hikers, crisscross the Sierra de La Laguna. Signposts are scarce—it's a good idea to scout an area first and ask questions locally about the best way to get from point A to point B. Although it's sometimes tempting to venture off established trails, that's a good way to get lost; you might also contribute to the destruction of delicate ecosystems. Light trails that don't seem to go anywhere may be cattle or coyote trails that connect surface water sources. See Sierra de La Laguna for information on specific trails.

Maps

Topographic maps, which chart trails and elevation differentials, are essential for extended hiking and backpacking. **Map Link,** 30 S. La Patera Lane, #5, Santa Barbara, CA 93117, tel. (805) 692-6777, fax (805) 692-6787, e-mail: custserv@maplink.com; **Map Center,** 2611 University Ave., San Diego, CA 92104, tel. (619) 291-3830; and **Treaty Oak,** P.O. Box 50295, Austin, TX 78763, tel. (512) 326-4141, e-mail: maps@treatyoak.com, carry a complete line of Baja topo maps in three scales (1:1,000,000, 1:250,000, and 1:50,000), sold separately according to region. The maps cost around US$6 each. The stores will mail out a Baja map list on request.

These same topographic maps are also available in Baja from any **Instituto Nacional de Estadística, Geografía e Informática** (INEGI) office for about US$3 per sheet. Some topos may be out of print, in which case you can usually obtain a photocopy of archival prints from an INEGI office for US$6. These maps show not only trails and contour lines, but villages not normally marked on other maps.

Although you won't need a great deal of Spanish to read the INEGI maps, you might need to know the following translations for the map legend:

brecha—gravel road

vereda—path

terracería transitable en todo tiempo—all-weather dirt road

terracería transitable en tiempo de secas—dirt road passable only in dry weather

carretera pavimentada—paved highway

carretera de más de dos carriles, caseta de pago—toll highway of more than two lanes

INEGI has one office in the Cape Region where you can obtain maps. It's in La Paz at Plaza Cuatro Molinos, Calle Altamirano 2790, Col. Centro, tel. (1) 123-1545 or 123-3150.

What to Bring

For a hike of a day or less, all you need is sturdy footwear (light, high-topped hiking boots are preferable to sneakers in rocky terrain) and whatever food or water you plan to consume for the day (count on at least two liters of water per person for chaparral or lower sierra day-hiking, more if the weather is hot).

Longer hikes obviously require more preparation and equipment. Bring enough clothing to remain comfortable at both ends of the temperature spectrum; on the Pacific side of the sierra, days tend to be warm, nights chilly. A three-season backpacking tent and a light sleeping bag rated for temperatures down to 2° C/35° F usually suffice for shelter.

Good hiking boots are essential. Thick lug soles with steel shanks are preferable, as they provide protection from sharp rocks and spiny plants. Bring along a first-aid kit that includes an elastic bandage for sprains and snakebite treatment, and a pair of tweezers for removing thorns and cactus spines. Also pack a flashlight, compass, waterproof matches, a knife, extra batteries, foul-weather gear, and a signal device (mirror or whistle).

Always carry plenty of water; a minimum of two liters per person per full day of walking, five in hot weather. Although springs and *tinajas* exist in the sierra, the water level varies considerably and you shouldn't count on finding water sources along the way. If you need drinking water from one of these sources, always boil it first for at least 10 minutes or treat it with iodine or a water filter designed to remove impurities. Bring enough food for the duration of your hike (count on about 1.5 pounds of dry food per person per day), plus one or two days extra. One to three nestable pans will suffice for up to six hikers, along with a spoon, small plastic bowl, and cup for each person.

Camping Tips

Campsites: In addition to all the usual rules for choosing campsites, don't camp beneath coconut palms (a falling coconut could knock down your tent or fracture your skull) or in arroyos (danger of flash floods).

Fires and Waste Disposal: Open fires are permitted just about anywhere in the Cape Region except within city limits. Dead or fallen hardwood is plentiful in the upper sierra; lower down, cactus skeletons—especially pitahaya and cholla—make excellent fuel. Scrap lumber suitable for firewood can sometimes be salvaged from town dumps. Imitate the locals and keep your fires small. Never leave hot coals or ashes behind; smother with sand—or water, if you can spare it—till cool to the touch.

Pack out all trash that won't burn, including cigarette butts; they take 10-12 years to decompose. Bury human waste six inches down, and don't use soap in streams or springs.

Island Camping: If you happen to have the blessed opportunity to camp on any of the Sea of Cortez islands like Espíritu Santo, Cerralvo, or Partida, check your bags thoroughly before landing on the island to make sure you haven't inadvertently brought along any animal species (including insects or insect eggs) that aren't native to the island. Such introduced species can wreak havoc on fragile island ecologies. Pack out all human waste as well as trash; carrying along a port-a-potty and deep-sixing its contents at sea after you leave the island is the most convenient way to deal with the former.

FISHING

The Cape Region's reputation as one of the world's best sportfishing regions is well deserved. Nowhere else will you find as many varieties of fish in an area as compact and accessible as the waters surrounding the Cape. Although it's most famous for acrobatic billfish—marlin, sailfish, and swordfish—and other deep-sea species, the Cape also offers opportunities for surf casters, small-boaters, and sport divers, as well as folks who don't yet know a rod from a reel.

Onshore Fishing

Most accessible to travelers, since it doesn't require a boat, is onshore or surf fishing, which you can enjoy anywhere along the coast you can get a line into the water.

Surf fishing is best on the Pacific coast between Playa El Migriño and El Carrizal (north of Todos Santos), at beaches along the Corridor, and almost anywhere on the Sea of Cortez between San José del Cabo and La Paz. Com-

WORLD FISHING RECORDS SET IN BAJA

The nonprofit International Game Fish Association (IGFA) tracks world records set for each species of game fish according to weight, weight/test ratio (fish weight to line test), place where the catch was made, and other significant record details. World-record catches achieved by Baja anglers for specific line classes include those for the following fish: Pacific blue marlin, striped marlin, Pacific sailfish, swordfish, roosterfish, dolphinfish (dorado), gulf grouper, California yellowtail, Pacific bonito, bigeye trevally, spotted cabrilla, spearfish, giant seabass, white seabass, California halibut, Pacific jack crevalle, black skipjack, yellowfin tuna, Pacific bigeye tuna, and chub mackerel. Baja anglers hold all-tackle records—highest

weight of any fish species regardless of line test—for gulf grouper, olive grouper, roosterfish, Pacific amberjack, white seabass, spotted cabrilla, rainbow runner, black skipjack, yellowfin tuna, Pacific jack crevalle, chub mackerel, and California yellowtail.

For information on IGFA membership and record entries, write to IGFA, 3000 E. Las Olas Blvd., Fort Lauderdale, FL 33316, website: www.igfa.com. Membership includes a copy of the IGFA's annual *World Record Game Fishes Book,* which contains a list of all current fishing records, as well as the bimonthly *International Angler* newsletter. IGFA members are also eligible for discounts on fishing charters offered by several sportfishing outfitters in Cabo San Lucas.

blue marlin

mon onshore fish include surfperch, cabezón, sand bass, ladyfish, halibut, corvina, opaleye, leopard shark, and triggerfish. Surf fishing the submarine canyons along the shore of the East Cape can actually yield roosterfish, California yellowtail, and yellowfin tuna for anglers using the right tackle, and onshore catches of dorado and even marlin are not unknown. All of these except the marlin are considered excellent food fish, and even the marlin is edible when smoked.

Inshore Fishing

Anyone with access to a small boat, either a skiff trailered in or a rented *panga* (an open fiberglass skiff that's usually five to six meters long and powered by a 40- to 60-hp outboard motor), can enjoy inshore fishing at depths of up to 50-100 meters. Common inshore catches include many of the surf fishes mentioned above, plus various kinds of groupers, seabass, bonito shark, sculpin (scorpionfish), barracuda, sierra, pompano, amberjack, red and yellow snapper, pargo, and cabrilla. Cabrilla must be released when caught.

Larger gamefish occasionally taken inshore are the bluefin and yellowfin tuna, yellowtail, do-

rado, jack crevalle, and roosterfish. Again, all fish mentioned make good eating.

Offshore Fishing

The bigger gamefish are found in deeper waters—over 200 meters (100 fathoms)—and require bigger tackle and more technique, including specialized trolling methods prescribed for each type of fish. Larger boats—fishing cruisers—are usually necessary simply because of the distance from shore to the fishing area. In the Cape Region, however, you can reach depths of over 200 meters less than 1.5 km offshore. These areas are accessible by skiff or *panga,* though strong seasonal currents are sometimes a problem, requiring a larger outboard motor. Contrary to the popular image of Cabo San Lucas sportfishing, it isn't necessary to use a boat equipped with fighting chairs to catch the big ones, although it's undoubtedly more comfortable.

Because of the special tackle and techniques involved in offshore fishing, many Cape visitors hire local fishing guides—who usually provide boats and tackle—to transport them to offshore fishing grounds. A sometimes less-expensive alternative involves signing up for fishing cruises that take groups of tourist anglers out on big powerboats.

Most offshore anglers go after striped, blue, or black marlin, sailfish, swordfish, wahoo, dorado, roosterfish, yellowtail, and tuna. These fish are large, powerful fighters, requiring the angler to have skill in handling rod and line. The billfish are the most acrobatic, performing high leaps and pirouettes when hooked; wahoo and roosterfish will also "greyhound," or perform a series of long, low jumps while swimming rapidly in one direction.

Of the billfish, only the swordfish is considered good eating. The rest are traditionally regarded as trophy fish, meant to be stuffed and mounted in the den or living room. To their credit, an increasing number of anglers these days release billfish after catch; many outfitters discourage or even forbid the taking of these beautiful creatures unless the fish has been badly injured in the fight.

The wahoo, dorado, roosterfish, yellowtail, and various tunas all make excellent eating.

Fishing Seasons

The Cape Region presents a complex set of fishing conditions that vary from month to month and year to year. Fish are biting somewhere in Cape waters year-round, but water temperature, ocean currents, weather patterns, fish migrations, and other variables mean you usually won't find the same type of fish in the same spot in both December and July. An unusually dry year in the American Southwest, for example, lessens the outflow of nutrients from the Colorado River into the Sea of Cortez, diminishing the store of plankton and other small marine creatures at the bottom of the Cortez food chain. This in turn affects populations of larger fish, from seabass to whale sharks.

Because of the numerous variables, all the "fishing calendars" can serve only as guidelines. Generally, the greatest variety and number of gamefish swim the widest range of Cape waters from April through October, when the water temperatures are very warm. In winter, many species migrate south, but fortunately for winter anglers, exceptions abound. The widely distributed California yellowtail, for example, is pre-

sent year-round, migrating up and do⌣ . of Cortez—La Paz and the East Cape . ter, central to northern Cortez in summer—⌣ well as the lower Pacific coast. Sierra peak season is winter, when they're found in abundance along the Pacific coast. Wahoo generally spend Dec.-April at the Cape, moving up toward Bahía Magdalena and the southern Cortez in the warmer months.

If your trip occurs between December and April, head for Cabo San Lucas or San José del Cabo; from May to November you can angle anywhere along a horseshoe-shaped loop extending from Bahía Magdalena on the Pacific side to above La Paz on the Cortez.

As a final caveat, remember that an unusually warm winter means better fishing all over Baja; likewise a particularly cold winter forces many fish far south, making even Cabo San Lucas, the "fisherman's paradise," less productive.

Tackle

Although bait and tackle are available at shops in La Paz and Cabo San Lucas, supplies are variable and you can't count on finding exactly what you want. The more expensive fishing fleets supply or rent good fishing gear, while the budget-oriented outfits provide spotty equipment. If you're inclined toward using one of the no-frills outfitters in order to economize, you ought to have your gear assembled before arrival.

A full fishing kit containing tackle for every conceivable Cape Region sportfishing possibility would probably weigh in excess of 70 kg. Seasoned anglers claim you can get by in just about any situation with four basic rigs: two trolling rods with appropriate reels and 50- to 80-pound-test monofilament line for offshore fishing; one medium-duty eight- or nine-foot rod and spinner with 30-pound mono for surf casting and onshore fishing; and a six-foot light spinning rig loaded with four- to eight-pound line for bait fishing, freshwater fishing, or light surf casting. Two trolling rigs are recommended because these are the rods used against fish most likely to yank your outfit into the sea; it's always best to have a spare.

No matter how many rods you bring into Mexico, you're legally permitted to fish with only one at a time. Electric reels are permitted for use by handicapped persons only.

...any given moment is high-
...properly equipped angler
...n an array of natural and ar-
frozen bait—including everything ... .o mackerel to clams—is usually availab.. ar the more frequented fishing
areas; you can also easily catch your own bait
with a light rig. A cooler is necessary for keeping
bait fresh; hired boats will usually supply them.
Among the vast selection of artificial lures available, the most reliable seem to be those peren-
nials that imitate live bait, such as spoons, lead-
heads, candybars, swimmers, and, for offshore
fishing, trolling heads. Bring along a few of each
in different colors and sizes. You can purchase a
few highly specialized lures, such as marlin heads
and wahoo specials, in Cabo San Lucas.

Tide Tables

Serious onshore-inshore anglers should bring
along a set of current tide tables so they can
decide what time to wake up in the morning.

Fishing Licenses

The red tape surrounding fishing in Mexico is
minimal. The basic requirement is that anyone
over 16 who intends to fish must possess a Mexican fishing license; technically, this includes all
persons aboard boats equipped with fishing tackle, whether they plan to fish or not. This is important to remember for anyone going along on
fishing trips as a spectator.

A single license is valid for all types of fishing,
anywhere in Mexico, and is issued for periods of
one day, one week, one month, or one year.
A license is usually included in the price of
sportfishing cruises, but not necessarily on
panga trips—if you don't have a license, be
sure to ask if one is provided before embarking
on a guided trip. The cost of a Mexican license
has risen steadily over the last few years but remains less expensive than most fishing licenses in the U.S. or Canada. Last time we checked
the cost was US$12.15 for a week, US$19 for a
month, and US$25.30 for an annual license.

Fishing licenses are available from a number of

FISH TRANSLATOR

Mexican guides who lead sportfishing trips often
use the local terms for gamefish; when they
don't, the English terms they use aren't always
correct. This works the other way, too—many
gringos use incorrect Spanish names for Baja fish,
which can cause confusion when asking about local
fishing conditions. Here is a key to some of the
more common translations:

albacore tuna—*albacora*
barracuda—*picuda*
black seabass—*mero prieto*
bluefin tuna—*atún de aleta azul*
blue marlin—*marlín azul*
dolphinfish (mahimahi)—*dorado*
grouper (generic)—*garropa*
halibut—*lenguado*
hammerhead shark—*cornuda*
jack crevalle—*toro*
ladyfish—*sabalo*
mackerel—*sierra, makerela*
manta ray—*manta*
octopus—*pulpo*
Pacific amberjack—*pez fuerte*

perch (generic)—*mojarra*
pompano—*palometa*
puffer (generic)—*bolete*
red snapper—*huachinango*
roosterfish—*papagallo, pez gallo*
sailfish—*pez vela*
seabass (cabrilla)—*cabrilla*
shark (generic)—*tiburón*
small shark—*cazón*
squid—*calamar*
stingray (generic)—*raya*
striped marlin—*marlín rayado*
swordfish—*pez espada*
triggerfish—*cochi*
wahoo—*sierra wahoo, peto*
whale shark—*pez sapo*
white seabass—*corvina blanca*
yellowfin tuna—*atún de aleta; amarilla*
yellowtail—*jurel*

Pez is the generic word for fish. Once fish has
been caught and is ready for cooking (or has been
cooked), it's called *pescado*.

sources, including tackle shops and Mexican insurance companies near the U.S.-Mexico border. They can be obtained by mail from the **Mexico Department of Fisheries (PESCA)**, 2550 Fifth Ave., Suite 101, San Diego, CA 92103-6622, tel. (619) 233-6956, fax (619) 233-0344, or from California branches of the **American Automobile Association (AAA)** and **Discover Baja Travel Club,** 3089 Clairemont Dr., San Diego, CA 92117, tel. (619) 275-4225 or toll-free (800) 727-BAJA, e-mail: discovbaja@aol.com.

Mexican Regulations
The general daily bag limit is 10 fish per person, including no more than five of any one species. Certain fish varieties are further protected as follows (per-day limits): one full-grown marlin, sailfish, or swordfish; two dorado, roosterfish, shad, tarpon, or shark. Extended sportfishing by boat is limited to three consecutive days if the daily bag limit is reached each of the three days.

Bag limits are the same for free divers as for rod-and-reelers. Only handheld spears and band-powered spearguns—no gas guns or powerheads—are permitted and no tanks or compressors may be used. A further weight limitation permits no more than 25 kg (55 pounds) of fish in a day's catch of five specimens, or one specimen of unlimited weight. Gill nets, purse nets, and every other kind of net except for handling nets are prohibited for use by nonresident aliens, as are traps, explosives, and poisons.

The taking of shellfish—clams, oysters, abalone, shrimp, and lobster—by nonresident aliens is officially prohibited. However, taking a reasonable amount—no more than can be eaten in a meal or two—is customarily permitted. This regulation is in place to protect Mexican fishing unions; even buying shellfish from local sources is prohibited unless you purchase from a public market or *cooperativa*. Obtain a receipt in case of inspection.

Totuavas, sea turtles, and cabrilla are protected species that cannot be taken by anyone. Nor can any fish be caught for "ornamental purposes" (e.g., for aquarium use). Mexican fishing regulations are subject to change; check with the Mexico Department of Fisheries for the latest version before embarking on a fishing expedition.

Two areas off limits to all fishing are Bahía Cabo San Lucas harbor and Pulmo Reef, the only official fish sanctuaries along the peninsular coast. Many other areas probably ought to be protected for educational and recreational purposes, since the government-regulated bag limits help to preserve fish species but not fish habitats. Fishing, boating, diving, and other aquatic activities can wreak havoc on lagoons and delicate reef systems—use special care when traversing these areas. Never drop an anchor or a fishing line on a coral reef; such contact can cause irreversible damage to reef systems.

U.S. Customs and California State Regulations
Once you've obeyed Mexican fishing regulations and bagged a load of fish, you still have to conform to U.S. Customs regulations if you wish to enter the U.S. with your catch. Fortunately, U.S. regulations conform with Mexican bag limits, so whatever you've legally caught south of the border can be transported north.

The U.S. state of California further requires anyone transporting fish into the state to present a completed California Declaration of Entry form, available at the border or at any international airport in California. To facilitate identification of the transported fish, some part of each fish—head, tail, or skin—must be left intact. In other words, you can't just show up at the customs station with a cooler full of anonymous fish fillets. You may also be asked to show a valid Mexican fishing license or a PESCA form confirming legal purchase of fish or shellfish. For more information, contact the California Department of Fish and Game, 1350 Front St., San Diego, CA 92101, tel. (619) 237-7311.

BOATING

Recreational boating along Baja's peninsular and island coastlines has been popular since the 1950s. In the days before the Transpeninsular Highway, it was one of the safest, if slowest, ways of traveling from California to the southern peninsula. Despite recent improvements in highway travel, interest in navigating Baja waters has only increased. The main difference now is that smaller vessels can be trailered or cartopped down the peninsula, saving days and weeks that might otherwise be spent just reaching your cruising destination.

An extremely wide range of pleasure boats plies Baja waters, from sea kayaks to huge motor yachts. The most heavily navigated areas lie along the northwest coast between San Diego and Ensenada and in the Cabo San Lucas to La Paz corridor, but even these waters are relatively uncrowded compared to the marinas and bays of California. Cabo San Lucas, the most popular southern Baja harbor, checks in only around 2,000 foreign-owned vessels per year, an average of less than six arrivals per day.

Cartopping

The most popular boats for short-range cruising, fishing, and diving are those that can be transported on top of a car, RV, or truck—aluminum skiffs in the 12- to 15-foot range. This type of boat can be launched just about anywhere; larger, trailered boats are restricted to boat launches with trailer access. The most appropriate outboard motor size for a boat this size is 15-20 hp; larger motors are generally too heavy to carry separately from the boat, a necessity for cartopping.

If you decide to transport a skiff or sea kayak on top of your vehicle, be sure to use a sturdy, reliable rack or loader with a bowline to the front bumper and plenty of tie-downs. The rough road surfaces typical of even Baja's best highways can make it difficult to keep a boat in place; crosswinds are also a problem in many areas. Frequent load checks are necessary.

Inflatables

Rigid inflatable boats (RIB), such as those manufactured by Achilles or Zodiac, are well suited to coastal navigation from Cabo San Lucas around to the East Cape. You can carry them on top or even in the cargo area of a large car or truck and inflate them with a foot pump or compressor as needed. A small 24-hp outboard motor is the best source of power. Inquire at **Pacific Marine Supply**, 4114 Napier St., San Diego, CA 92110, tel. (619) 223-7194, fax (619) 223-9054, e-mail: pacmarine@pacmarinesupply.com, for the latest gear.

NavTec Expeditions, 321 N. Main St., Moab, UT 84532, tel. (801) 259-7983, toll-free (800) 833-1278, organizes guided RIB trips in the Sea of Cortez along the coast of Baja California Sur for US$1,990 pp for seven nights/eight days.

Trailering

Larger boats that require trailering because of their weight, and which then must be floated from the trailer at a launch site, are much less versatile than cartop boats. On the entire peninsula fewer than 20 launches—five or six on the Pacific side, the remainder on the Sea of Cortez—offer trailer access. Another disadvantage to boat trailering is that Baja road conditions make towing a slow, unpleasant task. On the other hand, if one of these spots happens to be your destination and you plan to stay awhile, the added cruising range of a larger vessel might be worthwhile.

boaters moored at Bahía Santa María, The Corridor

Ocean Cruising

The typical ocean cruiser on the Pacific side is a 12- to 24-meter (40- to 80-foot) powerboat; on the Cortez side, 10- to 18-meter (35- to 60-foot) sailboats are popular. Properly equipped and crewed, these boats can navigate long distances and serve as homes away from home. Smaller motor-powered vessels are usually prevented from ocean cruising simply because of the lack of available fueling stations—their smaller fuel capacities greatly diminish cruising range. Sailboats smaller than nine meters (30 feet) have a similar problem because of the lack of storage space for food and water.

If you want to try your hand at ocean cruising, contact **Cortez Yacht Charters,** 3609 Hartzel Dr., Spring Valley, CA 91977, tel. (619) 469-4255, fax (619) 461-9303; or **Baja Coast SeaFaris,** Marquéz de León 933, La Paz, Mexico, tel. (800) 945-2742, e-mail: info@bajaseafaris.com.

Charts

The best nautical charts for Baja waters are those compiled by the U.S. government. They come in two series: the Coastal Series, which covers the entire Pacific and Cortez coastlines in three large charts (numbers 21008, 21014, and 21017) with a scale of around 1:650,000 each; and the Golfo de California Series, which offers much more detailed maps—in scales from 1:30,000 for La Paz to 1:290,610 for the entire Cape Region—of selected areas along the Cortez coast and around the Cape. Both series are based on nautical surveys conducted between 1873 and 1901, so many of the place names are out of date.

You can purchase these charts individually from the **Defense Mapping Agency,** Washington, DC 20315-0010, tel. (301) 227-2495, toll-free (800) 826-0342. Two of the Coastal Series are out of print, however, and others may eventually drop from sight as well. A much better and less expensive source of these charts is *Charlie's Charts: The Western Coast of Mexico (Including Baja),* which is a compilation of all U.S. nautical charts from San Diego to Guatemala, including those currently unavailable from the DMA. The charts have been extensively updated from the DMA originals, with more recent markings for anchorages, boat ramps, hazards, and fishing and diving spots. The spiral-bound

volume is available from **Charles E. Wood,** Box 1244, Station A, Surrey, BC, Canada V3W 1G0. It's also available in many California marine supply stores, and from Amazon.com.

Waterproof, tear-resistant double-sided plastic charts published by Fish-n-Map, 8535 W. 79th Ave., Arvada, CO 80005, tel. (303) 421-5994, fax (303) 420-0843, are available in four sheets: Sea of Cortez North Chart (San Felipe to Mulegé, with inset maps of Bahía de Los Angeles, Las Islas Encantadas, Bahía San Francisquito, Puerto Refugio, and Guaymas); Sea of Cortez South Chart (Loreto to Cabo San Lucas, with inset maps of Loreto south to Bahía Agua Verde, Bahía de La Paz, Isla Espírito Santo, and Cabo San Lucas); the Baja California Chart North Pacific (Tijuana to Bahía Tortugas, with inset maps of the Coronado Islands, San Quintín area, Isla San Benito, and Isla Guadalupe); and Baja California Chart South Pacific (Punta Eugenia to Cabo San Lucas). Each of these measures 24 by 36 inches (four by nine inches folded), costs US$6, and is available wherever Baja maps are sold.

Gerry Cruising Charts, P.O. Box 976, Patagonia, AZ 85624, tel. (520) 394-2393, produces 15 navigation charts for the entire Sea of Cortez (including the mainland Mexico side), plus a packet of charts for the Pacific side of Baja, costing US$30-45 depending on the number of charts per packet. Gerry Cunningham, who complied these charts, also wrote *The Complete Guide to the Sea of Cortez,* which comes in three volumes and costs US$29-31 per volume or US$75 for the whole set.

Tide Tables

Tide tables are published annually; to cover the entire Baja coastline you'll need two sets, one that pertains to the Pacific tides and one for the Sea of Cortez tides. Either or both are available from marine supply stores or **Map Link,** 25 E. Mason, Santa Barbara, CA 93101, tel. (805) 965-4402, fax (805) 962-0884. You can also order Sea of Cortez tide tables from the **University of Arizona** Printing and Publishing Dept., Room 102, West Stadium, Tucson, AZ 85721, tel. (602) 621-2572, fax (602) 621-6458.

Boat Permits

Any nonresident foreigner operating a boat in Mexican waters who intends to fish from that boat is required to carry a Mexican boat permit as well as a fishing permit. Even if you transport a boat to Baja with no fishing tackle and no plans to fish, it's a good idea to obtain a boat permit; first, because you might change your mind when you see all the fish everyone else is pulling in, and second, because you never know when you might end up carrying a passenger with fishing tackle. *All* boats used for fishing require a permit, whether cartopped, trailered, carried inside a motor vehicle, or sailed on the open seas.

Permits are available by mail from the Mexico Department of Fisheries or from the Discover Baja Travel Club. A boat permit is valid for 12 months; fees vary according to the length of the craft.

Temporary Import Permits

These aren't necessary for Baja but are required if you plan to take a boat to mainland Mexico, whether by land or water. You can obtain the permit from offices in La Paz or Santa Rosalía or from a Registro Federal de Vehículos office in Tijuana, Mexicali, Ensenada, or La Paz.

Port Check-ins

If you launch a boat at a Mexican port, specifically within the jurisdiction of a Captain of the Port (COTP), you must comply with official check-in procedures. This simply involves reporting to the COTP office and completing some forms. The only time it's a hassle is when the Captain isn't present; you may have to wait around a few hours. Some ports charge filing fees of up to US$15.

Anytime you enter another COTP's jurisdiction, you're required to check in. In everyday practice, boaters only go through this formality when spending the night at a port with a COTP office.

Checking out is not required until you leave the port of origin, i.e., the port at which you first launched. If you're on a cruise from a foreign country, you should check out at the last port with a COTP on your return itinerary. Current COTPs in Baja are located at Ensenada, Guerrero Negro, Bahía Magdalena (San Carlos), Cabo San Lucas, San José del Cabo, La Paz, Puerto Escondido, Loreto, Mulegé, Santa Rosalía, Bahía de los Angeles, and San Felipe.

Fuel, Supplies, and Repairs

At present only permanent marinas in Cabo San Lucas and La Paz (or farther north in Ensenada,

Puerto Escondido, and Santa Rosalía) offer fuel year-round. Elsewhere you must count on your own reserves or try your luck at canneries, boatyards, and fish camps, where prices will probably exceed official Pemex rates. Often at places other than marinas you'll have to go ashore and haul your own fuel back to the boat; come prepared with as many extra fuel containers as you can manage.

La Paz is the Cape Region's best source of marine supplies and repairs. As with all other motorized conveyances in Baja, it's best to bring along plenty of spare parts, especially props, filters, water pumps, shear pins, hoses, and belts. Don't forget to bring along at least one life jacket per person—statistics show that in 80% of all boating fatalities, the victims weren't wearing them.

SEA KAYAKING

Kayaking is one of the best ways to experience the Cape Region coasts, yet few American kayakers seem to make it this far south. Coves, inlets, water caves, and beaches inaccessible to skiffs or 4WD vehicles are easily approached in a kayak, especially on the Sea of Cortez. The Cortez is truly a world-class kayaking environment, as more and more kayakers discover each year. La Paz in particular is an excellent place to learn sea-kayaking skills because of the abundance of bays, coves, and islands nearby.

Kayaking on the Pacific side is for the experienced paddler only. High surf and strong currents require equal quantities of strength and expertise. Finding a beach campsite isn't too difficult, but reaching it through the surf might be.

Equipment

Sea kayaks can be rented from sports outfitters in La Paz and Cabo San Lucas. Outfitters in La Paz favor traditional closed-cockpit models designed for cold-water zones, even though nearby waters are quite warm most of the year. Cabo San Lucas outfitters often carry both closed-and open-cockpit styles. For extended winter touring, the closed-top boats are preferable—cool winds can make even warm spray feel cold on the skin. For shorter winter trips or summer excursions, the open-top has certain advantages. Since the paddler sits on top of the deck

Kayaking is a great way to explore coastal waters.

rather than underneath it, the open-top is much easier to exit and thus somewhat safer overall. Open-cockpit kayaks are also easier to paddle and more stable than traditional kayaks—just about anyone can paddle one with little or no practice. But they do maneuver a bit more slowly due to a wider beam and higher center of gravity.

If you're on your way to Baja by vehicle and need kayaking equipment or supplies, a convenient stop is **Southwest Sea Kayaks,** 2590 Ingraham St., San Diego, CA 92109, tel. (619) 222-3616, fax (619) 222-3671, e-mail: kayaked@aol. com. **Southwind Kayak Center,** 17855 Sky Park Circle, Irvine, CA 92614, tel. (714) 261-0200, e-mail: info@southwindkayaks.com, provides similar services. Both stores offer rentals and sales.

Maps and Tide Tables
Nautical charts are of little use for kayak navigation. A better choice is 1:50,000-scale topo maps, available from Map Link, Map Center, or Gerry Cruising Charts (contact information is provided under Boating, above). Tide tables are also invaluable.

Organized Kayak Trips
A great way to learn sea kayaking is to join an organized trip led by experienced kayakers. The Cape Region's best companies, **Baja Expeditions** and **Mar y Aventuras,** lead kayak trips out of La Paz year round; see the La Paz section for details.

Another good source of information on organized kayak trips and on Baja kayaking in general is **California Kayak Friends,** 14252 Culver Dr. No. 199, Irvine, CA 92604, tel. (818) 377-4314, e-mail: scckayak@earthlink.net. Membership in this nonprofit kayaking club costs $30 a year and includes a club roster and newsletter subscription.

WINDSURFING

From November through March, the Sea of Cortez is a windsurfer's paradise, particularly along the East Cape. La Paz is also a very good area, even in summer, when a strong breeze called El Coromuel comes in just about every afternoon. The best spots here lie along the mostly deserted beaches of the peninsula northeast of town—Punta Balandra to Punta Coyote. When nothing's blowing in the Bahía de La Paz vicinity, dedicated windsurfers can shuttle west across the peninsula to check out the action at Punta Marquéz on the Pacific side, only 72 km (45 miles) away.

Los Barriles on Bahía de Palmas, along the East Cape, is one of the more accessible windsurfing areas in southern Baja. The wind blows a steady 18-30 knots all winter long and wavesailing is possible in some spots. During the season, uphauling (pulling mast and sail up from the water) is usually out of the question due to chop and high winds, so the ability to waterstart

boardsailors on their
way into the blue

(mount and launch a sailboard from deep water) is a prerequisite for windsurfing in this area.

Los Barriles is also home to the **Baja Vela Highwind Center,** tel. (415) 322-0613, toll-free (800) 223-5443 in the U.S. and Canada, which offers highly rated instruction and package deals from mid-November through mid-March. Even if you're not a participant in one of its windsurfing vacations, you may be able to arrange for service and parts. Every January, Vela cosponsors the Vela-Neil Pryde Windsurfing Championships at Los Barriles.

The Pacific side of Baja generally demands more experience from the sailboarder. Those who can handle high surf and strong winds will love it. None of the Cape Region's Pacific shores, however, are protected from major swells, so the novice should attempt only fair-weather sailing.

SURFING

Cape Region surfers are blessed; they can enjoy both winter and summer wave action within a radius of roughly 100 km. In winter, a west-north-west groundswell combines with the year-round northwest windswell to stoke point breaks along the Pacific shore from Punta Marquéz all the way to Migriño. Some breaks, such as those at San Pedrito and Cerritos, are well known; others are found at "secret" spots that only locals are supposed to know about. Soul surfers will find these without much trouble.

During summer's southern swell, the place to be is the Corridor between Cabo San Lucas and San José del Cabo, where beach breaks predominate at dependable spots like Costa Azul ("Zipper's"). When the southern swell is really happening, surfable waves wrap right around San José del Cabo as far north up the Sea of Cortez as Los Barriles. More information on Pacific and Cortez breaks can be found in the appropriate destination sections.

Equipment

Surfing is a low-tech sport, so the scarcity of surf shops in Baja is not a major problem. For any extended trip down the coast, carry both a short and a long board—or a gun for the north-west shores of Isla Natividad or Islas de Todos Santos in winter. Longboards aren't used much in the Cape Region, however. Besides wax and a cooler, about the only other items you need to bring are a fiberglass-patching kit for bad dings and a first-aid kit for routine surf injuries. Most surf spots are far from medical assistance—don't forget butterfly bandages. Boards can be repaired at just about any boatyard on the coast, since most Mexican *pangas* are made of fiberglass and require a lot of patching.

Small surf shops in San José del Cabo and Cabo San Lucas sell boards, surfwear, and accessories. The best is San José's **Killer Hook.** You can buy Mexican-made boards—San Miguel and Cactus brands—for about US$50-75 less than what they cost north of the border, about US$100 less than retail for a comparable American or Japanese board.

Tide charts come in handy for predicting low and high tides; a pocket-sized tide calendar available from **Tidelines,** P.O. Box 431, Encinitas, CA 92024, tel. (760) 753-1747, charts daily tide changes from Crescent City, California, to Manzanillo, Mexico, with +/-corrections from a Los Angeles baseline.

SNORKELING AND SCUBA DIVING

The semitropical Sea of Cortez coral reefs at the southern tip of the Cape Region are among the least known dive locations in Mexico, yet because they're so close to shore they're also among the most accessible. Cape marinelife is concentrated in two types of environments: natural reefs, of either rock or hard coral; and shipwrecks, which develop into artificial reefs over time.

Heavy swells and surging along the Pacific coast mean that Pacific diving should only be tackled by experienced scuba divers or with an experienced underwater guide.

Cape Diving

Because it lies at the intersection of the Pacific and the Cortez, the Cape Region makes a particularly varied dive location. The Sea of Cortez alone offers one of the world's richest marine ecosystems; sea lions, numerous whale and dolphin varieties, manta rays, amberjacks, and schooling hammerhead sharks are all part of a thick food chain stimulated by cold-water upwellings amid the over 100 islands and islets that dot the Cortez. Larger species native to temperate northern waters mix with colorful, smaller species of tropical origin that have found their way north from Central and South American waters, thus providing underwater scenery that is especially vivid and varied.

Rock reefs are abundant throughout the lower Cortez islands near La Paz, where tidal conditions are generally calm and the water is relatively warm year-round. Marinelife is plentiful and varied at such sites. From La Paz south, onshore water temperatures usually hover between 21° C (70° F) and 29° C (85° F) year-round, making the southern Cortez the most popular diving destination on this side of Baja. Water visibility is best July-Oct., when it exceeds 30 meters (100 feet); this is also when the air

temperature is warmest, often reaching well over 32° C (90° F).

La Paz has several dive shops; popular local dive sites are numerous and include Playa Balandra (mostly snorkeling), Roca Suwanee, Isla Espíritu Santo, Isla Partida, the *Salvatierra* shipwreck, El Bajito Reef, Los Islotes, and El Bajo Seamount. El Bajo is famous for its summer population of giant manta rays. Schooling hammerhead sharks are also common during the summer months—they're very rarely aggressive toward divers when swimming in schools, so El Bajo makes an excellent observation area.

The Cabo Pulmo and Los Cabos areas are served by several small dive operations. The East Cape is known for Pulmo Reef, the only hard coral reef in the Sea of Cortez. This reef consists of a series of eight volcanic ridges inhabited by profuse coral life. The coral attracts a wide variety of fish of all sizes and colors; other smaller reefs, as well as shipwrecks, lie in the general vicinity. Because most underwater attractions are close to shore, this area is perfect for diving from small boats or open-cockpit kayaks. Some of the reef fingers can even be reached from shore.

Several coves along the coast toward Cabo San Lucas make good snorkeling sites. Bahía Cabo San Lucas itself is a protected marine park; the rocks and points along the bayshore are suitable for snorkelers and novice scuba divers while the deep submarine canyon just 45 meters offshore attracts experienced thrillseekers. This canyon is known for its intriguing "sandfalls," streams of falling sand channeled between rocks along the canyon walls. Nearby Playa Santa María and Playa Chileno, on the way east toward San José del Cabo, are popular snorkeling areas with soft corals at either end of a large cove.

Equipment

Dive shops throughout the Cape Region are well stocked with standard diving and snorkeling equipment. Novice divers won't need to bring anything; experienced divers who are picky about their equipment may want to bring along any specialized gear they're accustomed to. Since most equipment sold or rented in Cape dive shops is imported from the U.S., stocks vary from season to season. Purchase prices are also generally a little higher in Mexico than north of the border.

At Cabo San Lucas and around the Cape as far north as La Paz, a light wetsuit may be necessary from late November through March; shorties or ordinary swimsuits will suffice the rest of the year. In summer, many Sea of Cortez divers wear Lycra skins to protect against jellyfish stings.

Because divers and anglers occasionally use the same areas, a good diving knife is essential for dealing with wayward fishing line. Bring two knives so you'll have a spare. Also pack extra O-rings and bring a wetsuit patching kit if you plan to dive away from resort areas.

Air: Dependable air for scuba tanks is available in La Paz, Cabo Pulmo, and Cabo San Lucas. Always check the compressor first to make sure it's well maintained and running clean. Divers with extensive Baja experience usually carry a portable compressor not only to avoid contaminated air, but to use in areas where tank refills aren't available.

Recompression Chambers: Servicios de Seguridad Subacuática (Underwater Safety Services), tel. (1) 143-3666, operates a hyperbaric decompression chamber in Cabo San Lucas at Plaza Marina (next to Plaza Las Glorias). The facility is equipped with two compressors, an oxygen analyzer, closed-circuit TV, and a hotline to Divers Alert Network (DAN). If this facility isn't available, the next nearest full-time, dependable recompression facility is the **Hyperbaric Medicine Center** at the University of California Medical Center in San Diego,

chilipepper fish

tel. (619) 543-5222. The HMC is open Mon.-Fri. 7:30 a.m.-4:30 p.m. and for emergencies.

Cabo Diving Services, Apdo. Postal 195, Cabo San Lucas, BCS, tel. (1) 143-1110, claims it will soon be setting up another recompression chamber in Cabo San Lucas—call for the latest word.

Organized Dive Trips and Instruction

Cabo San Lucas boasts the Cape Region's greatest number of dive shops offering dive excursions. Many also offer instruction and PADI scuba certification.

In Cabo Pulmo on the East Cape, three small operations offer guided dive trips; one, **Pepe's Dive Center,** Apdo. Postal 532, Cabo San Lucas, BCS, tel. (1) 141-0001, toll free (877) 733-2252, also offers instruction and PADI certification at reasonable rates. If you're planning on doing a Pulmo dive, it's considerably less expensive to arrange it here than in Cabo San Lucas on the other end of the Cape, assuming you can arrange your own transportation.

La Paz has two or three reliable outfitters that offer guided dives and instruction/certification, relatively few considering the numerous offshore dive sites in the vicinity. The oldest, **Baja Expeditions,** 2625 Garnet Ave., San Diego, CA 92109, tel. (619) 581-3311, toll-free (800) 943-6967, fax (619) 581-6542, e-mail: travel@bajaex.com, offers well-organized, extended dive trips on live-aboard boats to El Bajo and other offshore sites June-November.

ACCOMMODATIONS

Places to stay in the Cape Region run the gamut from free beach camping to plush resort hotels. Visitors who plan on doing the Cape circuit will have a greater range of options at any given location if they bring along camping gear.

HOTELS AND MOTELS

Unlike the closely spaced, vertical high-rises of Cancún, Acapulco, and other major Mexican re-

sorts, Cape Region hotels tend more toward the organic than the geometric. Even in the Los Cabos area, they're more likely to hide behind a rocky cliff or occupy a secluded cove, spreading out along a sandy swath rather than towering over it. Often their shapes and colors mimic the surrounding environment.

For most Cape hotels, the high season runs Nov.-March. Some places charge a higher peak-season rate Jan.-March; in purely statistical terms, March usually scores the highest annual hotel occupancy. At many hotels and motels, midweek rates are lower than weekend rates.

Obviously one way to save money on accommodations is to visit the Cape in the off-season, i.e., April-October. The Cape Region's climate is livable year-round; summer temperatures of 37° C/100° F on the Cortez coast are usually mitigated by sea breezes and relatively low humidity. The exception is Aug.-Sept., when high temperatures and high humidity are the norm all along the Cortez coast (see Climate for further specifics).

Whatever the rack rate, you can usually get the price down by bargaining (except during peak periods, e.g., Christmas, spring break, and Easter). When making a reservation or checking in, be sure to clarify whether the room rate includes meals—occasionally it does. Asking for a room without meals is an easy way to bring the rate down, or you can simply ask if there's anything cheaper.

Most hotels add a 12% tax (10% valued-added tax, plus 2% lodging tax) to quoted rates. Some also add a 10% service charge. To avoid a 22% surprise over posted rates when you check out, be sure to ask whether the quoted rate includes tax and service.

Price categories used in this book are as follows:

Shoestring: under US$15
Budget: US$15-35
Inexpensive: US$36-55
Moderate: US$56-80
Expensive: US$81-120
Premium: US$120+

Unless otherwise specified, where rate ranges are quoted in this book, the lower figure represents the rate for the least expensive single room, while the upper figure is the rate for the most expensive standard double room. Other room choices may be available at rates between those two figures, and suites may be available at higher rates. If a single price is listed, it reflects the average price of a standard room, single or double occupancy. All listed rates are per room, per night.

Shoestring to Budget
Many hotels and motels in the Cape Region are considerably less expensive than their counterparts in the U.S., Canada, or Europe. Even Los Cabos rates tend to line up slightly lower than rates at most other beach resorts in Mexico (the

San José–Cabo San Lucas Corridor is an exception). In the budget range, you'll find a simple but clean room with private bath and double bed for around US$20-35 in La Paz, Cabo San Lucas, Todos Santos, and San José. Soap, towels, toilet paper, and purified drinking water are usually provided; in some places you may have to ask. Rooms in this price range don't always offer a/c (in San Lucas and San José they usually do) but fans may be available.

Lodging under US$15 per night is rare unless you stay at a *casa de huéspedes* or *pensión* (see below), where bathrooms are usually shared *(baño colectivo)*. Only La Paz, the state capital, has such rock-bottom facilities. Todos Santos also harbors one hostel with shoestring rates.

Inexpensive to Moderate
The largest number of hotels and motels in the Cape Region fall into the US$40-80 range. Some are older Mexican-style hotels just a bit larger than those in the budget range, while others are American-style motels. Everything in this price range comes with a/c.

Expensive to Premium
Higher-end places are found all along the coast from La Paz around to Cabo San Lucas. Prices for international-class accommodations average around US$80-120. Some of these places are good values, while others are definitely overpriced. When in doubt, stick to the less expensive hotels. Or ask about "specials"; places that normally cost US$150 a night are sometimes available at 50% discounts.

The most luxurious hotels in all of Baja—indeed among the best in all of Mexico—are found along the coast between San José del Cabo and Cabo San Lucas, in an area known as "The Corridor." Beach frontage, huge pools, spas, world-class restaurants, and golf course privileges are all part of the experience at these resorts. A few Cape resorts charge US$250 or more for particular rooms or suites. Las Ventanas al Paraíso, one of the latest and greatest of the Corridor palaces, starts at US$400 for a junior suite and tops out at US$3,000 a night for a three-bedroom presidential suite.

Hotel Reservation Services
Most of the hotels and motels mentioned in this guidebook will take advance reservations direct-

*Westin Regina Resort
Los Cabos*

ly by phone or mail. Some visitors may find it more convenient to use one of the following reservation services offered in the United States: **Baja Lodging Services,** tel. (619) 491-0693; **Baja Motion,** toll free tel. (877) 246-BAJA; or **Baja California Tours,** tel. (858) 454-7166 or toll-free (800) 336-5454, e-mail: bajatours@aol.com. Occasionally these agencies can arrange lower room rates or special packages not offered directly by the hotels themselves. Note that the life of these kinds of booking agencies tends to be very short—Baja California Tours is in fact the only hotel reservation agency specializing in Baja that has lasted through two editions of this guidebook. Your local travel agent may also be able to book lodging in Baja.

Delfin Hotels and Resorts, 330 High St., Santa Cruz, CA 95060, tel. (408) 459-9494 or toll-free (800) 524-5104, fax (408) 459-9574, website: www.cabohotels.com, handles reservations for several condominiums and hotels in San José del Cabo (La Jolla, Misiones del Cabo) and Cabo San Lucas (Suites Terrasol, Marina Cabo Plaza, Cabo Inn, and Casa Rafael's).

CASAS DE HUÉSPEDES AND PENSIONES

Aside from free or very basic campgrounds, *casas de huéspedes* (guesthouses) and *pensiones* (boardinghouses) are the cheapest places to stay in the Cape Region. Unfortunately for budgeteers they're found only in La Paz. The typical *casa de huéspedes* offers rooms with shared bath *(baño colectivo)* for US$5-10, US$8-13 with private bath. A *pensión* costs about the same and differs from a *casa de huésped* only in name. At either, most lodgers are staying for a week or more, but the proprietors are usually happy to accept guests by the night.

The main difference between these and budget hotels/motels—besides rates—is that they're usually located in old houses or other buildings (e.g., convents) that have been converted for guesthouse use. Soap, towels, toilet paper, and drinking water are usually provided, but you may have to ask.

Youth Hostel
A Hostelling International-affiliated youth hostel (*villa deportiva juvenil,* or youth sports villa) in La Paz offers shared dormitory-style rooms. Each guest is assigned a bed and a locker and has access to the hostel's sports facilities. Bathing facilities are communal and guests must supply their own soap and towels. The rate is US$5 (US$6 for non-HI members).

Staying at the hostel is a great way to meet young Mexicans and improve your Spanish; English is rarely spoken. About the only drawback is that the hostel is inconveniently located some distance from the center of town, so transportation can be a problem.

Condo/House Rentals and House-sitting
For long-term stays of a month or more—and occasionally for stays as short as a week—

house or condo rental may be significantly less expensive and more convenient than staying at a hotel or motel. Rents vary wildly according to facilities, neighborhood, and general location in Baja. The most expensive rentals are those found along The Corridor between San José and San Lucas. Expect to pay a minimum of US$500 a month in these beach areas (in some instances you could easily pay that for a weekend), more typically US$1,000-1,500 a month for something quite simple.

Some of the best deals on beach houses can be found in Los Barriles, Buena Vista, and Todos Santos. At any of these places you can rent a furnished one- or two-bedroom with kitchen starting at around US$350-500 a month, more for places with air-con or lots of modern appliances. Property management services and real estate companies in these areas can help you locate something in your price range—see the appropriate destination chapters for contact information.

Some of the same companies that manage rentals may be able to offer house-sitting opportunities in homes whose seasonal residents want someone to take care of their property while they're away. Living rent-free in Baja may sound wonderful, but keep in mind that many homeowners have a list of chores they want carried out on a regular basis, such as tending plants, feeding and exercising pets, and so on. A newsletter called **Caretaker Gazette,** P.O. Box 5887-M, Carefree, AZ 85377-0887, tel. (480) 488-1970, e-mail: caretaker@uswest.net, occasionally advertises house-sitting opportunities in Mexico.

CAMPING

The Cape Region has more campgrounds, RV parks, and camping areas for its size than any region in Mexico. Because the Cape's population density is so low, it's easy to find beach campsites offering idyllic settings and precious solitude, often free of charge. For travelers who like the outdoors, camping is an excellent way to slash accommodations costs. A recent tourist survey found that over half of Baja's foreign overnight visitors camp rather than stay in hotels.

Campgrounds and RV Parks
The Cape Region offers roughly 20 private campgrounds that charge fees ranging from around US$4 for a place with virtually zero facilities to as high as US$15 for a developed RV park with full hookups and recreation facilities. Most campgrounds charge around US$3-5 for tent camping, US$7-12 for full hookups.

If you can forgo permanent toilet and bathing facilities you won't have to pay anything to camp, since there's an essentially limitless selection of free camping spots, from beaches to deserts to mountain slopes. You won't necessarily need 4WD to reach these potential campsites, as plenty of turnouts and graded dirt *ramales* (branch roads) off the main highways can be negotiated by just about any type of vehicle.

The isolated, idyllic beaches of the Cape Region offer numerous camping opportunities.

FOOD AND DRINK

Much of what *bajacalifornianos* eat can be considered Northern Mexican cuisine. Because Northern Mexico is generally better suited to ranching than farming, ranch-style cooking tends to prevail in rural areas, which means that ranch products—beef, poultry, and dairy foods—are highly favored.

Unlike the northern mainland, however, just about any point in the Cape Region is less than a couple of hours' drive from the seashore, so seafood predominates here more than elsewhere in Northern Mexico—or probably anywhere else in Mexico for that matter. In most places on the Cape, seafood is more common than meat or poultry. If there's anything unique about Cape cuisine, it's the blending of ranch cooking with coastal culture, which has resulted in such distinctive food creations as the *taco de pescado* (fish taco).

WHERE TO EAT

The Cape's larger towns—La Paz, San José del Cabo, and Cabo San Lucas—offer everything from humble sidewalk taco stands to *gran turismo* hotel restaurants. Elsewhere the choices are fewer and more basic. In small towns there may be only two or three restaurants serving standard Mexican dishes or, if near the coast, *mariscos* (seafood). Sometimes the best meals on the road come from what you improvise after a visit to a local *tienda de abarrotes* (grocery store).

Most hotels on the Cape have restaurants; in small towns and remote areas these may be among the best (and only) choices. A few hotel restaurants, such as the Westin Regina Resort's Arrecife Restaurant or The Restaurant at Las Ventanas al Paraíso, both found in The Corridor between San José and San Lucas, are worthwhile culinary destinations in and of themselves. In Cabo San Lucas, the Cape's vacation capital, many restaurants cater to tourist tastes by serving a hybrid menu of common Mexican dishes, seafood, and burgers.

Costs

In this guidebook we've tried to give some guidance as to the approximate meal cost at most sit-down restaurants. At "inexpensive" places you can count on spending less than US$7 for an entrée (or for a *comida corrida,* where available), while a "moderate" meal will cost up to US$15, "expensive" over US$15.

Local Color

Taquerías, small, inexpensive diners where tacos are assembled before your eyes (sort of the Mexican equivalent to the old-fashioned American

Streetside grills provide aromatic ambience and great food.

hamburger stand), tend to be found in areas with lots of foot traffic—near bus terminals, for example. The good ones are packed with taco-eaters in the early evening. In La Paz and San José del Cabo, another economical alternative is the *lonchería*—a small, cafe-style place that usually serves *almuerzo* (late breakfast/early lunch) and *comida* (the main, midday meal). *Loncherías* typically are open 11 a.m.-5 p.m. Municipal markets in La Paz and San José feature rows of *loncherías* serving inexpensive basic meals and *antojitos* (snacks or one-plate dishes). Some *loncherías* offer *comida corrida,* a daily fixed-price meal that includes a beverage, an entree or two, side dishes, and possibly dessert.

Cafes or *cafeterías* are similar to *loncherías* except that they may open earlier and serve *desayuno* (breakfast) in addition to other meals.

A *cenaduría* is yet another simple, cafe-style restaurant, this time concentrating on *la cena,* the evening meal. Often the menu will be similar to that of a *lonchería*—mostly *antojitos*—but the hours are later, typically 5-10 p.m.

Ordering and Paying

You really don't need much Spanish to get by in a restaurant (in most hotel restaurants, you won't need any at all). Stating what you want, plus *por favor* (please), will usually do the trick (e.g., *dos cervezas, por favor,* "two beers, please"). Don't forget to say *gracias* (thank you). The menu is called *el menú* or, much less commonly in Baja, *la carta.* As a last resort, you can always point to what you want on the menu.

La cuenta is the bill. A tip *(la propina)* of about 10-15% is expected at any restaurant with table service; look to see if it's already been added to the bill before placing a tip on the table.

WHAT TO EAT

Tortillas

A Mexican meal is not a meal without tortillas, the round, flat, pancake-like disks eaten with nearly any nondessert dish, including salads, meats, seafood, beans, and vegetables. Both wheat-flour and cornmeal tortillas are commonly consumed in the Cape Region. Among Northern Mexicans, it is said that meat and poultry dishes taste best with flour tortillas while vegetable dishes go best with

corn. Most restaurants offer a choice of the two. If you order tortillas without specifying, you may get *¿de harina o de maíz?* as a response.

Although prepackaged tortillas are available in *supermercados* (supermarkets), most Mexicans buy them fresh from neighborhood *tortillerías* or make them at home. Many restaurants and cafes in the Cape region, and virtually all *loncherías* and *taquerías,* serve only fresh tortillas—tortillas made the same day, or the night before. If you're used to prepackaged tortillas, which is what most Mexican eateries in the U.S. or Canada serve, you're in for a pleasurable surprise when you raise a fresh, hot, homemade tortilla to your nose for the first time.

Incidentally, a tortilla has two sides, an inside and an outside, that dictate which direction the tortilla is best folded when wrapping it around food. The side with the thinner layer—sometimes called the *pancita,* or belly—should face the inside when folding the tortilla. If you notice the outside of your tortilla cracking, with pieces peeling off onto the table, you've probably folded it with the *pancita* outside instead of inside.

Antojitos and Main Dishes

Antojitos literally means "little whims," thus implying snacks to many people. However, the word also refers to any food that can be ordered, served, and eaten quickly—in other words, Mexican fast food. Typical *antojitos* include tamales, enchiladas, burritos, *flautas, chiles rellenos, chalupas, picadillo,* quesadillas, *tortas,* and tacos.

The main dish or *el plato fuerte* of any meal can be a grander version of an *antojito,* a regional specialty from another part of Mexico (*mole poblano,* for example), or something the *cocineros* (cooks) dream up themselves. Typical entrees are centered around meats, seafood, or poultry.

Breakfasts

Menus at tourist restaurants are often confusing because some of the same "breakfast" dishes may end up on more than one section of the menu. Mexicans have two kinds of breakfasts, an early one called *desayuno,* eaten shortly after rising, and a second called *almuerzo* that's usually taken around 11 a.m. To further confuse the issue, Spanish-English dictionaries usually translate *almuerzo* as "lunch," while bilingual menus often read "breakfast."

The most common Mexican *desayuno* is simply *pan dulce* (sweet pastry) or *bolillos* (torpedo-shaped, European-style rolls) with coffee or milk. Cereal is also sometimes eaten for *desayuno;* e.g., *avena* (oatmeal), *crema de trigo* (cream of wheat), or *hojuelas de maíz* (corn flakes).

The heavier eggs-and-frijoles dishes known widely as "Mexican breakfasts" in the U.S. and Canada are usually taken as *almuerzo,* the late breakfast, which is most typically reserved for weekends and holidays. Eggs come in a variety of ways, including *huevos revueltos* (scrambled eggs), *huevos duros* (hard-boiled eggs), *huevos escafaldos* (soft-boiled eggs), *huevos estrellados* (eggs fried sunny side up), *huevos a la mexicana* (also *huevos mexicanos,* eggs scrambled with chopped tomato, onion, and chiles), *huevos rancheros* (fried eggs served on a tortilla), and *huevos divorciados,* two *huevos estrellados* separated by beans, each egg usually topped with a different salsa.

Eggs also come *con chorizo* (scrambled with ground sausage), *con tocino* (with bacon), or *con jamón* (with ham). All egg dishes usually come with frijoles and tortillas. The biggest *almuerzo* package on the menu is typically called *almuerzo albañil* ("brickmason's *almuerzo"*) or *huevos albañil* ("brickmason's eggs"); this means eggs with one or more varieties of meat on the side.

ANTOJITOS

birria—lamb or goat stew in a sauce spiced with chiles, cinnamon, cloves, cumin, and oregano

burrito—a flour tortilla rolled around meat, beans, or seafood fillings; Baja's lobster burritos are legendary

chalupa—a crisp, whole tortilla topped with beans, meat, etc. (also known as a *tostada*)

chile relleno—a mild poblano chile stuffed with cheese, deep-fried in egg batter, and served with a ranchero sauce (tomatoes, onions, and chiles)

enchilada—a corn tortilla dipped in chile sauce, then folded or rolled around a filling of meat, chicken, seafood, or cheese and baked in an oven

enfrijolada—same as *enchilada* except dipped in a sauce of thinned refried beans instead of chile sauce

entomatada—same as *enchilada* except dipped in a tomato sauce instead of chile sauce

flauta—a small corn tortilla roll, usually stuffed with beef or chicken and fried

gordita—a small, thick, corn tortilla stuffed with a spicy meat mixture

huarache—literally, "sandal"; a large, flat, thick, oval-shaped tortilla topped with fried meat and chiles

menudo—a thick soup made with cows' feet and stomachs (and less commonly, intestines), and seasoned with *chiles de árbol,* oregano, and fresh chopped onion; reputedly a sure hangover cure

pozole—hominy stew made with pork or chicken and garnished with radishes, oregano, onions, chile powder, salt, and lime

picadillo—a spicy salad of chopped or ground meat with chiles and onions (also known as *salpicón*)

quesadilla—a flour tortilla folded over sliced cheese and grilled; ask the cook to add *chiles rajas* (pepper strips) for extra flavor

sope—a small, thick, round corn cake with dimpled edges, topped with a spicy meat mixture and crumbled cheese

taco—a corn tortilla folded or rolled around anything and eaten with the hands; *tacos de pescado,* or "fish tacos," are a Baja specialty

tamal—plural *tamales;* cornmeal *(masa)* dough wrapped in a corn husk and steamed; sometimes stuffed with corn, olives, pork, or turkey

torta—a sandwich made with a Mexican-style roll (*bolillo/birote* or the larger *pan telera*); one of the most popular is the *torta de milanesa,* made with breaded, deep-fried veal or pork

COOKING METHODS

Entrees, whether meat, poultry, or seafood, are most commonly prepared in one of the following styles:

adobo, adobada—marinated or stewed in a sauce of vinegar, chiles, and spices

a la parrilla—broiled or grilled

albóndigas—meatballs

al carbón—charcoal-grilled

a la veracruzana—seafood, often *huachinango* (red snapper), cooked with tomatoes, onions, chiles, and olives

al mojo de ajo—in a garlic sauce

al pastor—slowly roasted on a vertical spit

al vapor—steamed

asado/asada—grilled

barbacoa—pit-roasted

con arroz—steamed with rice

encebollado—cooked with onions

entomado—cooked with tomatoes

empanizada—breaded

frito—fried

guisado—in a spicy stew

machaca—dried and shredded

One of the cheapest and tastiest *almuerzos* is *chilaquiles,* tortilla chips in a chile gravy with crumbled cheese on top. Eggs or chicken can be added to *chilaquiles* as options. Another economical choice is *molletes,* which consists of a split *bolillo* spread with mashed beans and melted cheese, served with salsa on the side.

Meats

Common meats include *carne de res* (beef), *puerco* (pork), and *borrego* (lamb). *Jamón* (ham), chorizo (sausage), and *tocino* (bacon) are usually reserved for *almuerzo.* Steak may appear on menus as *bistec, bistek, biftec,* or "steak." *Venado* (deer meat or venison) and *conejo* (rabbit) are commonly served on ranchos. Poultry dishes include *pollo* (chicken), *pavo* (turkey), and, less frequently, *pato* (duck) and *codorniz* (quail).

Seafood

Pescado (fish) entrees on the menu are often seasonal or dependent on the "catch of the day."

Often just the word *pescado* and the method of cooking will appear (e.g., *pescado al mojo de ajo*). If you need to know exactly what kind of fish, just ask *"¿Hay qué tipo de pescado?"*—although in some cases the only response you'll get will be something generic like *"Pescado blanco"* ("white fish"). For specific fish names, see the special topic Fish Translator.

Baja's number-one seafood specialty is the *taco de pescado* (fish taco). If you've never tried one, you're most likely wondering "What's the big deal—a fish taco?" Eat one, though, and you're hooked for life. Short, tender, fresh fish fillets are dipped in batter and fried quickly, then folded into a steaming corn tortilla with a variety of condiments, including *salsa fresca* (chopped tomatoes, onions, chiles, and lime juice), marinated cabbage (similar to coleslaw in the U.S.), guacamole (a savory avocado paste), and sometimes a squirt of mayonnaise or *crema* (fresh Mexican cream). *¡La última!* Any kind of white-fleshed fish can be used—the best fish tacos are those made from yellowtail *(jurel),* halibut *(lenguado),* or mahimahi *(dorado).*

Shellfish dishes *(mariscos)* popular on Baja menus include: *ostiones* (oysters), *almejas* (clams), *callos* (scallops), *jaibas* (small crabs), *cangrejos* (large crabs), *camarones* (shrimp), *langosta* (lobster), *langostina* (crayfish, also called *cucarachas*), and *abulón* (abalone). They can be ordered as *cocteles* (cocktails—steamed or boiled and served with lime and salsa), *en sus conchas* (in the shell), or in many other ways.

Beans

The beans (frijoles) preferred in the Cape Region, as on the northern mainland, are pinto beans, usually dried beans boiled until soft, then mashed and fried with lard or vegetable oil (usually the former). Often this preparation is called *frijoles refritos,* or "refried beans," although they're not really refried except when reheated. Sometimes the beans are served whole, in their own broth, as *frijoles de olla* (boiled beans) or with bits of roast pork as *frijoles a la charra* (ranch-style beans). Frijoles can be served with any meal of the day, including breakfast.

Cheese

Even the most remote rancho will usually have some cheese *(queso)* around, so if your appetite isn't stimulated by the *iguana guisada* simmering on the hearth, you can usually ask for *chiles rellenos* (mild poblano chiles stuffed with cheese and fried in an egg batter) or quesadillas (cheese melted in folded flour tortillas). A meal of beans, tortillas, and cheese provides a complete source of protein for travelers who choose to avoid meat, poultry, or seafood for health, economic, or moral reasons.

Vegetables and Vegetarian Food

Although vegetables are sometimes served as side dishes with *comidas corridas,* with restaurant entrees, or in salads *(ensaladas),* they're seldom listed separately on the menu. Many types of vegetables are grown in the Cape Region, particularly in the lower elevations on the east side of the Sierra de La Laguna and in the vicinity of Todos Santos and Pescadero. Several farms in the Todos Santos area specialize in organic produce.

It's difficult but not impossible to practice a vegetarian regime in Baja. Lacto-vegetarians can eat quesadillas (ask for corn tortillas, which unlike most flour tortillas do not contain lard) or enchiladas de queso (cheese enchiladas). With some luck, you'll stumble across restaurants that can prepare a variety of interesting cheese dishes, including *queso fundido con champiñones* (melted cheese with mushrooms, eaten with tortillas) and quesadillas made with *flor de calabaza* or squash flower. Some places make beans without lard *(sin manteca)* but you'll have to ask to find out. Pizza restaurants are common through-out urban Baja. Many larger towns have at least one vegetarian/health food store (usually called *tienda naturista*) with a small dining section as well as bulk foods.

Ovo-lacto-vegetarians can add egg dishes and flan to their menus. Vegans for the most part will do best to prepare their own food. Look for shops with signs reading *semillas* (seeds) to pin down a good selection of nuts and dried beans. Of course you'll find plenty of fresh fruits and vegetables in markets and grocery stores (see Buying Groceries, below).

Soup

The general menu term for soup is *sopa,* although a thick soup with lots of ingredients is usually a *caldo* or *caldillo. Menudo* is a soup of hominy *(nixtamal)* and cow's feet and stomach (or, less commonly, intestine) in a savory, reddish-brown broth, served with chopped onions, chiles, and crumbled oregano. It's seen through-out Mexico and is highly prized as a hangover remedy. *Pozole* is a similar soup with a much lighter-colored broth; some varieties of *pozole* are made with chicken instead of tripe.

Other tasty soups include *sopa de tortillas, sopa azteca,* and *sopa tlapeño,* all variations of artfully seasoned chicken broth garnished with *totopos* (tortilla wedges) and sliced avocado.

Salsas and Condiments

Any restaurant, cafe, *lonchería,* or *taquería* will offer a variety of salsas. Sometimes only certain salsas are served with certain dishes, while

fruit vendor, Cabo San Lucas

at other times one, two, or even three salsas are stationed on every table. Often each place has its own unique salsa recipes—canned or bottled salsas are rarely used. The one ingredient common to all salsas is chile peppers; these vary in heat from mild to incendiary.

There are as many types of salsas as there are Mexican dishes—red, green, yellow, brown, hot, mild, salty, sweet, thick, thin, blended, and chunky. The most typical is the *salsa casera* (house salsa), a simple, fresh concoction of chopped chiles, onions, and tomatoes mixed with salt, lime juice, and cilantro. This is what you usually get with the complimentary basket of *totopos* (tortilla chips) served at the beginning of every Mexican meal. Another common offering is *salsa verde* (green sauce), made with a base of tomatillos (small, tart, green tomato-like vegetables). Some salsas are *picante,* or spicy hot (also *picosa*), so it's always a good idea to test a bit before pouring the stuff over everything on your plate.

Whole pickled chiles are sometimes served on the side as a condiment, especially with tacos. Salt *(sal)* is usually on the table, although it's rarely needed since Mexican dishes tend to be prepared with plenty of it. Black pepper is *pimiento negro,* and if it's not on the table it's normally available for the asking. Butter is *mantequilla,* sometimes served with flour tortillas.

In *taquerías,* guacamole (mashed avocado blended with onions, chiles, salt, and sometimes other ingredients) is always served as a condiment. In restaurants it may be served as a salad or with tortilla chips.

Desserts and Sweets

The most popular of Mexican desserts, or *postres,* is a delicious egg custard called flan. It's listed on virtually every tourist restaurant menu, along with *helado* (ice cream). Other sweet alternatives include pastries found in *panaderías* (bakeries) and the frosty offerings at the ubiquitous *paleterías.* Strictly speaking, a *paletería* serves only *paletas,* flavored ice on sticks (like American popsicles but with a much wider range of flavors), but many also serve *nieve,* literally "snow," which is flavored grated ice served like ice cream in bowls or cones.

Dulcerías, or candy shops, sell a huge variety of sticky Mexican sweets, usually wrapped individually. Often brightly decorated, *dulcerías* are oriented toward children and sometimes carry inexpensive toys as well as sweets. The larger ones sell piñatas—colorful papier-mâché figures filled with candy and small gifts and hung at parties, where children are allowed to break them with sticks, releasing all the goodies inside. Traditionally piñatas are crafted to resemble common animals, but these days you'll see all kinds of shapes, including Power Rangers and Batman.

In Todos Santos, once an important sugarcane-growing area, a local specialty is *panocha,* a candy made from raw sugar.

BUYING GROCERIES

The cheapest way to feed yourself while traveling around the Cape Region is the same way you save money at home: Buy groceries at the store and prepare your own meals. While they may not have any dining spots to speak of, even the smallest towns will have a little grocery store or corner market. A ripe avocado, a chunk of *queso fresco,* and a couple of *bolillos* can make a fine, easy-to-fix meal.

The humblest type of store is the small family-owned *tienda de abarrotes,* usually recognizable by the single word *abarrotes* (groceries) printed somewhere on the outside (*tienda* means "store"). These stock the basics—tortillas, dried beans, flour, herbs and spices, bottled water, a few vegetables, possibly *bolillos* and *queso fresco*—as well as limited household goods like soap and laundry detergent. As at the 7-Eleven back home, the food at the average *tienda de abarrotes* is not particularly inexpensive.

A better deal, where available, is the government-sponsored Diconsa, an acronym for Distribuidora Conasupo, S.A. Diconsas carry many of the same items as *tiendas de abarrotes,* but at government-subsidized prices. Not every item is cheaper, however, so it pays to shop around. The "Tienda Rural" is very similar. Larger, supermarket-style Conasupos are called Conasupers. Even less expensive are markets operated by ISSSTE (Instituto de Seguridad y Servicios Sociales para Trabajadores del Estado).

Privately run, American-style supermarkets, found in La Paz, San José, and Cabo San Lucas,

paletería y nevería

are called *supers* or *supermercados.* Like their American counterparts, they're usually well stocked with a wide variety of meats, baked goods, vegetables, household goods, and beer and liquor, including many common U.S. brands. The supermarket at Plaza Aramburo in Cabo San Lucas has a better variety of foodstuffs than many American supermarkets! As in the rest of North America, supermarket prices are often lower than those of smaller grocery stores.

La Paz and San José support *mercados municipales* (municipal markets), large warehouse-type structures where meat, fruit, and vegetable producers sell their goods directly to the public. Prices are often very good at these markets but it helps if you know how to bargain.

Panaderías

Although you can often buy a few bakery items at the aforementioned stores, the best place to buy them is at their source—a *panadería* (literally, "breadery," i.e., bakery). The typical *panadería* produces tasty *bolillos* (Mexican rolls), *pastels* (cakes), and *pan dulce* (cookies and sweet pastries). To select bakery items from the shelves of a *panadería,* simply imitate the other customers—pick up a pair of tongs and a tray from the counter near the cash register and help yourself, cafeteria-style.

Tortillerías

Unless you make them yourself, the best tortillas are found where they make them fresh every day. Restaurants, *tiendas,* and home cooks will purchase from the local *tortillería* to avoid spending hours at a *metate* (grinder) and *comal* (griddle). The automated process at a *tortillería* uses giant electric grinders and conveyor belts to transform whole corn into fresh tortillas, which you purchase by weight, not number. A kilo yields about 40 average, 12-cm (five-inch) tortillas; you can order by the *cuarto* or *medio* (quarter or half kilo). The government-subsidized prices are low (currently about 53 cents per kilo).

NONALCOHOLIC BEVERAGES

Water

Bottled drinking water is usually available at every *tienda de abarrotes* or supermarket throughout the region. If you're car camping, renting a house, or staying in one place for a long time, it may be more convenient to use the 20-liter (roughly five-gallon) reusable plastic containers of drinking water available in most Mexican towns. These typically cost US$6 for the first bottle of water and bottle deposit, then US$1.20 for each 20-liter refill. This is much cheaper than buying individual liter or half-liter bottles, which often cost as much as US$1 apiece, and you won't be throwing away so much plastic. The water will be easier to dispense if you also buy a *sifón* (siphon) designed for that purpose. These are available for around US$2.50 at many grocery stores.

The water and ice served in restaurants in the Cape Region is always purified—it's not necessary to order *agua mineral* (mineral water) unless you need the minerals. Likewise, the water used as an ingredient in "handmade" drinks, e.g., *licuados* or *aguas frescas,* also comes from purified sources. Actually, most Cape residents—Mexicans and foreigners alike—drink right out of the tap because the source, Sierra de La Laguna spring water, is perfectly safe.

Soft Drinks

Licuados are similar to American "smoothies"—fruit blended with water, ice, honey or sugar, and sometimes milk or raw eggs, to produce something like a fruit shake. Any place that makes *licuados* will also make orange juice *(jugo de naranja).*

Aguas frescas are the colorful beverages sold from huge glass jars on the streets of larger cities, or at carnivals, especially during warm weather. They're made by boiling the pulp of various fruits, grains, or seeds with water, then straining it and adding sugar and large chunks of ice. *Arroz* (rice) and *horchata* (melon-seed) are two of the tastiest *aguas.*

American soft drinks *(refrescos)* like 7UP, Coke, and Pepsi are common; their Mexican equivalents are just as good. An apple-flavored soft drink called Manzanita is popular.

Hot Drinks

Coffee is served in a variety of ways. The best, when you can find it—ranchos sometimes serve it—is traditional Mexican-style coffee, which is made by filtering near-boiling water through fine-ground coffee in a slender cloth sack. Instant coffee *(nescafé)* is often served at small restaurants and cafes; a jar of instant coffee may be sitting on the table for you to add to hot water. When there's a choice, a request for *café de olla* (pot coffee) should bring you real brewed coffee. When you order coffee in a Mexican restaurant, some servers will ask *de grano o de agua?* (literally "grain or water?"), meaning "instant or brewed?" One of the better Mexican brands found in supermarkets is Café Combate. If you'd like a darker roast than normally available, buy a bag of green coffee beans (available at most supermarkets) and roast your own in a dry iron skillet.

Café con leche is the Mexican version of café au lait, i.e., coffee and hot milk mixed in near-equal proportions. *Café con crema* (coffee with cream) is not as available; when it is, it usually means a cup of coffee with a packet of nondairy creamer on the side. Espresso machines are popping up everywhere in the resort areas of Cabo San Lucas and San José del Cabo; most of the time the so-called "espressos" and "cappuccinos" produced bear only a passing resemblance to the real thing.

Hot chocolate *(chocolate)* is fairly common on Mexican menus. It's usually served very sweet and may contain cinnamon, ground almonds, and other flavorings. A thicker version made with cornmeal—almost a chocolate pudding—is called *champurrado* or *atole.*

Black tea *(té negro)* is not popular among *bajacalifornianos* although you may see it on tourist menus. Ask for *té helado* or *té frío* if you want iced tea. At home many Mexicans drink *té de manzanilla* (chamomile tea), *té de yerba buena* (mint tea), or *té de canela* (cinnamon tea) in the evenings.

ALCOHOLIC BEVERAGES

Drinking laws in Mexico are minimal. The legal drinking age in Mexico is 18 years, and it's illegal to carry an open container of alcoholic beverage in a vehicle. Booze of every kind is widely available in bars, restaurants, grocery stores, and *licorerías* (liquor stores). *Borracho* means both "drunk" (as an adjective) and "drunkard."

Cerveza

The most popular and available beer brand in southern Baja and the Cape Region is Pacífico, from Mazatlán, just across the Sea of Cortez from La Paz. Tecate, brewed in the town of the same name in northern Baja, is the second most popular label. Both brands are good-tasting, light- to medium-weight brews, with Tecate holding a slight edge (more hops) over Pacífico. You can't compare either of these with their export equivalents in the U.S., since Mexican breweries produce separate brews for American consumption that are lighter in taste and lighter on the alcohol content—it's always better in Mexico.

Other major Mexican brands such as Corona Extra (the number-one selling beer in mainland Mexico, and number one imported beer in the

THE LIQUID HEART OF MEXICO

Mexico's national drink has been in production, in prototypical form, since at least the time of the Aztecs. The Aztecs in fact called themselves Mexicas in direct reference to the special spiritual role mescal—tequila's forerunner—played in their culture via Mextli, the god of agave (the desert plant from which *pulque,* mescal, and tequila are derived). These names, as interpreted by the Spanish, eventually yielded "Mexico."

The Spaniards levied a tax on tequila as early as 1608, and in 1795, King Carlos IV granted the first legal concession to produce tequila to Don José María Guadalupe Cuervo. The liquor's name was taken from the Ticuila Indians of Jalisco, who mastered baking the heart of the *Agave tequiliana weber,* or **blue agave,** and extracting its juice, a process employed by tequila distilleries today. Native to Jalisco, this succulent is the only agave that produces true tequila as certified by the Mexican government. Contrary to the myth that all true tequila must come from Tequila, Jalisco, Mexican law enumerates specific districts in five different Mexican states where tequila may be legally produced.

All liquors labeled "tequila" must contain at least 51% blue agave distillates. Sugarcane juice or extracts from other agaves usually makes up the rest. Many tequila aficionados will caution you to look for the initials NOM—for *Norma Oficial Mexicana*—on the label to be sure it's "real" tequila, but we've never seen a bottle of tequila sold in Mexico that didn't bear those letters.

Despite the fact that tequila sales are booming today, much of the tequila-making process is still carried out *a mano* (by hand). In the traditional method, the mature heart of the tequila agave, which looks like a huge pineapple and weighs 50-150 pounds, is roasted in pits for 24 hours, then shredded and ground by mule- or horse-powered mills. After the juice is extracted from the pulp and fermented in ceramic pots, it's distilled in copper stills to produce the basic tequila, which is always clear and colorless, with an alcohol content of 38-40%.

True "gold" tequilas are produced by aging the tequila in imported oak barrels to achieve a slightly mellowed flavor. The *reposado* or "rested" type is oak-aged for at least two months, while *añejo* or "aged" tequila must stay in barrels at least a year. Inferior "gold" tequilas may be nothing more than the silver stuff mixed with caramel coloring—always look for *reposado* or *añejo* on the label if you want the true gold.

José Cuervo, Sauza, and Herradura are well established, inexpensive to medium-priced tequila labels with international notoriety. Of these three, Herradura is said to employ the most traditional methods; tequila connoisseurs generally prefer it over the other two. In 1983 Chinaco, based in the state of Tamaulipas, became the first label to pro-

agave field

GREG BULL

duce a tequila made from 100% blue agave, a formula now considered standard for all high-end tequilas. Many tasters claim a label called Reserva del Patrón (sold simply as "Patrón" north of the Mexican border) is the finest and smoothest tequila tipple of them all. Other very fine *tequilas reposadas* include Don Eduardo, Ecuario Gonzales, La Perseverancia, Don Felipe, and our personal favorite for flavor and price, Las Trancas. To emphasize the limited production nature of these private reserve distillations, these brands are usually sold in numbered bottles with fancy labels. Less expensive but also very good are the Jimador, Centenario, and Orendain labels. As with wine, it's all a matter of personal preference; try a few *probaditos* ("little tastes" or shots) for yourself to determine which brand best tickles your palate. The fancier tequilas may be served in brandy snifters instead of the traditional tall, narrow shot glass *(caballito).*

Mescal and the Worm

The distillate of other agave plants—also known as magueys or century plants—is called mescal (sometimes spelled "mezcal"), not to be confused with the nondistilled mescal—*pulque*—prepared in pre-Hispanic Mexico. The same roasting and distilling process is used for today's mescal as for tequila. Actually, tequila is a mescal, but no drinker calls it that, just as no one in a U.S. bar orders "whiskey" when they mean to specify scotch or bourbon. Although many states in Mexico produce mescal, the best is often said to come from the state of Oaxaca.

The caterpillar-like grub or *gusano de maguey* (maguey worm) floating at the bottom of a bottle of mescal lives on the maguey plant itself. They're safe to eat—just about anything pickled in mescal would be—but not particularly appetizing. By the time you hit the bottom of the bottle, though, who cares? Maguey worms are often fried and eaten with fresh corn tortillas and salsa—a delicious appetizer.

Tequila Drinks

The usual way to drink tequila is straight up, followed by a water or beer chaser. Licking a few grains of salt before taking a shot and sucking a lime wedge afterward makes it go down smoother. The salt raises a protective coating of saliva on the tongue while the lime juice scours the tongue of salt and tequila residues.

Tequila con sangrita, in which a shot of tequila is chased with a shot of *sangrita* (not to be confused with *sangría,* the wine-and-fruit punch), is a slightly more elegant method of consumption. Sangrita is a bright red mix of orange juice, lime juice, grenadine, red chile powder, and salt.

An old tequila standby is the much-abused margarita, a tart Tex-Mex cocktail made with tequila, lime juice, and Cointreau (usually "Controy" or triple-sec in Mexico) served in a salt-rimmed glass. A true margarita is shaken and served on the rocks (crushed or blended ice tends to kill the flavor) or strained, but just about every gringo in Baja seems to drink "frozen" margaritas, in which the ice is mixed in a blender with the other ingredients.

If you detect a noticeable difference between the taste of margaritas north or south of the border, it may be because bartenders in the U.S. and Canada tend to use bigger and less flavorful Persian limes *(Citrus latifolia)* while in Mexico they use the smaller, sweeter key or Mexican lime *(Citrus aurantifolia swingle).* A "Baja margarita" substitutes Baja's own damiana liqueur for the triple-sec. The damiana herb is said to be an aphrodisiac.

Tequila is a pallid flame that passes through walls and soars over tile roofs to allay despair.

—ÁLVARO MÚTIS,
TEQUILA: PANEGYRIC AND EMBLEM.

U.S.), Dos Equis (XX), Superior, Carta Blanca, Bohemia, and Negra Modelo are available in tourist restaurants, but you'll notice the locals stick pretty much to Tecate and Pacífico, perhaps out of regional loyalty.

The cheapest sources for beer are the brewery's agents or distributors (look for signs saying *agencia, subagencia, cervecería,* or *depósito*) where you can return deposit bottles for cash or credit. You can buy beer by the bottle *(envase),* can *(bote),* six-pack *(canastilla),* or case *(cartón).* A 24-bottle *cartón* of Pacífico or Corona costs US$8.50, not counting the refundable bottle deposit. Large, liter-size bottles are called *ballenas* (whales) or *caguamas* (sea turtles) and are quite popular. When buying beer at an *agencia* or *depósito,* specify *fría* if you want cold beer; otherwise you'll get beer *al tiempo* (at room temperature). Many *depósitos* offer free ice with the purchase of a case of beer.

Wine

Baja is one of Mexico's major wine-production areas and Baja wines are commonly served in restaurants. A broad selection of varietals is available, including cabernet sauvignon, chardonnay, chenin blanc, pinot noir, barbera, tempranillo, and zinfandel. These and other grapes are also blended to produce cheaper *vino tinto* (red wine) and *vino blanco* (white wine). Better vintages may be labeled *reserva privada* (private reserve). When ordering wine in Spanish at a bar, you may want to specify *vino de uva* (grape wine), as *vino* alone can refer to distilled liquors as well as wine. *Vino blanco,* in fact, can be interpreted as cheap tequila.

Two of the more reliable and reasonably priced labels are L.A. Cetto and Santo Tomás, both produced in northern Baja. Better but more expensive—and hard to find—are Baja California's Monte Xanic and Viñas de Camou. If you can find it, Monte Xanic's 1995 Cabernet y Merlot is considered one of the finest wines ever produced in Mexico. Camou makes an excellent *coupage* of cabernet franc, cabernet sauvignon, and merlot, labeled Gran Vino de Château Camou.

Cabo San Lucas has a very good wine bar called Sancho Panza, part of Plaza Marina attached to Hotel Plaza Las Glorias, where you can taste almost any Baja vintage.

Liquor

Tequila is Mexico's national drink and also the most popular distilled liquor in Baja. If you're keen on sampling Mexico's best, head for Pancho's Restaurant in Cabo San Lucas, said to have the largest selection of tequilas in the entire country.

The second most popular liquor is brandy, followed closely by *ron* (rum), both produced in Mexico for export as well as domestic consumption. A favorite rum drink is the *cuba libre* (free Cuba), called *cuba* for short—a mix of rum, Coke, and lime juice over ice. Similar is the *cuba de uva,* which substitutes brandy for rum. Other hard liquors—including gin, vodka, and scotch—may be available only at hotel bars and tourist restaurants.

CANTINAS AND BARS

Traditionally, a cantina is a Mexican-style drinking venue for males only, but in modern urban Mexico the distinction between "bar" and "cantina" is becoming increasingly blurred. True cantinas are rare in the Cape Region. La Cañada del Diablo in Todos Santos is a rare example of a *cantina familiar* or "family cantina," where everyone is welcome. In the smaller towns of the interior, you may occasionally stumble upon a *palapa*-roofed, palm- or *carrizo*-walled structure festooned with blinking Christmas lights. Inside are a few tables and chairs and a handful of *borrachos;* if any women are present, they're either serving the booze or serving as hired "dates." The only drink

---

BAR LINGO

cantinero/cantinera—bartender
cerveza—beer
una fría—a cold one
envase, botella—bottle
casco—empty bottle
una copita, uno tragito—a drink
vaso, copa—glass
la cruda—hangover
sin hielo—without ice
con hielo—with ice
botanas—snacks

choices will be beer, Mexican brandy, and cheap tequila or *aguardiente*—moonshine. Often when you order tequila in a place like this, you'll be served a large glass of *aguardiente,* considered an acceptable substitute.

Bars, on the other hand, are found in most hotels and in the downtown districts of La Paz, San José, and Cabo San Lucas. They've developed largely as social venues for tourists or for a younger generation of Mexicans for whom the cantina is passé. A bar, in contrast to a cantina, will offer a variety of beer, wine, and distilled liquor. By Mexican standards, bars are considered very upmarket places to hang out, so they aren't extremely popular—many young Mexicans would rather drink at a disco where they can dance, too.

HEALTH AND SAFETY

By and large, Baja California's Cape Region is a healthy place. Sanitation standards are high compared to many other parts of Mexico, and the tap water quality in many areas is superior to that in most of California. The visitor's main health concerns are not food or water sources but avoiding mishaps while driving, boating, diving, surfing, or otherwise enjoying the Cape's great outdoor life. Health issues directly concerned with these activities are covered under the relevant sections in this book.

FOOD AND WATER

Visitors who use common sense will probably never come down with food- or water-related illnesses while traveling in Cabo. The first rule is not to overdo it during the first few days of your trip—eat and drink in moderation. Shoveling down huge amounts of tasty, often heavy Mexican foods along with pitchers of margaritas or strong Mexican beer is liable to make anyone sick from pure overindulgence. If you're not used to the spices and different ways of cooking, it's best to ingest small amounts at first.

Second, take it easy with foods offered by street vendors, since this is where you're most likely to suffer from unsanitary conditions. Eat only foods that have been thoroughly cooked and are served either stove-hot or refrigerator-cold. Many gringos eat street food without any problems whatsoever, but it pays to be cautious, especially if it's your first time in Mexico. Concerned with the risk of cholera, the Baja California Sur state government in July 1992 banned the sale of ice cream or ceviche by street vendors.

Doctors usually advise against eating peeled, raw fruits and vegetables in Baja. Once the peel has been removed, it is virtually impossible to disinfect produce. Unpeeled fruits and vegetables washed in purified water and dried with a clean cloth are usually okay. After all, plenty of Mexican fruit is consumed daily in Canada and the United States.

Hotels and restaurants serve only purified drinking water and ice, so there's no need to ask for mineral water or refuse ice. Most residents, both foreign and Mexican, drink the tap water, which comes from uncontaminated underground springs. To be safe, however, first-time visitors are advised not to consume tap water except in hotels where the water system is purified (look for a notice over the washbasin in your room). Most grocery stores sell bottled purified water. Water purification tablets, iodine crystals, water filters, and the like aren't necessary for Cape travel unless you plan on backpacking.

Turista
People who've never traveled to a foreign country may undergo a period of adjustment to the new gastrointestinal flora that comes with new territory. There's really no way to avoid the differences wrought by sheer distance. Unfortunately, the adjustment is sometimes unpleasant.

Mexican doctors call gastrointestinal upset of this sort *turista* since it affects tourists but not the local population. The usual symptoms of *turista*—also known by the gringo tags "Montezuma's Revenge" and "the Aztec Two-Step"—are nausea and diarrhea, sometimes with stomach cramps and a low fever. Again, eating and drinking only in moderation will help prevent the worst of the symptoms, which rarely persist more than a day or two. And if it's any consolation, Mexicans often get sick the first time they go to the U.S. or Canada.

Prevention and Treatment: Many Mexico travelers swear by a preventive regimen of Pepto-Bismol begun the day before arrival in country. Opinions vary as to how much of the pink stuff is necessary to ward off or tame the foreign flora, but a person probably shouldn't exceed the recommended daily dose. Taper off after four days or so until you stop using it altogether.

If you come down with a case of *turista,* the best thing to do is drink plenty of fluids. Adults should drink at least three liters a day, a child under 37 kg (80 pounds) at least a liter a day. Lay off tea, coffee, milk, fruit juices, and booze. Eat only bland foods—nothing spicy, fatty, or fried—and take it easy. Pepto-Bismol or similar pectin-based remedies usually help. Some people like to mask the symptoms with a strong over-the-counter medication like Immodium AD (loperamide is the active ingredient), but though this can be very effective, it isn't a cure. Only time will cure traveler's diarrhea.

If the symptoms are unusually severe (especially if there's blood in the stools or a high fever) or persist more than one or two days, see a doctor. Most hotels can arrange a doctor's visit or you can contact a Mexican tourist office, U.S. consulate, or Canadian consulate for recommendations.

SUNBURN AND DEHYDRATION

Sunburn probably afflicts more Cabo visitors than all other illnesses and injuries combined. The sunlight in Baja can be exceptionally strong, especially along the coast. For outdoor forays, sun protection is a must, whatever the activity. The longer you're in the sun, the more protection you'll need.

A hat, sunglasses, and plenty of sunscreen or sunblock make a good start. Bring along a sunscreen with a sun protection factor (SPF) of at least 25, even if you don't plan on using it all the time. Apply it to *all* exposed parts of your body—don't forget the hands, top of the feet, and neck. Men should remember to cover thinned-out or bald areas on the scalp. Sunscreen must be reapplied after swimming or after periods of heavy perspiration.

If you're going boating, don't leave shore with just a bathing suit. Bring along an opaque shirt—preferably with long sleeves—and a pair of long pants. Since you can never know for certain whether your boat might get stranded or lost at sea for a period of time (if, for example, the motor conks out and you get caught in an offshore current), you shouldn't be without extra clothing for emergencies.

It's also important to drink plenty of water or nonalcoholic, noncaffeinated fluids to avoid dehydration. Alcohol and caffeine—including the caffeine in iced tea and cola—will increase your potential for dehydration. Symptoms of dehydration include darker-than-usual urine or inability to urinate, flushed face, profuse sweating or an unusual lack thereof, and sometimes headache, dizziness, and general feeling of malaise. Extreme cases of dehydration can lead to heat exhaustion or even heatstroke, in which the victim may become delirious or convulse. If either condition is suspected, get the victim out of the sun immediately, cover with a wet sheet or towel, and administer a rehydration fluid that replaces lost water and salts. If you can get the victim to a doctor, all the better—heatstroke can be serious.

Rehydration Formula: If Gatorade or a similar rehydration fluid isn't available you can mix your own by combining the following ingredients: one liter purified water or diluted fruit juice; two tablespoons sugar or honey; one-quarter teaspoon salt; and one-quarter teaspoon baking soda. If soda isn't available, use another quarter teaspoon salt. The victim should drink this mixture at regular intervals until symptoms subside substantially. Four or more liters may be necessary in moderate cases, more in severe cases.

MOTION SICKNESS

Visitors with little or no boating experience who join offshore fishing cruises sometimes experience motion sickness caused by the movement of a boat over ocean swells. The repeated pitching and rolling affects a person's sense of equilibrium to the point of nausea. Known as "seasickness" *(mareo),* it can be a very unpleasant experience not only for those green at the gills but for fellow passengers anxious lest the victim spew on them.

The best way to prevent motion sickness is to take one of the preventives commonly available from a pharmacist: promethazine (sold as Phenergan in the U.S.), dimenhydrinate (Dramamine), or scopolamine (Transderm Scop). The latter is available as an adhesive patch worn behind the ear—the time-release action is allegedly more effective than tablets. These medications should be consumed *before* boarding the vessel, not after the onset of symptoms. It's also not a good idea to eat a large meal before getting on a boat.

If you start to feel seasick while out on the bounding main, certain actions can lessen the likelihood that it will get worse. First, do not lie down. Often the first symptom of motion sickness is drowsiness, and if you give in to the impulse you'll almost certainly guarantee a worsening of the condition. Second, stay in the open air rather than below decks—fresh air usually helps. Finally, fix your gaze on the horizon; this will help steady your disturbed inner ear, the proximate cause of motion sickness.

BITES AND STINGS

Mosquitoes and *Jejenes*

Mosquitoes breed in standing water. Since standing water isn't that common in arid Baja, neither are mosquitoes. Exceptions include palm oases, estuaries, and marshes when there isn't a strong breeze around to keep mosquitoes at bay. The easiest way to avoid mosquito bites is to apply insect repellent to exposed areas of the skin and clothing whenever the mossies are out and biting. For most species, this means between dusk and dawn.

The most effective repellents are those containing a high concentration of DEET (N,N-diethyl-metatoluamide). People with an aversion to applying synthetics to the skin can try citronella (lemongrass oil), which is also effective but requires more frequent application.

More common than mosquitoes in estuarial areas are *jejenes,* tiny flying insects known as "no-see-ums" among Americans—you almost never see them while they're biting. The same repellents effective for mosquitoes will usually do the trick with *jejenes.*

For relief from the itchiness of mosquito bites, try rubbing a bit of hand soap on the affected areas. *Jején* bites will usually stop itching in less than 10 minutes if you refrain from scratching

them. Excessive scratching of either type of bite can lead to infection, so be mindful of what your fingers are up to.

In spite of the presence of the occasional mosquito, the U.S. Centers for Disease Control has declared all of Baja California Sur malaria-free.

Wasps, Bees, and Hornets

Although stings from these flying insects can be very painful, they aren't of mortal danger to most people. If you're allergic to such stings and plan to travel in remote areas of Baja, consider obtaining antiallergy medication from your doctor before leaving home. At the very least, carry a supply of Benadryl or similar over-the-counter antihistamine. Dramamine (dimenhydrinate) also usually helps mitigate allergic reactions.

For relief from a wasp/bee/hornet sting, apply a paste of baking soda and water to the affected area. Liquids containing ammonia, including urine, also help relieve pain. If a stinger is visible, remove it—by scraping, if possible, or with tweezers—before applying any remedies. If a stung limb becomes unusually swollen or if the victim exhibits symptoms of a severe allergic reaction—difficulty breathing, agitation, or hives—seek medical assistance.

Ticks

If you find a tick embedded in your skin, don't try to pull it out—this may leave the head and pincers under your skin and lead to infection. Covering the tick with petroleum jelly, mineral oil, gasoline, kerosene, or alcohol will usually cause the tick to release its hold in order to avoid suffocation.

Burning the tick with a cigarette butt or hot match usually succeeds only in killing it—when you pull the tick out, the head and pincers may not come with it. Use the suffocation method and if the beast still doesn't come out, use tweezers.

Scorpions

The venom of scorpions *(alacranes)* varies in strength from individual to individual and species to species, but the sting is rarely dangerous to adults. It can be very painful, however, and can result in partial numbness and swelling that can last several days. In Baja, the small yellow scorpions inflict more painful stings than the larger, dark-colored ones.

The best treatment begins with persuading the victim to lie down and relax to slow the spread of the venom. Keep the affected area below the level of the heart. Ice packs on the sting may relieve pain and mitigate swelling; aspirin also helps.

Children who weigh less than about 13 kg (30 pounds) should receive medical attention if stung by a scorpion. Doctors in La Paz, San José, and Cabo San Lucas usually have ready access to scorpion antivenin *(anti-alacrán),* but it should only be administered under qualified medical supervision. Mexicans often keep on hand a bottle of alcohol containing dead scorpions; applied to a scorpion sting, this alcohol solution reportedly acts as an effective antivenin.

Scorpions prefer damp, dark, warm places—dead brush, rock piles, fallen logs—so exercise particular caution when placing your hands in or near such areas. Hands are the scorpion's most common target on the human body; you should wear gloves when handling firewood in Baja.

Other favorite spots for scorpions are crumpled clothing and bedding. In Gulf Desert areas of the Cape, always check your bed sheets or sleeping bag for scorpions before climbing in. In the same environments, shake out your shoes and clothing before putting them on.

Poisonous Sea Creatures
Various marine animals can inflict painful stings on humans. In Baja, such creatures include jellyfish, Portuguese men-of-war, cone shells, stingrays, sea urchins, and various fishes with poisonous spines.

The best way to avoid jellyfish and Portuguese men-of-war is to scope out the water before going in—if you see any nasties floating around, try another beach. You can avoid stingrays by shuffling your feet in the sand as you walk in shallow surf—this will usually cause rays resting in the sand to swim away.

To avoid cone-shell and sea-urchin stings, wear shoes in the water; several sport-shoe manufacturers now produce specialized water shoes, e.g., Nike's Aqua Socks. You can also often spot cones and urchins in clear water, especially when wearing a diving mask. Anglers should take care when handling landed fish to avoid poisonous spines.

The treatment for stings from all of the above is the same: Remove all tentacles, barbs, or spines from the affected area; wash the area with rubbing alcohol or diluted ammonia (urine will do in a pinch) to remove as much venom as possible; and wrap the area in cloth to reduce the flow of oxygen to the wound until pain subsides. If an acute allergic reaction occurs, get the victim to a doctor or clinic as quickly as possible.

Stingrays: Painful stingray wounds may require the famous hot-water treatment. If pain persists after thoroughly cleaning the wound, soak the affected limb in the hottest water the victim can stand. Continue soaking until the pain subsides—this can sometimes take up to an hour. The local folk remedy in Baja is to treat the wound with the sap of the *garambullo* cactus, often available from *botánicas* if not from a nearby patch of desert. Some stingray wounds may require medical treatment, even stitches.

MEDICAL ASSISTANCE

The quality of basic medical treatment, including dentistry, is relatively high in Cape cities and larger towns; ask at a tourist office or at your consulate for recommendations. Public IMSS hospitals can be found in La Paz, San José, and Cabo San Lucas; Cabo's hospital is quite modern. There are public IMSS clinics or Red Cross (Cruz Roja) stations in nearly every other town. In many areas the Red Cross can be reached by dialing 132 (toll-free) from any pay phone.

Emergency Evacuation
Over the years, several American companies have offered emergency 24-hour airlift service

(accompanied by licensed physicians and nurses) from anywhere in Mexico to U.S. hospitals. Few have lasted more than a year or two. One of the longer-running operations is **Aeromedevac,** 4420 Rainier Avenue, Suite 200, San Diego, CA 92120, tel. (619) 284-7910, (800) 462-0911 toll-free in the U.S., 001(800) 832-5087 toll-free from Mexico, fax (619) 284-7918. Aeromedevac will accept collect calls. Payment for the service can be made with a credit card or through your health insurance company.

Other companies with similar services include **Air Evac Services, Inc.,** 2630 Sky Harbor Blvd., Phoenix, AZ 85034, tel. (602) 244-9327, (800) 280-EVAC toll-free in the U.S. and Canada, fax (602) 302-6726; and **Advanced Aeromedical Air Ambulance Service,** P. O. Box 5726, Virginia Beach, VA 23471, tel. (757) 481-1590, (800) 346-3556 toll-free in the U.S. and Canada, fax (757) 481-2874, e-mail: aeromed@norfolk.infi.net.

For information on other air evacuation services, contact the **Association of Air Medical Services,** 110 North Royal Street, Suite 307, Alexandria, VA 22314, tel. (703) 836-8732, fax (703) 836-8920, e-mail: information@aams.org.

SAFETY

Statistics clearly show that violent crime is much less common in Mexico than almost anywhere in the United States. In Baja California Sur crime statistics are estimated to be over 90% lower than the U.S. national average. Yet Americans seem to be the most paranoid of all visitors to Mexico.

Historical reasons, to a large degree, account for this paranoia. Chief among them is the general border lawlessness that was the norm in the early 20th century—an era of border disputes and common banditry on both sides of the border. Americans living along the border came to fear *bandidos* who stole livestock and occasionally robbed the Anglo ranchers themselves, while the Mexicans feared American cattle rustlers, horse thieves, gunslingers, and the infamous Texas Rangers, a private militia whose conduct at the time fell somewhere between

Hell's Angels motorcycle gang and the Los Angeles Police Department.

Soon after this era had begun to wane, as politics on both sides of the border stabilized, the U.S. Prohibition experiment sent millions of Americans scrambling into Mexican border towns for booze. In the illicit atmosphere, boozers were soon rubbing elbows with gamblers and whoremongers, and it wasn't long before Mexican border towns gained an even more unsavory reputation.

Once Prohibition was lifted, Americans no longer had reason to come to Mexico solely for drinking purposes, and the border towns began cleaning up their acts. Among the uninformed and inexperienced, however, the border-town image remains, sadly mixing with the equally outdated *bandido* tales to prevent many Americans from enjoying the pleasures of life south of the border.

Historically the Cape Region has never had any banditry to speak of; neither the author nor anyone in the author's acquaintance has ever been robbed in the Cape (or, for that matter, anywhere in Baja). Compared to Hawaii or Florida, the Cape is many, many times safer in terms of crimes committed against tourists.

Help: The Secretaría de Turismo (SECTUR) maintains a 24-hour travelers' aid "hotline" for emergencies of all kinds: tel. 5250-0123 or 5250-0151.

Precautions

Visitors to Cabo should take the same precautions they would when traveling anywhere in their own countries or abroad. Keep money and valuables secured, either in a hotel safe or safety deposit box, or in a money belt or other hard-to-reach place on your person. Keep an eye on cameras, purses, and wallets to make sure you don't leave them behind in restaurants, hotels, or campgrounds. At night, lock the doors to your hotel room and vehicle.

Private campgrounds usually have some kind of security, if only a night watchman, to keep out intruders. Secluded beach campsites seem to be safe due to their seclusion—around the Cape Region it's rare for crime to occur in such areas. Nonetheless, don't leave items of value lying around outside your tent, camper, or RV at night.

IMMIGRATION AND CUSTOMS

ENTRY REGULATIONS

Tourist Permits

Citizens of the U.S. or Canada (or of 38 other designated countries in Europe and Latin America, plus Singapore) visiting Mexico solely for tourism are not required to obtain a visa. Instead they must carry validated "tourist cards" (*forma migratoria turista* or FMT), which aren't actually cards but slips of paper. These are available free at any Mexican consulate or Mexican tourist office, from many travel agencies, on flights to Mexico, or at the border. The tourist card is valid for stays of up to 180 days and must be used within 90 days of issue. Your card becomes invalid once you exit the country—you're supposed to surrender it at the border—even if your 180 days hasn't expired. If you'll be entering and leaving Mexico more than once during your trip, you should request a multiple-entry tourist card, available from Mexican consulates only.

To obtain the FMT you will need proof of citizenship—a birth certificate (or certified copy), voter's registration card, certificate of naturalization, or passport. A driver's license doesn't qualify.

Validation: Once you cross the border (or land at an airport on an international flight), your tourist card must be validated by a Mexican immigration officer. You can arrange this at any *migración* office in Baja (many *municipio* seats have them), but it's accomplished most conveniently at the border crossing itself or at the immigration office in Ensenada (right around the corner from the tourist information booth on Blvd. Costero). Note: FMTs are occasionally inspected at the army checkpoint at the north end of Guerrero Negro, so you'd best have your papers in order before entering Baja California Sur.

At airports you will pass through immigration, where an officer will stamp your paperwork with the date of entry and the number of days you're permitted to stay in Mexico.

Make sure you receive enough days to cover your visit. Some immigration officers, especially those at airports near tourist resorts, may fill in your FMT for 30 days, figuring that's sufficient for most holidays. If you want more than 30 days, it's best to mention it to the officer in advance.

Tourist Fee: In mid-1999, the Mexican government began collecting a 150-peso (around US$16 at the most recent dollar-peso exchange rate) from all tourists entering the country. If you fly in, this fee is tacked on to your airfare. If you arrive by land, you can pay this fee at any bank in Mexico. The bank will issue a receipt, which you must show when you leave the country. In normal practice—at least so far—it's rare that anyone checks to see that you've paid the tourist fee. This laxity may change when Mexican authorities realize that very few road travelers bother to pay the fee, or perhaps they'll be satisfied that everyone who flies into Mexico pays the fee.

The 150-peso fee is quite reasonable when you consider that Mexicans visiting the U.S. must pay US$45 for a tourist visa, even if their visa application is denied. Of course, comparing Mexican immigration into the U.S. with U.S. immigration into Mexico—whether legal or otherwise—is comparing apples to oranges, as relatively few Americans visit Mexico with the intention of sending Mexican pesos back home.

Minors: Before 1991, Mexican regulations required children under the age of 18 crossing the border without one or both parents to carry a notarized letter granting permission from the absent parent, or both parents if both were absent. This regulation is no longer in effect, but we've heard that some Mexican border officers, as well as airline check-in crews, are still asking for the letter, apparently unaware the regulation has been rescinded. Hence, unaccompanied minors or minors traveling with only one parent should be prepared for all situations with notarized letters. In cases of divorce, separation, or death, the minor should carry notarized papers documenting the situation.

In reality, minors with tourist cards are rarely asked for these documents. Children under 15 may be included on their parents' tourist card, but this means that neither the child nor the parents can legally exit Mexico without the other.

Tourist Visas

Tourists from countries other than the 40 countries for which no visa is necessary will need to obtain tourist visas in advance of arrival in Mexico. If you apply in person at a Mexican consulate, you usually can obtain a tourist visa on the day of application. Requirements include a valid passport, a roundtrip air ticket to Mexico, three photos, and a visa fee of US$29. If you apply in person, the Mexican Consulate General in San Diego can usually issue tourist visas on the day of application.

Foreign visitors who are legal permanent residents of the U.S. do not need visas to visit Mexico for tourism. A free tourist card can be obtained by presenting your passport and U.S. residence card to any travel agency or at the airport or border crossing.

Business Travel

Citizens of Mexico's NAFTA (North American Free Trade Agreement) partners, the U.S. and Canada, are not required to obtain a visa to visit Mexico for business purposes. Instead you can receive a free NAFTA business permit *(forma migratoria nafta* or FMN) similar to a tourist card at the point of entry (border crossing or airport); it's valid for 30 days. At the port of entry you must present proof of nationality (valid passport or original birth certificate plus a photo identification or voters registration card) and proof that you are travelling for "international business activities," usually interpreted to mean a letter from the company you represent, even if it's your own enterprise.

Those who arrive with the FMN and wish to stay over the authorized period of 30 days must replace their FMN with an FM-3 form at an immigration office in Mexico. The FM-3 is valid for a period of up to one year, for multiple entries, and may be extended. Note that the FMN is not valid for persons who will be earning a salary during their stay in Mexico.

Citizens of other countries visiting for business purposes must obtain an FM-3 visa endorsed for business travel, which is valid for one year.

Overstays

If you overstay your visa and are caught, the usual penalty is a fine of US$50 for overstays up to a month. After that the penalties become more severe. It's rare that a Mexican border official asks to see your FMT or visa when you're leaving the country. Your main risk comes if you get into trouble with the police somewhere in Mexico and they ask to see your immigration documents. Having expired papers will only further complicate your situation in such cases, so the best policy is to stay up to date in spite of the apparent laxity of enforcement.

Pets

Dogs and cats may be brought into Mexico if each is accompanied by a **vaccination certificate** that proves the animal has been vaccinated or treated for rabies, hepatitis, pip, and leptospirosis. You'll also need a **health certificate** issued no more than 72 hours before entry and signed by a registered veterinarian.

Since 1992 the requirement that the health certificate be stamped with a visa at a port of entry or at a Mexican consulate has been repealed. The certificate is still necessary; the visa isn't.

Upon recrossing the border into the U.S., the U.S. Customs Service will ask to see the vaccination certificate.

Visitante Rentista and Inmigrante Rentista Visas

FM-3 visas may be issued to foreigners who choose to live in Mexico on a "permanent income" basis. This most often applies to foreigners who decide to retire in Mexico, though it is also used by artists, writers, and other self-employed foreign residents. With this visa you're allowed to import one motor vehicle as well as your household belongings into Mexico tax-free.

The basic requirements for this visa are that applicants must forgo any kind of employment while living in Mexico and must show proof (bank statements) that they have a regular source of foreign-earned income amounting to at least US$1,000 per month (plus half that for each dependent over the age of 15, e.g., US$1,500 for a couple). A pile of paperwork, including a "letter of good conduct" from the applicant's local police department, must accompany the initial application, along with an immigration tax payment (US$60) and various application fees totaling about US$75.

The visa must be renewed annually but the renewal can be accomplished at any immigration office in Mexico. After five years in Mexico, you have to start over, or move up to the FM-2 or *inmigrante rentista* visa, which has higher income requirements and signifies an intent to stay longer. After five years on an FM-2, an *inmigrante rentista* is eligible to apply for *inmigrado* status, which confers all the rights of citizenship (including employment in Mexico), save the rights to vote and hold public office.

Many foreigners who have retired in Mexico manage to do so on the regular 180-day tourist visa; every six months they dash across the border and return with a new tourist card (issued at the border) on the same day. This method bypasses all the red tape and income requirements of the retirement visa. If you own a home in Baja, however, some local immigrations officials may interpret the law to mean that you must have an FM-2 or FM-3 visa—not an FMT or tourist visa—to be able to stay in that home for any period of time whatsoever. Although it's clear from a straight reading that Mexico's immigration laws do not require any special visas for home ownership (just as you don't need a particular visa to own property in the U.S. or Canada), each immigration district behaves like an individual fiefdom at the mercy of the local immigration chief.

Monthly income requirements for both *rentista* visas are keyed to the Mexican daily minimum wage (400 times minimum wage for the FM-2, 250 times for the FM-3), hence figures may vary according to the current dollar-peso exchange rate.

Reentering the U.S.

Overseas visitors need a passport and visa to enter the United States. Except for diplomats, students, or refugees, this means a nonimmigrant visitor's visa, which must be obtained in advance at a U.S. consulate or embassy abroad. Residents of Western European and Commonwealth countries are usually issued these readily; residents of other countries may have to provide the consulate with proof of "sufficient personal funds" before the visa is issued.

Upon arrival in the U.S., an immigration inspector will decide how long the visa will be valid—the maximum for a temporary visitor's visa (B-1 or B-2) is six months. If you visit Mexico from California (or from anywhere else in the U.S.) for stays of 30 days or less, you can reenter the U.S. with the same visa, provided the visa is still valid, by presenting your stamped arrival/departure card (INS form I-94) and passport to a U.S. immigration inspector. If your U.S. visa has expired, you can still enter the country for a stay of 29 days or less on a transit visa—issued at the border—but you may be required to show proof of onward travel, such as an air ticket or ship travel voucher.

BORDER CROSSINGS

Baja California's U.S.-Mexico border has five official border crossings: Tijuana (open 24 hours a day), Otay Mesa (open 6 a.m.-10 p.m.), Tecate (6 a.m.-midnight), Mexicali (24 hours), and Los Algodones (6 a.m.-10 p.m.). Tijuana is the largest and also the most heavily used, connecting Baja with U.S. Interstate 5, which extends all the way up the U.S. west coast to the Canadian border. For several years now, border officials have been considering longer hours for the nearby Otay Mesa crossing to ease congestion at Tijuana.

At any of the border crossings, you'll find the shortest waits (15-30 minutes at Tijuana) are between 10 a.m. and 3:30 p.m. or after 7 or 8 p.m. on weekdays. Weekends are the worst days in either direction, except late at night or before dawn, when traffic is light. If you're on your way out of Baja and find yourself near the border during rush hours, it might be best to find a restaurant and wait it out. A Saturday or Sunday morning wait at the Tijuana crossing can be as long as two hours in either direction; it's always longer going north.

If you're on foot, crossing is usually a breeze. Public and chartered buses also get through more quickly, utilizing special traffic lanes.

Mexican Consulate in San Diego

San Diego's Mexican Consulate General, 1549 India St., San Diego, CA 92101, tel. (619) 231-8414 or 231-8427, is relatively close to the Tijuana border crossing, about 30-45 minutes by car. The staff can assist with visas, immigration problems, special-import permits, and questions concerning Mexican customs regulations. The consulate's hours are Mon.-Fri. 9 a.m.-1 p.m.

CUSTOMS

Entering Mexico

Officially, tourists are supposed to bring only those items into Mexico that will be of use during their trip. This means you can bring in practically anything as long as it doesn't appear in large enough quantities to qualify for resale. Firearms and ammunition, as well as boats, require special permits (see Sports and Recreation.)

Technically speaking, you're not supposed to import more than one still camera, one movie camera, and one video camera, and no more than 12 rolls of film or blank videocassettes for each. Anything more is supposed to require permission from a Mexican consulate. In everyday practice, however, Mexican customs officials rarely blink at more film or an extra camera or two. Professional photographers and others who would like to bring more cameras and film into Mexico can apply for dispensation through a Mexican consulate abroad. Regarding audio equipment, you're limited to one compact disc (CD) player and one audio cassette player (or combo), two laserdiscs, and up to 20 CDs or recording cassettes. Other per-person limitations include one musical instrument, one tent and accompanying camping gear, one set of fishing gear, a pair of skis, two tennis rackets, five "toys," and one sailboard.

Other limits include: three liters of liquor or wine; two cartons (20 packs) of cigarettes or 25 cigars or 200 grams of tobacco.

Other than the above, you're permitted to bring in no more than US$300 worth of other articles. You will be subject to duty on personal possessions worth more than US$300, to a maximum of US$1,000 (except for new computer equipment, which is exempt up to US$4,000).

Foreign-registered motor vehicles—cars, trucks, RVs, motorcycles, etc.—do not require permits for travel anywhere on the Baja California peninsula. However, if you plan to take a vehicle registered outside Mexico onto one of the vehicle ferries that sail from Baja to the mainland, or if you plan to drive farther east than San Luis Río Colorado in Sonora, you must obtain an auto permit. These are available from any Mexican consulate abroad, or at the border, or from the ferry office in La Paz.

LET'S NAFTA

Now that NAFTA is in effect, customs regulations for goods produced in the U.S., Canada, or Mexico are supposed to evolve toward more leniency. However, our experience indicates that Mexican customs officers consistently ignore the NAFTA duty schedules and continue to collect duties at an improvised flat rate that is higher than what the treaty specifies.

At Los Cabos International Airport, for example, a hand-lettered sign in the airport immigration office declares "20% tax on all U.S.-made goods"—a direct contravention of NAFTA, which has reduced most duties on U.S.- or Canada-made goods to well below 20%. The treaty has in fact totally eliminated duties on many items, and by 2009 there are supposed to be no duties, period, on any goods produced within the NAFTA sphere.

The only way to get around the illicit flat rate is to carry a copy of the NAFTA tax schedule for any items you wish to import and then haggle with customs inspectors, using the document as evidence to support your side. Aside from American or Canadian exporters or customs brokers, very few visitors will want to go to this much trouble. What's left is a cat-and-mouse game in which visitors neglect to declare taxable goods, while Mexican customs inspectors invent "special" rates on the spot that usually run somewhere between the lower legal rate and the higher illegal rate.

For the most part such hassles only involve long-term visitors or residents who are bringing in appliances and other large-ticket items.

If you're bringing a vehicle across the border, you will need Mexican auto insurance. For further information on vehicle permits and insurance, see Getting There and Getting Around.

Returning to the U.S.

Visitors returning to the U.S. from Mexico may have their luggage inspected by U.S. Customs officials. The hassle can be minimized by giving brief, straight answers to the officials' questions (e.g., "How long have you been in Mexico?" "Do you have anything to declare?") and by cooperating with their requests to open your luggage, vehicle storage compartments, and any-

BUYING OR LEASING PROPERTY IN THE CAPE REGION

With certain restrictions, the Mexican government allows both resident and nonresident foreigners to own Mexican real estate—both land and buildings. Under the Constitution of 1857, foreign ownership of land by direct title is permitted only in areas more than 100 km (62 miles) from any international border and 50 km (31 miles) from any seacoast. In Baja California Sur, this limits prospective buyers to areas in the interior of the peninsula, where services—water, electricity, sewage, telephone—are often nonexistent.

However, since 1973 the Mexican government has offered a way for foreigners to acquire lots—including coastal property—that fall outside the geographic limits. The Ministry of Foreign Affairs issues permits to foreigners allowing them to create limited real estate trusts, administered by Mexican banks, with themselves as beneficiaries. Originally, these trusts were valid for 30-year nonrenewable terms only. In 1989 the government further liberalized real estate regulations so that the trusts (called *fideicomisos*) could be renewed at the end of each 30-year term for an additional 30-year term, with no limit on the number of renewals. *Fideicomisos* can be bought and sold among foreigners, at market rates, just like fee-simple property. In December 1993 the basic term for bank trusts was lengthened to 50 years, a period long enough to begin attracting U.S. housing lenders. Until recently U.S. lenders had remained aloof from the *fideicomiso* market;

mortgages are now available for financing up to 70% of appraised property values with terms of 15-20 years. Lending rates run around three percent higher than in the U.S., and closing costs for a mortgage deal are high.

Needless to say, Baja real estate prices have increased substantially as a result of this change in policy. The priciest coastal properties are those near the U.S.-Mexico border and on the Cape, but prices are still substantially below what's available in coastal California. The outlook for Cape Region real estate at the moment is bright; purchases made at the right time, in the right place, can be very good investments, but just like at home it pays to shop around carefully.

Lots large enough for a two- or three-bedroom home in the La Paz area are available for US$15,000 and up. In Cabo San Lucas or San José, house lots cost at least three times this, though condos are available for not much more. Elsewhere on the Cape—on the East Cape or north of Todos Santos—survivalist types can find beach hideaways with no services for even less; in remote areas, total annual lease payments run as low as US$1,000, sometimes less. With a desalinator, generator or solar cells, propane stove, refrigerator, and perhaps an airplane to get in and out, you can live in considerable style. Historic Cape pueblos such as Todos Santos, San Antonio, and Santiago offer lots of promise because they're developing so

home under construction in The Corridor

gradually and, for the most part, with taste and sensitivity for the land and culture. In terms of creature comforts, these towns lie somewhere between the convenience of Los Cabos and the remoteness of beach camps.

Precautions

Before you rush off to grab Cape land, you should be aware that a lot of people get burned in Mexican real estate deals. It's best to deal through an established, reputable real estate agent. The American company Century 21 has opened a Baja franchise, and although it generally represents only the more expensive properties, Century 21 people can be helpful with information on real estate trusts. Mexican tourist offices in Baja often carry information on residential property. And it's wise to talk to current owner-residents about which real estate companies have the best and worst reputations.

In condominium and subdivision situations a master *fideicomiso* is created. Only as the units are sold does the trust pass to the buyer, and then only if proper procedures are followed—which they often aren't. If you buy a condo or subdivision unit, you should receive a document naming you as beneficiary, thus transferring property from the master trust holder to the buyer. If you don't, you'll have to get the master trust holder's signature before you can sell or otherwise transfer the property to someone else.

Many sellers ask that the full purchase price be paid up front. Because a large number of gringos buy land in Mexico with cash, some Mexicans assume this is customary for all Americans and Canadians. Paying up front is not the typical procedure for Mexicans themselves, who usually make down payments and send in monthly time payments; mortgage terms similar to those found in Canada and the U.S. are available in Mexico, though they are difficult for nonresidents to obtain. Even if you have the cash, don't hand over more than half the full amount until you have the *fideicomiso* papers in hand.

Once again, investigate the realtor thoroughly before signing on the dotted line. Mexico doesn't require salespersons or brokers to obtain any sort of real estate license, hence many Americans and Canadians who couldn't make the grade back home now work in Mexico.

Time Shares

Time-share salespeople are the scourge of Cape resort areas, especially San José del Cabo and Cabo San Lucas, where they hang out on street corners and in hotel lobbies, hounding every tourist who passes by. These hustlers, who are sometimes gringos, will try almost anything to convince you to sign on the dotted line, on the spot—including denying that what they're selling is a time share (latest euphemism: "vacation club"). Fortunately the situation has improved in the last couple of years, and the time-share touts seem a bit more low-key than they used to be.

It pays to hold off on any decision until you've made inquiries among current time-share residents at the development and checked with your consulate to see if there have been any complaints. Time-share developments typically begin selling when construction has just begun—sometimes they don't get finished, or when they do they don't shape up as promised. Also, because time-share owners aren't year-round residents, they usually lack both a sense of community and a sense of responsibility toward the local environment. For the developer, time shares mean huge profits, as the same space is sold repeatedly in one-week segments. Since land in Baja is relatively inexpensive, considering the charming scenery and climate, it seems to attract get-rich-quick developers who show a decided lack of respect for the fragile Baja environment. Finally, keep in mind that from an investment perspective, time shares don't appreciate in value as much as single-owner properties, if they appreciate at all (not very likely).

This is not to say there aren't any good time-share opportunities on the Cape. But as with any real estate deal, it pays to proceed cautiously. Don't be cajoled into buying without considering all the options.

---

thing else they want opened. Sometimes the officers use dogs to sniff luggage and/or vehicles for contraband and illegal aliens.

Nearly 3,000 items—including all handicrafts—made in Mexico are exempt from any U.S. Customs duties. Adults over 21 are allowed one liter (33.8 fluid ounces) of alcoholic beverages and 200 cigarettes (or 100 cigars) per person. Note that Cuban cigars may not be imported into the U.S. and will be confiscated at the border if discovered. Since an estimated nine out of 10 cigars sold as Cubans in Mexico are reportedly fake, it's not worth the hassle, especially since a good hand-rolled cigar from

Veracruz can challenge most Cubans. All other purchases or gifts up to a total value of US$400 within any 31-day period can be brought into the U.S. duty-free.

Plant and Animal Prohibitions: The following fruits and vegetables cannot be brought into the U.S. from Mexico: oranges, grapefruits, mangoes, avocados (unless the pit is removed), and potatoes (including yams and sweet potatoes). All other fruits are permitted (including bananas, dates, pineapples, cactus fruits, grapes, and berries of all types).

Other prohibited plant materials are straw (including packing materials and items stuffed with straw), hay, unprocessed cotton, sugarcane, and any plants in soil (this includes houseplants).

Animals and animal products that cannot be imported include wild and domesticated birds (including poultry, unless cooked), pork or pork products (including sausage, ham, and other cured pork), and eggs. Beef, mutton, venison, and other meats are permitted at up to 50 pounds per person.

Customs regulations can change at any time, so if you want to verify the regulations on a purchase before risking duties or confiscation at the border, check with a U.S. consulate in Baja before crossing.

Returning to Canada
Duty-frees include 200 cigarettes (or 50 cigars, or 250 grams of tobacco), and 1.14 liter of booze. Exemptions run from C$20 to C$500 depending on how long you've been outside Canada. To reach the maximum exemption of C$500 you must be gone at least one week. Since Canada is also signatory to NAFTA, customs legalities will change over the next decade.

LEGAL MATTERS

All foreign visitors in Mexico are subject to Mexican legal codes, which are based on Roman and Napoleonic law. The most distinctive features of the Mexican judiciary system, contrasted with Anglo-American systems, are that the system doesn't provide for trials by jury (the judge decides) nor writs of habeas corpus (though you must be charged within 72 hours of incarceration). Furthermore, bail is rarely granted to an

arrested foreigner—for many offenses, not even Mexican nationals are allowed bail. Hence, once arrested and jailed for a serious offense, it can be very difficult to arrange release. The lesson here is: Don't get involved in matters that might result in your arrest. This primarily means anything having to do with drugs or guns.

The oft-repeated saw that in Mexico an arrested person is considered guilty until proven innocent is no more true south of the border than north. As in Canada or the U.S., an arrested person is considered a criminal *suspect* until the courts confirm or deny guilt. You have the right to notify your consulate if detained.

Mexican federal police (*federales* and *judiciales*) as well as the Mexican army, mostly under pressure from the U.S., occasionally set up roadblocks to conduct searches for drugs and for arms. Such roadblocks used to be rare in Baja, but have recently increased in number. On recent Transpeninsular drives I've been stopped at six of seven different military checkpoints *(puestos de control)* between Tijuana and Cabo San Lucas. In each case the soldiers were courteous, and the vehicle searches were brief and cursory.

If your vehicle is stopped at a *puesto de control,* be as cooperative as possible. If there are any irregularities or if you object to the way in which the procedure is carried out, make note of the incident—including whatever badge numbers, names, or license numbers you can obtain discreetly—and later file a report with the Mexican Attorney General for Tourist Protection. So far I've not heard of any problems encountered by foreign visitors, although I was told a couple of Americans were arrested for carrying unregistered firearms—a serious federal offense in Mexico—in 1996.

La Mordida
In the past, Mexican police had a reputation for hassling foreigners, especially those who drove their own vehicles in Mexico. Tales of the legendary *mordida* (literally, "bite"), or minor bribe, supposedly a necessary part of navigating one's way around Mexico, swelled way out of proportion to reality but were nonetheless based on real incidents.

For several years now, the Mexican police have for the most part ceased singling out foreigners for arrest, partly as a result of anticorruption efforts by the federal government but more importantly because of a conscious effort to attract more tourists. Most foreign visitors who drive in Mexico these days complete their trips without any police hassles. (See Getting Around, following, for tips on traffic laws and dealing with traffic police.)

Military

In recent years the Mexican government has replaced many federal police officers around the country with active-duty army officers in an effort to clean up corruption among nonmilitary law enforcement agencies. In Baja all 84 *judiciales* involved in antidrug operations were replaced with army officers in 1996. Opinions are sharply divided as to whether this is having a net positive or negative effect on law enforcement, but it's a fact that you can see more military personnel around the country than at any time since 1920 in Mexico. Roadblock inspection points or *puestos de control* along major and minor highways have become increasingly common. All manner of vehicles—buses, trucks, private autos—may be stopped and searched at such inspection points; if you get stopped the best thing to do is simply be patient until it's over, usually in five minutes or less. For the most part, soldiers stationed at these checkpoints perform their duties in a serious but respectful manner. Typically they speak very little English and this usually works in favor of the non-Spanish-speaking foreign visitor, as it means they can't ask very many questions.

In Case of Arrest

If you get into trouble with Mexican law, for whatever reason, you should try to contact your nearest consulate in Baja. Embassies and consulates for each town are listed under the respective destination chapters. You can also contact the local state tourism offices—see the sections on each town for phone numbers and addresses. In Baja California Sur, the state tourism office in La Paz is the best place to look for help. These agencies routinely handle emergency legal matters involving visiting foreigners; you stand a much better chance of resolving legal difficulties with their assistance.

MONEY, MEASUREMENTS, AND COMMUNICATIONS

CURRENCY

The unit of exchange in Mexico is the **peso,** which comes in paper denominations of N$10, N$20, N$50, N$100, N$200, N$500. Coins come in denominations of five, 10, 20, and 50 centavos, and N$1, N$2, N$5, and N$10.

Prices

The N$ symbol (standing for "new pesos" to differentiate from pre-1993 "old pesos") is often used for indicating peso prices. Occasionally you may also encounter the $ symbol for pesos. While it's unlikely you'll ever confuse dollar and peso prices because of the differing values, you should ask when in doubt. Sometimes the abbreviation m.n. will appear next to a price—this means *moneda nacional* (national money) and also refers to pesos.

Since coins smaller than one peso are often scarce, payments often must be rounded off to the nearest peso or at least to the nearest 50 centavos. For a marked price of N$8.55, for example, you actually have to pay only N$8.50; for a N$8.75 price you may have to pay N$9.

Dollars vs. Pesos

Most places on the Cape will take U.S. dollars as well as pesos. Paying with pesos, however, usually means a better deal when the price is fixed in pesos; if you pay in dollars, the vendor can determine the exchange rate. If a can of motor oil, for example, is marked at N$18, and the bank rate is N$9 per dollar, you'll pay US$2 for the oil with pesos changed at the bank. However, if you ask to pay in dollars, the vendor may charge US$2.50 since vendors have the right—by custom rather than law—to charge whatever exchange rate they wish. If you're bargaining for price, it really doesn't matter what currency you use.

Some stores in smaller towns prefer not to take dollars since this means keeping track of two currencies and makes banking more complicated. Pemex stations sometimes refuse dollars—attendants are usually too busy to stop and calculate rates.

For anything larger than a N$100 note, getting change can sometimes be a problem in small towns, so try to carry plenty of notes and coins in denominations of N$50 or smaller. Small change is commonly called *morraya.*

Devaluation

The Mexican peso has been in a deflationary spin since 1976, when the government decided to allow the national currency to "float" on the international money market. From 1976 to 1987 the exchange rate slid from eight pesos to the dollar to over 2,000. In 1988 the Bank of Mexico instituted measures to slow the decline to less than a centavo per day by the end of 1992. Following the switch to the new peso in '93, the peso actually gained in value against the U.S. dollar, until the 1995 devaluation sliced it down again. This was bad news for peso-spending Mexicans, but good news for dollar-holding bargain hunters.

The fluctuating exchange rate means you should keep an eye on the exchange rate when traveling in Mexico. Use credit or ATM cards whenever possible—these always feature the best exchange rate. Sometimes the peso falls by the time the transaction is posted to your card account, meaning you'll save a little more money.

The devaluation continues to work in favor of the dollar-holder; the dollar bought roughly 30% more in 2000 than it did in 1994.

CHANGING MONEY

Banks

Banks offer the best exchange rate for buying pesos, and they all offer the same rate, set by the Bank of Mexico. This rate is usually posted behind the counter where foreign exchange is handled. Banks also accept a wide range of foreign currencies, including Swiss francs, German marks, British pounds, Japanese yen, and Canadian dollars. Either cash or travelers checks are accepted. The main drawbacks with banks are the long lines and short hours (Mon.-Fri. 9 a.m.-1:30 p.m.); the foreign-exchange service usually closes at noon or 12:30 p.m.

Moneychangers

The second-best rate is at the *casa de cambio* or private moneychanging office. The *casa de cambio* either knocks a few pesos off the going bank rate or charges a percentage commission. It pays to shop around for the best *casa de cambio* rates since some places charge considerably more than others. Rates are usually posted; *compra* refers to the buying rate for US$ (how many pesos you'll receive per dollar), while *vende* is the selling rate (how many pesos you must pay to receive a dollar). As with banks, the difference between the buying and selling rates is the moneychangers' profit, unless they charge commissions on top of it.

Moneychangers are usually open much later than banks; some even work evening hours, which makes them immeasurably more convenient than banks. American dollars are generally preferred, though many *casas* will also accept Canadian dollars. However, Canadians should always keep a reserve supply of U.S. dollars for instances when Canadian currency isn't accepted. Moneychangers usually accept travelers checks; some border-town *casas,* however, accept only cash.

Only the larger towns and tourist centers offer moneychanging offices. In smaller towns you'll have to resort to a bank or local merchant. Many storekeepers will be happy to buy dollars at a highly variable and sometimes negotiable rate. Few will take travelers checks, however, unless you make a purchase.

Moneychangers at Mexican airports offer notoriously low rates. Try to buy pesos in advance if arriving by air, or pay with dollars until you can get to a bank or *casa de cambio.*

Hotels

Hotels, motels, *pensiones,* and other lodgings generally offer the lowest exchange rates. If you're trying to save money, avoid changing currency where you stay. Pay for your room in pesos if possible, since the same low rate often applies to room charges paid in dollars.

Credit Cards

Plastic money (primarily Visa and MasterCard) is widely accepted in the Cape Region at large hotels, at restaurants catering to tourists or businesspeople, at car rental agencies (you can't rent a car without a credit card), and at shops in tourist centers or large cities. Usually card displays at the cash register or on the door will announce that *tarjetas de crédito* (credit cards) are accepted. If in doubt, flash one and ask *"¿Se aceptan tarjetas de crédito?"* or simply *"¿Está bien?"* A reference to *efectivo* means "cash." Credit cards are not accepted at Pemex stations.

Paying for goods and services in Baja with credit cards that are paid through U.S. or Canadian banks can save you money since the exchange rate will usually dip farther in the dollar's favor by the time the transaction is posted at your bank. Many shops and some hotels, however, add a three- to six-percent surcharge to bills paid with a card, which more than offsets the exchange rate differential.

Cash advances on credit card accounts—a very useful service for emergencies—are available at Mexican banks.

Debit Cards and ATM Cards

Many banks now accept MasterCard or Visa debit cards ("cash" or "check" cards) as well as ATM (automatic teller machine) cards on the Plus or Cirrus systems. Using an ATM card to obtain pesos from ATMs in Mexico is much more convenient than cashing travelers checks. Some banks that issue ATM cards charge transaction fees for use of another bank's ATMs; check with your bank to see if these are reasonable. Some banks allow a certain number of free ATM transactions a month before service fees are charged. So far Mexican banks don't appear to charge a fee for withdrawing cash from their ATMs with cards from other banks, but this may change over time. ATMs are called *cajeros automáticos* (automatic cashiers) in Mexico.

At this time the most reliable machines seem to be those operated by **Banamex, Bancomer, Bital, Bancrecer, Banorte,** and **Serfín,** whose ATMs accept cards coded for the Visa, MasterCard, Cirrus, and Plus systems as well as intra-Mexico systems.

MONEY MANAGEMENT

Estimating Costs

Inflation in Mexico currently runs around 18% per annum, in large part due to the continued weakening of the peso on international markets, but also because of a slight relaxation of wage and price controls. This means that when estimating travel costs based on prices quoted in this book, some allowance must be made for inflation. Although peso prices will increase in direct proportion to the inflation rate, this isn't necessarily so for prices figured in dollars, since the dollar continues to gain in value against the peso.

Because of fluctuations in the peso-dollar ratio, and in an effort to keep prices up to date, all prices in this book are quoted in dollars. This doesn't mean, however, that there won't be any increase in prices by the time you arrive. A couple of phone calls to hotels for price quotes should give you an idea of how much rates have increased, if at all; this difference can be applied as a percentage to all other prices for a rough estimate of costs.

Tipping

A tip of 10-15% is customary at restaurants with table service unless a service charge is added to the bill. Luggage handling at hotels or airports warrants a tip of 50 cents per bag. A few hotels maintain a no-tipping policy; details will be posted in your room. The tipping of chambermaids is optional—some guests tip and some don't. Remember that these folks typically earn minimum wage; even a small tip may mean a lot to them.

You don't need to tip Pemex station attendants unless they wash your windows, check the oil, or perform other extra services beyond pumping gas. The equivalent of 25-50 cents in pesos is sufficient. When the change due on a gasoline purchase is less than N$1 it's customary to let the attendant keep the change.

Taxes

The Mexican government collects an *impuesta al valor agregado* (IVA) or "value added tax" of 10% on all goods and services in Baja, including hotel and restaurant bills and international phone calls. On the mainland the same tax is 15%, so Baja is a bargain in this respect. Although by American standards this may seem high, this tax hike brings Mexico more in line with other countries that employ such value-added taxes—such as France, where the VAT runs over 20%.

Hotels add a further two-percent lodging tax. Most hotel rate quotes include taxes, but to make sure you might ask *"¿Se incluyen los impuestos?"*

Bank Accounts

For long-term stays in Mexico—six months or more—visitors might consider opening a Mexican bank account. Now that peso deflation has been slowed, a *small* peso account seems quite safe; Mexico, in fact, hasn't had a single bank failure in 60 years. Interest earnings are refreshingly high compared to current rates in the U.S., Canada, or Europe. You can also open a U.S. dollar account at many banks, then convert to pesos at your leisure; these are much safer in the sense that you won't lose out if the peso dives, but they don't earn much interest.

Bancomer, BanCrecer (BanOro), Bital, and several other banks will accept personal checks drawn on U.S. banks from their account-holders. Probably the biggest advantage is that you won't have to worry about the short foreign-exchange hours kept by Mexican banks; you can bank right up until closing or use an ATM card.

Retirees age 55 and older living in Mexico may open an interest-bearing "Friendship Senior Checking Program" account at California Commerce Bank in Los Angeles that allows them to cash CCB checks at any branch of Banamex. Checks are free, and neither bank charges for check cashing. CCB is owned by Banamex but fully insured under FDIC.

MEASUREMENTS AND STANDARDS

Weights and Measures

Mexico uses the metric system as the official system of weights and measures. This means the distance between La Paz and San José del Cabo is measured in kilometers, cheese is weighed in grams or kilograms, a hot day in Cabo San Lucas is 32° C, gasoline is sold by the liter, and a big fish is two meters long. A chart at the end of this book converts pounds, gallons, and miles to kilos, liters, and kilometers, and vice versa.

Bajacalifornianos used to dealing with American tourists often use the Anglo-American and metric systems interchangeably. Even rancheros in remote areas occasionally use *millas* (miles) as a measure.

In this book, distances are rendered in kilometers, often followed by miles in parentheses for the benefit of American readers and for checking against American odometers. All road markers

in Mexico employ the metric system. Dimensions and weights are usually quoted using the metric system, but boat lengths and fishing line tests are quoted in feet and pounds (due to the influence of American boaters and anglers).

Time

Baja California Sur lies in the mountain time zone. All of Mexico now observes daylight saving time from the first Sunday in April to the last Sunday in October.

Time in Mexico is often expressed according to the 24-hour clock, from 0001 to 2359 (one minute past midnight to 11:59 p.m.). A restaurant posting hours of 1100-2200, for example, is open from 11 a.m. to 10 p.m.

Electricity

Mexico's electrical system is the same as those in the U.S. and Canada: 110 volts, 60 cycles, alternating current (AC). Electrical outlets are of the American type, designed to work with appliances with standard double-bladed plugs. Small towns in some rural areas may experience brief interruptions of electrical service or periods of brownout (voltage decrease). In a few villages, gasoline-powered generators are the only sources of electricity and may be turned off during the day.

TELEPHONE SERVICES

The national telephone company, TelMex, privatized in 1990 and has improved its services considerably over the last decade. Local phone calls are relatively cheap—a one-peso coin will pay for a phone-booth call—as are long-distance calls *within* Mexico. If you can find a working phone—many public phones seem permanently "out of order"—connections are usually good, though you may have to wait a while to get through to the operator during busy periods like Sundays and holidays.

If you don't want to use a phone booth or a hotel phone (hotels usually add their own surcharges to both local and long-distance calls), you can make a call during business hours from a TelMex office. Only large towns offer TelMex offices with public telecommunications facilities; a small town may offer a private telephone office (usually called *caseta de teléfono* or *caseta de larga distancia*), often set up in the corner of a local shop, where you can make calls. Like hotels, private telephone offices add surcharges to calls, but rates are usually reasonable.

A public pay phone service called Ladatel (acronym for "Larga Distancia Teléfono") offers phone booths where you can pay for local or long-distance calls with a *tarjeta de teléfono* (phone card) issued by TelMex or by TelNor. You can purchase debit cards in denominations of N$5, N$10, N$20, N$30, and N$50 at many pharmacies, convenience stores, supermarkets, bus terminals, and airports.

Long-Distance Domestic Calls

At the moment TelMex long-distance rates anywhere within Mexico—regardless of distance—cost a flat rate of about 33 cents per minute during daylight hours, half that after 8 p.m. Mon.-Sat. and all day Sunday. To make a long distance call within Mexico, dial 01 plus the area code and number.

In January 1997, the Ministry of Communications and Transport began allowing other telecommunications companies to compete with TelMex for long distance services. So far the competition has had virtually no effect on calling within Mexico, as very few Mexican residents—including private phone offices—have chosen to use them. If you have a calling card number for Sprint, AT&T, MCI, Bell Canada, or British Telecom, you can

TELEPHONE CODES

Long-distance operator (national): 020
Time: 030
Directory Assistance (local): 040
Mexico City area code: 05
Police, Red Cross, Fire: 060
Spanish-English emergency information: 07
International operator: 090

LONG-DISTANCE DIRECT DIALING FROM MEXICO VIA TELMEX:

station to station (in Mexico): 01 + area code + number
person to person (in Mexico): 02 + area code + number
station to station (U.S. and Canada): 00 + 1 + area code + number
person to person (U.S. and Canada): 09 + 1 + area code + number
station to station (other international): 00 + area code + number
person to person (other international): 09 + area code + number

OTHER LONG DISTANCE COMPANIES:

AT&T: 01-800 288-2872 or 001-800-462-4240
MCI: 01-800-021-8000 or 001-800-674-7000
Sprint: 001-800-877-8000

BAJA CALIFORNIA AREA CODES

All of Baja California (Norte) now shares the same area code, 6; all of Baja California Sur now uses the area code 1.

In case you're given an old five- or six-digit phone number for a place in Baja, here are the previous area codes:

Tijuana: 66
Rosarito: 661
Ensenada: 61
Mexicali: 65
Tecate: 665
San Felipe: 657
Guerrero Negro/Mulegé: 115
Loreto: 113
La Paz: 112
San José del Cabo/Cabo San Lucas/ Todos Santos: 114
San Quintín: 616

Calling Mexico from Abroad

Mexico country code: 52

To call Mexico direct from outside the country, dial your international access code + 52 + number. Example: to call the number 5255-0631 in Mexico City from the U.S., dial 011 (international access code) + 52 (Mexico country code) + 6 (Baja California area code) + 684-0461 (phone number in Tijuana).

use it to make long-distance calls. Each of these has its own access code for direct dialing.

International Calls

To direct dial an international call via TelMex, dial 00 plus the area code and number for a station-to-station call or 09 plus area code and number for a person-to-person or other operator-assisted call. Long-distance international calls are heavily taxed and cost more than equivalent international calls from the U.S. or Canada.

To reach toll-free (800) numbers in Mexico, dial 01 first. Dial 001 first for numbers in the U.S., or 091 for Canada.

See the Telephone Codes chart for access numbers that will connect you with operators from AT&T, MCI, or Sprint for calling card or credit card calls.For Canada Direct, dial 01-800-010-1990, and for BT Direct dial *791 ("star" 791).

The appropriate long-distance operator can then place a collect call on your behalf or charge the call to your account if you have a calling card for that service. If you try these numbers from a hotel phone, be sure the hotel operator realizes the call is toll-free; some hotel operators use their own timers to assess phone charges.

Warning: TelMex international rates now run about the same as AT&T's, sometimes cheaper depending on time of day and call destination. Since the deregulation of Mexican telephone service, several unscrupulous U.S.-based long-distance phone companies have set up shop in Mexico to take advantage of undiscerning tourists. The English-language signs next to the phone usually read "Call the U.S. or Canada Collect or With a Credit Card" or "Just Dial Zero to Reach the U.S. or Canada." Another clue is that the name of the company is not posted on the sign. If you try asking the operators on the line who they represent, you'll find the same company often operates under several different names in the same area, charging at least 50% more per international call than TelMex, AT&T, MCI, or Sprint—or even many times more, as much as US$10-20 for the first minute, plus US$4 each additional minute, even on weekends. A percentage of these charges usually goes to the hotel or private phone office offering the service. At most private phone offices it's cheaper to use TelMex, even if you have to pay a service charge on top of TelMex rates, than to use these price-gouging U.S. companies. Or

use MCI, Sprint, AT&T, or one of the other more well-known international companies. Unless you're independently wealthy, always ask which company is being used before you arrange an international call through a hotel or private phone office. Some Mexican hotels are now cooperating with these cutthroat American companies— the tip-off is a card next to the phone that says you can use credit cards to make a call to the U.S. or Canada.

Collect Calls

For international service, calling collect often saves hassles. In Spanish the magic words are *por cobrar* (collect), prefaced by the name of the place you're calling (e.g., *"a los Estados Unidos, por favor—por cobrar"*). This will connect you to an English-speaking international operator. For best results, speak slowly and clearly. You're supposed to be able to obtain an international operator directly by dialing 09, but this number doesn't always work.

Long-Distance Numbers

Area codes in Mexico are in a period of transition. Before January 2000, some area codes had three digits and some had two, while Mexico City, Monterrey, and Guadalajara each had one-digit area codes. Starting in 2000, all area codes are supposed to go to one digit. These single-digit area codes consist of the first digit of the old two- or three-digit codes. The leftover digits—one or two depending on the original area code— are to be added to the local phone number, bumping them up to seven or eight digits.

The number (114) 2-4274 in La Paz, for example, is now (1) 142-4274. In Tijuana, the number (66) 81-7000 will be (6) 681-7000. This means the current area code for La Paz is 1, while the code for Tijuana is now 6. In effect, under the new system all of Baja California Norte now shares one area code, 6, while all of Baja California Sur comes under the area code 1. Should you need to call Mexico City, the number (5) 235-7678 is now 5235-7678, i.e., there is now no area code for Mexico City.

In everyday practice, these code changes make no difference when calling long distance, as you must still dial the same numbers. They do make a difference when making local calls, however. See Local Numbers for explanation on what to do when dialing locally.

All international calls out of the U.S. or Canada to Mexico require the 011 prefix. 52 is the country code for Mexico, so if you're dialing the number (1) 142-4274 in La Paz, from the U.S./Canada, you'll have to dial 011 52 1 142-4274.

Local Numbers

As of January 2000, all telephone numbers in both states of Baja California, and most phone numbers elsewhere in Mexico, will consist of seven digits. Exceptions are Mexico City, Monterrey, and Guadalajara, whose phone numbers will feature eight digits. The "old" way of writing the numbers will most likely persist until Mexicans begin changing phone books, stationery, business cards, and street signs.

This means if you are in La Paz, and intend to call what would formerly have been written as (114) 2-4274 (or simply 2-4274, without the old area code) under the earlier system, you must dial 142-4274. In other words, simply add the last two digits of the old three-digit area code.

There's no standard way of hyphenating the numbers in Mexico. You may see the number in our La Paz example written as 1424274, 14-24274, 14-24-274, and so on.

Internet Resources

Numerous online service providers offer information on the Cape Region, and the number of World Wide Web sites with data on the region seem to be multiplying monthly. You can expect a general text search under the keywords "Los Cabos" to turn up at least 12,400 references, perhaps many more. A recent search we made via Yahoo! found over 300 websites dedicated to various aspects of the Cape Region. Many of these are commercial sites established by tour operators or hotels, while others are personal websites created by Cabo travel devotees. The ratio of commercial to noncommercial sites is liable to increase over time if current Internet trends continue.

You'll do better to narrow your search by starting with a few known URLs (universal resource locators) and working from there using links to other resources. See Baja on the Web in the Resources section for a list of some we've found. Remember that all URLs mentioned here are subject to change without notice; a couple of them even changed addresses while we were compiling this section. You can of course use your own Web browser to conduct searches. Yahoo (www.yahoo.com), Webcrawler (http://query.webcrawler.com), and Alta Vista (www.altavista.com) work well for blind searches.

Moon Handbooks' website (www.moon.com) contains occasional excerpts from this book and other Moon titles, ordering information, an online travel newsletter, and links to various related sites.

E-mail and Internet Access

If you're bringing computer and modem to the Cape Region with hopes of staying on the infobahn, on-line options are limited to a small number of local Internet service providers and a few international ones. Baud rates can be slow—we have trouble logging on at speeds of 28.8M or greater, bottlenecked by low bandwidth and line interrupts in the Mexican phone system. With fiber optics well underway in some parts of the peninsula, this is changing rapidly, though much depends on the kind of equipment installed at any given town linked with fiber optics.

CompuServe Interactive, America Online, and IBM Global are the only "internaional" providers so far that include local access phone numbers on Mexico. CompuServe Interactive (CSi) claims the largest market share and is available at up to 56.6M baud (28.8M in everyday practice); because it beats all the competition in terms of computer networking infrastructure, so far it is the most reliable. Mexico's own TelMex and TelNor, both associated with Prodigy, are close seconds. Unfortunately all of CompuServe Interactive's modes and access numbers are in mainland Mexico—Puebla, León, Guadalajara, and Mexico City—all long-distance calls from Baja. AOL has a connection in San José del Cabo.

RJ11 phone jacks are the standard in newer hotels, but in older hotels, motels, and *casas de huéspedes* the phones may still be hardwired. A pocketknife and pair of alligator clips are useful for stripping and attaching wires, or bring along an acoustic coupler. You can also take your laptop to a local phone office and ask to plug into their system. Most phone offices are cooperative if you're polite and explain what you're up to. We've encountered a few small-town offices that seemed to fear that our laptop would suck all the electrical power in the town dry, or that we would call Mongolia and charge it as a local call. Sometimes a good bit of explanation is necessary. If the office telephone is hard-wired, ask if they have a fax machine, since all fax units use standard RJ11 jacks.

Cybercafes where you can log on using public terminals to send and receive e-mail or browse the Web are multiplying slowly in La Paz, San José del Cabo, Cabo San Lucas, and Todos Santos. No doubt more public Internet access points will appear over the next few years. All allow access to any Web-based e-mailing such as Yahoo! or MSN Hotmail, or you can often check your account back home by logging onto the website of your own Internet service provider.

If you're looking for a local ISP, the most reliable one in the Cape Region currently appears to be Cabo.net.

POSTAL SERVICE

The Mexican postal service, though reliable, is relatively slow. Delivery time has been shortened by 75% since 1989, the year a full government subsidy for Sepomex (Servicio Postal Mexicana) was discontinued and the Ministry of Communications and Transport ordered the agency to become self-sufficient. Average delivery time between Mexico and the U.S. or Canada is about 10 days, while to Europe you must figure two weeks. Mail sent to Mexico from outside the country generally reaches its destination more quickly.

Most towns in the Cape Region have a post office *(oficina de correos)* where you can receive general-delivery mail. Have correspondents address mail in your name (last name capitalized), followed by a/c Lista de Correos, Correo Central, the town name, and the state; e.g., Joe CUMMINGS, a/c Lista de Correos, Correo Central, La Paz, Baja California Sur, Mexico. Mail sent this way is usually held 10 days. If you want your mail held up to 30 days, substitute the words "Poste Restante" for Lista de Correos in the address, e.g. Joe CUM-MINGS, a/c Poste Restante,

Correo Central, La Paz, Baja California Sur, Mexico. If you have the postal code for the town or city, insert it just after the state name. Since delivery time is highly variable, it's best to use poste restante just to be safe.

In small towns and villages, residents often don't use street addresses, simply the addressee's name followed by *domicilio conocido* (known residence) and the name of the town or village. Even in large towns and cities, addresses may bear the name of the street without a building number (*sin número,* abbreviated as "s/n"), or will mention the nearest cross streets (e.g., *ent. Abasolo y Revolución,* or "between Abasolo and Revolución").

Many foreigners who are seasonal Cape residents have their mail sent in care of a hotel or RV park. You can rent boxes at many Mexican post offices but the initial application process often takes several weeks. Todos Santos, Cabo San Lucas, and La Paz have private mail companies that also rent boxes with minimal red tape.

For mail to the U.S., many residents save their letters and parcels until a friend or relative makes a trip across the border. A letter mailed to Los Angeles from Cabo San Lucas will take as much as two weeks, while one mailed from Chula Vista, California (opposite Tijuana) will take only two days. Old Baja hands usually do the same, handing over mail to travelers returning to the States.

The Mexican post office offers an express mail service (EMS) called Mexpost. International rates are relatively high; a Mexpost express letter to the U.S. or Canada, for example, costs US$16, to Europe US$20. Mexpost claims to deliver almost anywhere in Mexico within 48 hours, to major cities around the world within 72 hours. A Mexpost parcel cannot exceed 1.05 meters along any one dimension or weigh more than 20 kg.

UPS, Airborne Express, DHL, FedEx, and other courier services now operate in La Paz and Cabo San Lucas. So far DHL and UPS seem to offer the lowest prices and best services. Local companies such as Estafeta and Aeroflash are also available but reliability does not appear to match the international services.

SERVICES AND INFORMATION

BUSINESS HOURS

The typical small business is open Mon.-Fri. 9 a.m.-2 p.m., closed until 4 or 5 p.m., then re-opened until 7 or 8 p.m. Retail businesses are usually open on Saturday as well. Official government offices typically maintain an 8:30 a.m.-3:30 p.m. schedule, although Secretary of Tourism offices usually open again from 5-7 p.m.

Banks are open Mon.-Fri. 8:30 a.m.-1:30 p.m., but the foreign currency exchange service usually closes around noon—probably to lock in the exchange rate before afternoon adjustments.

TRAVEL SERVICES

Tourist Information

Mexico's federal tourist bureau, the Secretaría de Turismo (SECTUR), has an office in La Paz where you'll find a variety of free brochures, maps, hotel and restaurant lists, and information on local activities. It's between Km 6 and 5 on Mexico 1 (Av. Abasolo); tel. (1) 122-1199, fax (1) 122-7722.

Outside Mexico the government staffs 12 Mexican Government Tourism Offices (MGTO) to handle requests for tourist information. Seven of these offices are located in the United States. The information they provide on the Cape Region, however, is minimal. We've recently heard that the MGTO may be undergoing a structural change, combining private and public participation, and that henceforth it may be called the Mexico Tourist Promotion Council.

Travel Clubs

Baja's popularity as a boating and RV destination has spawned two California-based travel clubs that specialize in recreational travel on the peninsula and along the Pacific coast of mainland Mexico. Membership benefits include discounts (usually 10-20%) at various hotels, restaurants, and other tourist-oriented establishments in Mexico; discounted group auto and boat insurance; the opportunity to participate in such club events as tours and fiestas; and subscriptions to newsletters containing tips from other club members, short travel features, and the latest information on road conditions and Mexican tourism policy. The clubs can also arrange tourist cards, boat permits, and fishing licenses by mail.

Discover Baja specializes in road travel and publishes a monthly newsletter, while Vagabundos del Mar is oriented toward boaters and RVers, and publishes its newsletter every two months. Discover Baja, the larger of the two clubs, invites members or potential members to visit its San Diego area office on the way to Baja for up-to-date road and weather information. Contact **Discover Baja** at 3089 Clairemont Dr., San Diego, CA 92117, tel. (619) 275-4225, toll-free (800) 727-BAJA, e-mail: info@discoverbaja.com, website: www.discoverbaja.com. Write or call **Vagabundos del Mar** 190 Main St., Rio Vista, CA 94571, tel. (800) 474-BAJA, fax (707) 374-6843, e-mail: vags@compuserve.com, website: www.bajavags.com.

MAPS

For general road travel in the Cape Region, the maps in this guidebook should suffice. If you're planning to drive farther north than La Paz, you can pick up one of the many Baja California maps available to visitors. Two maps are particularly well suited to general-purpose Baja road travel. One is published by the Automobile Club of Southern California and is available from most AAA offices; maps are free to AAA members. This map is easy to read, accurate, and detailed enough for any border-to-cape auto trip. Its excellent graphics include topographic shading.

The AAA map is accurate along Mexico 1, but inaccurate or out of date for many places on other highways or on smaller, unpaved roads. Even on or near Mexico 1, "dead" ranches that dried up 10-15 years ago haven't been removed. At the same time thriving ranches like La Garita on Mexico 19, for example, may not be marked on the map. Remote coastal areas are particularly spotty. Still it can be recommended for ordinary Tijuana-to-Cabo highway navigation.

International Travel Map Productions (ITM) publishes a well-researched map that's a bit harder to find, especially in the United States. Map and travel stores may carry it, or it can be ordered from ITM, P.O. Box 2290, Vancouver, BC V6B 3W5, Canada. In spite of its smaller scale (one inch: 15.78 miles or 25.4 km), the ITM map is far more detailed than the AAA map and all distances are entered in kilometers as well as miles. Many dirt roads, trails, and destinations unmarked on the AAA map appear on the ITM map. In addition, the map features contour lines in 200-meter intervals and is annotated with useful historical and sightseeing information. The main drawback of this map is that it's so detailed it's difficult to read. In addition, the

map's graphics scheme uses far too much red, a color particularly difficult to read in low light (e.g., under a car dome light).

Topographical Maps
Since differences in elevation often determine backcountry route selection, hikers, kayakers, mountain bikers, and off-road drivers should consider obtaining topographical maps in advance of their arrival in the Cape Region. For information on what's available and where to get it, see Hiking and Backpacking, above. Topo maps are difficult to come by in the Cape Region; in La Paz, the Instituto Nacional de Estadística Geografía e Informática (INEGI), in Plaza Cuatro Molinos at Calle Altamirano 2790, tel. (1) 123-1545 or 123-3159, sells topo maps for Baja California Sur at around US$4 a sheet.

GETTING THERE

BY AIR

International Flights
The Cape Region boasts two international airports: **Los Cabos International Airport** (airport code: SJD) near San José del Cabo, and **Márquez de León International Airport** (LAP) near La Paz. Both field flights from the U.S.—the only country with direct international flights to the Cape—as well as from mainland Mexico.

Los Cabos (SJD), a modern airport about 15 km (nine miles) north of San José, receives daily direct flights from Houston, Los Angeles, Oakland, Phoenix, San Diego, and San Francisco, with connections to many other U.S. cities. Many other cities in the U.S. post flights to Los Cabos with one or more stopovers along the way, usually Mexico City or Monterrey. Los Cabos is well connected by air with mainland Mexico.

International flights to La Paz (LAP) arrive from El Paso, Los Angeles, Phoenix, San Antonio, and Tucson—all but Los Angeles require stops along the way. La Paz is very well connected with mainland Mexico, however.

For specific information on regularly scheduled flights to the aforementioned airports, see the La Paz and San José del Cabo Getting There sections.

Air/Hotel Packages
Airlines serving Baja often offer package deals that include airfare, hotel, and airport transfers at money-saving prices. A typical package will include three nights hotel accommodations, airfare, and airport transfers for about the same as airfare alone. Contact the airlines directly to inquire about such packages, or check with a good travel agent. Newspaper travel sections often carry advertisements for air/hotel deals in Los Cabos.

Suntrips, tel. (800) SUNTRIPS, combines roundtrip air between San Francisco and Los Cabos with three nights hotel accommodations beginning at US$269. Considering that roundtrip airfare alone to Los Cabos can cost US$350 or more, these are bargain rates. Fares are subject to change, of course; these are only examples.

BY LAND

Most Cape visitors arrive by air, but a significant number—many of them repeat visitors— drive all the way down the peninsula from the U.S.-Mexico border. Public transportation by Mexican bus is also possible from the border.

Full details on the transpeninsular road trip— by private vehicle and by bus—are available in Moon Handbooks' *Baja*.

San Diego to Tijuana
Greyhound Bus Lines, tel. (619) 239-9171 in San Diego, operates around 20 buses a day, nearly round the clock, from the San Diego bus terminal to Tijuana's downtown bus terminal. The fare is US$6 one-way or US$9 roundtrip. Greyhound also runs a number of buses daily to Tijuana's Central de Autobuses—where you'll find the greatest selection of buses heading to Baja California Sur—for about the same fare. San Diego's bus terminal is located at 120 W. Broadway.

The cheapest bus to the border from San Diego is the Metropolitan Transit System's city bus no. 932, which travels from the downtown area (Centre City) to San Ysidro every 30 minutes from 5:30 a.m. to 9:30 p.m. (6 a.m.-9 p.m. weekends and holidays) for just US$1.50. Because it makes several stops along the way, the city bus takes an hour and 20 minutes to reach San Ysidro. For schedule information, call (619) 233-3004.

Buses to La Paz
See Intercity Bus Service, below, for details on bus routes between the border and the Cape Region.

AIRLINES SERVING THE CAPE REGION

Note: All routes are subject to change; call the airlines for the latest information.

AERO CALIFORNIA, TEL. (800) 237-6225

- **to La Paz:** nonstop flights from Chihuahua, Culiacán, Guadalajara, Hermosillo, Los Mochis, Mazatlán, Monterrey, and Tijuana; connecting flights from Los Angeles and Mexico City
- **to Los Cabos:** flights from Los Angeles, Guadalajara, and Monterrey

AEROLITORAL, TEL. (800) 237-6639

- **to La Paz:** nonstop flights from Ciudad Obregón, Hermosillo, Loreto, Los Mochis, and Mazatlán; connecting flights from Chihuahua and Monterrey
- **to Los Cabos:** flights from Los Mochis, La Paz, Loreto, Chihuahua, Culiacán, Ciudad Obregón, and Hermosillo

AEROMÉXICO, TEL. (800) 237-6639

- **to La Paz:** nonstop flights from Culiacán, Guaymas, Mexico City, and Tijuana; connecting flights from Guadalajara and Phoenix
- **to Los Cabos:** flights from Mexico City and San Diego

ALASKA AIRLINES, TEL. (800) 426-0333

- **to La Paz:** nonstop flights from Los Angeles; connecting flight from Seattle
- **to Los Cabos:** nonstop flights from Los Angeles, Phoenix, and San Francisco; connecting flight from Seattle

AMERICAN AIRLINES, TEL: (800) 321-2121

- **to Los Cabos:** daily flights from Dallas/Ft. Worth

AMERICA WEST, TEL. (800) 433-7300

- **to Los Cabos:** nonstop flights from Phoenix; connecting flights from many U.S. cities

CONTINENTAL, TEL. (800) 523-3273

- **to Los Cabos:** nonstop flights from Houston; connecting flights from many U.S. cities

MEXICANA AIRLINES, TEL. (800) 531-7921

- **to Los Cabos:** nonstop flights from Guadalajara, Los Angeles, and Monterrey

From Mainland Mexico

Transportes Norte de Sonora (TNS) and **Autotransportes del Pacífico** operate long-distance express buses to Mexicali and Tijuana from various towns in Guanajuato, Nayarit, Sonora, Chihuahua, Michoacán, Jalisco, Sinaloa, Zacatecas, Querétaro, and México City.

Green Tortoise

To those who have never traveled by Green Tortoise, it's difficult to describe the experience. Imagine a sort of youth hostel on wheels, with a bit of a '60s spirit, and you'll begin to get the idea. The buses are refurbished Greyhounds with convertible beds and tables, comfortable but a bit of a tight squeeze at night when everyone's lying down. That's also when the bus travels. It's a great way to meet people.

Green Tortoise operates nine-day (from US$329) and 14-day (from US$399) trips to Baja Nov.-March that begin in San Francisco (pickups in L.A. and San Diego are possible) and range as far south as La Paz. Prices are very reasonable and include transportation and lodging on the bus, plus guided hikes and side trips to remote Baja beaches. The food fund adds another US$7-8 per day to the trip; communal meals cover about 70% of the meals—some meals are left to the participants. The trips include an optional windsurfing and sailing program available for an additional fee. All things considered, it's a travel bargain and a novel introduction to Baja.

For further information, contact Green Tortoise, 494 Broadway, San Francisco, CA 94133, tel. (415) 956-7500, toll-free (800) 867-8647, e-mail: tortoise@greentortoise.com, website: www.greentortoise.com.

Driving

If you're contemplating the drive and have limited time, figure on making it from Tijuana to Cabo in three eight-hour days (Cataviña first night, Santa Rosalía or Mulegé second night) or two and a half dawn-to-dusk days (Guerrero Negro first night, La Paz second night). If you stretch your itinerary to include a week's driving time each way, you'll have a safer trip and more of an opportunity to enjoy the sights along the way.

The red tape for driving into Baja is minimal. No vehicle permits of any kind are required, no matter how long you stay in Baja, unless you plan to cross to the mainland by road (via San Luis Río Colorado) or ferry (Santa Rosalía or La Paz).

Insurance: Before driving into Baja, drivers should arrange for Mexican vehicle insurance. No matter what your own insurance company may tell you, Mexican authorities don't recognize foreign insurance policies for private vehicles in Mexico.

Vehicle insurance isn't required by law in Mexico but it's a good idea to carry a Mexican liability policy anyway; without it, a minor traffic accident can turn into a nightmare. Short-term insurance—as little as one day's worth—can be

San Francisco's vagabond poet Tony Sheldon and the 1954 GM Green Tortoise

arranged at any of several agencies found in nearly every border town between the Pacific Ocean and the Gulf of Mexico. One reliable insurer of long standing is **Lewis & Lewis,** 8929 Wilshire Blvd., Ste. 220, Beverly Hills, CA 90211, tel. (310) 657-1112, toll-free (800) 966-6830, fax (310) 652-5849, e-mail: mexauto@gte.net. Lewis & Lewis' premiums for a multiple-entry, one-year, comprehensive policy for Baja/Northwest Mexico start at around US$130 for under US$5,000 in coverage and rise to US$516 for US$100,000 worth of coverage; liability only costs US$74 per year.

Those in a hurry might prefer **Instant Mexico Insurance Services.** IMIS sits at the last exit before the San Ysidro/Tijuana border crossing at 223 Via de San Ysidro, tel. (619) 428-4714, toll-free (800) 638-0999. It's open 24 hours and in addition to insurance offers tourist cards, fishing and boating permits, maps, guidebooks, and other Baja requisites.

The Discover Baja and Vagabundos del Mar travel clubs (see Services and Information for addresses and phone numbers) offer lower group insurance rates for members only—check with each for the latest deals. These group policies are offered on a yearly basis only; they can't be purchased by the day, week, or month.

Whichever policy you choose, always make photocopies of it and keep originals and copies in separate, safe places. It's also a good idea to carry a photocopy of the first page—the "declaration" or "renewal of declaration" sheet—of your home-country policy, as Mexican law requires you cross the border with at least six months' worth of home-country insurance.

Temporary Vehicle Import Permits

If you're only driving in the states of Baja California and Baja California Sur, you won't need one of these. However, if you plan to take a vehicle aboard a ferry bound for the mainland from Santa Rosalía or La Paz, you will need a temporary vehicle import permit before you'll be allowed to book a ferry ticket. To receive this permit, simply drive your vehicle to a Mexican customs office (this can be done at any official border crossing or in La Paz) and present the following: a valid state registration for the vehicle (or similar document certifying legal ownership), a driver's license, and a credit card (Visa, Mas-

terCard, American Express, or Diner's Club) issued outside Mexico.

If you are leasing or renting the vehicle, you'll also have to present a leasing or rental contract made out to the person bringing the vehicle into Mexico. If the vehicle belongs to someone else (e.g., a friend or relative), you must present a notarized letter from the owner giving you permission to take the vehicle to Mexico. Contrary to rumor, you aren't required to present the "pink slip" or ownership certificate unless the state registration certificate is for some reason unavailable.

Once Mexican customs officials have approved your documents, you'll proceed to a Banjército (Banco del Ejército or Military Bank) office attached to the customs facilities and your credit card account will be charged US$12 for the permit fee. This fee must be paid by credit card; cash is not accepted. If you don't have a credit card, you'll have to post a bond (one to two percent of the vehicle's blue-book value) issued by an authorized Mexican bond company—a very time-consuming and expensive procedure. Banjército is the bank used for all Mexican customs charges; the operating hours for each module are the same as for the border crossing at which it's located.

Once the fee has been charged to your credit card, the permit is issued, with a validity period equal to that shown on your tourist card or visa. You may drive back and forth across the border—at any crossing—as many times as you wish during the permit's validity. You are supposed to surrender the permit at the border when your trip is over, however.

In the U.S., further information on temporary vehicle importation can be obtained by calling (800) 446-8277. Under an agreement between the American Automobile Association (AAA) and the Mexican government, U.S. motorists with credit cards are able to obtain both tourist cards and auto permits from AAA offices in Texas, New Mexico, Arizona, and California. In reality all AAA does is fill out the papers for you; you still have to stop at the border, walk into the customs office, and get the papers validated. When we tried doing this with AAA forms, Mexican customs rejected them because AAA had translated some of the forms, which was deemed unacceptable. In addition, the AAA office we used in California filled the forms in incorrectly, writing in the section marked "For Official Use Only."

La Paz–
Mazatlán ferry

We had to start from scratch, so the trip to AAA was wasted time.

If you're renting a car with Mexican license tags, none of the above is necessary, of course.

BY FERRY FROM MAINLAND MEXICO

Two passenger-vehicle ferry services currently connect La Paz with the Mexican mainland—one runs from Topolobampo, the other from Mazatlán. With passenger/vehicle ferries anyone driving on the mainland can reach the Cape Region without a time-consuming trip all the way around the Sea of Cortez. Many drivers from the American west coast use Baja ferry services as an alternative way of reaching the mainland, since it allows them to avoid traffic-heavy Mexico 15 (or its expensive toll equivalent, Mexico 15-D) on the way to Mazatlán and points farther south.

A third ferry service is available between Santa Rosalía in central Baja and Guaymas, Sonora, on the mainland. Moon Handbooks' *Baja* and *Northern Mexico* contain complete information on this route.

We've found the ferries to be comfortable and efficient in all classes. In heavy seas you may want to consider taking motion sickness tablets before boarding.

Fares and Classes

About a decade ago the vehicle ferry system was privatized under the directorship of Grupo SEMATUR (Servicios Maritimos y Turísticos) de California, S.A., and fares are now market-priced rather than subsidized. The fares listed here were valid as of 2000; allow for average inflation, roughly 18% per year, when making ferry plans.

Passenger fares are based on class: *salón* (bus-style reclining seats in various general seating areas), *turista* (shared bunk rooms with washbasins), and *cabina* (small, private cabins with two single berths and toilet facilities). Some ferryboats also feature an additional *especial* class with large, deluxe cabins. Fares for children under 12 are 50% of adult fares.

Vehicle fares are based on the length of the vehicle—the longer the rig, the higher the fare. All fares must be paid in pesos. Sample tariffs range from US$30 for a motorcycle on the La Paz–Topolobampo route to as much as US$750 for a trailer rig over nine meters (30 feet) long from La Paz to Mazatlán. Passenger and vehicle fares are separate.

You must drive the vehicle into the cargo hold yourself; this is usually the most unpleasant part of the journey, as most of the vehicles crossing are Mexican 18-wheeled trucks; the diesel fumes that accumulate in the hold while everyone gets in position (as directed by the ferry crew) can be intense. Soldiers or federal police are present on the piers at both ends of the journey, searching for arms and illegal drugs with the help of trained dogs.

Note: Signs at all vehicle ferry ticket offices warn that passenger tickets will not be issued to pregnant women.

Reservations

Generally speaking, if you show up at the ferry terminal one day in advance of your desired voyage, you should be able to get passenger tickets. To book vehicle passage, you must hold a valid temporary vehicle import permit (see above).

Salón seats are sold on a first-come, first-served basis; *turista* can be reserved three days or more in advance; a *cabina* or *especial* can be reserved a month or more in advance. During holiday periods—especially Semana Santa (the weeks before Easter Sunday) and Christmas week, when you might want to avoid ferry service altogether—you should try to pick up your tickets at least a week or two in advance. Reservations must be confirmed 15 days before departure date for the La Paz–Mazatlán and La Paz–Topolobampo routes.

SEMATUR operates ticket offices at each of its ferry piers for advance as well as day-of-departure sales. Mexican travel agencies authorized to handle ticket reservations and sales in La Paz are: Viajes Transpeninsulares, tel. (1) 122-0399; Viajes Perla, tel. (1) 122-8666; and Viajes Cabo Falso, tel. (1) 122-4131. In Los Mochis: Festival Tours, tel. (6) 818-3986. In Mazatlán: Turismo Coral, tel. (6) 981-3290; and Viajes Attiq, tel./fax (6) 914-2400. In Mexico City: Festival Tours, tel. 5682-7043.

SEMATUR's toll-free information and reservation telephone number in Mexico is (800) 696-9600; this number can be dialed from the U.S. and Canada with the prefix 011-52 instead of 01. Ferry schedules and fares are also posted on www.ferrysematur.com.mx.

Topolobampo–La Paz

Topolobampo is a small port town that serves the Los Mochis area. An interesting way to reach Baja's Cape Region from, say, Texas is to take the Chihuahua al Pacífico train via Creel and the Barrancas del Cobre ("Copper Canyon," Mexico's equivalent of the Grand Canyon) to Los Mochis, then the Topolobampo ferry to La Paz. Ferries on this route are mostly devoted to cargo, with a smaller *salón* section. During holiday periods, more passenger space is usually available.

The ferry leaves Topolobampo daily (except Sunday) at 10 p.m. and arrives in La Paz about 8 a.m. Eastbound, the ferry departs La Paz the same days at 11 a.m., arriving at Topolobampo around 7 p.m. On Monday, Tuesday, Friday, and Saturday, only *salón* class is available, and the fare is US$15. When other classes are made available, *turista* costs US$30, *cabina* US$45, and *especial* US$61.

Motorhomes on this route are charged US$191; autos under five meters (15 feet) US$128. Motorcycles pay US$28. Trailer rigs pay US$167-434.

Mazatlán–La Paz

At the moment this is the most full-service passenger-vehicle ferry available between Baja and the mainland. Each of the three craft that regularly ply this route offers *salón, turista, cabina,* and *especial* classes plus a restaurant/bar, disco, small video lounge, deck bar, and cafeteria. The most popular place to hang out, in good weather, is the stern deck bar where there's a view, a well-stocked bar, and a CD jukebox. On Wednesdays (eastbound) and Thursdays (westbound), only *salón* class is available.

Ferries depart each port daily at 3 p.m., arriving on the other side at around 9 a.m. Fares run US$23 *salón,* US$45 *turista,* US$68 *cabina,* and US$91 *especial.*

Vehicle tariffs are: autos under five meters (15 feet) US$210; motorhomes US$314; motorcycles US$47; trailer rigs US$273-713.

GETTING AROUND

If you've driven your own vehicle down to the Cape Region, you'll have a ready set of wheels for exploring all the Cape offers. If not, cars are easily rented in La Paz, San José del Cabo, and Cabo San Lucas. You can also visit almost every town by public intercity bus.

BY AIR

Charter Flights
Companies that can arrange small-plane charters to almost any legally open airfield in Baja from Southern California include: Air Charter Express, 6714 Avenida Andorra, La Jolla, CA 92037, tel. (619) 993-5861; Gunnell Aviation, 3100 McDonnell Douglas Loop North, Santa Monica, CA 90405, tel. (310) 452-0999; AeroCargo, Brown Field, San Diego, CA 92173, tel. (619) 661-6099, toll-free (800) 335-2252, fax (619) 661-2597; and Lundy Air Charter, 1860 Joe Crosson Dr., El Cajon, CA 92020, tel. (619) 562-4181.

In the Cape Region, charter flights may be arranged through **Aereo Calafía,** tel. (1) 143-4302, in Cabos San Lucas.

BY BUS

Intercity Bus Service
Baja's reliable intercity bus transportation covers the peninsula from Tijuana to Cabo San Lucas. The longest direct ride available is the Tijuana–Cabo San Lucas route (about 30-32 hours), operated once daily by **Autotransportes Águila.** Many people break the bus trip up with an overnight stop in La Paz (25-28 hours from the Tijuana) and change to one of the many La Paz–Cabo San Lucas buses the following day.

Transportes Norte de Sonora (TNS) operates buses between Tijuana, Tecate, Mexicali, and points farther west, including destinations on the Mexican mainland as far away as Mexico City.

Special express buses with hostess service and a/c are used on long-distance trips. Shorter trips may or may not have a/c, but the buses are always tolerably comfortable. Schedules aren't always scrupulously kept but even smaller bus terminals may feature public phones, restrooms, and cafes. The infamous "chicken buses" of Southern Mexico and Central America don't exist in Baja.

Fares are moderate. A Tijuana–La Paz ticket on a *primera* or first-class bus costs about US$69; second class is half that. The La Paz–Cabo San Lucas run is US$7-9, depending on whether you go via San José del Cabo or Todos Santos. Reservations aren't necessary—and in most cases aren't accepted—for bus travel. Buses usually depart several times daily, so you simply show up at the bus terminal around the time you want to leave. Buses ply the 35-km (22-mile) stretch between San José del Cabo and Cabo San Lucas frequently, all day long, for US$2 each way.

All the Spanish you need for riding a bus is *boleto* (ticket), the name of your destination (have a map handy just in case), and a reasonable command of spoken Spanish numbers for quoted fares (although the fare is always posted somewhere on the ticket office wall).

City Buses and *Colectivos*
La Paz has a comprehensive city bus system with fares averaging 20-40 cents, payable in pesos only. City buses come in a variety of sizes and shapes, from 12-passenger vans *(colectivos)* to painted school buses and huge modern vessels with automatic doors. The destination or general route—typically a street name—is usually painted somewhere on the front of the bus or displayed on a marquee over the front windshield.

Printed bus schedules are either hard to come by or nonexistent. If you can't figure out which bus to take by comparing the destination sign with a map, just ask other waiting bus passengers or, if your Spanish isn't up to that, make inquiries at the tourist office.

TAXI

Route Taxis
La Paz also features *taxis de ruta,* specially licensed cars that follow set routes similar to and

Intercity bus service in Baja is extensive and reliable.

often paralleling the bus routes. These vehicles are usually large American station wagons that hold up to 12 passengers. Unlike city buses, you can flag them down anywhere along the route. The destination is usually painted in whitewash on the windshield but locals often distinguish the route by the taxis' two-tone color scheme. A *roja y crema* may run from the central bus station to a market on the outskirts of town while a *negro y azul* may travel from the plaza to the main shopping district. Other than the terminating points of the route at either end, there are no predetermined taxi stops; passengers must let the driver know where they want off. As on city buses, route taxi fares are the same no matter where you disembark. Usually they're only a bit higher than bus fares.

Hire Taxis

Regular hire taxis congregate at hotels and designated taxi stands in La Paz, Todos Santos, San José del Cabo, and Cabo San Lucas. Sometimes fares are posted at the hotel or taxi stand, but often you must ask for a fare quote. If possible, try to find out the fare from hotel staff or a friendly resident before approaching a taxi driver—you'll feel more secure about not getting ripped off. If the quoted fare doesn't match what you've been told in advance, you can negotiate or try another driver. Fortunately, most Cape taxi drivers will quote the correct fare immediately.

In smaller towns with no buses or route taxis you may sometimes find a few regular hire taxis

hanging out by the town plaza. They're generally used for reaching out-of-town destinations, since anyplace without a city bus system is small enough to wander around on foot. Although the locals pay a set fare based on distance, gringos are sometimes quoted a much higher fare. Dig in and negotiate until it's reasonable. Even if you can afford the higher fare, you owe it to other foreign visitors not to encourage price-gouging.

CYCLING

Among cyclists, Baja California Sur's Cape Region is the most popular area in all of Mexico. Traffic is relatively light, the scenery is striking, and cyclists can pull over and camp just about anywhere.

Touring or mountain bike? If you plan to stay on paved highways, a touring bike would be the better choice, as it's lighter and faster than a mountain bike. On the other hand, the Cape offers so many great off-highway rides—like the lower sierra and the Camino Rural Costero along the East Cape—that anyone who has the time and equipment should consider a mountain bike. Off-road riding requires a stronger frame, higher clearance, and wider tires.

Many interesting trail rides lie within the 386-km (240-mile) loop that circles the Cape from La Paz to Cabo San Lucas via the Sierra de La Laguna and back via Todos Santos and the west coastal plains. The lower eastern escarpment of the sierra in particular—west of Santiago and Miraflores—is fat-tire heaven, offering rides through tropical-arid thorn forests and, if you can handle steep grades and bike portage, sub-alpine meadows. The other side of the mountains, behind Pescadero on the West Cape, can also be very rewarding. The unpaved road network along the coast between San José and La Paz will astound even the most jaded dirt bikers as it takes them past deserted white-sand coves with coral reefs, over jagged desert peaks, and then down into lush San Juan de los Planes.

Because the Cape sun can be particularly strong when you're on paved surfaces, which both reflect and radiate heat, you may find an 11 a.m.-3 p.m. siesta necessary no matter what time of year you ride. Don't forget to bring sunglasses and plenty of high-SPF sunscreen.

Equipment and Repairs

Whether you're riding a mountain or touring bike, you'll need the same basic essentials to handle long-distance Baja riding. If you plan to camp along the way, you'll need the usual camping and first-aid gear, selected to fit your panniers. Camping is often your only choice on long coastal trips, since all cyclists can't necessarily make the mileage from hotel to hotel. On the other hand, if you're only doing the Cape loop you can easily bike from hotel to hotel.

Helmets are particularly important; a head injury is even more serious when you're in the middle of nowhere. A helmet will also keep direct sun off the top of your skull. A rearview mirror is a must for keeping an eye on motorists coming from behind on narrow roads. A locking cable is preferable to a clunky U-lock for long-distance trips since it weighs less, although bicycle theft isn't much of a problem in Baja. The only other security you might need is a removable handlebar bag for carrying camera and valuables; you can take the bag with you when stopping at restaurants or *tiendas* and fill it with snacks for eating on the fly.

Water is an uppermost consideration on overnight trips. No matter what the time of year, cyclists should carry four one-liter bottles of water per day. The one-liter bottles used for cycling are more puncture-resistant than water containers designed for camping. Punctures are al-

ways a concern in Baja because of all the trees and plants bearing spines.

Tires: The puncture threat means you should outfit your bike with heavy-duty tires and tubes. Bring along two or three spare tubes, one spare tire, a tire gauge, and a complete tire repair kit. You should also carry duct tape and moleskin—or commercial plastic booting—to use as booting material against sidewall cuts caused by sharp rocks or cactus.

Rack: Check nuts and bolts daily and retighten as necessary. Applying Locktite should lessen the need for retightening—carry a small supply along with extra nuts and bolts. Bailing wire can be used for improvised repairs; carry two or three meters along with wirecutters.

Other Repairs: Bike shops can be found in La Paz and Cabo San Lucas. Although the Mexicans who run these shops can sometimes perform miraculous repairs using nothing resembling a bike's original parts, it's safer to come prepared with spares, especially for parts that aren't easily jury-rigged. At a minimum, carry a spare freewheel, a rear derailleur, and all the wrenches and screwdrivers necessary to work on your bike. If in addition you bring along several extra spokes, cables, and a spare chain, you'll be ready for just about any repair scenario.

Bicycle Transportation

All airlines that fly to the Cape Region will allow you to check bikes as luggage as long as they're boxed. Bus lines will transport bikes of paying passengers in bus luggage compartments for no additional cost, but again bikes should be boxed. For return trips from Baja, you should be able to pick up a box from bicycle shops in La Paz or Cabo San Lucas, or build your own from discarded cardboard boxes.

Guided Bicycle Trips

If you're unsure of your off-road cycling skills, you might want to tackle the Cape with an experienced cycle guide. Several tour operators now run cycling programs in Baja. **Backroads,** 1616 Fifth St., Berkeley, CA 94710-1740, tel. (510) 527-1555, fax (510) 527-1444, organizes fully outfitted, six- and seven-day mountain-biking trips in the Cape Region for around US$800-1,100.

DRIVING IN THE CAPE REGION

Before the 1973 completion of the Transpeninsular Highway (Mexico 1), only hardened off-road vehicles with equally sturdy drivers ever made it to the Cape. Nowadays, with paved Mexico 1 and paved Mexico 19 forming a loop around the Cape, the region is perfectly safe for ordinary folks driving ordinary passenger cars, as long as they employ a little ordinary common sense. For the adventurer, miles of unpaved roads remain that will take you as far from civilization as anyone would care to go. Such off-highway digressions are perfect for those who might agree with one of naturalist Joseph Krutch's famous Baja fiats:

Baja California is a wonderful example of how much bad roads can do for a country. Bad roads act as filters. They separate those who are sufficiently appreciative of what lies beyond the blacktop to be willing to undergo mild inconvenience from that much larger number of travelers which is not willing. The rougher the road, the finer the filter.

CAPE DISTANCES

La Paz to San Pedro via Mexico 1: 24 km (15 miles), 30 minutes

San Pedro to Todos Santos via Mexico 19: 51 km (32 miles), 45 minutes

Todos Santos to Cabo San Lucas via Mexico 19: 72 km (45 miles), 90 minutes

La Paz to Cabo San Lucas via Mexico 1 and Mexico 19: 147 km (92 miles), two hours

La Paz to Los Barriles via Mexico 1: 105 km (65 miles), one hour 45 minutes

Los Barriles to San José del Cabo via Mexico 1: 81 km (50 miles), 90 minutes

San José del Cabo to Cabo San Lucas via Mexico 1: 34 km (21 miles), 30 minutes

La Paz to Cabo San Lucas via Mexico 1: 221 km (137 miles), two hours 30 minutes

---

Cape Roads

Two paved national highways grace the Cape Region: Mexico 1 (the Transpeninsular, from Tijuana to Cabo San Lucas) and Mexico 19 (between Cabo San Lucas and San Pedro, via Todos Santos). Both of these highways seem to be better maintained than their counterparts in central and northern Baja—this may be due to the fact that northern Baja roads are much more heavily trafficked, while central Baja may be too remote for regular upkeep by Mexican road crews.

The only paved state highway is BCS 286, the relatively short blacktop running between La Paz and San Juan de los Planes. These three highways enable drivers to visit all of the Cape's major towns and resort areas, including La Paz, Los Barriles, Santiago, San José del Cabo, The Corridor (the 28-km/18-mile stretch between San José and Cabo San Lucas), Cabo San Lucas, and Todos Santos.

An as-yet-unnamed paved road leads east of Mexico 1 at Las Cuevas to a point about six miles south of the East Cape community of La Ribera. Eventually, according to local authorities, this paved road will extend all the way down the East Cape to San José. Meanwhile a decent, unpaved, fair-weather road parallels this coastline.

The lower eastern escarpment of the Sierra de La Laguna is bisected by Mexico 1, which offers the only paved-road access to the mountains.

Off-Highway Travel

The Cape's unpaved roads vary considerably, from rutted jeep tracks to elevated, graded, gravel boulevards. The trouble with the graded unpaved roads is that they tend to degenerate quickly between gradings into washboard surfaces impossible to drive at anything but very low speeds (8-16 kph/5-10 mph)—unless you want to risk crushed vertebrae and a dropped transmission.

The effect of these unpaved roads on you and your vehicle depends a lot on what you're driving. Some off-highway Baja navigators drive pickups with customized shocks and suspension that enable a driver to float over the worst washboard surfaces. Other drivers—like many of the local residents who can't afford heavy-duty, customized rigs—learn to drive slowly and appreciate the scenery.

road to La Candelaria

The best unpaved roads are probably those that have evolved more or less naturally, with little or no grading. When the weather's dry, some of these roads ride better than the Transpeninsular. Of course, unpaved roads may sometimes start out nicely but get worse with each passing mile, to the point where even the most intrepid explorers are forced to turn around. At other times, a road will suddenly improve after a long stretch of cavernous potholes and caved-in sides. Weather is a big determining factor; even the best ungraded, unpaved roads are often impassable during or following a hard rain.

How do you know when to turn around? There's always an element of risk when driving down a dirt road for the first—or even the hundredth—time, but it helps to ask around before embarking on a road that doesn't see much traffic. A good road map can also assist with such decisions. The AAA map (see Services and Information, above) classifies unpaved roads into four categories: gravel, graded, dirt, and poor. The annotated ITM map uses a similar but more specific fourfold system: gravel, graded, unimproved dirt, and vehicular track. Although neither of these maps is entirely up to date or 100% accurate, using one or both in conjunction with local input will greatly improve your decision-making. A topographical map could be of considerable value to a 4WD navigator as well, since sometimes it's the steep canyon grades that spell defeat.

Even with the best planning there's always the possibility of getting stuck in muddy or sandy areas. Anyone engaging in serious off-highway driving should carry along a sturdy shovel for digging out mired wheels. Another handy trick for negotiating soft ground is to let the air out of your tires to a pressure of around 12-15 psi. This really works, but you should also carry along a 12-volt air compressor, one that will plug into the cigarette lighter, for pumping the tires back up after you're on firm ground again.

Driving Precautions

The first rule of Baja driving, no matter what kind of road you're on, is *never* take the road for granted. Any highway in Baja, including the Transpeninsular, can serve up 100 meters of smooth, seamless blacktop followed immediately by 100 meters of contiguous potholes or large patches of missing asphalt. A cow, horse, or burro could be right around the next curve, or a large dog can leap out in front of your vehicle just as you fasten your eyes on a turkey vulture drying its wings on top of a tall cardón.

The speed limits set by the Mexican government—80 kph (48 mph) on most highways—are very reasonable for Baja's highway conditions. Obey them and you'll be much safer than if you try to keep the speedometer needle in the spot you're accustomed to. Wandering livestock, relatively narrow highway widths (six to eight meters/19-25 feet max), and inconsistent highway maintenance mean you simply can't drive at U.S./Canada speeds.

Many Cape roadways suffer from a conspicuous lack of shoulders. This doesn't mean you won't find any places to pull off—gravel turnouts appear fairly regularly, and in many areas you can drive directly onto the roadside from the highway. It just means you can't count on a safe margin in an emergency situation. At the very least, an emergency turnout will raise a lot of rocks and dirt—small dangers in themselves—and in some spots, like in the sierras around San Antonio, leaving the highway can launch you and your vehicle into a thousand-foot freefall. Guardrails are often flimsy or nonexistent.

Yet another reason not to take the road for granted are the high numbers of sometimes un-

---

ROADSIDE RELIGION

Along Baja's roadways you'll occasionally see small roadside crosses—sometimes in clusters—or shrines. Often placed at fatal accident sites, each cross marks a soul's point of departure from this world. Larger shrines containing Christ or Virgin figures are erected to confer blessings or protection on passing motorists. These vary from simple enclosures made of vegetable oil cans to elaborate sculptural designs.

In the brush beside the track there was a little heap of light, and as we came closer to it we saw a rough wooden cross lighted indirectly. The cross-arm was bound to the staff with a thong, and the whole cross seemed to glow, alone in the darkness. When we came close we saw that a kerosene can stood on the ground and that in it was a candle which threw its feeble light upward on the cross. And our companion told us how a man had come from a fishing boat, sick and weak and tired. He tried to get home, but at this spot he fell down and died. And his family put the little cross and the candle there to mark the place. And eventually they would put up a stronger cross. It seems good to mark and to remember for a little while the place where a man died. This is his one whole lonely act in all his life. In every other thing, even in his birth, he is bound close to others, but the moment of his dying is his own.

—JOHN STEINBECK,
THE LOG FROM THE SEA OF CORTEZ.

---

marked blind curves and blind hilltops frequently encountered. Never assume a clear path around a curve or over a hilltop—potential obstructions include an oblivious 18-wheeler or bus passing in the opposite direction, wandering livestock, rockslides, or road washouts. To be on the safe side, keep toward the outside edge of your own lane. Commercial truck drivers in Mexico roar down the road as if they're exempt from all speed limits, almost always flying at least 40 kph over the posted limit.

Rule number two is never drive the highways at night. Except along the Corridor portion of Mexico 1 between San José and Cabo San Lucas, highways have no lighting. In addition, reflectors and even painted lines are absent from many highway sections; even if no other vehicles besides your own were on the road at night, you could easily overshoot an unexpected curve. Add to this the fact that many poorly maintained local vehicles have nonfunctioning headlights, taillights, or brakelights, and it should be obvious that trying to make highway miles after sundown is crazy. Some locals do it, but they're used to local conditions and know the roads relatively well. Still, a high proportion of car accidents in Baja—around 80% according to insurance companies—occur at night.

Specific Hazards: When you see road signs marked Vado or Zona de Vados, slow down. The word *vado* is most often translated as "dip," but in Baja it usually means more than a slight depression in the road—it's any place where the road intersects an arroyo, or dry stream wash. The danger lies not only in the sudden grade drop but in the potential for running into a recently accumulated body of water. Some *vados* feature measuring sticks marked in meters; when water is present, you'll know roughly how deep it is. If you come to a *vado* full of water with no measuring stick, get out of your vehicle and measure the depth yourself using a mesquite branch or other suitable object. *Vados* aren't always signposted, so stay alert—they appear even on relatively flat terrain.

In towns, pueblos, *ejidos,* or anywhere else people live in Mexico, you'll encounter *topes* (speed bumps). Often unpainted and unsigned, they can really sneak up on you. Some *topes* are real industrial-strength tire-poppers, so always take it very slow when traversing them.

You'll notice that Mexican drivers seem to have more respect for speed bumps than for stop signs or traffic lights.

Highway Signs

One of the pleasures of driving in the Cape Region is the relative absence of signs cluttering the roadside. Billboards, in fact, are virtually nonexistent. The Mexican government does have a system of highway signs, however, based on common international sign conventions followed throughout most of the world; these can be very helpful as long as you know what they mean. Most display self-explanatory symbols (e.g., a silhouette of a man holding a shovel means "men working").

Cautionary sign captions are especially helpful, including Curva Peligrosa (Dangerous Curve), Despacio (Slow), and Zona de Vados (Dip Zone). Other common highway signs include: Desviación (Detour), No Tire Basura (Don't Throw Trash), Conserve Su Derecha (Keep to the Right), Conceda Cambio de Luces (Dim Your Lights), No Rebase (No Passing), and No Hay Paso (Road Closed).

Along the highways as well as on many secondary roads, you can measure driving progress with the assistance of regularly spaced kilometer markers, usually black lettering on a reflective white background.

If you're having tire trouble, look for homemade signs reading "Llantera," which indicate tire repair shops.

ROAD SIGNS

ALTO — STOP	RAILROAD CROSSING	**CEDA EL PASO** — YIELD RIGHT OF WAY	**TOPES** — SPEED BUMPS
CIRCULACION — ONE WAY	**DOBLE CIRCULACION** — TWO WAY	**E** — PARKING	**NO** — NO PARKING
DIP (across arroyo)	DIP (across arroyo)	**PARADA** — BUS STOP	**CONSERVE SU DERECHA** — KEEP TO THE RIGHT

Traffic Offenses

Although Mexican traffic police don't go out of their way to persecute foreign drivers, it may seem that way when you're the foreigner who's stopped. The more cautiously you drive, the less likely you'll inadvertently transgress local traffic codes. This would seem like obvious advice, but for some reason many visiting motorists in Baja drive as if they thought there were no traffic laws in Mexico. Most of these people seem to have California plates.

If you're stopped by a *tránsito* (traffic cop), the first rule is to behave in a patient, civil manner. The officer might then let you off with just a warning. If the officer decides to make a case of it, you'll be asked to proceed to the nearest police post or station, where a fine will be assessed and collected. This is a perfectly legal request. But if the cop suggests or even hints at being paid on the spot, you're being hit up for *la mordida*, the minor bribe.

In Baja, requests for *la mordida* from foreigners—for traffic offenses, at least—have become increasingly rare, and the government is making admirable progress toward stamping the practice out altogether. If confronted with such a situation, you have two choices. Mexico's Attorney General for the Protection of Tourists recommends you insist on going to the nearest station to pay the fine, and that as you pay you request a receipt. Such a request may result in all charges being dropped. If you don't feel like taking the time for a trip to the station, you can choose to negotiate the "fine" on the spot. Doing so, however, won't contribute to the shrinking of the *mordida* phenomenon.

Speeding citations are rare, but when they are issued the fine is usually equivalent to one day's Mexican minimum wage (currently about US$4) per each kilometer per hour above the speed limit you were estimated to be driving. Aside from speeding on Mexico 1-D, driving the wrong direction on one-way streets and running stop signs are the two most common traffic violations among foreign drivers in Baja. Some intersections may display no vertical stop ("Alto") signs at all, only broad stripes painted on the pavement indicating where vehicles are supposed to stop. The best practice is to assume you're supposed to stop at every single intersection in the city, which is pretty close to the truth. A sign reading "Cuatro Altos" means the intersection is a four-way stop.

Insurance

It's very important to carry a Mexican liability-insurance policy on your vehicle while driving in Baja. In case of an accident, such a policy could keep you from going to jail. For details on Mexican insurance, see Driving, above.

Fuel

The only automotive fuel commercially available in Mexico is sold at government-owned Pemex stations. Unlike many parts of Mexico, Pemex stations are fairly plentiful in the Cape Region, though it's always best to top off your tank whenever it reaches the half-empty mark and there's a Pemex station at hand.

Three kinds of fuel are available: an unleaded fuel with an octane rating of 87 (Magna Sin); a high-test unleaded rated at 89 (Premium), and diesel. All three are priced by Pemex according to standard rates and shouldn't vary from station to station. Since Pemex is government-owned, you don't see the week-to-week price fluctuations common in countries where oil companies are privately owned and rates are influenced by small changes in international oil prices. All are roughly equivalent in price to their U.S. or Canadian counterparts, depending on where you're accustomed to purchasing fuel. The price should always be marked in pesos on the pump. Nearly all Pemex pumps in Baja now give readouts calibrated for the new peso, and they zero out automatically when the fuel nozzle is lifted from the pump.

Make sure the pump is zeroed before the attendant starts pumping your gasoline/diesel. If the nozzle hasn't been returned to the pump since the last sale, you could find your fuel total added to the previous customer's. This seems to be less of a problem than in previous years; stations in the border towns are still the places most likely to overcharge. It helps to get out of your vehicle to keep an eye on the pumping procedures. If you're confused by the pump readout, currency conversion, or price per liter, carry a handheld calculator to make sure it all adds up; a calculator held in clear view will deter most potential grifters. As more new pumps are added they will be calibrated to read in new pesos to conform to the currency. This should make calculations considerably easier. A new scam for gas over-charging (to us) at modern, auto-zeroing pumps is to use a gas hose that comes from an open pump on the opposite side, so you can't see whether the readout starts at zero.

Fuel must be paid for in cash. On the mainland a few stations are now taking Mexican bank cards such as Carnet. It's probably only a matter of time before Carnet acceptance at Pemex stations spreads to other cities across the nation, with perhaps Visa and MasterCard close behind. For the moment, however, be sure to carry plenty of pesos for fuel purchases. Mexican currency is the overwhelming preference of most Pemex stations; some stations near the U.S.-Mexico border take U.S. dollars, but the rate is always rounded down.

Rumors about the quality of Pemex fuels sometimes suggest an extra fuel filter or additive is necessary. This may have been the case 15 or more years ago, but nowadays Pemex fuel seems to perform well in all types of vehicles.

The main problem with Pemex fuel remains its availability, although in recent years the situation has improved. Long lines at small-town stations—the lines at the Mulegé Pemex are legendary—and the occasional selling out of all types of fuel at a particular station are not uncommon. To notify customers, the hose will usually be draped over the top of a pump when it's empty. Major culprits for pump sell-outs are American RV caravans; if 10 or 15 RVs fuel up at a Pemex station when it's between deliveries, the station may have to shut down until the next Pemex tanker arrives.

Liquefied Petroleum Gas (LPG): LPG fuel is available in Baja. The price per liter is about the same as for Magna Sin when bought for vehicular purposes. LPG sold for heating and cooking is subsidized and costs less than in the U.S. or Canada. The difficulty is finding it. Look for signs reading *butano*.

Oil

Motor oil is widely available at *tiendas* and Pemex stations throughout the Cape. If your vehicle takes anything lower (thinner) than 30-weight, however, you'd better bring along your own; most places stock only 30- or 40-weight oil.

Parts and Repairs

Good auto shops and mechanics are available in La Paz, San José, and Cabo San Lucas. Elsewhere, if you have a breakdown, it's either do it yourself or rely on the mercy of passing drivers. In areas where you can find a mechanic, the following makes can usually be serviced: Chevrolet, Dodge, Ford, Nissan, Toyota, and

---

WORDS AND PHRASES TO KNOW

Driving

Full, please (at a gasoline station)—
  Lleno, por favor.
My car has broken down.—*Se me ha
  descompuesto el carro.*
I need a tow.—*Necesito un remolque.*
Is there a garage nearby?—*¿Hay un garage
  cerca?*
Is the road passable with this car (truck)?—
  ¿Puedo pasar con este carro (esta troca)?
With four-wheel drive?—*¿Con doble
  tracción?*
It's not passable.—*No hay paso.*
traffic light—*el semáfora*
traffic sign—*el señal*
gasoline (petrol)—*gasolina*
gasoline station—*gasolinera*
oil—*aceite*
water—*agua*
flat tire—*llanta desinflada*
tire repair shop—*llantera*

Auto Parts

fan belt—*banda de ventilador*
battery—*batería*
fuel (water) pump—*bomba de gasolina
  (agua)*
spark plug—*bujía*
carburetor—*carburador*
distributor—*distribuidor*
axle—*eje*
clutch—*embrague*
gasket—*empaque, junta*
filter—*filtro*
brakes—*frenos*
tire—*llanta*
hose—*manguera*
starter—*marcha, arranque*
radiator—*radiador*
voltage regulator—*regulado de voltaje*

Volkswagen. For anything else, you should carry spare filters, plugs, points, hoses, belts, and gaskets—even for the shortest of trips.

Green Angels

The Secretaría de Turismo operates a fleet of green trucks called Angeles Verdes (Green Angels) that patrol Baja's highways and offer professional assistance to anyone with automotive problems. Each truck carries a first-aid kit, a shortwave radio, gasoline, and a variety of common auto parts. They're usually staffed by two uniformed employees, one of whom may speak some English. The drivers will perform minor repairs for the cost of the parts and can provide towing for distances up to 24 km (15 miles). If they can't remedy the problem or tow your vehicle to a nearby mechanic, they'll give you a lift or arrange for other assistance.

The trucks supposedly patrol assigned highway sections at least twice a day; the author's experience is that the Green Angels are much more commonly seen in south-central Baja, where they're most needed due to the longer distances between towns.

Trailers and RVs

The Cape is a popular destination for RVers. Not only are there plenty of RV parks with services, but you can pull off the road and camp just about anywhere outside the cities, with few restrictions. Those restrictions that do exist are largely physical; numerous places simply can't accommodate a wide trailer or motorhome because of narrow roadways, steep grades, or sharp curves. Even the Transpeninsular is tight in some places. In fact, you shouldn't even attempt a Baja trip in any rig wider than three meters (nine feet).

The type of rig most suited to Baja travel is probably a well-equipped camper or van. With a bed, two five-gallon water containers, a small propane stove and refrigerator, and a portable toilet, you can travel just as independently as someone driving a 40-foot motorhome. Add a deep-cycle RV battery under the hood and you can run a variety of electrical appliances for at least a week without turning over your engine. For extra power, mount a solar panel on top of the cab or camper.

More complete information on managing the entire transpeninsular journey by RV is available in Moon Handbooks' *Baja* .

Car Rental

You can rent cars in La Paz, San José del Cabo, and Cabo San Lucas. At many agencies, various Volkswagen models are all that's available. Most rental places charge daily rates of around US$25-29 for a VW bug or Chevy Pop, US$45-50 for a VW Golf or Nissan Tsuru II (Sentra), US$61-68 for a Jeep Wrangler, and US$50-65 for a VW *combi* (van), plus per-km fees ranging 10-30 cents per kilometer. Often a little negotiating will result in getting these same daily rates without any kilometer charges. Rates in-

automotive angels

clude Mexican liability insurance, but not collision damage. For added collision coverage, figure an extra US$8-16 a day.

If you're planning on driving long distances, you can save money by arranging a flat rate with no kilometer costs. If you can rent by the week, the savings increase considerably. The best deal in Baja on an advance reservation is from Avis International: a new, made-in-Mexico Chevy Pop (no a/c or radio) for US$119 per week, with unlimited free kilometers. You can try calling **Avis International,** U.S./Canada tel. (800) 331-1212, Mexico tel. (800) 7-0777, in advance to see what kind of specials they may be running. You might be able to negotiate an equally low rate on a walk-up basis from any of the agencies at Los Cabos International.

The VW bug, incidentally, is one of the best non-4WD passenger cars for Baja travel since its engine is air-cooled (no radiator boil-overs) and over the drive wheels (good traction), and its road clearance is a bit above average. The "old" classic VW bug is still manufactured in Puebla, Mexico; you can buy a brand new one from any Mexican Volkswagen dealer for around US$7,000.

Besides the Jeep Wranglers available in Baja, you can rent a Toyota 4Runner from **M&M Jeeps,** tel. (619) 297-1615, fax (619) 297-1617, in San Diego for US$200 a day. M&M will allow you to drive its vehicles anywhere in Baja, and can arrange for vehicle pickup—for an extra charge—if you'd prefer to drive one way only.

Another company that rents vehicles for Baja driving is **California Baja Rent-A-Car,** 9245 Jamacha Blvd., Spring Valley, CA 91977, tel. (619) 470-7368, (888) 470-7368 toll-free in the U.S. and Canada, fax (619) 479-2004, e-mail: info@cabaja.com or reservations@cabaja.com. California Baja offers Jeep Cherokees, Jeep Wranglers, GMC Suburbans, Ford Explorers, and GMC Hummers, plus a variety of passenger

vans and convertibles. Sample rates start at US$40 a day plus 35 cents per mile (the first 100 miles are free) for a subcompact, including Mexican insurance and transportation from San Diego International Airport. A Wrangler rents for US$100 a day plus 40 cents per mile (100 free miles per day), while a Toyota mini-motorhome that sleeps six costs US$140 daily (100 free miles per day). Drop-offs in Cabo San Lucas, La Paz, or Loreto can be arranged for an extra charge.

Motorcycles

The entire Cape Region is excellent motorcycle country. The winding sierra roads are especially challenging, and since traffic is generally light you can really let it rip. Another advantage of motorcycle travel is that if your bike gets mired in soft ground, you can almost always extricate it without assistance.

As with automotive travel in Baja, pre-departure planning is important. You should be able to carry enough gear in two panniers and a backpack (tied down on the rear) for a trip all the way down the peninsula.

Good motorcycle mechanics are hard to find in the Cape Region—you should be entirely self-reliant to make this trip safely and successfully. Besides the usual camping and first-aid gear, bikers should carry all tools needed for routine maintenance, spare brake shoes, a tire repair kit, spare levers, an extra battery, a clutch cable, spare light bulbs, a four-liter reserve gas can, and a spare helmet visor.

The same driving precautions that apply to four-wheel driving should be followed by bikers as well. Special care should be taken when negotiating blind curves since buses and trucks in Mexico aren't used to seeing motorcycles on the highway. As with bicycle touring, motorcyclists may find that an 11 a.m.-3 p.m. siesta is necessary to avoid the sun's worst rays.

LA PAZ AND VICINITY

Ensconced along the largest bay on Baja's Sea of Cortez coast, La Paz is a city of 180,000 noted for its attractive *malecón* (waterfront walkway) backed by swaying palms and pastel-colored buildings, its splendid sunsets, easygoing pace, sunny climate, and its proximity to uncrowded beaches and pristine islands. Many Baja travelers—Mexicans and gringos alike—cite La Paz (Peace) as their favorite city on the Baja California peninsula; a few even go as far as to pronounce it their favorite in all of Mexico. Nowadays Cabo San Lucas, 221 km (137 miles) farther south, receives more attention than La Paz in the American press, which suits La Paz fans fine since it means fewer tourists.

Of all the cities in Baja, La Paz is steeped most profoundly in mainland Mexico's traditions; it was the first major European settlement on the peninsula and has long been a haven for Mexicans dissatisfied with life on the mainland. Many *paceños* (La Paz natives) are descendants of mainlanders who sailed to La Paz to avoid the political turmoil of the 19th and early 20th centuries. And it's not uncommon to meet more-recent Mexican émigrés who decided to resettle in La Paz after becoming fed up with the political machinations in modern-day Mexico City, Guadalajara, or Monterrey. *Paceños* are proud of the many ways in which their city lives up to its name.

The city offers a wide variety of accommodations and dining venues, well-stocked supermarkets, marine supply stores, and a ferry terminal with daily departures for Mazatlán and Topolobampo across the Sea of Cortez. Parking can be a bit tight, and minor traffic snarls are common in *el centro,* the city center, but can be avoided by using Blvd. Forjadores, a wide avenue skirting the southern section of the city. Along the bay, La Paz remains much as John Steinbeck described it in 1941:

La Paz grew in fascination as we approached. The square, iron-shuttered colonial houses stood up right in back of the beach with rows of beautiful trees in front of them. It is a lovely place. There is a broad promenade along the water lined with benches, named for dead residents of the city, where one may rest oneself. . . . [A] cloud of delight hangs over the distant city from the time when it was the great pearl center of the world. . . . Guaymas is busier, they say, and Mazatlán gayer, but La Paz is antigua.

Climate and Travel Seasons
The most pleasant time of year to visit La Paz is mid-October through June, when days are balmy

and evenings are cool. In January, maximum temperatures average 22° C (72° F), minimum temperatures 14° C (57° F). Temperatures for July average 35° C (96° F) maximum, 24° C (75° F) minimum, but daytime highs of over 38° C (100° F) aren't unusual. Hot summer afternoons are moderated by the daily arrival of the *coromuel,* a strong onshore breeze that bedevils yachties trying to escape the harbor but cools down the rest of the population.

La Paz and vicinity average only around 15 cm (six inches) of rainfall per year, over half generally falling during the Aug.-Sept. *chubasco* (tropical storm) season. Full-fledged *chubascos* with gale-force winds actually reach La Paz only every couple of years. Most of the time the area receives only the remote influences of storms centered along mainland Mexico's lower west coast.

Over the last few years, February has been La Paz's peak tourist month. Even then you should be able to find a hotel room easily since the average occupancy rate runs around 50% all year-round.

HISTORY

Early Spanish Contact
When the Spanish first landed on the shores of Bahía de La Paz in the early 16th century, the area was inhabited by migrating bands of Guaicura and Pericú, who allegedly called their homeland "Airapi." Hunters and gatherers, these Amerindian groups lived mostly on shellfish, small game, and wild plants. As artifacts on display at La Paz's Museum of Anthropology demonstrate, they were also skilled weavers and potters.

Into this peaceful scene entered the first European, a Basque mutineer named Fortún Jiménez who commandeered the Spanish ship *Concepción* on the Sea of Cortez in 1533. Originally under the command of Capt. Diego Becerra, the *Concepción* had been sent to explore the sea on behalf of Spain's most infamous conquistador, Hernán Cortés. After executing the captain, Jiménez landed at Bahía de La Paz in early 1534, where he and 22 of his crew were killed by Amerindians while filling their water casks at a spring. The survivors sailed the *Concepción* back to the mainland, where the ship

Hernán Cortés

was immediately captured by Cortés's New Spain rival, Nuño de Guzmán. At least one crew member managed to escape and returned to Cortés with descriptions of a huge, beautiful bay filled with pearl-oyster beds.

Cortés himself landed at the northeast end of the bay, probably at Pichilingue near the present ferry terminal, in May 1535 and named it Puerto de Santa Cruz. Cortés was able to effect a truce with local Amerindians, but his attempt at establishing a permanent Spanish colony lasted only through 1538, when the colonists were forced to abandon the peninsula due to supply problems.

The next Spaniard to visit the bay was famed explorer Sebastián Vizcaíno, who landed here in 1596 during his long voyage around the peninsula's perimeter and north to California. Because he and his crew were treated so well by the Pericú, Vizcaíno named the bay Bahía de la Paz (Bay of Peace).

Pirates and Colonization
Baja California remained free of Spaniards another 100 years before the successful establishment of a mission colony at Loreto to the north. By this time, English and Dutch pirates were plundering New Spain's Manila galleons as

they returned from the Orient weighted down with gold, silks, and spices. One of the freebooters' favorite staging areas was Bahía de La Paz, which contained numerous *ensenadas* (coves) and inlets perfect for concealing their swift corsairs. When Spanish crews put in for water, the pirates raided the galleons, often using their knowledge of strong afternoon winds to attack the ships when they were effectively pinned down.

Increased pirate activity in the late 17th and early 18th centuries created the need for a Spanish presence in the Cape Region. In 1719 Padre Juan de Ugarte, then President of the Missions, contracted a master shipbuilder to construct a ship for the specific purpose of exploring the Sea of Cortez coast and improving supply lines with the mainland. The barque *El Triunfo de la Cruz,* assembled of native Baja hardwood at the

Mulegé estuary, made its first sailing to Bahía de La Paz in 1720 with Ugarte and Padre Jaime Bravo as passengers.

Ugarte and Bravo founded the mission community of Nuestra Señora del Pilar de La Paz at the current city site. The padres didn't find the Pericú to be as friendly this time around; the mission lasted only until 1749, when it was abandoned following a series of Amerindian rebellions. By this time, another mission and a presidio had been founded farther south at San José del Cabo—a better location for monitoring pirate activity.

La Paz Reborn

Left with European diseases and without the support of the mission system, the local Pericú population dwindled quickly. By 1811, Mexican ranchers and *pescadores* who had settled along

ENGLISH PIRATES ON THE SEA OF CORTEZ

Sir Francis Drake, Thomas Cavendish, William Dampier, Woodes Rogers, Thomas Dover, and other English privateers left behind a colorful Baja legacy. In spite of Spain's repeated attempts to colonize the peninsula, throughout the Spanish colonial period the pirates probably gained more wealth in the Californias than the Spanish themselves. For 250 years they plagued the Manila galleons off the coast of the Californias, finding the bays and lagoons of Baja's Cape Region perfect hiding places from which to launch attacks on treasure-laden ships.

In La Paz, using their knowledge of the strong breeze that blows into the harbor every summer afternoon, the pirates attacked Spanish galleons while the vessels were effectively trapped in the bay. Four centuries after the first Manila–Acapulco voyages, this afternoon wind is still known as *El Coromuel,* named for the Puritan Cromwells—father and son—who ruled successively as Lord Protectors of England.

The Disappearance of the *Desire*

The most notorious of the Pacific privateers was Sir Thomas Cavendish, whose greatest feat of plunder occurred at Cabo San Lucas in 1587. There his two English vessels, *Desire* and *Content,* commandeered the Spanish galleon *Santa Ana* follow-

ing a protracted sea battle. Cavendish set fire to the *Santa Ana* after looting its cargo holds and setting its crew and passengers ashore. The Spanish crew later retrieved the burned hulk and restored it for a return to Acapulco.

The plundered treasure, meanwhile, was divided between the *Desire* and *Content.* The ships set sail for England immediately, but during the first night of their triumphant voyage the *Desire* disappeared. Cavendish reported in England that the captain and crew of the *Desire* must have scuttled the ship on a nearby island and disappeared with the loot. Neither the wreckage of the vessel nor the treasure was ever discovered; some historians speculate that at least part of the missing wealth remains buried near the Cape.

A Visit by Robinson Crusoe

In 1709, famed corsair Woodes Rogers landed in La Paz after rescuing a seaman who'd been marooned five years on a deserted island off Chile's coast. The rescued man was Alexander Selkirk, whose island sojourn became the inspiration for Daniel Defoe's *Robinson Crusoe,* published in 1719. Selkirk was aboard Rogers's *Dover* when the crew captured the Spanish galleon *Encarnación* off Cabo San Lucas in 1709; he served as sailing master on the ship's return voyage to England the following year.

THE PEARLS OF LA PAZ

Pearls develop from sand grains or other small particles that manage to get between an oyster's mantle and its shell. The oyster secretes a substance that cushions it from the irritation of the particle—if the grain moves freely during the secretion buildup, the pearl is more or less spherical; if it stays in one place or is embedded in the shell, it becomes a "baroque" pearl. Even when an oyster doesn't contain a pearl, the interior of the shell is valued for its rainbow luster, known as mother-of-pearl. Only particular mollusk varieties within the family Pteridae, found only in certain coastal areas off East Asia, Panama, and Baja California, can form pearls.

Pearl gathering in the New World goes back at least 7,000 years. When the Spanish found Indians along the Sea of Cortez coast wearing pearls and pearl shells as hair ornaments in the early 16th century, they quickly added pearls to the list of exploitable resources in Mexico. Finding the source of the luminescent, milky-white spheres—oyster beds—became a priority of marine expeditions off Mexico's west coast.

After a Spanish mutineer reported the presence of pearls in Bahía de la Paz in 1533, harvesting them became one of Cortés's primary interests in exploring Baja's lower Sea of Cortez coast. Between 1535, when Cortés finally managed to establish a temporary settlement at Bahía de la Paz, and 1697, when Jesuit padres began missionizing the Baja penin-

sula, untold thousands of pearls were harvested. The Jesuits, however, strongly objected to any secular exploitation of the peninsula, preferring to keep Baja within the domain of the Church. Hence during the mission period (1697-1768), pearling was restricted to sporadic illegal harvests; still, many pearls found their way to Europe, where they encrusted the robes of bishops and Spanish royalty.

In the mid-19th century, following the secularization of Baja missions, the Baja pearl industry was revived by *armadores* (entrepreneurs) who hired Yaqui divers from Sonora to scour the shallow bays, coves, and island shores between Mulegé and La Paz. The invention of diving suits in 1874 revolutionized pearling by allowing divers access to deeper waters. By 1889 the world pearling industry was dominated by Compañía Perlífera de Baja California, based in La Paz.

Intensive harvesting rapidly depleted the oyster beds, and between 1936 and 1941 most of the remaining pearl oysters were wiped out by an unknown disease. Many La Paz residents today believe the disease was somehow introduced by the Japanese to eliminate Mexican competition in the pearl industry, but it's more likely the disease simply took advantage of an already weakened population.

The mystique of La Paz pearls continued long after the industry's demise. John Steinbeck based his novella *The Pearl* on a famous pearl story he heard while visiting La Paz in 1941.

the Bahía de La Paz started their own town, which they named La Paz after the bay. After Loreto was severely damaged during a hurricane in 1829, the capital of Baja California Sur was moved to burgeoning La Paz, where it's remained ever since.

During the Mexican-American War (1846-48), U.S. troops occupied the city; the soldiers left when the Californias were split by the 1848 Treaty of Hidalgo. But American general William Walker, dissatisfied with the treaty and hoping to add another slaveholder state to counter the growing U.S. abolitionist movement, formed his own army of "New York Volunteers" and retook La Paz in November 1853. Proclaiming himself "President of the Republic of Sonora," Walker lasted only six months; he and his mercenaries

fled upon hearing that the U.S. wouldn't back their claims, and that the Mexican Army was on its way to La Paz from the mainland. Walker was tried in the U.S. for violation of neutrality laws, fined, and two years later was executed by the Nicaraguan army for attempting a similar takeover of Nicaragua.

La Paz remained a sleepy tropic seaport, known only for pearl harvesting, until it was declared a duty-free port following WW II. After an epizootic disease killed off the entire pearl-oyster population, the city's economic focus turned to farming and trade with the mainland. During Mexico's postwar economic boom, mainland Mexicans crossed the Sea of Cortez in droves to buy imported merchandise; enchanted by La Paz itself, many stayed on.

In the 1950s, La Paz became well-known as a fishing resort and was visited by a succession of North American literati and Hollywood celebrities, thus initiating the city's reputation as an international vacation spot. But until the Transpeninsular Highway was completed in 1973, the city remained for the most part a tourist destination for mainland Mexicans.

Statehood was bestowed on the Territory of Baja California Sur in 1974, and La Paz was made state capital. Linked by air, ferry, and highway to mainland Mexico and the U.S., the city has grown considerably yet managed to maintain its tropic port ambience. As a tourist destination, it remains more Mexican than foreign—of the 130,000 leisure visitors who visit La Paz annually, Mexican nationals typically outnumber foreigners three to one.

SIGHTS

Museo de Antropología

Baja California history buffs shouldn't miss this well-designed museum at Calles 5 de Mayo and Altamirano, tel. (1) 122-0162. Three floors of exhibits cover Cape Region anthropology from prehistoric to colonial and modern times. On display are fossils, minerals, Amerindian artifacts, dioramas of Amerindian and colonial life, and maps of rock-painting sites throughout central and southern Baja. Labels are in Spanish only.

A small gift section offers Spanish-language books in the fields of anthropology, archaeology, and art history, including such hard-to-find volumes as the *Catalogo Nacional de los Monumentos Históricos Inmuebles de Baja California Sur,* an inventory of historical buildings in the *municípios* of San Antonio, San José del Cabo, Santiago, and Todos Santos.

Next to the museum is an older building that has served La Paz as a hospital, prison, and, more recently, the **Biblioteca Justo Sierra,** a children's library. Behind the library is an ethnobotanical garden dedicated to the exhibition of medicinal herbs and sculpture from the region.

The museum is open daily 9 a.m.-5 p.m.; admission free.

Plaza Constitución (Jardín Velazco)

La Paz's tidy downtown *zócalo* is enclosed by Av. Independencia and Calles 5 de Mayo, Revolución de 1910, and Madero. At the southwest side of the plaza is the post-missionary-style **Catedral de Nuestra Señora de La Paz,** which replaced La Paz's original mission church in 1861. Although the twin-towered brick edifice looms over the plaza, it lacks the charm of earlier Jesuit missions. Inside, only an image of Nuestra Señora del Pilar and a few theological books survive from the earlier 1720 mission. A couple of blocks southwest of the plaza, on Calle Zaragoza between Arrival and Lerdo de Tejada, you'll find a plaque commemorating the original mission site.

At the northwest side of Plaza Constitución, opposite the cathedral, is the **Biblioteca de História de las Californias** (Library of Califor-

Catedral de Nuestra Señora de La Paz

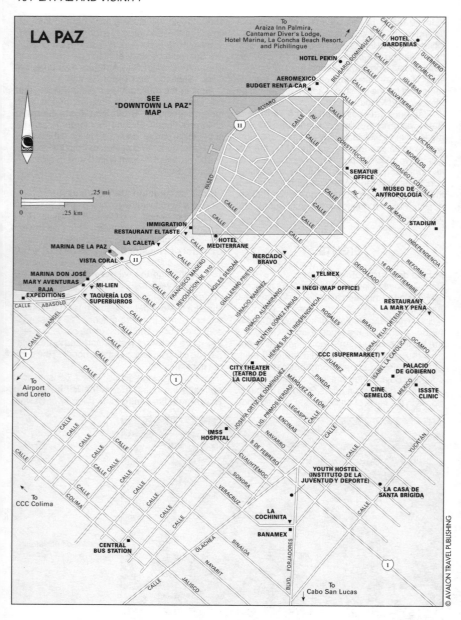

LA PAZ

SEE "DOWNTOWN LA PAZ" MAP

To
Araiza Inn Palmira,
Cantamar Diver's Lodge,
Hotel Marina, La Concha Beach Resort,
and Pichilingue

HOTEL GARDENIAS

HOTEL PEKIN

AEROMEXICO
BUDGET RENT-A-CAR

0 ____ .25 mi
0 ____ .25 km

SEMATUR OFFICE

★ MUSEO DE ANTROPOLOGÍA

STADIUM

IMMIGRATION
RESTAURANT EL TASTE
LA CALETA

HOTEL MEDITERRANE

MERCADO BRAVO

TELMEX

INEGI (MAP OFFICE)

RESTAURANT LA MAR Y PEÑA

MARINA DE LA PAZ

VISTA CORAL

MARINA DON JOSÉ
MAR Y AVENTURAS
BAJA EXPEDITIONS

MI-LIEN

TAQUERÍA LOS SUPERBURROS

CCC (SUPERMARKET)

PALACIO DE GOBIERNO

CITY THEATER
(TEATRO DE LA CIUDAD)

CINE GEMELOS

ISSSTE CLINIC

To
Airport
and Loreto

IMSS HOSPITAL

To
CCC Colima

YOUTH HOSTEL
(INSTITUTO DE LA JUVENTUD Y DEPORTE)

LA CASA DE SANTA BRÍGIDA

LA COCHINITA

BANAMEX

CENTRAL BUS STATION

To
Cabo San Lucas

© AVALON TRAVEL PUBLISHING

nias' History). Housed in the 1880s-era former Casa de Gobierno (Government House), the library is filled with Spanish- and English-language volumes on Alta and Baja California history. The general public is welcome to use the library for research; it's open Mon.-Fri. 9 a.m.-6 p.m., Saturday 9 a.m.-3 p.m. For library information, call (1) 122-0162.

La Unidad Cultural Profesor Jesús Castro Agúndez

This cultural center at Calles Farías and Legaspy, in the Cuatro Molinos (Four Windmills) district, includes an art gallery, community art school, city archives, and the **Teatro de la Ciudad** (City Theater), tel. (1) 125-0207, a 1,500-seat performing-arts facility that hosts musical, theatrical, and dance performances throughout the year. Next to the theater, four windmills pay tribute to a time when La Paz relied on wind power to pump water and generate electricity.

Also at the complex is **La Rotonda de los Sudcalifornianos Illustres,** a circle of sculpted figures representing Baja California Sur's most celebrated heroes—most of them teachers and soldiers.

Malecón

One of the city's major attractions is the pleasant five-km *malecón,* a seawall promenade along

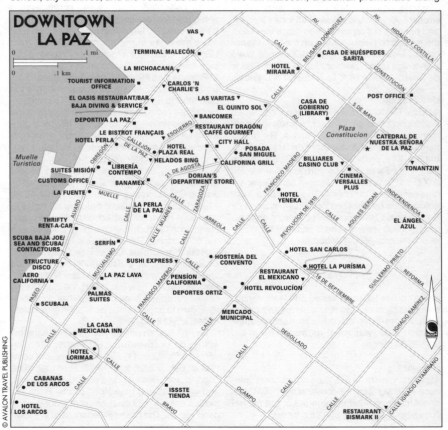

DOWNTOWN LA PAZ

0   .1 mi
0   .1 km

VAS
TERMINAL MALECÓN
LA MICHOACANA
TOURIST INFORMATION OFFICE
CARLOS 'N CHARLIE'S
EL OASIS RESTAURANT/BAR
BAJA DIVING & SERVICE
LAS VARITAS
EL QUINTO SOL
DEPORTIVA LA PAZ
BANCOMER
RESTAURANT DRAGÓN/ CAFFÉ GOURMET
LE BISTROT FRANÇAIS
HOTEL PERLA
HOTEL PLAZA REAL
CITY HALL
POSADA SAN MIGUEL
LIBRERÍA CONTEMPO
HELADOS BING
CALIFORINA GRILL
SUITES MISIÓN
CUSTOMS OFFICE
BANAMEX
DORIAN'S (DEPARTMENT STORE)
LA FUENTE
MUELLE
LA PERLA DE LA PAZ
HOTEL YENEKA
THRIFTY RENT-A-CAR
SCUBA BAJA JOE/ SEA AND SCUBA/ CONTACTOURS
SERFÍN
SUSHI EXPRESS
HOSTERÍA DEL CONVENTO
HOTEL SAN CARLOS
STRUCTURE DISCO
LA PAZ LAVA
PENSIÓN CALIFORNIA
HOTEL LA PURÍSIMA
AERO CALIFORNIA
RESTAURANT EL MEXICANO
DEPORTES ORTIZ
HOTEL REVOLUCIÓN
PALMAS SUITES
SCUBAJA
MERCADO MUNICIPAL
LA CASA MEXICANA INN
HOTEL LORIMAR
CABANAS DE LOS ARCOS
ISSSTE TIENDA
HOTEL LOS ARCOS
RESTAURANT BISMARK II

HIDALGO Y COSTILLA
BELISARIO DOMINGUEZ
CASA DE HUÉSPEDES SARITA
HOTEL MIRAMAR
CONSTITUCIÓN
POST OFFICE
CASA DE GOBIERNO (LIBRARY)
5 DE MAYO
Plaza Constitución
CATEDRAL DE NUESTRA SEÑORA DE LA PAZ
BILLIARES CASINO CLUB
TONANTZIN
CINEMA VERSALLES PLUS
FRANCISCO MADERO
REVOLUCIÓN DE 1810
AQUILES SERDAN
INDEPENDENCIA
EL ÁNGEL AZUL
GUILLERMO PRIETO
REFORMA
16 DE SEPTIEMBRE
IGNACIO RAMIREZ
DEGOLLADO
OCAMPO
BRAVO
CALLE IGNACIO ALTAMIRANO

Muelle Turístico

ESQUERRO
OBREGÓN
CALLEJÓN DE LA PAZ
21 DE AGOSTO
ZARAGOZA
AREOLA
CALLE MIJARES
MUTUALISMO
FRANCISCO MADERO
ALVARO
PASEO

© AVALON TRAVEL PUBLISHING

the northwest side of Paseo Alvaro Obregón extending from Calz. 5 de Febrero (Mexico 1 south) to the northeastern city limits. Palm-shaded benches are conveniently situated at intervals along the walkway for watching sailboats and yachts coming in and out of the bay. The best time of day for peoplewatching is around sunset, when the city begins cooling off, the sun dyes the waterfront orange, and *paceños* take to the *malecón* for an evening stroll or jog. Snacks and cold beverages are available at several *palapa* bars along the way.

Recently the city has transformed the former Muelle Fiscal into the Muelle Turístico (Tourist Pier) by adding an archway over the entry, cobblestone paving, potted plants, and well-lit wrought-iron seating areas. With locals strolling and hanging out on the pier on warm evenings, the revitalized pier has taken on the feel of a traditional Mexican plaza. Over the entrance to the pier, a sign reads "Bienvenidos a La Paz, Puerto de Ilusión" (Welcome to La Paz, Port of Dreams).

Universities

As Baja California Sur's educational center, La Paz supports a large number of schools at the primary, secondary, and tertiary levels. The prominent **Universidad Autonomía de Baja California Sur** (University of South Baja California), on Blvd. Forjadores, has an enrollment of around 2,000 and reputable programs in agriculture, engineering, and business. The **Instituto Tecnológico de La Paz** (Technological Institute of La Paz), also on Blvd. Forjadores, enrolls approximately 3,000 students and is primarily known for its commercial-fishing department.

HOTELS

La Paz offers the most varied and least expensive selection of places to stay of any city in Baja. Room rates are quite reasonable for a seaside area, with most rooms falling in the US$25-65 range.

Shoestring

Accommodations in this price range come without a/c—a significant inconvenience July-October. And since most of them are in the central commercial zone they can be a bit noisy.

As old as the city itself, **Pensión California,** Calle Degollado 209, tel. (1) 122-2896, is housed in a former 18th-century convent between Revolución de 1910 and Madero. The interior courtyard of this rambling Moorish-style building contains a tropical garden of sorts and a display of old and new paintings that lend a distinctly Bohemian feel to the atmosphere. Rooms are basic—little more than a few worn sticks of furniture, fan, and hot shower—but reasonably comfortable. Practically every backpacker on the Baja circuit turns up at the Pensión California at one time or another. Rates: US$7 s/d, US$10 d; discounts possible for long-term stays.

The same family operates **Hostería del Convento,** Calle Madero Sur 85, tel. (1) 122-3508, in another former convent right around the corner. It has a similarly funky and faded feel, with a bit more greenery in the courtyard. Rates: from US$8 s to US$24 for a room sleeping up to eight; long-term discounts available.

Posada San Miguel, Calle Domínguez 1510, tel. (1) 122-1802, is a colorful colonial-style inn built around a tiled courtyard. The 13 basic, almost bare rooms have fairly hard beds, but the ornate entryway—decorated with historical photos of La Paz—is a major plus. You may want to borrow a broom to sweep your room before settling in. Rates: US$9 s, US$11 d.

Seemingly undiscovered by visiting budget travelers is the family-run **Casa de Huéspedes Sarita,** Calle Domínguez 254, tel. (1) 122-4274, which offers a cozy front balcony sitting area and clean rooms with attached bath. The public areas aren't particularly charming, but the beds are comfortable. Rates: US$7 s, US$11 d.

Hotel San Carlos, Calles Revolución and 16 de Septiembre, tel. (1) 122-0444, has dingy but cheap rooms with balcony and fan. Not recommended except as a last resort, the San Carlos has all the appearances of a *hotel de paso,* better known to anglophones as a "short-time hotel." Rates: US$13 s/d.

La Paz has an official youth hostel at the **Instituto de la Juventud y el Deporte** (Villa Juventil La Paz), tel. (1) 122-4615, a sports complex on Blvd. Forjadores (Km 3) near Calz. 5 de Febrero. Facilities include a pool, gym, cafeteria, and volleyball and basketball courts. Beds are single bunks in gender-segregated, four-person dorm rooms. The hostel is distant from the town center and about the same cost for two people as a more centrally located shoestring hotel, considering the cost per bed. But it's closer to the main bus terminal than the downtown lodgings. All ages welcome. Rates: US$3 a night, US$2.50 with a Hostelling International card.

Shoestring-Budget

In a quieter district a five-minute drive from the center of town, **La Casa de Santa Brígida,** Márquez de León 1715, tel. (1) 122-8818, between Chiapas and Yucatán, offers clean rooms with two single beds and modern hot-water bathrooms. Guests may enjoy a public TV room, convention center, chapel, and shady garden. An attached dining room serves reasonably priced meals. Rates: US$15 s, US$30 d, plus tax. Discount rates available for families and groups.

Budget

One of the better downtown lodgings in this price category is the well-kept and efficient **Hotel La Purísima,** Calles 16 de Septiembre and Serdán, tel. (1) 122-3444, fax (1) 125-1142, which occupies a four-story, red-and-white building near the municipal market. All rooms feature a/c, fan, and TV, and service is excellent. Foreign travelers appear to be rare in this hotel, so it's a good choice for visitors looking to immerse themselves in urban Mexican hotel culture. Rates: US$20 s, US$24 d, US$28 t, US$31 q.

Hotel Revolución, Revolución 85 (between Degollado and 16 de Septiembre), tel. (1) 125-8022, occupies two of three stories in an orange-and-green structure. Its 16 rooms are adequate, but not as good and not much cheaper than the Purísima's. Rates: US$17 s, US$19 d, US$23 t.

Although in name it's a hotel, **Hotel Yeneka,** Calle Madero 1520 (between Calle 16 de Septiembre and Av. Independencia), tel./fax (1) 125-4688, looks and operates much like a guesthouse. Long known on the backpacker circuit, the Yeneka is built around a courtyard filled with tropical vegetation, a rusting Model T, and an amazing collection of other items giving the appearance of an ongoing garage sale. Almost everything is painted green; a pet monkey swings from tree to tree. The proprietors can arrange snorkeling, diving, fishing, boating, and horseback-riding excursions. Rooms are very basic and a bit scruffy. Rates: US$19 s.

Around the corner from Hotel Los Arcos, the friendly **Hotel Lorimar,** Calle Bravo 110, tel. (1) 125-3822, fax (1) 125-6387, is a longtime budget favorite with European, Canadian, and American visitors. Its 20 a/c rooms are clean and well-maintained. The proprietors speak English but are happy to let you practice your Spanish; they can also arrange kayaking and diving trips through local outfitters. The Lorimar is just a block off the *malecón;* guests often meet in the cozy upstairs dining area to exchange travel tips. Rates: US$19 s, US$23 d, US$27 t, US$31 q, tax included.

The **Hotel Plaza Real,** Callejón de La Paz and Calle Esquerro, tel. (1) 122-9333, fax (1) 122-4424, a block off the *malecón* and right around the corner from the Hotel Perla, is a three-story, modern hotel popular with middle-class Mexican businesspeople. Rooms have a/c and TV, and the downstairs coffee shop is a popular local spot for breakfast and Mexican food. Rates: US$35 s/d.

Also a block off Paseo Obregón, the three-story, apartment-style **Hotel Miramar,** Calles 5 de Mayo and Domínguez, tel. (1) 122-8885, fax (1) 122-0672, features clean, modern rooms with fan, a/c, minibar, and TV with VCR. Some rooms come with balconies and bay views at no extra charge, so be sure to ask what's available. The parking lot is a plus. Rates: US$30 s/d, tax included.

Hotel Pekin, Paseo Obregón at Calle Guadalupe Victoria, tel. (1) 125-5335, fax (1) 125-0995, occupies a vaguely Asian two-story building facing the *malecón.* It offers clean rooms with a/c and TV (some with bay views) and is attached to a Chinese restaurant of similar name (Nuevo Pekin). Rates: US$22 s, US$25 d, US$27 t.

In a residential neighborhood in the northwest part of the city, the friendly **Hotel Gardenias,** Calle Serdán Norte 520, tel. (1) 122-3088, fax (1) 125-0436, is a large, modern, two-story hotel built around a pleasant courtyard and pool. Popular among Mexicans, the Gardenias offers 56 clean rooms with a/c and TV. Note: Although the hotel's street address reads Calle Serdán, the entrance is actually on Guerrero between Serdán and Gmo. Prieto. Rates: US$25 s, US$30 d.

Highway Hotels: If you're blazing through town on your way south to Los Cabos, two budget hotels along the highway here make convenient stops. Opposite Casa Blanca RV Park, **Motel Villa del Sol,** near Km 5 on Mexico 1, tel. (1) 124-0298, fax (1) 125-3883, is a motel-style complex with rooms encircling a parking area. Rooms have a/c, bath, and TV. Rates: US$22 d. Farther in toward the city at Km 3.5, well-kept **Motel Calafía,** tel. (1) 122-5811, fax (1) 125-4900, has similarly arranged rooms. Rates: US$17 d.

Inexpensive
The three-story, blue-and-white stucco **Hotel Mediterrané,** Calle Allende 36, tel./fax (1) 125-1195, e-mail: mail@hotelmed.com, enjoys a good location, just a half block from the *malecón*. The small, well-managed hotel features large, airy, sparkling-clean rooms with a/c, refrigerator, and TV/VCR; each room is named for a different Greek island. There's also a rooftop sundeck with lounge chairs. Kayaks and canoes are on hand for guests who would like to paddle in the bay. Bicycles are available for land-lovers. La Pazta restaurant is attached downstairs. Rates: US$45-50 s/d.

North of downtown, **Club El Moro** at Km 2, La Paz-Pichilingue Rd., tel. (1) 122-4084, is a white-washed, Moorish-style place on landscaped grounds. All rooms and kitchenette-equipped suites come with a/c, satellite TV, and private terrace. Other amenities include a pool, restaurant, and bar. Buses heading downtown pass the hotel frequently during daylight hours; otherwise it's a two-km (1.2-mile) walk to the town center. Rates: standard room US$40, studio suite US$50, junior suite US$60, suite with loft US$70, two-bedroom suite US$80. Weekly and monthly rates available on request.

Moderate
The venerable **Hotel Perla,** Paseo Obregón 1570, tel. (1) 122-0777 or toll-free (800) 716-8799, fax (1) 125-5363, e-mail: perla@lapaz. cromwell.com.mx, has long been one of the city's most popular hotels. In 1941, Max Miller, author of *Land Where Time Stands Still,* wrote:

> *The Hotel Perla is the place to stay. For an American there's no other choice unless he wishes to rent a room with a Mexican family or live in a Mexican board-and-rooming house. . . . [T]he Mexicans themselves expect an American to stay at the Hotel Perla. If he doesn't stay there when he first arrives, then he's in La Paz for no good reason. He's under suspicion.*

The two-story, tile-roofed hotel enjoys a prime location right at the center of the *malecón* and just a few steps away from the main shopping district. La Terraza, the hotel's downstairs, open-air restaurant, remains a favorite gathering place for La Paz residents and visitors alike, while the upstairs nightclub draws a mostly local crowd. The mezzanine floor features a small pool. The clean, plainly decorated rooms have high ceilings, a/c, TVs, and telephones. Indoor parking is available on the ground floor. On the downside, La Perla has continued to raise its prices at a pace beyond that of normal inflation, and the hotel now seems rather overpriced by La Paz standards. Rates: US$77 s/d, US$16 for each additional person, including federal tax.

Another *malecón* standby around since the dawn of La Paz's tourist industry is **Cabañas de**

COURTESY ROSEWOOD RESORTS

los Arcos, Paseo Obregón 498, tel. (1) 122-2744 or (800) 6-8644 in Mexico, fax (1) 125-4313. Built in 1954, during La Paz's heyday as an exotic playground for Hollywood celebrities, *paceño*-owned Los Arcos became the city's first center for sportfishing trips. Today you can choose from among 52 a/c rooms in the original cabaña section (fireplaces), junior suites behind the cabaña section (no fireplaces), and rooms and suites in the much larger **Hotel Los Arcos** section less than 100 meters down the street. Like the cabañas, rooms in the new hotel section face the *malecón* and bay. Both the new and original sections have swimming pools; the new one also offers a coffee shop, restaurant, bar, gift shop, sauna rooms, massage service, and whalewatching, diving, and sportfishing tours. Considering the nicer rooms and additional hotel amenities, Los Arcos is better value than La Perla. Cabaña rates: junior suites US$60 s/d, US$70 t, cabañas US$75 s/d, t US$85. Hotel rates: standard rooms US$75 s/d, US$85 t, bay-view rooms US$80 s/d, US$90 t, junior suites US$85-105. To make reservations in the U.S., call (949) 450-9000 or (800) 347-2252, fax (949) 450-9010.

The new **El Ángel Azul,** Independencia 518, tel./fax (1) 125-5130, e-mail: bajasierra@lapaz. cromwell.com.mx, is housed in a historic building that once served as the La Paz courthouse. Carefully restored with INAH guidance, the hotel offers just three guest rooms around a large, landscaped courtyard, and a restaurant/café/bar with Mexican and Swiss cuisine. The work of local artists is showcased throughout. Secure parking is available. Rates: US$65 s/d, plus tax.

Club Hotel Cantamar Diver's Lodge, P.O. Box 782, La Paz 23000, tel. (1) 122-1826, tel./fax (1) 122-7010, fax (1) 122-8644, e-mail: bajadiving@cromwell.com.mx, is next to the ferry terminal in Bahía Pichilingue. The four-story lodge features 16 rooms and two suites, a marina (under construction), pool, bar, and snack bar, as well as a boat ramp, kayak rentals, private beach, fishing fleet, dive shop, scuba shop, and recompression chamber. Dive packages are available for three to seven nights, at a cost of US$240-591 d. Included are round-trip airport transfers and lunch on dive days. Rates: US$65 s/d, US$110 for suites.

At Km 2.5 on the La Paz-Pichilingue Rd., almost opposite Marina Palmira, the palm-encir-cled **Araiza Inn Palmira,** tel. (1) 121-6200, (800) 6-8777 for reservations in Mexico, (800) 929-2402 in the U.S./Canada, fax (1) 121-6227, caters to conventioneers as well as vacationers with its large meeting rooms, banquet halls, and quiet garden rooms. Other facilities include a pool, tennis court, restaurant, bar, and disco. Rates: from US$75 s/d.

Moderate-Expensive

South of the *malecón* and Marina de La Paz is **Hotel La Posada de Engelbert,** Calles Nuevo Reforma and Playa Sur (Apdo. Postal 152, La Paz, BCS or P.O. Box 397, Bonita, CA 91908), tel. (1) 122-4011, U.S. tel./fax (888) 476-9351. Originally built by pop crooner Engelbert Humperdinck for the Hollywood set, the recently renovated Posada offers 25 large, Mexican colonial-style suites and fireplace-equipped *casitas*. All rooms have satellite TV, phone, and a/c. A pool, tennis court, activities center, restaurant, and *palapa* bar fill out the compound. The quiet waterfront atmosphere is a plus. Rates: US$75 junior suites, US$95-110 casitas.

Expensive

You'll pay a bit more to stay right on the water rather than along the *malecón*. None of the bayfront hotels are within easy walking distance of the *malecón* or downtown La Paz, although taxis are always available.

Opposite the Araiza Inn Palmira (adjacent to the plush Marina Palmira) at Km 2.5, La Paz-Pichilingue Rd., stands the **Hotel Marina,** tel. (1) 121-6254 or toll-free in Mexico (800) 685-8800, fax (1) 121-6177, where facilities include tennis courts, a large pool, and an outdoor bar; boat slips are available nearby for visiting yachties. Also see Apartments, Condos, and Long-Term Rentals, below. Rates: from US$89 s/d. For U.S. reservations call (800) 826-1138 or e-mail: infor@hotelmarina.com.mx,

La Concha Beach Resort & Condos, tel. (1) 121-6161, U.S. tel. (800) 999-BAJA, fax (619) 294-7366, e-mail: laconcha@juno.com, sits on Playa Caimancito (near Km 5, La Paz-Pichilingue Rd.), the city's closest swimming beach. All of the 154 well-kept rooms have bay views. On the premises are two pools, tennis courts, an aquatic sports center, restaurant, bar, and gift shop. The swimming pool in La Concha's newer condo section (see Apartments, Suites, and Long-Term Rentals, below) is nicer than the original hotel pool; both pools are open to hotel guests. The resort's Cortez Club offers water sports, including fishing, diving, kayaking, and windsurfing. Rates: US$91-106 s/d, depending on the season (low season rates are in effect Aug.-Sept. only).

Premium

Southwest of town, at Km 5.5 on northbound Mexico 1 (it turns north eventually), the eight-story **Crowne Plaza Resort,** tel. (1) 124-0830 or reservations (800) 0-0999, fax (1) 124-0837, e-mail: crowne@lapaz.cromwell.com.mx, offers 158 bayside Mediterranean-style suites. Amenities include nonsmoking rooms, three swimming pools, sauna baths, pool tables, a gym, squash court, jacuzzi, tennis facilities, massage room, restaurant/bar, and car-rental agency. The hotel stands opposite the state tourism office and next to the site of the long-awaited FIDEPAZ marina. Rates: US$150-575 d, plus 12% tax.

BED AND BREAKFAST INNS

Inexpensive

Managed by a friendly, bilingual *paceña,* **Palmas Suites,** Calle Mutualismo 314, tel./fax (1) 122-4623, e-mail: palmas@yupimail.com, offers seven large apartments with kitchenettes, each available by the day, week, or month. Casually furnished, each apartment will accommodate up to three people without additional charges. Breakfasts are served in an enclosed patio area out front of the apartments. Palmas Suites sits only a block off the *malecón* and is within convenient walking distance of shops and restaurants. Rates: US$35/day s with a full breakfast or US$40 d with two continental breakfasts, US$225 s or US$260 d per week, or US$470 s/d per month. One two-bedroom apartment is also available for US$70/day with two continental breakfasts, US$260/week, US$750/month.

Inexpensive-Moderate

A half block off the *malecón,* **La Casa Mexicana Inn** (formerly Casa La Paceña), Calle Bravo 106 (between Madero and Mutualismo), tel./fax (1) 125-2748, is a well-decorated, American-operated B&B in a converted house. The

three rooms have a/c, fans, VCRs, and private baths; the largest overlooks a fountain and garden. Rates include a breakfast of delicious home-baked pastries. For U.S. reservations, call (707) 869-2374, or e-mail: inn@casamex.com. Closed June-October. Rates: US$50-75 s/d.

APARTMENTS, CONDOS, AND LONG-TERM RENTALS

Inexpensive

Suites Misión, on Paseo Obregón between Arrival and Bañuelos, offers spacious two-bedroom furnished apartments for rent by the week or the month. All have a/c, a small TV, and a kitchenette; linens are provided. Rates: US$38 pp per night.

Moderate

Operated by La Concha Resort, **La Concha Hotel and Suites,** Belisario Domínguez at Salvatierra, tel. (1) 123-3948, is an apartment-style complex in a residential neighborhood downtown. Each huge, two-bedroom apartment features a/c, TV, phone, full-sized kitchen, and two bathrooms. Security parking is available. Rates: US$53.50 daily without use of the kitchen, or US$75 daily with kitchen use. You can also rent by the month for US$990, not including electricity (charged separately).

Moderate-Expensive

The **Vista Coral** condos at Marina de La Paz, past the southwest end of the *malecón,* may have some apartments available for rent by the night. Inquire at the friendly Marina de La Paz office, tel. (1) 122-1646, fax (1) 125-5900.

Expensive-Premium

La Concha Beach Resort & Condos, Mexico tel. (1) 121-6161 or 121-6121, fax (1) 121-6218, U.S. tel. (619) 260-0991 or (800) 999-BAJA, fax (619) 294-7366, is on Playa Caimancito near Km 5 on La Paz-Pichilingue Road. La Concha rents large one- to three-bedroom condos each with a/c, TV, and kitchenette, but without direct-dial telephone; you must go through the resort switchboard to dial out. Condo residents have full use of hotel facilities, including two pools, a beach, restaurant/bar, and water-sports center.

Rates: US$115-155 a night; long-term discounts available.

Suites Marina, adjacent to Marina Palmira and Hotel Marina at Km 2.5, La Paz-Pichilingue Rd., tel. (1) 121-6254, fax (1) 121-6177, contains modern, well-designed, Mediterranean-style junior suites with kitchenettes. Rates: US$120-135 standard suite; US$150-170 master suite.

Rental Agent
La Paz Real Estate, Apdo. Postal 288, La Paz, BCS, tel./fax (1) 125-9599, maintains a list of local house and apartment rentals, most of them available by the month. Staff members speak English as well as Spanish.

CAMPING AND RV PARKS

Free beach camping is available north of the Pichilingue ferry terminal at Playa Pichilingue, Playa Balandra (Puerto Balandra), Playa El Tecolote, and Playa El Coyote. Except for El Tecolote, none of these beaches has fresh water; all supplies must be brought from La Paz. Two restaurants at El Tecolote supply food and beverages.

Several trailer parks spread west from city's edge out onto Mexico 1. Starting from the farthest away, just before Km 15 in El Centenario comes **Los Aripez (Oasis de Aripez) RV Park,** tel. (1) 124-6090, VHF channel 22. Popular among transpeninsular voyagers making short La Paz stopovers, 26 full-hookup slots here cost US$10 for two, plus US$2 per each additional person; facilities include hot showers, flush toilets, laundry, restaurant, bar, and boat access to Ensenada de La Paz. No tent sites are available. Open year-round.

Five km (three miles) west of the city on Mexico 1, across from Motel Villa del Sol, is the well-maintained **Casa Blanca RV Park,** tel. (1) 124-0009, fax (1) 125-1142, where over 46 full-hookup sites are US$10 a night for two persons plus US$2 for each additional guest. The facility includes showers, flush toilets, a pool, tennis courts, spa, laundry, restaurant, and a small market. Open Nov.-May. The Casa Blanca is up for sale; rates, facilities, and opening months could change drastically if a new management takes over.

A kilometer closer to the city center and surrounded by a high wall, **El Cardón Trailer Park,** at Km 4 (Apdo. Postal 104, La Paz, BCS), tel. (1) 124-0078, fax (1) 124-0261, features 80 shaded, well-tended *palapa* sites with full hookups for US$10 for two, plus US$1 each additional person; tents permitted. El Cardón offers a pool, groceries, recently renovated bathrooms with flush toilets and hot showers, a dump station, and laundry. Open year-round.

Off Av. Abasolo (Mexico 1) not far from the bayshore is the upscale, 96-slot **La Paz RV Park,** Apdo. Postal 482, La Paz, BCS, tel. (1) 122-4480 or 122-8787, fax (1) 122-9938. Full hookups alongside concrete pads or tent sites on the ground cost US$10 for two plus US$3 per additional guest; facilities include showers, flush toilets, potable tap water, a small pool, jacuzzi, tennis court, laundry, restaurant, and bar. Open Nov.-May only. To find this RV park, go east on Av. Abasolo and turn left (toward the bay) just before the VW dealer, then turn left before Posada Engelbert and continue three or four blocks.

A bit farther east toward the city center, off Calle Nayarit on the bay, is the smallish, palm-planted **Aquamarina RV Park,** Apdo. Postal 133, La Paz, BCS, tel. (1) 122-3765 or 122-3761. A favorite among boaters and divers, Aquamarina features its own marina, complete with boat ramp, storage facilities, and air for scuba tanks, plus showers, flush toilets, potable tap water, a pool, and laundry facilities. Nineteen full-hookup sites cost US$11 for two, plus US$2 per additional guest. Open Nov.-May only. The Aquamarina also offers three apartments for rent.

FOOD

La Paz offers dining venues for all tastes and budgets, and, as might be expected in a coastal city, the seafood selection is particularly good.

American
Visiting and resident yachties crowd **The Dock Café,** Marina de La Paz, at the corner of Topete and Legaspy, tel. (1) 125-6626, a small, casual diner serving fried chicken, hamburgers, fish and chips, bagels, salads, steaks, American breakfasts, some Mexican dishes, and homemade apple pie. The food quality is uneven and

service can be slow, however. A blues trio occasionally performs in the evening. Moderately priced. Open Mon.-Sat. 8 a.m.-10 p.m., Sunday 8 a.m.-1 p.m. (It's usually closed for two weeks at the end of August/beginning of September.) Also at the marina is **Penthouse Racing Club,** a small restaurant/bar atop the Chandlery marine supply store.

La Fabula Pizza serves American-style pizza and Italian specialties at six locations: Paseo Obregón 15 (at Av. Independencia), tel. (1) 122-4101; 5 de Mayo 310, tel. (1) 122-5603; Isabel La Católica at Allende, tel. (1) 122-4153; Blvd. Kino 2530, tel. (1) 122-8641; Fco. Mújica at Colima, tel. (1) 125-7741; and Calz. 5 de Febrero 535-B, tel. (1) 122-0830. Moderately priced. Open daily for lunch and dinner.

Restaurant Grill Campestre, opposite the FIDEPAZ building on Mexico 1 North, near Km 55, tel. (1) 124-0454, is popular with gringos and Mexicans alike for barbecued ribs, Cobb salad, and other American specialties. Moderately priced. Open daily for lunch and dinner.

At **Viejo Oeste,** Legaspy at Topete, tel. (1) 122-6191, near Marina de La Paz, the house specialty is American-style steaks, but the large *palapa* restaurant is popular with local residents. Moderately priced. Open Mon.-Sat. 11 a.m.-11 p.m.

Though mostly a takeout place, **Romeo's Pizza,** Calle Madero 830 (between León and Legaspy), tel. (1) 125-9495 or 122-4550, offers a few tables on the sidewalk in front. Good standard pizza. Inexpensive to moderate. Open Tues.-Sun. 11 a.m.-10 p.m.

Antojitos

In the afternoons, the downtown area centered around the *malecón* and Calle 16 de Septiembre features street vendors serving fish tacos and *cocteles.* One of the best stands for fish, shrimp, clam tacos, and *aguas frescas* is **Super Tacos de Baja California Hermanos González.** Formerly at the corner of Arrival and Esquerro opposite the Banamex, it has moved down the street south a bit to a spot beneath a big tree, opposite the side entrance of La Perla department store. The famous stand is still packed around lunchtime.

Taquería los Faroles, near the Hostería del Convento on Calle Madero (no phone), is a clean,

inexpensive diner serving fish tacos, *milanesa, flautas, sopes,* tostadas, *licuados,* and midday *comida corrida.* Open daily 11 a.m.-7 p.m.

Taquería Los Superburros, over on Abasolo between 5 de Febrero and Navarro, serves hamburgers, tacos, quesadillas, *huaraches,* and *papas rellenas.*

During the daytime, the cluster of *loncherías* in the **Mercado Municipal Francisco E. Madero,** Revolución and Degollado, serves as a very inexpensive grazing spot for *antojitos* and *comidas corridas.* **Mercado Bravo,** at the corner of Bravo and G. Prieto, also holds a few *loncherías.*

Asian

La Cochinita, Forjadores and Veracruz, tel. (1) 122-1600, is an extremely clean fast-food spot serving generous portions of Mexicanized Japanese dishes. It's a very popular lunch spot with the locals. Open daily 10 a.m.-9 p.m.

Restaurant Dragón, 16 de Septiembre at Esquerro, tel. (1) 122-1372 (upstairs over Caffé Gourmet), is generally considered the best of the five or six Chinese restaurants in La Paz's tiny Chinatown. It's also the most upscale (though not expensive) and is an important lunch spot for local *políticos.* The menu is basically Cantonese, with Mexican influences. Not the place to wear shorts and T-shirt. Open daily 1-9:30 p.m.

If you're looking for basic Chinese takeout, try **Mi-Lien,** on Abasolo between 5 de Febrero and Navarro, tel. (1) 122-5165, next to Taquería Los Superburros. Inexpensive. Open daily 11 a.m.-10 p.m.

Sushi Express, Madero and Degollado, tel. (1) 122-3425, specializes in fresh sushi, teppanyaki, and tempura. Free delivery. Inexpensive. Open Wed.-Mon. 1-11 p.m.

Teriyaki San, 5 de Febrero at Ramírez, tel. (1) 122-1674, is a clean, efficient, a/c fast-food joint with inexpensive Japanese food. Open daily noon-9 p.m.

Cafés

A great place to enjoy coffee and pastries in air-conditioned comfort is **Caffé Gourmet,** Esquerro and 16 de Septiembre, tel. (1) 122-6037. The menu offers a long list of hot and cold coffee drinks, chai, smoothies, Italian sodas, pies, cookies, and pastries along with cigars and liquors.

Expresso Café, on Obregón north of Oasis, is also air-conditioned, and the menu contains a whole page of coffee drinks, hot and cold, plus deli sandwiches, salads, snacks and pastries.

A tiny place with a couple of outdoor tables and a recently added a/c area, **Café del Trópico,** Calle 16 de Septiembre, a half block southeast of the *malecón,* serves Veracruz-style coffee (including decaffeinated) made from fresh-roasted and fresh-ground Veracruz coffee beans. It's open daily 8 a.m.-1:30 p.m. and 5:30-9 p.m.

International

Housed in a U-shaped colonial around a courtyard, **Le Bistrot Français,** Calle Esquerro 10, between Callejón de La Paz and 16 de Septiembre, is a new place featuring French-influenced cuisine. Dishes include *tartas* (quiche-like pies, offered in seafood and squash-blossom versions), salads, soups, seafood, steaks, ribs, and a tempting dessert menu. You can dine indoors or alfresco in the leafy courtyard. Open daily 7 a.m.-11 p.m.

The Malecón de Vista Coral, also known as Plaza Vista Coral, is a good spot for those seeking eclectic dining alongside the harbor. **Bougainvillea Restaurant,** Malecón de Vista Coral 5, tel. (1) 122-7744, is the most upmarket of several popular eateries in a new dining/entertainment area next to the Vista Coral development. The Bougainvillea caters to discriminating palates with sharp service and such culinary arcana as peppered tuna sashimi and grilled lobster in orange chipotle sauce. Fabulous pizza from wood-fired ovens. Moderate to expensive. Open daily noon-midnight.

At **Café Bar Capri,** Malecón de Vista Coral (Local 4), between Márquez de León and Topete, tel. (1) 123-3737, you'll find crepes, baguettes, *antojitos,* cakes and desserts, exotic drinks, books, music, art, and a bay view. Colorful tables inside and out fill with locals who stop by for early evening drinks. Inexpensive to moderate. Open Tues.-Sun. 7 a.m.-12:30 a.m.

China Gourmet, Malecón de Vista Coral 3, tel. (1) 125-2824, serves health-conscious stir-fries, omelettes, and salads, as well as a selection of fruit drinks, coffees, and chai (Indian-style milk tea), at umbrella-shaded tables facing the harbor.

Kiwi Restaurant Bar, on the *malecón* between 5 de Mayo and Constitución, tel. (1) 123-3282, offers a good bay view and a varied menu of seafood, Mexican, and international recipes. On weekends the restaurant occasionally features live music. Moderately priced. Open daily 8 a.m.-midnight.

La Pazta, on Calle Allende adjacent to Hotel Mediterrané, tel. (1) 125-1195, is simply decorated with works of art, pastel stucco, and exposed brick. The light and airy restaurant offers breakfast, lunch, and dinner. The evening menu features a long list of pastas, pizzas, fondues, and other Swiss and Italian specialties. The extensive wine list includes Italian, U.S., Chilean, and *bajacaliforniano* labels. Moderately priced. Open daily 7 a.m.-11 p.m.

The new **El Ángel Azul,** Independencia 518, tel. (1) 125-5130, in the hotel of the same name, features Mexican as well as Swiss cuisine. Open Tues.-Sun. 8 a.m.-10 p.m. Closed Monday.

Overlooking the shop-lined pedestrian street off of 16 de Septiembre, **California Grill,** 21 de Agosta, offers such gringo favorites as nachos, soups, several types of spaghetti, steaks (US$9), barbecued pork ribs (US$8), chicken cordon bleu, chicken fajitas, seafood (US$6.50-11), hamburgers (US$4), and a salad bar.

The venerable **El Taste,** Paseo Obregón at Juárez, tel. (1) 122-8121, features steaks, Mexican food, and seafood. It's patronized by a mostly tourist and expat clientele. Moderate to expensive. Open daily for breakfast, lunch, and dinner.

Outdoors beneath the Hotel Perla, **La Terraza,** Paseo Obregón 1570, tel. (1) 122-0777, features an extensive menu of seafood, Mexican, steak, and Italian dishes. A steady crowd of both tourists and locals comes for the best people-watching in town, as well as for the reasonably tasty, reasonably priced food.

VAS, on the *malecón* at Paseo Obregón between 5 de Mayo and Independencia, tel. (1) 122-7510, is a middle-class spot featuring international dishes, fish and seafood specialties, salads, soups, and breakfasts. Inexpensive to moderate. Open Tues.-Sun. 8 a.m.-10 p.m.

El Oasis Restaurant and Bar, Paseo Obregón 115 (between 16 de Septiembre and Callejón de La Paz, next to Carlos'n Charlie's), tel. (1) 125-7666, is a sidewalk patio restaurant with a large menu of seafood, steaks, and Mexican dishes. Moderately priced. Open daily 11 a.m.-1 a.m.; live music in the evening.

La Paz Gourmet, on Calle Bravo near Mutualismo, is a "street deli" operating Nov.-July only. Look for homemade salads, quiche, frittata, deli-style sandwiches, full luncheon plates, muffins, cookies, and more, to go or to eat at two tables set up at streetside. Moderately priced; open Mon.-Sat. 10 a.m.-4 p.m.

Mexican

A popular coffee-shop-style place, **Restaurant Plaza Real,** Hotel Plaza Real, Calle Esguerro at Callejón de La Paz, tel. (1) 122-9333, offers moderate prices, efficient service, and good Mexican food. The fresh orange juice is quite refreshing on a hot day. Open Sun.-Fri. 7 a.m.-11 p.m., Saturday 7 a.m.-1 p.m.

Next to Hotel Perla on Callejón de La Paz, **Cafe El Callejón** has all sorts of breakfast specials and *antojitos.* The menu features many types of *huaraches,* including a Oaxaca-style version with beans, cream, and cheese, or traditional with cheese, beans, and *nopalitos.* A variety of coffees are offered, including decaf. You can dine at outdoor tables under umbrellas on the *callejón*—a great spot to peoplewatch.

Café San Francisco, next to the Hotel Mediterrané on Calle Allende, tel. (1) 122-7479, serves cheap and tasty Mexican meals in a clean, bright, and airy atmosphere. Open 7:30 a.m.-9 p.m. daily; *comida corrida* available 1-4 p.m.

Carlos'n Charlie's, Obregón at 16 de Septiembre, tel. (1) 122-9290, is part of the same chain as Squid Roe and Señor Frog's, but the atmosphere is much more low-key than the typical Grupo Anderson enterprise. The interior decor features old Mexican movie posters, while the menu emphasizes good Mexican fare, seafood (try the *ceviche paceño*), and steak dishes. Much of the clientele is Mexican. The terrace tables usually catch a breeze. Moderate to expensive. Open daily noon-midnight.

In a courtyard behind La Fabula on Obregón, **Peña La Pitahaya de Janicua,** Obregón 15, tel. (1) 126-2234, is an almost hidden spot with a bohemian ambience and a Mexican menu. Artwork and Mexican crafts are on display throughout, and there's live Latin folk music nightly.

Rosticería California, Serdán between Degollado and Ocampo, tel. (1) 122-5118, is a popular downtown eatery famous for roast chicken, which can be ordered by the piece, half, or whole, or as *brochetas,* teriyaki with rice, or "cordon bleu." All orders are available to go, or you can dine at booths inside or beneath *palapas* outside. Rosticería California has other branches around town, including a nicer one on the west side of Calz. Olachea, south of Calle Cuauhtémoc. Inexpensive. Open daily 10 a.m.-10 p.m.

Super Pollo makes a good, economical choice for *pollo asado al carbón estilo Sinaloa* (Sinaloa-style grilled chicken), sold with tortillas and salsa. Eat in or take out at three locations: Calz. 5 de Febrero at Gómez Farías, tel. (1) 122-5588; 5 de Mayo at Gómez Farías, tel. (1) 122-6988; and Blvd. Forjadores at Loreto, tel. (1) 123-1858. Open daily 11 a.m.-10 p.m.

Restaurant El Mexicano, Calle Serdán at 16 de Septiembre, tel. (1) 122-8965, serves *menudo,* seafood, standard Mexican dishes, and *comida corrida;* nothing special but it's cheap. Open daily 7:30 a.m.-10 p.m.

The simple but pretty restaurant/bar **El Zarape,** Av. México 3450 (between Oaxaca and Nayarit), tel. (1) 122-2520, features a tiled entryway and a menu of traditional Mexican dishes. On Saturday evenings El Zarape hosts a *cazuelada,* i.e., a buffet of *cazuelas* (large, open clay pans) filled with *moles* and other specialties of Central and Southern Mexico. On Sunday evenings a more modern Mexican buffet brings together recipes from all over the republic. Moderately priced. Open daily noon-midnight.

Seafood

Operated by local seafood wholesalers Mar y Peña, **Restaurant La Mar y Peña,** Calle 16 de Septiembre between Isabel la Católica and Albañez, tel. (1) 122-9949, is a small a/c place with a terrific menu that features practically everything that swims, including several *machaca* (dried and shredded) versions. The *sangría preparada* (homemade sangria) is also good. Credit cards accepted. Moderately priced. Open daily 9 a.m.-10 p.m.

The casual, family-run **Bismark II,** Degollado at Ramírez, tel. (1) 122-4854, specializes in lobster, abalone, and *carne asada.* All meals start with the restaurant's unique *totopos*—instead of chips, they're fried whole tortillas, served with a smooth guacamole. The ceviche is also very good. Moderately priced. Open daily 8 a.m.-10 p.m.

Perched at water's edge toward the southwest end of the *malecón, palapa*-roofed **La Caleta,** Paseo Obregón at Pineda, tel. (1) 123-0287, is one of the city's most romantic spots for an evening meal. Look for fresh seafood and standard Mexican dishes. Moderately priced; occasional live music. Open weekdays 10 a.m.-11 p.m., weekends till 2 a.m.

South of the Aero California office on Obregón is **El Cangrejo Loco,** a tiny restaurant with a few tables on the sidewalk. It's a simple place with seafood (try the excellent *cocteles*) priced at a reasonable US$4.25-10.50.

One of the better hotel restaurants, **Restaurant Bermejo,** Los Arcos Hotel, Paseo Obregón, tel. (1) 122-2744, overlooks the *malecón*—ask for a window table. The Italian chef prepares a varied menu of seafood, steaks, and pastas. If you've had a successful day fishing, the restaurant will prepare your catch for US$6 pp, including all the dinner accompaniments. Moderate to expensive; open daily noon-midnight.

Under an *enramada* just north of Nuevo Pekin, the rustic **Restaurant Bar Mariscos Dos Mares,** Alvaro Obregón, serves basic but fresh seafood dishes. The slightly less rustic **Mar de Cortéz,** 5 de Febrero and Prieto, tel. (1) 122-7274, is also a clean, *palapa*-roofed place specializing in seafood.

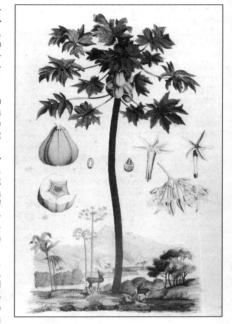

papaya

Vegetarian
El Quinto Sol, Domínguez and Av. Independencia, tel. (1) 122-1692, is a natural food/vegetarian store with a café section serving *tortas, comida corrida,* pastries, salads, granola, fruit and vegetable juices, and yogurt.

Tonantzin, 5 de Mayo at Serdán (one block east of the plaza), offers whole-wheat bread, yogurt, *licuados,* juices, and herbs. Open Mon.-Sat. 8 a.m.-8 p.m., Sunday 8 a.m.-3 p.m.

Groceries
The **Mercado Municipal Francisco E. Madero,** Revolución at Degollado, houses a collection of vendor stalls purveying fresh fish, meats, fruit, vegetables, and baked goods at nonsubsidized free-market prices. Since prices are usually posted, no bargaining is necessary. Opposite the market on Degollado, **Panaficadora Lilia** sells fresh *bolillos* and *pan dulce* daily. Nearby at the corner of Revolución and Bravo is a *tortillería.*

Other traditional markets include **Mercado Bravo** (Bravo at G. Prieto) and **Mercado Abastos** (on Blvd. Las Garzas).

The government-subsidized **ISSSTE Tienda,** Calle Revolución de 1910 at Bravo, has the city's best grocery prices, although the selection varies according to what ISSSTE purchased cheaply that week. The **Tienda Militar** (Military Store), on Calle 5 de Mayo at Padre Kino, offers a larger selection than ISSSTE Tienda and is almost as inexpensive.

La Paz supermarkets include two large **CCC** (Centro Comercial California) outlets—one on Av. Abasolo at Colima, the other on Isabel La Católica at Bravo. These carry American-brand packaged foods as well as Mexican products, but prices are about a third higher than what you'd usually pay elsewhere in town. Another good supermarket chain is **Supermercado Aramburo,** with three branches: 16 de Septiembre at Altamirano, Madero at Hidalgo y Costilla, and Durango 130 Sur (between Ocampo and Degollado).

The latest and greatest addition in this category is **Plaza Ley** on the eastern outskirts of town on Las Garzas at Teotihuacán. Part of a Sinaloa-based chain, this store carries a huge selection of groceries as well as clothing, gardening supplies, small appliances, books, videos, housewares, and more.

Natural Foods
El Quinto Sol, Domínguez at Av. Independencia, offers natural juices, wheat gluten, soybean meat substitutes (including soybean *chorizo*), whole-wheat flour, herbs, yogurt, and ice cream, as well as a few ready-to-eat items like *tortas* and salads. **Los Girasoles,** Calle Revolución between Hidalgo y Costilla and Morelos, tel. (1) 122-5590, operates a bakery and sells veggie sandwiches, yogurt, granola, vitamins, and various whole grains. **Tonantzin,** 5 de Mayo at Serdán, is similar.

Semilla y Cereales Camacho, on the north side of Calle Revolución de 1910 about a half block southwest of the Mercado Municipal Francisco E. Madero, stocks an intriguing selection of herbal medicines as well as cereals, dried fruits, jams, nuts, culinary herbs, dried chiles, and various beans.

Ice Cream, Sweets, Coffee Beans
Downtown La Paz is packed with *tiendas* selling *nieves* (Mexican-style ice cream) and *paletas* (popsicles). **Paletería y Nevería La Michoacana** (formerly Mr. Yeti) is a big one, with branches on Paseo Obregón and Calle Madero. A personal favorite is tiny **La Fuente,** on Paseo Obregón between Degollado and Muelle; though small, this place offers a huge variety of flavors (including *capirotada,* a Mexican bread pudding), as well as *licuados, aguas frescas,* and all-fruit *paletas.*

For American-style ice cream, head for the reliable **Helados Bing,** at Esquerro and Callejón de La Paz (opposite Hotel Plaza Real), or **33 Helados,** Paseo Obregón near Calle Hidalgo y Costilla.

Three *dulcerías* (sweet shops) lie on three corners of the intersection of Calles Ocampo and Serdán. On the fourth corner is a large school, the obvious target market for these sweet shops. **Dulcería Perla** has a complete selection of traditional and modern Mexican sweets, while **Dulcería Aladino** on the opposite corner specializes in candy-filled piñatas, including a few in the shape of Pokémon characters.

Fresh-roasted coffee beans can be purchased at the outlets of **Cafe Combate** (Calle 5 de Mayo 1056), **Café Batalla** (Calle 5 de Mayo at Belisario Domínguez), and **Cafe Marino** (Jalisco at Yucatán). We'd give Café Batalla the edge, but better yet are the fresh-roasted Veracruz beans from **Café del Trópico** on Calle 16 de Septiembre (see Cafés, above).

ENTERTAINMENT

Bars
Bar Pelicanos, overlooking the *malecón* in Hotel Los Arcos, is a large, sedate watering hole popular among tourists and old hands. It's worth at least one visit to peruse the old photos along the back wall; subjects include a motley array of unnamed vaqueros and revolutionaries, as well as Pancho Villa, Gen. Blackjack Pershing, Pres. Dwight Eisenhower, Emiliano Zapata, and Clark Gable, who poses with a marlin. The bar is open daily 10 a.m.-1 a.m.

On the beach side of Paseo Obregón, three blocks west of Hotel Los Arcos, is the casual and sometimes lively *palapa* bar **La Caleta,** where the clientele is predominantly local. Yachties from the nearby Marina de La Paz occasionally arrive via Zodiac rafts, which they park on the adjacent beach. Drinks are reasonably priced, especially during the 4-8 p.m. happy hour, and there's usually live music after 9 p.m. or so.

On Calle Esquerro near the Hotel Perla, the slightly seedy **Peña Folklórico Misión** (also known as Bar Misión) features live *norteña* bands nightly.

Tequilas Bar and Grill, in a rustic house next to Palmas Suites on Calle Mutualismo, is an intimate bar with pool tables and a small private room popular with local politicians.

Caliente Race & Sports Book, on Paseo Obregón, has the usual array of satellite-linked TV monitors for viewing international sports events—and betting on them if the mood strikes you. It's open Mon.-Fri. 10 a.m.-midnight, Sat.-Sun. 9:30 a.m.-midnight.

Discos and Nightclubs

Living up to its laid-back reputation, La Paz isn't big on discos. A slightly older crowd frequents **Las Varitas,** Av. Independencia 111, tel. (1) 125-2025, downtown near El Quinto Sol natural foods store and Plaza Constitución. The club offers dancing to recorded and live music.

Carlos'n Charlie's, on Paseo Obregón, has an attached dance club that experiences occasional waves of popularity, especially on Thursday evenings when women are admitted without having to pay the usual cover charge. **Bahía Rock,** next to the Crowne Plaza Resort at Km 5.5, packs a crowd Friday and Saturday nights. **Structure,** Paseo Obregón at Ocampo, is a newer disco with an as-yet-unproven track record. **Nightclub La Cabaña,** at the Hotel Perla, usually offers live *norteña* and *tecnobanda* music and attracts a local crowd.

Out on Plaza Vista Coral, you'll find **What?!** a rock club/sports bar/discotheque.

Billiards

Billares Casino Club, Calle Revolución de 1910 at Av. Independencia (opposite the southwest corner of the plaza), has some of the nicest playing tables and cues I've seen in Mexico. To play costs US$3 per hour—upscale by Mexican standards. Local shooters are happy to demonstrate the two most popular games: *billiares,* a three-ball game played on a table with no pockets; and "pool," wherein ball numbers 3-15 are lined up along the edge of the table and sunk in order (the person who sinks the 15 wins). Some players are also familiar with eight-ball as played in the United States.

Bullfights and *Charreadas*

The municipal stadium at Constitución and Verdad occasionally hosts *corridas de toros* in the late winter months, usually Feb.-March.

Paceños are more active in *charrería* than in bullfighting, and you can attend *charreadas* (Mexican-style rodeos) at **Lienzo Charro Guadalu-**

pano, just south of the city on the west side of Mexico 1 south (heading toward San Pedro). For information on the latest schedules for *charreadas* and *corridas de toros,* contact the state tourism office between Km 6 and 5 on Mexico 1 (Av. Abasolo), opposite the FIDEPAZ Marina, tel. (1) 124-0199. A *gran charreada* is usually held to celebrate Cinco de Mayo (5 May).

Cinemas

La Paz has two movie theaters. **Cinema Versalles Plus,** Revolución de 1910, south of the plaza, shows first-run movies on four screens. The two-screen **Cine Gemelos** can be found on Isabel La Católica between Allende and Juárez.

EVENTS

La Paz's biggest annual celebration is **Carnaval,** held for six days before Ash Wednesday in mid-February. Carnaval is also held in the Mexican cities of Mazatlán, Ensenada, and Veracruz, but Carnaval connoisseurs claim La Paz's is the best—perhaps because the city's *malecón* makes a perfect parade route.

As at all Mexican Carnavals, the festival begins with the Quema de Mal Humor, or "Burning of Bad Humor," in which an effigy representing an unpopular public figure is burned. Other events include the crowning of La Reina del Carnaval (Car-

costumed Carnaval celebrant in La Paz

naval Queen) and El Rey Feo (Ugly King), colorful costumed parades, music, dancing, feasting, cockfights, and fireworks. The festival culminates in El Día del Marido Oprimido, or "Day of the Oppressed Husband" (23 and a half hours of symbolic freedom for married men to do whatever they wish), followed by a masquerade ball on the Tuesday evening before Ash Wednesday.

Also prominent on the city's yearly events calendar is the **Fiesta de La Paz** (officially known as "Fiesta de la Fundación de la Ciudad de La Paz"), held 3 May, the anniversary of the city's founding. The state tourist office can provide up-to-date details on festival scheduling and venues.

SHOPPING

Before the city's duty-free status was recalled in 1989, imported merchandise could be purchased in La Paz free of import duties and sales tax. Nowadays sales tax is commensurate with the rest of Mexico's. But the city still offers some of Baja's best shopping in terms of value and variety, starting with the downtown department stores of **Dorian's** (Calle 16 de Septiembre at Esquerro) and **La Perla de La Paz** (Calle Arrival at Mutualismo). Dorian's resembles a typical middle-class, American-style department store; La Perla is more of a discount department store, featuring a good supply of coolers (ice chests), toiletries, housewares, liquors, and pharmaceuticals at low prices.

Along Paseo Obregón in the vicinity of the Hotel Perla and Hotel Los Arcos are a number of souvenir and handicraft shops of varying quality. One of the better ones is **Artesanías La Antigua California,** Paseo Obregón 220, which sells quality folk arts and crafts from the mainland. **México Lindo,** next to Carlos'n Charlie's, is also good for *artesanías.* **Curios Mary,** Arreola 25 at Obregón, tel. (1) 122-0815, specializes in Majorcan pearls.

Attached to Palmas Suites, **Uget,** Mutualismo 314, tel. (1) 122-4623, is a new shop featuring decorative hand-painted Mexican tiles, as well as rustic bathroom and kitchen accessories and hardware.

Away from the city center, the **Centro de Arte Regional,** Calle Chiapas at Encinas, produces and sells pottery, while **Artesanía Cuauhté-moc,** Av. Abasolo between Jalisco and Nayarit, weaves rugs, blankets, wall-hangings, tablecloths, and other cotton or wool items. Custom orders are possible, and customers are welcome to watch the weavers at their looms in back of the shop. Opposite Artesanía Cuauhtémoc on Av. Abasalo, **Casa María** carries a good selection of *artesanías,* rustic furniture, and decorating accessories.

For tourist-variety souvenirs, especially *playeras* (T-shirts), a good choice is **Bye-Bye,** four blocks east of Hotel Perla on Paseo Obregón. For bottom-dollar bargains on clothing, housewares, and leather, browse the **Mercado Municipal Francisco E. Madero,** Revolución de 1910 at Degollado. Inexpensive electronics, watches, and jewelry are available at a string of shops along Calles Domínguez and Madero between Av. Independencia and Calle 16 de Septiembre, and along a pedestrian alley off Calle 16 de Septiembre near Dorian's department store.

Deportes Ortiz, on Calle Degollado almost opposite Pensión California, tel. (1) 122-1209, carries a modest selection of camping, diving, and other sports equipment. **Santander,** a large store at the corner of Serdán and Degollado, tel. (1) 125-5962, stocks a wide variety of useful *artesanías,* including saddles, guitars, and *huaraches.*

BEACHES

Bahía de La Paz is scalloped with 10 signed, public beaches. Most inviting are the seven beaches strung out northeast of La Paz along Península de Pichilingue—they get better the farther you get from the city.

Playa Palmira, around four km (2.5 miles) east of downtown La Paz via the La Paz-Pichilingue Rd., has been taken over by the Araiza Inn Palmira and Marina de Palmira, leaving little remaining beachfront. A kilometer farther, the small but pleasant **Playa El Coromuel** offers restaurant/bar service, a waterslide, *palapas,* and toilets.

In front of La Concha Beach Resort near Km 5, **Playa Caimancito** (named for an offshore rock formation that resembles a small gator) features a rock reef within swimming distance of the grayish beach. Although it's close to the city and resort developments, you can see a surprising number of tropical fish here; incoming tide is the best time for swimming or snorkeling. The bus fare to these three beaches from the *malecón* bus terminal in downtown La Paz is 55 cents.

Playa del Tesoro, 14 km (8.5 miles) from the city, is another casual, semiurban beach with *palapas* and a sometimes-open, often-closed restaurant. The beach was purportedly named

BEACHES AND ISLANDS NEAR LA PAZ

for a cache of silver coins unearthed by crews building a road to the Pichilingue ferry terminal near the beach. Just southwest of El Tesoro, a dirt road leads to hidden **Playa Punta Colorada,** a small, quiet cove surrounded by red-hued hills that protect it from the sights and sounds of the La Paz-Pichilingue Road. Buses from downtown La Paz cost US$1.65.

At Km 17, just beyond the SEMATUR ferry terminal, is **Playa Pichilingue,** the only public beach in the La Paz vicinity with restrooms available 24 hours for campers. The beach also has a modest *palapa* restaurant.

After Pichilingue the once-sandy track has been replaced by pavement as far as Playa Tecolote. The turnoff for **Playa Balandra** appears five km (three miles) beyond Pichilingue, then it's another 800 meters (half mile) to the parking area and beach. Several *palapas,* brick barbecue pits, and trash barrels have been installed by the city. Depending on the tide, the large, shallow bay of Puerto Balandra actually forms several beaches, some of them long sandbars. Ringed by cliffs and steep hills, the bay is a beautiful and usually secluded spot, perfect for wading in the clear, warm waters. Clams are abundant, and a coral reef at the south end of the bay offers decent snorkeling. Climb the rock cliffs—carefully—for sweeping bay views. Camping is permitted at Balandra, but oftentimes a lack of breeze brings out the *jejenes* (no-see-ums), especially in the late summer and early fall. The beaches sometimes draw crowds on weekends.

About three km (1.5 miles) beyond the Playa Balandra turnoff is **Playa El Tecolote,** a wide, long, pretty beach backed by vegetated dunes. Because Tecolote is open to the stiff breezes of Canal de San Lorenzo, the camping here is usually insect-free. Two *palapa* restaurants, **El Tecolote** and **Palapa Azul,** sell seafood and cold beverages and rent *pangas,* beach chairs and umbrellas, fishing gear, and plastic canoes. Free municipal *palapas* and barbecue grills dot the beach north and south of the restaurants. If you visit during the week the place is almost deserted. Only three buses per day go as far as Tecolote and Balandra, departing the *malecón* terminal at noon, 1 p.m., and 3 p.m. and returning at 5:30 p.m.; the fare is US$2.15.

Isla Espíritu Santo, 6.5 km (four miles) away, is clearly visible in the distance; for around

US$40-50 you can hire a *panga* from Palapa Azul to cross the channel (see Islands, below).

Farther Afield

From Tecolote the road returns to sand as it winds across the peninsula for about 13 km (eight miles) before ending at remote **Playa Coyote.** Along the way shorter roads branch off to rocky coves suitable for camping. Don't tackle this road expecting to find the perfect white-sand beach; the farther northeast from Tecolote you go, the stonier and browner the beaches become.

South of Playa Coyote you can navigate a network of sand roads to Puerto Mejia and **Las Cruces.** Named for three crosses topping a bluff near the cove where Cortés supposedly landed, Las Cruces served as a supply port for Isla Cerralvo pearl beds during the pearl era. It was abandoned in the 1930s after the pearl-bearing oysters died out. In 1949, Abelardo L. Rodríguez III, grandson of a former Mexican president, designed and built at Las Cruces a fly-in getaway resort for Hollywood celebrities, including Desi Arnaz and Bing Crosby. The 20,000-acre resort was incorporated as Club de Caza y Pesca Las Cruces (Las Cruces Hunting and Fishing Club) in 1961 and today remains a private association counting around 225 members. Although the resort's popularity peaked in the 1950s and '60s, some of the fabulous beach villas are still occupied on occasion. The road's final approach is so difficult (intentionally so, according to rumors) that few people arrive by road; instead guests use the resort's private airstrip or arrive by yacht. Membership is conferred by invitation and sponsorship only.

Península El Mogote

This 11-km (seven-mile) thumb of land juts across the top of Ensenada de La Paz directly opposite the city. The southern shore of the peninsula is rimmed by mangroves, while the north side facing the open bay offers clean water and a long beach sullied only by everyday flotsam. It's not uncommon to see dolphins swimming by. Local myth says that if you eat the wild plums of the *ciruelo (Cryptocarpa edulis)* growing on El Mogote's sand dunes, you'll never want to leave La Paz.

Road access to El Mogote is problematic; the easiest way to reach the peninsula is by kayak from Marina de La Paz area (see Kayaking, below, for more information). Most kayakers land on the mangrove side facing Ensenada de La Paz then walk across the peninsula's narrow isthmus to reach the bay/ocean side.

ISLANDS

The large and small islands clustered just north of Península de Pichilingue offer an amazing variety of recreational possibilities both in and out of the water. The 22.5-km-long (14-mile-long) Isla Espíritu Santo and its smaller immediate neighbor to the north, Isla Partida, are excellent destinations for all manner of watercraft from sea kayaks to yachts. Sandy beaches and large coves along the western shores of both islands provide numerous opportunities for small-craft landings and camping. In full sun, the sand-bottom reflections of these bays create such a bright, translucent color that white seagulls flying over them are transformed into glowing blue-green UFOs.

Caleta El Candelero, Isla Espíritu Santo

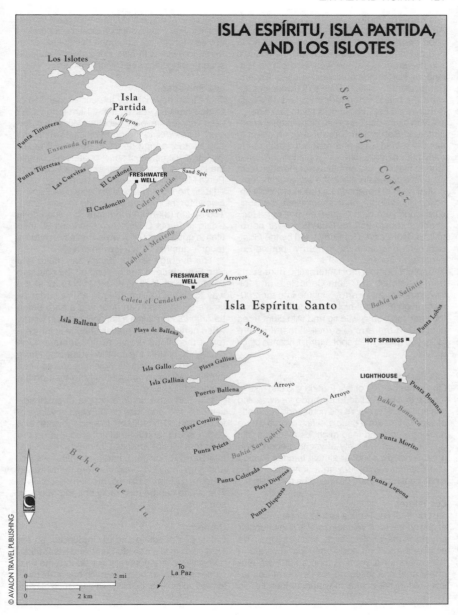

ISLA ESPÍRITU, ISLA PARTIDA, AND LOS ISLOTES

Los Islotes

Isla Partida

Punta Tintorera

Arroyos

Ensenada Grande

Punta Tijeretas

Las Cuevitas

El Cardonel

FRESHWATER WELL

Sand Spit

El Cardoncito

Caleta Partida

Arroyo

Bahía el Mesteño

FRESHWATER WELL

Arroyos

Caleta el Candelero

Isla Espíritu Santo

Bahía la Salinita

Punta Lobos

Isla Ballena

Playa de Ballena

Arroyos

HOT SPRINGS

Isla Gallo

Playa Gallina

LIGHTHOUSE

Punta Bonanza

Isla Gallina

Puerto Ballena

Arroyo

Bahía Bonanza

Playa Coralito

Arroyo

Punta Prieta

Bahía San Gabriel

Punta Morito

Punta Colorada

Playa Dispensa

Punta Lupona

Punta Dispensa

Bahía de la

Sea of Cortez

© AVALON TRAVEL PUBLISHING

0   2 mi

0   2 km

To La Paz

Isla Espíritu Santo

Around Isla Espíritu Santo, rock reefs provide good **snorkeling** at: Punta Prieta, at the north end of Bahía San Gabriel toward the island's southwestern tip; at the west end of Isla Ballena, an islet off the northwest coast of Espíritu Santo; at three islets in Caleta El Candelero, toward the island's northern end; and off Punta Bonanza on Espíritu Santo's southeast side.

Even if you don't snorkel, picturesque, sand-bottomed **Bahía San Gabriel** is worth a visit to see the ruined walls of a pearlery dating to the early 20th century. The low walls form an inner lagoon that fills and empties with the tides, creating little waterfalls along the edges of the bay.

Just north of Ensenada La Ballena (directly opposite Isla Ballena), near a spot where the Guaicura found year-round water, several small rock shelters known as **Las Cuevitas** bear petroglyphs. More caves formerly used by the Guaicura can be found in the dry arroyo behind Ensenada La Ballena.

Espíritu Santo's most interesting **hike** starts from the beach at Caleta Candelero and follows a deep, rocky arroyo inland into the 200-meter-high (650-foot-high) volcanic bluffs. Along the way you'll pass wild fig and wild plum trees clinging to the arroyo's rock sides; if you're lucky you might even spot a rare, endemic black jackrabbit.

Isla Partida

On the northern tip of Isla Partida you can hike to the top of a bluff called **El Embudo** for sweeping sea and island views. At the north and south ends of Isla Partida are a couple of fish camps where drinking water and food might be available, but don't count on it. Plenty of yachts frequent the area. A narrow sandbar almost bridges Partida and Espíritu Santo, leaving a tight channel for small boat movement between the two islands.

Los Islotes

Just north of Isla Partida lie Los Islotes, a cluster of guano-covered volcanic rock islands popular among divers, anglers, birds, and sea lions. The sea lions and their pups often join divers and snorkelers for a swim. A lone adult male elephant seal has taken up residence at Los Islotes. While this animal may appear friendly, his great size, strength and large teeth have the potential to inflict serious injury; local dive operators advise that you not approach this animal or attempt to swim with him. For further details on scuba-diving sites see Diving, below.

Isla San José

Other than day visits by the occasional Sea of Cortez cruising vessel, this 24-km-long island sees very few travelers, whether Mexican or foreign. It lies well to the north of Isla Partida and Los Islotes, a long boat trip from La Paz. To save travel time, most small-boaters heading to the island launch from either Punta Coyote or Punta Mechudo, both reached via a rough graded road from San Juan de la Costa (see Fishing, below, for information on getting to San Juan). The 60-km (37-mile) road from San Juan de la Costa to Punta Coyote takes at least 90 minutes in good conditions, while Punta Mechudo is roughly another 11 km (seven miles).

The average skiff or *panga* can make **Isla San Francisco,** a small island off the southern tip of Isla San José, in about an hour, or all the way to Bahía La Amortajada at the larger island's south end in an hour and a half. Bahía La Amortajada makes a fair anchorage in winter, when northern winds prevail. A ridge in the center of the island crests at 500 meters, high enough to protect the southwestern coast from those cold winter winds, which means you can expect warmer temperatures here than on the mainland opposite.

Isla San José holds a couple of small settlements: Isla San José de la Palma, a village of fewer than 50 inhabitants toward the north end of the island, and a smaller fish camp on the rock-reef islet of Arrecife Coyote, northwest of Isla San Francisco. Limited supplies—water and gas—may be available from the Mexican fishermen at these camps, but don't count on it. The island can be miserably hot and buggy in summer.

Camping

Caleta El Candelero and El Cardoncito, on the west sides of Isla Espíritu Santo and Isla Partida, respectively, are generally considered the best camping beaches because each has a freshwater well suitable for bathing. To be certain of haul-

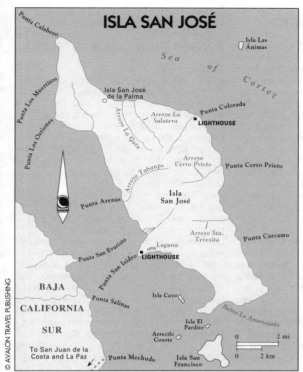

ISLA SAN JOSÉ

© AVALON TRAVEL PUBLISHING

Partida by kayak; the shallow channel between the two islands is only a few hundred meters across. Playa Tecolote or the smaller beaches just to its east are good put-in points for kayak trips to the island. Because of winds and tidal currents, this isn't a trip for the novice paddler. Even experienced sea kayakers on a first voyage to the island should follow someone who knows the tricky interplay of currents, shoals, tides, and winds. Two outfitters in La Paz lead kayak trips to the islands with experienced guides; see Kayaking, below, for contact information.

Several travel agencies in La Paz arrange two-hour powerboat jaunts to Isla Espíritu Santo and Isla Partida for around US$40-50 pp including lunch. At Palapa Azul on Playa Tecolote, you can arrange a four-hour trip around the west side of Espíritu Santo to a large island bay (Ensenada Grande) on Isla Partida and to the sea lion colony at Los Islotes; the cost for this trip, US$90 for up to six persons, includes lunch. A one-way shuttle out to the island costs US$50. **Mar y Aventuras,** Calle Topete 564 (between 5 de Febrero and Navarro, near Marina Don José and Marina de La Paz), tel./fax (1) 123-0559, U.S. tel. (406) 522-7595 or (800) 355-7140, fax (406) 522-7596, e-mail: sea@kayakbaja.com, offers a *panga* trip to Espíritu Santo and Los Islotes for US$150 per boat, roundtrip.

Whether booking with an agency in town or at the beach, inquire about the quality and contents of the lunch. If the lunch situation sounds iffy or awful (one prominent La Paz company a few years ago served one lousy sandwich of white bread glued to two slices of processed American cheese), demand more food or carry your own lunch. Life preservers are another variable worth inquiring about; some boats don't carry them.

ing some water out, you should bring your own bucket and 4.5 meters (15 feet) of rope. For drinking purposes you should bring enough purified water for the duration of your stay. If you must drink from the well, treat the water with purification tablets/iodine or boil it for at least 10 minutes.

Because these islands are part of an ecological preserve, you are supposed to obtain permission from the La Paz SEMARNAP office, Paseo Obregón at Héroes del 47 (between downtown La Paz and Club El Moro), tel. (1) 122-2418, before setting up camp.

Getting to the Islands

Punta Lupona, on the southern tip of Espíritu Santo, lies within kayaking range—just 6.5 km (four miles)—from Península de Pichilingue. Once at Espíritu Santo, it's easy to explore Isla

SPORTS AND RECREATION

Fishing

Outer bay and offshore fishing in the La Paz area are very good; a boat is mandatory since onshore and surf-fishing opportunities are limited. The bay and canals west of the islands hold roosterfish, pargo, cabrilla, needlefish, bonito, amberjack, jack crevalle, yellowtail, sierra, and pompano. Beyond Isla Espíritu Santo are the larger gamefish, including dorado, grouper, marlin, tuna, and sailfish. Yellowtail usually run in the area Jan.-March, while most other gamefish reach peak numbers April-November. Canal de Cerralvo, around the east side of Península de Pichilingue, provides excellent fishing for roosterfish and *pargo colorado* Jan.-July.

Any of the major La Paz hotels will arrange fishing trips; one of the oldest operations is **Jack Velez Sportfishing Charters,** Apdo. Postal 402, La Paz, BCS, tel. (1) 122-2744 or 121-5577, fax (1) 125-5313, which maintains a desk at Hotel Los Arcos. Another established outfit is **Fisherman's Fleet,** tel. (1) 122-1313, also with a desk at Los Arcos. Both offer fully equipped boats with guides, tackle, ice, and fish-cleaning and -filleting service at daily rates ranging from US$180 (for a 22-foot *panga*) to US$350 (for a 30-foot cabin cruiser).

You can also arrange guides and boats at the pier just east of the Pichilingue ferry terminal. From here, *panga* fishing trips in the bay generally cost US$80-90 a day for two people, while trips beyond Isla Espíritu Santo or to Canal de Cerralvo cost around US$160. Long-range fishing cruises run US$200-300 a day and usually accommodate up to four anglers.

Anglers with a sturdy set of wheels and their own tackle can drive the desolate road north from El Centenario (west of La Paz on the way to Ciudad Constitución) to **Punta El Mechudo** and **San Evaristo** at the northernmost end of Bahía de La Paz, where the onshore and inshore fishing—for grouper, snapper, pargo, cabrilla, sierra, dorado, and yellowfin—is almost as good as in the Canal de Cerralvo. Most visiting anglers camp on either side of Punta El Mechudo. The road is paved for the first 40 km (25 miles) as far as the phosphate-mining town of San Juan de la Costa, then it becomes graded gravel interspersed with ungraded sand for the final 53 km

(33 miles) to San Evaristo. This road is best traversed by high-clearance vehicles only.

Fishing tackle is available at **Deportiva La Paz,** Paseo Obregón 1680, tel. (1) 122-7333.

Boating

With a huge, protected bay, one private and four public marinas, and several boatyards and marine supply stores, La Paz is Baja California's largest and best-equipped boating center.

At the west end of the *malecón* (Calle Topete at Legaspy) is **Marina de La Paz,** Apdo. Postal 290, La Paz, BCS, tel. (1) 125-2112 or 122-1646, fax (1) 125-5900, VHF 16, e-mail: marinalapaz@bajavillas.com, owned by original *panga* designer Malcolm "Mac" Shroyer. Facilities include a launch ramp, fuel dock (diesel), market with groceries and marine supplies, café, water and electricity outlets, cable TV, laundry, showers, restrooms, a chandlery, and boat and vehicle storage. Club Cruceros de La Paz, e-mail: cruceros@baja.com, website: www.clubcruceros.com, is a local non-profit association that maintains a clubhouse at the marina and offers incoming mail service. The 80 slips range 30-110 feet in length and are 16 feet deep. Daily rates range from US$15.50 for a 24- to 50-foot craft to US$50 for a 65- to 70-foot craft. The daily rate is discounted June-Oct.; monthly rates start at US$285. Showers cost US$1.30 daily. Cable TV is US$1 per day or US$15 per month. Parking for slip clients is US$1 daily or US$22 per month. Marina de La Paz is the most popular marina in the bay and is often full Nov.-May; call or write in advance to check for vacancies before sailing in.

Northeast of town, on the Canal de La Paz at Km 2.5, the well-planned **Marina Palmira,** Apdo. Postal 34, La Paz, BCS, tel. (1) 121-6297, fax (1) 121-6142, VHF 16, currently offers 140 electricity-supplied slips accommodating yachts up to 100 feet long and 12 feet deep, as well as dry-storage facilities, a market, laundry, water, showers, bathrooms, a pool, jacuzzi, tennis court, two restaurants, a bar, 24-hour security, parking for one car per registered guest, a public phone, marine supplies, a fuel dock (diesel as well as gas), and boat launch. Crewed and bareboat yacht charters are available. Daily slip rates range US$15-60 depending on the size of the boat; monthly rates are US$11.50 per foot for slips of 60 and 80 feet, and US$12.50 per foot for

islets near Isla Espíritu Santo

slips of 100 feet, plus 10% tax. Electrical service costs extra. Condos and hotel rooms adjacent to the marina are available for rent by the day, week, or month.

The **Marina Don José,** at the end of Calle Encinas, one street south of Marina de La Paz, tel. (1) 125-9720, fax (1) 122-3640, offers mooring facilities for up to 25 boats but is usually full. On the premises are a *tienda,* outdoor restaurant, and four charter boats offering diving and sportfishing. The marina has recently upgraded its facilities; rates now run US$8.80 per foot per month.

Still under construction is La Paz's fourth docking facility, the government-financed **FIDEPAZ Marina.** It's on the waterfront near the state tourist office at the west end of Canal de La Paz. According to FIDEPAZ officials, the facility—if ever actually completed—will offer over 400 slips. Yet another pipe dream is a marina called **Costa Baja;** it's north of the Marina Palmira and still in the planning stages.

You can launch trailered and cartopped boats at Marina de La Paz, Marina Palmira, Marina Don José, Aquamarina RV Park, and Pichilingue. Smaller boats and kayaks can put in at any of the public beaches.

Parts and Repairs: Marina de La Paz is the best local source of information about boating needs; **Ferretería Marina SeaMar,** tel. (1) 122-9696 (SeaMar Marine Chandlery in English), a marine supply store opposite the marina entrance, stocks many everyday nautical items and is open Mon.-Fri. 8:30 a.m.-1:30 p.m. and 3-6 p.m., Saturday 8:30 a.m.-1:30 p.m. A booklet by Janet Calvert entitled *La Paz Boater's Guide to Goods and Services,* available at the marina, contains a thorough list of all boatyards, outboard-motor shops, and marine supply stores in La Paz. Boaters at the marina can also offer recommendations for the best places to obtain boat parts and repairs. Another marine supply store is the relatively new **López Marine Supply,** Vista Coral Plaza, tel. (1) 125-4160.

Buying a *Panga:* La Paz is the *panga* capital of Mexico. Until 1968, when American Mac Shroyer designed and built the first molded fiberglass *pangas,* many Sea of Cortez fishermen still used dugout canoes of Amerindian design; glass *pangas* made in La Paz are now sold all over Mexico. **Embarcaciones Arca,** tel. (1) 122-0874, fax (1) 122-0823, makes and sells *pangas* at a factory on Calle Gmo. Prieto between Juárez and Allende. The standard *panga* is sold in 16- to 26-foot lengths, but the factory can accommodate special orders as long as 36 feet. The standard *panga* outboard motor is a "cinco-cinco caballos," 55 horsepower. Prices run US$3,000-4,000 each, depending on whether canopy, stowage compartment, or other options are included. You can also buy *pangas* through **California Marine Boats,** Colima and Madero, tel./fax (1) 125-5184, e-mail: info@calmarineboats.com.

Boat Charters

Baja Coast SeaFaris, e-mail: jim@bajaseafaris.com, can organize customized charters aboard its *Irish Mist* sailing yacht and *Marco Polo* power cruiser. A six-day, seven-night trip includes visits to Espíritu Santo, Isla Partida, and Los Islotes, with stops along the way for swimming with sea lions, kayaking, sailing, beachcombing, birdwatching, snorkeling, or fishing. The cost of this trip on either boat is US$1,235 pp. The eight-night, nine-day "Baja Bash" trip is similar and costs US$1,635 pp. Rates include all onboard meals, snacks, and cocktails, lodging at Los Arcos Hotel on the last evening, and airport transfers. Scuba diving can also be arranged. Reservations should be made at least four months in advance for trips during the spring, fall, or major holidays.

Kayaking

Two local outfits operate excellent guided kayak trips in the region. **Baja Expeditions,** Calle Sonora 586 (just off Av. Abasolo), tel. (1) 125-3828, U.S. tel. (800) 843-6967, e-mail: travel@bajaex.com, offers seven-day sea-kayaking tours around Isla Espíritu Santo (March-May and Oct.-Jan. only), seven-day kayaking/whalewatching trips in Magdalena Bay, or 10-day coastal paddles between Loreto and La Paz. A more adventurous 10-day, open-water kayak trip hops among the islands of Espíritu Santo, Los Islotes, San José, Santa Cruz, and Santa Catalina. These trips are available Oct.-April only. Rates range from US$895 pp for the seven-day Espíritu Santo trip to US$1,200 pp for the Magdalena Bay trip. All rates based on double occupancy.

Mar y Aventuras, Calle Topete 564 (between 5 de Febrero and Navarro, near Marina Don José and Marina de La Paz), tel./fax (1) 123-0559, U.S. tel. (406) 522-7595 or (800) 355-7140, fax (406) 522-7596, e-mail: sea@kayak-baja.com, is geared toward kayak renters and day-trippers as well as persons interested in multiday guided tours. Five-day expeditions around Isla Espíritu Santo (Oct.-April only) cost US$700-800 depending on the number of participants. In addition to the longer trips, it offers several shorter excursions, such as a six-hour bay kayak tour to visit Peninsula El Mogote's mangrove and beach areas for just US$35 pp including lunch, an all-day paddling and snorkeling trip to Playa Balandra for US$40 pp, and a more ambitious all-day outing around the various hidden beaches and outlying islands of La Paz for US$55 pp. Custom-designed kayak trips of any length can be arranged.

Experienced kayakers can also rent kayaks from Mar y Aventuras for paddling to El Mogote or to the islands on their own. The company rents kayaks for US$40 a day or US$165 for six nights, including PFD, paddle, bilge pump, and spray deck. Also available for rent are snorkeling

gear, wetsuits, dry bags, tents, small stoves, and sleeping bags. Boat shuttles out to Isla Espíritu Santo (US$200-250 roundtrip) as well as truck shuttles to Playa Tecolote for beach launches to Espíritu Santo (US$40 per vehicle one-way) can be arranged.

Baja Quest (see Diving) organizes six-day kayaking/hiking/camping trips around Isla Espíritu Santo (December only). The price is US$870 pp, including hotel. A three-day package runs US$740 pp.

Diving

The granddaddy of all dive outfits in La Paz is Fernando Águilar's **Baja Diving and Service,** Paseo Obregón 1665-2 or Independencia 107-B, tel. (1) 122-1826 or 122-7010. Besides offering equipment sales and rental, Águilar organizes dive trips to the *Salvatierra* wreck, Los Islotes, or other nearby sites for US$77 a day including guide, transportation, lunch, unlimited sodas and beer, weight belt, and two tanks. Dive trips to El Bajo and Isla Cerralvo cost US$87. For all trips, add US$15 for full gear. Basic scuba certification costs US$90; a complete open-water diving certification course is available for US$280. In addition, BBS offers snorkeling trips for US$40 to Playa Encantada and the sea lion colony, as well as windsurfing equipment and instruction. Available rental equipment includes regulators, BCDs, wetsuits, masks, snorkels, fins, tanks, weight belts, booties, and portable air compressors. Baja Diving and Service also operates the only recompression chamber available to sport divers in La Paz.

Baja Expeditions, Calle Sonora 586 (just off Av. Abasolo), tel. (1) 125-3828, offers day-long and live-aboard dive programs in the La Paz vicinity. Most of these—particularly the live-aboard trips on the a/c, 86-foot *Don José*—are booked out of the U.S. office, 2625 Garnet Ave., San Diego, CA 92109, tel. (619) 581-3311 or (800) 843-6967, fax (619) 581-6542, e-mail: travel@bajaex.com, but it's occasionally possible to sign up in La Paz when space is available. From 28 May-30 Nov. the company runs eight-day expeditions aboard the *Don José;* US$1,295 pp for standard rooms to US$1,495 pp for superior rooms (double occupancy). Three eight-day excursions specifically dedicated to viewing the magnificent whale shark are offered in May and June for US$1,495 pp, double occupancy.

Day excursions aboard Baja Expeditions' 50-foot *Río Rita* dive boat can be booked in La Paz at a rate of US$115 per day, which covers three dives, breakfast, lunch, snacks, and happy hour. A rate of US$335-355 pp buys a three-day package complete with three nights of hotel accommodations (at Los Arcos, La Concha Beach Resort, or Hotel Marina) and two days of diving.

DIVING AND SNORKELING AROUND LA PAZ

Some of Baja's best dive sites lie in the vicinity of La Paz, but most are accessible only by boat. Along the western shores of **Isla Espíritu Santo** and **Isla Partida** are several good diving reefs. Bahía San Gabriel, a large cove along Espíritu Santo's southwest shore, features a shallow boulder reef (San Rafaelito) at its northern end suitable for both scuba diving and snorkeling. Similar rock reefs—along with submarine caves—can be found farther north off Espíritu Santo's western shore near Caleta El Candelero, extending from the west side of **Isla Ballena**. The latter islet also features a black coral forest and is protected from strong prevailing winds. All of these sites lie one to two hours from La Paz by boat.

One of the most colorful dive sites in the vicinity is **Los Islotes**, the tiny islet group off the north end of Isla Partida. Boulder reefs and underwater pinnacles off the north and northeast shores draw large marine species, including schools of hammerhead sharks, manta rays, and other pelagic (open-ocean) fish. A nearby cove is home to around 300 sea lions that seem to enjoy swimming alongside divers and performing tricks for the camera. Late in the breeding season (Jan.-May) is the best time to visit the colony, since this is when the adolescent pups are most playful. The south side of Los Islotes is well protected from prevailing winds virtually year-round.

To the southwest of Los Islotes lies **El Bajito**, a large rock reef that extends to within six meters (20 feet) of the sea's surface; the base of the reef meets a sandy bottom at about 24-28 meters (80-90 feet). The diverse marinelife frequenting the reef includes grouper, cabrilla, and an unusually large number of morays living among the many cracks and crevices in the reef; attached to the rocks are gorgonians, sea fans, and a variety of other invertebrates. Wind protection here is scant.

A group of three sea pinnacles called **El Bajo** (also known as Marisla Seamount), about 13 km (8.2 miles) northeast of Los Islotes, is renowned for the presence of large pelagics such as marlin, sharks (hammerhead, blacktip, tiger, and silvertip), dorado, corvina, and manta rays. Mantas frequent El Bajo from July to mid-October and here seem unusually friendly. Whale sharks, the largest fishes in the world, are occasionally seen near El Bajo during the same months, as are pilot whales. Depths range 18-43 meters (60-140 feet). Boats typically take two to three hours to reach El Baja from La Paz.

Due to strong tidal currents and lack of wind protection, El Bajito and El Bajo are best left to experienced open-ocean divers.

The wreck of the *Salvatierra*, a 91-meter (300-foot) La Paz–Topolobampo ferry that went down in the Canal de San Lorenzo in 1976, presents one of the more challenging dives. The hull lies about two and a half km (one and a half miles) southeast of the southern tip of Isla Espíritu Santo at a depth of approximately 10 fathoms (18 meters/60 feet). Encrusted with sponges, sea fans, mollusks, and gorgonians, the wreck attracts numerous varieties of tropical fish, including groupers, barracuda, angelfish, goatfish, parrotfish, moray eels, and rays.

Southeast of Península de Pichilingue, the somewhat more remote **Isla Cerralvo** offers several additional diving opportunities. **La Reinita**, a rock reef off the island's northern shore, attracts large pelagic fish. Even more remote—generally reached by live-aboard boat trips—are **Isla Santa Cruz** and **Islas Las Animas** to the north. The former is known for rock reefs at depths of around 17 meters (35 feet) with a profusion of sea horses, while the latter reportedly offers the greatest variety of diving experiences—caves, hammerheads, whale sharks, sea lions—of any site in the Sea of Cortez. Only Baja Expeditions leads Santa Cruz and Animas dives at the moment.

As elsewhere in the Sea of Cortez, the optimum diving months are May-Aug., when visibility reaches 30 meters (100 feet) or more and water temperatures run around 27° C (80° F). In September tropical storms are an obstacle and during the late fall and winter months high winds and changing currents reduce visibility to 10-15 meters (35-50 feet). A light wetsuit is necessary any time except June-August.

Operated by a Mexican-Japanese couple, **Baja Quest,** Sonora 174 (between Topete and Rangel), tel. (1) 123-5320, fax (1) 123-5321, e-mail: bajaqust@balandra.uabcs.mx, offers four-night, three-day dive-trip packages, including hotel and airport transfers, for US$325-743 depending on hotel and number of people. It can also arrange customized live-aboard dive packages in the Sea of Cortez May-Oct., with stops at Isla Espíritu Santo, El Bajo, San Francisquito, Las Animas, and Isla Cerralvo. Accommodation consists of two nights at a hotel and two nights aboard the *Garota.* During the five-day trip, three days of diving and all meals, refreshments, and beer are included. Prices run US$653-767 depending on hotel and number of people. Another package consisting of three nights on board, two nights at a hotel, and four days of diving costs US$775-870. Baja Quest also organizes five-day dive-cruise and camping combinations (May-Oct. only) for US$799 pp.

Other dive operators in town include: **Scuba Baja Joe,** Ocampo and Obregón 460, tel. (1) 122-4006, fax (1) 122-4000; **Scubaja,** Nicolás Bravo and Obregón, tel./fax (1) 122-7423, e-mail: info@scubaja.com; **Centro de Buceo Carey** Vista Coral 17, tel./fax (1) 123-2333; **Sea and Scuba** Obregón 460, Suite 208 at Ocampo, tel. (1) 123-5233; and **Toto's Dive Shop and Service,** on Guerrero between Revolución de 1910 and Serdán, tel. (1) 122-7154, fax (1) 123-4521.

Diving equipment and airfills are sold at **Deportiva La Paz,** Paseo Obregón 1680, tel./fax (1) 122-7333. The shop doesn't organize dive trips.

Cycling
Katún, Paseo Obregón 460, Local 204, tel. (1) 123-4888, rents Trek 903 mountain bikes for US$7 an hour or US$10 for three hours. The proprietors will supply handdrawn maps of local bike trails with any rental on request.

Biciclettas Dino, on the east side of Obregón, north of Calle Nayarit, stocks bicycle parts and offers repair service.

Organized Tours
Contactours, Obregón 460, second floor, tel. (1) 123-2212, between Ocampo and Degollado, organizes several package land tours in the La Paz area. The "city tour" takes you through the downtown area, stopping at a pottery factory, a weaver, a couple of museums, the cathedral, shops, and the public market. The 10 a.m.-4 p.m. tour costs US$15. The company also organizes beach tours, whalewatching tours, and snorkeling/diving tours through the auspices of Scubaja.

INFORMATION AND SERVICES

Tourist Offices
Baja California Sur's **Coordinación Estatal de Turismo** office lies between Km 6 and 5 on Mexico 1 (Av. Abasolo) opposite the Crowne Plaza Resort, tel. (1) 124-0100 or 124-0103, fax (1) 124-0722, e-mail: turismo@lapaz.cromwell.com.mx. The friendly staff speaks English and can assist with most tourist inquiries; the Attorney for the Protection of Tourists is also stationed here. The office maintains an information booth on the *malecón* near Calle 16 de Septiembre, where you can pick up maps and brochures. Office and booth are open Mon.-Sat. 8 a.m.-7 p.m.

Newspapers
Two Spanish-language dailies are published in La Paz: *Diario Peninsular* and *El Sudcaliforniano.* Neither is any great shakes as Mexican newspapers go.

Librería Contempo, a bookstore on Calle Arrival at Paseo Obregón, carries *The News* and *Mexico City Times* from Mexico City as well as a few American magazines.

Changing Money
Several banks and moneychangers can be found on Calle 16 de Septiembre near the *malecón.* As elsewhere in Baja, the banks provide currency-exchange service only Mon.-Fri. before noon. Both Bancomer and Banamex have ATMs.

Moneychangers *(casas de cambio)* stay open till early evening and on Saturday but are closed on Sunday, when your only alternative is to change money at a hotel at lower rates. Pesos are a must for everyday purchases in La Paz; city merchants are not as receptive to U.S.-dollar transactions as their counterparts in Cabo San Lucas simply because they're not as used to them.

USEFUL LA PAZ
TELEPHONE NUMBERS

La Paz area code: 1
Police: 122-0781
Fire Department: 122-7474
Red Cross: 122-1111
Green Angels: 125-9677
Highway Patrol: 122-0369
IMSS Hospital: 122-7377
Tourist Attorney: 122-5939
State Tourism Office: 124-0100 or 124-0103
Immigration: 124-6349
Ferry Office: 125-4666
COTP: 122-0243 or 122-4037

The local American Express representative is **Turismo La Paz,** Calle Esquerro 1679 (behind Hotel Perla and just around the corner from Hotel Plaza Real), tel. (1) 122-8300 or 122-7676, fax (1) 125-5272. Hours for AmEx service are Mon.-Fri. 9 a.m.-2 p.m. and 4-6 p.m., Saturday 9 a.m.-2 p.m.

Post, Telephone, and Courier
The main post and telegraph office is at Revolución and Constitución, a block northeast of the cathedral; open Mon.-Fri. 8 a.m.-1 p.m. and 3-7 p.m., Saturday 8 a.m.-1 p.m.

DHL, Av. Abasolo at Nayarit, tel. (1) 125-3994 or 122-6987, is the most reliable courier service in the city. The company will pick up packages at no extra charge.

E-mail and Internet Access
Baja Net (www.baja.net.mx) maintains an Internet café at Calle Madero 430, tel. (1) 125-9380, where you can use its computer terminals and pay by the hour or by the year.

Language Courses
If you'd like to study Spanish while you're in La Paz, **Centro de Idiomas, Cultura y Comunicación (CICC),** Calle Madero 2460 and Legaspy, tel. (1) 125-7554, fax (1) 125-7388, e-mail: cicclapaz@yahoo.com, offers classes at all levels, from beginner to advanced. The standard course costs US$1,386 and includes four weeks of intensive classes (25 hours per week),

a homestay with a Mexican family, two meals per day, airport transfer, study material, and all related excursions and activities. Longer or shorter courses, or courses without a homestay, can be arranged.

Laundry
If you need to do some laundry, **La Paz Lava** at Ocampo Pte. and Mutualismo is a good choice. This clean, modern self-service laundromat is within walking distance of the *malecón,* so you can stroll along the waterfront while waiting for your clothes. La Paz Lava also provides delivery service to home or hotel.

Immigration
If you're planning to cross the Sea of Cortez by ferry and haven't yet validated your tourist card, stop by the immigration office on Paseo Obregón between Allende and Juárez, tel. (1) 124-6349. It's usually open Mon.-Fri. 9 a.m.-5 p.m. The immigration office at the airport is open seven days a week, while the one at the Pichilingue ferry terminal is open only an hour or so before each ferry departure.

GETTING THERE

By Air
Márquez de León International Airport (LAP) is 12 km south of the city; the airport access road leaves Mexico 1 at Km 9. Although it's a small airport, facilities include a couple of gift shops, two snack bars, rental car booths, LADATEL phones (cards available for purchase from the snack bar), and a fax/telegraph service.

La Paz's principal air carrier, **Aero California,** on Obregón, between Bravo and Ocampo, tel. (1) 125-1023, flies daily to and from Chihuahua, Culiacán, Guadalajara, Hermosillo, Los Mochis, Mazatlán, Monterrey, and Tijuana, along with connecting flights from Los Angeles and Mexico City.

Aeroméxico, Paseo Obregón between Hidalgo y Costilla and Morelos, tel. (1) 124-6366 or 124-6367 (arrival and departure information), or tel. (1) 122-0092 (reservations only), offers daily nonstop flights to La Paz from Culiacán, Guaymas, Mexico City, and Tijuana, as well as connecting flights from Guadalajara and Phoenix.

Subsidiary **Aerolitoral,** tel. (800) 3-6202 toll-free in Mexico, tel. (800) 237-6639 in the U.S., offers nonstops from Ciudad Obregón, Hermosillo, Loreto, Los Mochis, and Mazatlán, and connecting flights from Chihuahua and Monterrey.

Alaska Airlines, tel. (800) 426-0333 in the U.S., fields nonstop flights to/from Los Angeles with connecting flights to/from Seattle.

Airport Transportation: A company called **Transporte Terrestre** operates yellow-and-white vans between the city and the airport. The standard fare is US$8 *colectivo* (shared), US$14 private service for up to four persons. A regular taxi to the airport should cost around US$15. Some hotels operate airport vans that charge just US$3-4 pp.

By Land
Intercity Bus: From the **Central Camionera,** Calle Jalisco at Av. Independencia, **Águila,** tel. (1) 122-7898, runs northbound buses to Ciudad Constitución (US$8, hourly 7 a.m.-8 p.m.), Puerto San Carlos (US$10, twice daily), Puerto López Mateos (US$11, once daily), Loreto (US$15, twice daily), Mulegé (US$21, twice daily), Santa Rosalía (US$23, twice daily), San Ignacio (US$30, twice daily), Vizcaino Junction (US$34, twice daily), Guerrero Negro (US$36, twice daily), San Quintín (US$54, twice daily), Ensenada (US$56, four times daily), Tijuana (US$69, three times daily), Tecate (US$72, three times daily), and Mexicali (US$79, twice daily).

Southbound, Águila buses depart from the Terminal Malecón six times daily (8 a.m.-8:30 p.m.) to the central Cape Region towns of El Triunfo (US$2.50), San Antonio (US$2.60), San Bartolo (US$3.50), Los Barriles, (US$4), Santiago (US$5.50), and Miraflores (US$6), continuing on to San José del Cabo (US$10) and Cabo San Lucas (US$9). More direct buses to Cabo San Lucas via Todos Santos operate eight times daily between 6:30 a.m. and 7:30 p.m. for US$6. The fare as far as Todos Santos is US$2.75.

By Sea
The ferry port at Pichilingue, 16 km (9.5 miles) northeast of downtown La Paz via Mexico 11, serves vehicle and passenger ferries between La Paz and the mainland destinations of Topolobampo (for Los Mochis) and Mazatlán. **SEMATUR** runs the ferries on those routes. We've

heard of tentative plans to begin a new route between La Paz and Puerto Vallarta, replacing the old Cabo San Lucas-Puerto Vallarta ferry discontinued several years ago.

You can book SEMATUR ferry tickets in advance at: the ferry terminal, tel. (1) 122-9485; the city ticket office, Calle 5 de Mayo at Gmo. Prieto, tel. (1) 125-3833 or 125-4666, fax (1) 125-6588 (open Mon.-Fri. 8 a.m.-1 p.m. and 4-6 p.m., weekends 8 a.m.-1 p.m.); or Turismo La Paz, at the Hotel Perla, tel. (1) 122-7676 or 122-8300.

For fares and schedules, see By Ferry from Mainland Mexico in the On the Road chapter.

Vehicle Permits: A temporary vehicle import permit is necessary for vehicular travel on the Mexican mainland. These permits aren't needed for Baja California travel, but if you've driven down to La Paz and decide you'd like to take your wheels on a mainland-bound ferry, you'll need to get one before buying a ticket. The whole process operates more smoothly in Tijuana, so if you anticipate using the ferry service, doing the paperwork in advance will save time and hassle.

If for whatever reason you decide to take the ferry and haven't done the paperwork in advance, you can obtain the proper permit in La Paz from the **Aduana Maritima** office at the north end of the Pichilingue ferry terminal; open 9 a.m.-1 p.m. and 5-7 p.m. To receive the permit, you will need the original and three copies of your vehicle title or registration, a major credit card (in the vehicle owner's name), your driver's license, and your passport with valid Mexican visa. You can also try the Aduana Maritima office at Paseo Obregón and Ignacio Bañuelos, opposite the Muelle Turístico on the *malecón,* tel. (1) 122-0730, but applying at this office is usually a more cumbersome procedure than applying at the ferry office. The permit can usually be processed on the spot, but budget a couple of days anyway, just in case all the right bureaucrats aren't in.

Private Boats: La Paz is an official Mexican port of entry, so the COTP office near Marina Palmira has authority to clear yachts for movement throughout Mexican waters. Unless you plan to anchor outside, the easiest way to arrange this is to check in at Marina de La Paz or Marina Palmira and let the marina staff process all port clearance papers. For Marina de La Paz clients, clear-in service is free, clear-out is US$10; for nonclients the charges are US$5 in, US$15 out. Only one clearance in and out is required for entering and exiting the country; between Mexican ports the same papers can be presented. See Sports and Recreation, above, for information on La Paz marinas.

GETTING AROUND

You can reach most points of interest downtown on foot. For outlying areas, you can choose city buses or taxis, or rent a car.

City Bus

Regular city buses and *colectivos* radiate in all directions from the *zona comercial* surrounding the Mercado Municipal on Calle Degollado. Each bears the name of either the principal street along its run or the district where the route begins and ends. Any bus marked "El Centro," for example, will end up near the Mercado Municipal at Revolución and Degollado. Bus fare anywhere in town is around 25 cents.

From Terminal Malecón, Paseo Obregón 125, **Transportes Águila** runs 11 buses between La Paz and various points along Península de Pichilingue. Fares range from 55 cents to US$2.15 depending on your destination, and buses depart almost hourly 7 a.m.-7 p.m. Call (1) 122-7898 for more information.

Taxi

Taxis can be found throughout El Centro, the downtown area between Calles 5 de Mayo and Degollado (especially along the west end of Calle 16 de Septiembre in the shopping district), and in front of the tourist hotels. On the *malecón* (Paseo Obregón), the main taxi stands are in front of Hotel Los Arcos and Hotel Perla. The average taxi hire downtown costs around US$2-3. La Paz taxis don't have meters, so it's sometimes necessary to haggle to arrive at the correct fare.

Longer trips are more economical if you use a shared taxi van or *colectivo*. A *colectivo* from the Central Camionera to the center of town, for example, costs US$1.40 pp; by private taxi it's as much as US$5. Route taxis *(taxis de ruta)* operate along the main avenues parallel to city buses for 25-35 cents pp.

Car Rental

Several La Paz travel agencies can arrange auto rental, but rates are generally lower if you deal directly with a rental agency. Local agencies include: **Baja California Autorentas,** Obregón 826 (between Salvatierra and Victoria), tel. (1) 125-7662; **Avis,** on Av. Obregón between Pineda and Márquez de León, tel./fax (1) 122-2651; **Dollar,** at the corner of Obregón and Pineda, tel. (1) 122-6060, (1) fax 122-6040; **Budget,** at Obregón 582-1 between Hidalgo y Costilla and Morelos, tel. (1) 122-7655, fax (1) 123-3622, and at Obregón 1775, tel. (1) 122-7655, fax (1) 125-6686; **Hertz,** Paseo Obregón 2130-D, tel. (1) 122-5300 or 122-0919; and **Thrifty,** Paseo Obregón and Lerdo de Tejada, tel. (1) 123-5151 or 124-6365. Daily rental rates typically run higher than in Los Cabos, and companies tend to levy per-kilometer charges on top of the daily rate. All companies offer significant discounts for rentals of six days or more.

Avis, Budget, Thrifty, and Hertz operate service counters at La Paz International Airport.

Fuel: La Paz is blessed with seven Pemex stations, all offering Magna Sin (unleaded), Premium, and diesel.

Motor Scooter Rental

The **Moto Rentas Bermejo's** stand on the *malecón* right in front of Bermejo's Souvenir Shop, just north of Baja Diving Service, rents "motos" for an exorbitant US$12 per hour, US$35 for five hours, or US$50 per day.

SOUTHEAST OF LA PAZ

State highway BCS 286 begins south of La Paz off Mexico 1 (at Km 211) and leads southeast 43 km (26 miles) to the agricultural center of San Juan de los Planes. Along the way this paved road climbs over the northeastern escarpment of the Sierra de La Laguna (here sometimes given its own name, Sierra de las Cacachilas), then descends toward the coastal plains, offering a panoramic view of aquamarine Bahía de la Ventana and Isla Cerralvo in the distance. At the crest of the ridge you'll pass stands of live oak, several ranches, and the village of **La Huerta** (Km 17 on BCS 286). When the weather in La Paz seems intolerably hot, a drive up into the Sierra de las Cacachilas is a good way to cool off.

Bahía de la Ventana

At Km 38 a paved road branches northeast off BCS 286 and leads eight km (five miles) and 11 km (6.8 miles), respectively, to the fish camps of La Ventana and El Sargento on Bahía de la Ventana. Along the way it passes a small salt-works. Windsurfing is very good at La Ventana due to the strong northeasterlies channeled through Canal de Cerralvo to the north. Onshore and inshore fishing is good all the way along the L-shaped bay; farther offshore in the Canal de Cerralvo, catches of marlin, skipjack, and dorado are common in the summer months. The gently sloped beach offers easy small-boat launching. If you don't fish, the bayshore still makes a worthwhile destination for blessedly secluded camping, swimming, and snorkeling, especially in the spring and fall (summers are hot). Isla Cerralvo (see below) lies about 16 km (10 miles) offshore.

La Ventana Campground, along the beach just north of the village of La Ventana, offers simple tent/camper sites, trash barrels, toilets, and showers for US$3 a night. Boats can easily be beach-launched here; Dec.-March the campground is taken over by windsurfers. Many people are buying or leasing beach lots in the area and planting breeze-block cubes on them.

Construction has recently begun on the new **Ventana Bay Resort.** The resort reportedly will feature bungalow-style guest rooms set around a clubhouse, along with private residences, restaurants, a bar, pool, jacuzzi, tennis courts, and a full-service windsurfing and diving shop operated by Baja Adventures. For further information, contact Casa Miramar, tel. (1) 141-0271 in Buena Vista, U.S. tel. (800) 533-8452, e-mail: mr-bill@windriders.com.

Basic supplies are available in El Sargento, which boasts a Centro de Salud (public health

clinic), baseball diamond, soccer field, and a place where you can buy barrel gas.

San Juan de los Planes

Los Planes, as it's usually called, has several markets, a café, and around 1,500 inhabitants supported by farming (cotton, tomatoes, beans, and corn) or by fishing at nearby bays.

Bahía de los Muertos

This pretty, curved bay with primitive beach camping is reached by a graded road running east 21 km (13 miles) from San Juan de los Planes. Historians don't know why a 1777 Spanish map named this shore "Bay of the Dead," but the name gained substance when a Chinese ship beached here in 1885. The ship had been refused entry at La Paz harbor because the crew was suffering from yellow fever; after putting in at this bay, all 18 crewmen died. Mexican fishermen buried the bodies above the tideline and marked their graves with wooden crosses, a few of which still stand. In the early 20th century, a community of American farmers tried unsuccessfully to cultivate the desert surrounding the bay; some died of thirst or hunger, adding to the bay's list of *muertos.*

You can pitch a tent or sleep under the stars anywhere along the north end of Bahía de los Muertos for no charge.

Ensenada de los Muertos, an abandoned port at the north end of the bay, was built in the 1920s for the shipping of ore from El Triunfo mines in the Sierra de La Laguna.

Punta Arenas de la Ventana

A lesser road branches northeast about four km before Los Muertos and leads eight km (five miles) to beautiful Punta Arenas de la Ventana. Defunct until recently, **Las Arenas Resort,** 8080 La Mesa Blvd., Suite 205, La Mesa, CA 91941, U.S. tel. (619) 460-4319 or (888) 644-RESORT, fax (619) 460-4918, e-mail: info@lasarenas.com, has reopened under new ownership as an all-inclusive fishing and diving resort. Las Arenas offers 40 spacious beachfront suites with ceiling fans and large bathrooms; all open onto private balconies with ocean views. Fishing *pangas* are available for US$150-225 per day depending on size, while cruisers go for US$300-325 per day. Tackle rents for US$10 pp per day, and fishing licenses are available at the resort for US$8 per day or US$15 per week. The resort will fillet and freeze your catch for free. Transportation between the La Paz airport and Las Arenas is available for US$45 pp roundtrip, or US$315 roundtrip for one to four people from the Los Cabos airport (group discounts available). Rates: US$100 pp single occupancy, US$80 pp double occupancy, additional persons US$35 per night. All rates include three meals per day but do not include tax (12%) or service (10%).

The waters off Punta Arenas reputedly offer Baja's best roosterfish angling; wahoo, amberjack, grouper, dorado, and billfish are also in abundant supply. Guided *panga* trips may be available from the beach next to the resort, where local *pangeros* moor their boats, for US$50-75 per day. A bit south of the resort, off **Punta Perico** (Parakeet Point), is a lively reef with varied depths of 3-25 meters (10-82 feet).

Alternate Routes

Bahía de los Muertos can be reached from the south via a 47-km (29.5-mile) dirt road between Los Barriles and San Juan de los Planes. The road is wide and flat from Los Barriles as far as Punta Pescadero and El Cardonal—13 km (8.5 miles) and 22 km (13.5 miles), respectively. North of El Cardonal, the road begins to rise along the Mesa Boca Alamo, eventually cutting inland and ascending steeply into the jagged, red Sierra El Carrizalito. Several miles of the road here wind around narrow, adrenaline-pumping curves with steep drop-offs. Contrary to popular belief, 4WD is not a necessity for this section of road, but careful driving and good road clearance are. Twenty-four km (15 miles) from El Cardonal, the road leaves the mountains and meets the paved end of BCS 286.

San Juan de los Planes, La Ventana, Punta Arenas de la Ventana, and Bahía de los Muertos can also be reached from Mexico 1 via a graded, unpaved road from San Antonio. The road's east end begins on BCS 286 about 3.5 km (2.2 miles) south of the turnoff for La Ventana and El Sargento. See El Triunfo and San Antonio in the Central Cape section for details.

Isla Cerralvo

Across Bahía de la Ventana and Canal de Cerralvo lies Isla Cerralvo, one of the largest islands in the Sea of Cortez. At the time of early Spanish exploration, the island held large pearl-oyster beds and was inhabited by a small group of Pericú. Later the rugged island reportedly became a favored final resting place for the *vagabundos del mar,* Amerindians who roamed the Sea of Cortez in dugout canoes until well into the 20th century.

Today Cerralvo remains one of the least visited of Baja's large coastal islands, simply due to its location on the far side of the Península de Pichilingue. Coral-encrusted **Roca Montaña,** off the southeastern tip of the island, is an excellent diving and fishing location, as is **Piedras Gordas,** marked by a navigation light at the southwestern tip. Depths at these sites range 3-15 meters (10-50 feet). Other good dive sites include the rock reefs off the northern end (average depth 18-21 meters/60-70 feet), which feature a good variety of reef fishes, sea turtles, and shipwrecks. One of the reefs, **Arrecife de la Foca,** features an unidentified shipwreck with "Mazatlán" marked on the hull. **La Reina,** another reef at the north end of the island, is the site of a large steel-hulled freighter that sank half a century ago. Barely a hundred meters off the island's west shore are two adjacent rock reefs known as **La Reinita.**

Access to Isla Cerralvo is easiest from Bahía de la Ventana or Punta Arenas, where beach launches are possible. From La Paz, it's a long haul around the Península de Pichilingue via Canal de San Lorenzo.

CENTRAL CAPE

Along Mexico 1 between La Paz and San José del Cabo are a number of mining-turned-farming towns with cobblestone streets and 19th-century stone-and-stucco architecture. Nestled among well-watered arroyos in the Sierra de La Laguna, these neglected settlements now support themselves growing citrus, avocado, mangoes, corn, and sugarcane, and, to a lesser extent, serving the needs of passing travelers. Many of the families living in the central Cape Region are descended from Spanish settlers of the 18th and early 19th centuries. Others are newcomers—including a few Americans and Canadians—drawn by the area's solitude and simplicity.

SAN PEDRO TO SAN BARTOLO

San Pedro

This town of only 377 inhabitants appears—and quickly disappears—just before the junction of Mexico 1 and Mexico 19. *Carnitas* connoisseurs swear by **El Paraíso de San Pedro** and **Carnitas y Chicharones San Pedro,** two unassuming roadside cafés on the highway's west side. The junction itself is reached at Km 185; if Cabo San Lucas is your destination, you must decide whether to take Mexico 19 via Todos Santos or

the Transpeninsular Highway (Mexico 1) via El Triunfo, San Antonio, San Bartolo, Santiago, and Miraflores.

Unless you're in a hurry to reach Cabo San Lucas, Mexico 1 is the most scenic choice for drivers of autos and light trucks. South of San Pedro, Mexico 1 winds through the Sierra de La Laguna and features a succession of dizzying curves and steep grades. Hence for trailers, RVs, and other wide or lengthy vehicles, Mexico 19 is the better choice since it runs along relatively flat terrain.

El Triunfo and San Antonio

During the Jesuit missionary period, this section along the lower northern slopes of the sierra was earmarked for cattle ranching. But mining concessions moved in following the discovery of silver in 1748, and San Antonio quickly grew into a town of 10,000 people, many of them Yaqui laborers. Then known as Real de Minas de Santa Ana, it was the first nonmission town founded in Baja. The Spanish crown took over the mines in 1769 and struggled to turn a profit from a relatively low quality of ore. When Loreto was heavily damaged by a hurricane in 1829, San Antonio briefly served as capital of the Californias before the capital was transferred to La Paz in 1830.

In 1862 better gold and silver deposits were uncovered at El Triunfo (Triumph), seven km (4.5 miles) north of San Antonio. By 1878 the large Progreso mining concern had established seven gold and silver mines around the village, attracting a number of Mexican, French, English, Italian, German, and American immigrants. The company paid for the region's first post office and installed the first electrical and phone lines to La Paz.

Both San Antonio and El Triunfo bustled with frontier commerce through the end of the 19th century, when the ore began running out. Then a hurricane flooded the mines in 1918 and sounded the death knell; by 1925 both towns were virtually abandoned. Today El Triunfo has only around 400 residents, most of them involved in small-scale mining (extracting ore from leftover tailings) or the weaving of palm baskets. A few *artesanías* can be found on the main road through town. San Antonio, set in a lushly planted valley that descends eastward all the way to the Sea of Cortez, has developed into a farming community with around 800 residents, a Pemex station, post office, and a few markets.

A number of historic adobe buildings in both towns have been restored, including El Triunfo's Casa Municipal and San Antonio's unusual 1825 church exhibiting train and paddlewheeler motifs. A fun time to visit San Antonio is 13 June, the feast day of St. Anthony, when everyone from both San Antonio and El Triunfo turns out for music and dancing.

Near San Antonio, between Km 156 and 157, a road heads north off Mexico 1 and leads 22 km (13.6 miles) to BCS 286, the highway to San Juan de los Planes and La Paz. This is the shortest way to reach Bahía de los Muertos and La Ventana from the Central Cape. The road is signed for "Los Planes" coming from the south along Mexico 1, but not from the north. Although the road surface starts out with asphalt, it quickly becomes a wide, graded dirt road traversable by most vehicles. Once you hit BCS 286, turn left for La Paz, right for Los Planes and the Cortez coast.

San Bartolo
Beginning just past Km 128, San Bartolo (pop. 550) is the greenest and lushest of the central Cape settings, thanks to a large spring gushing straight out of a mountainside into the arroyo. To complete the tropical picture, many homes sport thatched roofs. Mangoes, avocados, and other fresh fruits are available at roadside stands or in town. **Restaurant Los Burritos, Restaurant El Paso,** and **Dulcería El Oasis** on the east side of the highway serve meals. El Oasis sells regional *dulces* made of fruit such as guava or mango, as well as homemade cheese, *empanadas, bistec ranchero,* quesadillas, and the coldest beer in town.

San Bartolo's patron saint day is 19 June, conveniently close to San Antonio's.

From San Bartolo, a 26-km unpaved road follows an arroyo lined with huge *güeribos* to the tiny settlement of **San Antonio de la Sierra.** This

desert ornamented with agave

arroyo in turn leads to the arroyo and ranch settlement of **Santo Domingo,** where rustic ranch furniture, leather, and fruit candy are produced.

RV Park: Relatively new **Rancho Verde RV Haven,** between Km 143 and 142, Mexico 1, tel. (888) 516-9462 in the U.S., e-mail ranchoverdebill@aol.com, offers 3,100 acres of mountain desert wilderness for camping, biking, or just taking time out during a transpeninsular road journey. Spaces cost US$11 with full hookups and hot showers, or US$7 if you're self-contained. This admits up to three persons per site; a fourth is charged US$2 per night, and children under 10 stay free. Food service isn't ordinarily available, but the friendly Mexican staff can prepare simple *antojitos* on request.

SANTIAGO

The largest of the central Cape Region towns, Santiago (pop. 2,500) was founded as Misión de Santiago el Apóstol in 1723 by Italian padre Ignacio María Nápoli. The mission was abandoned in the latter half of the 18th century following a series of Pericú rebellions, and only in relatively recent times has agriculture revived the arroyo community.

A two-km road flanked by vegetable plots, leafy fruit orchards, and blue fan palms leads west from Mexico 1 (Km 85) across the wide, flat Arroyo de Santiago, dividing the town into Loma Norte and Loma Sur (North and South Slopes). Santiago and environs serves the region as an important source of palm leaves for making *palapa* roofs. *Palmeros* claim the fan-shaped fronds are best cut during a full moon, as rising sap makes the palm leaves last longer. Properly dried and stored, 250 palm leaves equals one *carga* or load, for which the *palmeros* receive US$30-50 depending on leaf quality.

Various *tiendas* line the town plaza; the town also offers a Pemex station, hotel, supermarket stocked with local fruit and vegetables, post office, telegraph office, church, and the only zoo on the peninsula south of Mexicali.

Among the residents of the small but nicely landscaped **Parque Zoológico** are a peccary, bear, coyote, fox, monkey, parrots, and ducks. Some of the animals are Cape Region natives. The park is open daily 6 a.m.-6 p.m. in summer,

till 5 p.m. the rest of the year. Admission is free, though donations are gladly accepted. To bypass the town center and proceed directly to the zoo, take the left fork just after crossing the dry arroyo near the town entrance, then take the next left fork onto a levee road that curves along the south end of town to the zoo.

Also in town, a small, rustic museum adjacent to the church at the corner of Calzada Misioneros and Calle Victoria contains colonial artifacts and local fossils. It's open Mon.-Fri. 8 a.m.-1 p.m.; free admission.

Santiago celebrates its patron saint day, the feast day of St. James, on 25 July.

Accommodations and Food
Budget: Casa de Huéspedes Palomar, tel. (1) 122-0604, south of the plaza on the east side of Calzada Misioneros, offers six tidy rooms around a courtyard for US$16 s/d a night. The Palomar's highly regarded restaurant, decorated with local fossils, serves seafood, enchiladas, and burgers Mon.-Sat. 11:30 a.m.-8 p.m. Entrées start at US$6; *pescado mojo de ajo,* fish cooked in garlic butter, is a house specialty. At last pass the only sign we saw out front simply read "Restaurant Bar."

Vicinity of Santiago
The dirt road to the zoo continues southwest nine km (5.5 miles) to the village of **Agua Caliente** (also known as Los Manantiales), where a hot spring in a nearby canyon (about seven km, four miles west of the village) has been channeled into a concrete tub for recreational purposes. Camping is permitted in the canyon. Ask directions to two other hot springs in the area: **El Chorro** (west of Agua Caliente) and **Santa Rita** (north). The network of roads behind Santiago passes through dense thornforest in some spots and it's easy to get lost unless you keep a compass on hand or a good fix on the sun. If you can bring along a copy of the Mexican topographic map for this area (Santiago 12B34), all the better; each of these locales is clearly marked. Do not attempt these roads at night. If you continue south along the sandy road past Agua Caliente, you'll reach the town of Miraflores after 8.7 km (5.4 miles).

At the north end of Santiago, another dirt road leads northwest to **Rancho San Dionísio** (23.5

To
Cañon San Dionisio
and La Laguna

To
El Triunfo
and La Paz

▲ Cerro el Tepetate

Palo Verde

Santiago

GRADED
ROAD

SANTA RITA
(HOT SPRINGS) ■

El Encinal

San Jorge

San Jorge

Mesa Cerralvo

1

Agua Caliente

Las Cabras

EL CHORRO
(HOT SPRINGS) ■

Agua
Caliente

Las Escobas

Las
Vinoramas

Mesa las Vinoramas

Cerro la Ventanita ▲

**SANTIAGO
TO MIRAFLORES**

To
Cañon San Bernardo

Boca de la Sierra

GRADED ROAD

0   2 mi

0   2 km

Miraflores

AIRSTRIP ✈

El
Ranchito

San Martín

Mesa el Capulín

La Tinaja

1

Mesa los Difuntos

GRADED
ROAD

MOON

Caduaño

Boca de la Sierra

To
Cañon San Pablo

To
San José del Cabo

© AVALON TRAVEL PUBLISHING

km/14.5 miles), where the Cañon San Dionísio approach to Picacho La Laguna begins. See Sierra de La Laguna, below, for sierra hiking details.

At **Las Cuevas,** five km (3.1 miles) northeast of Santiago on Mexico 1 (around Km 93), is the turnoff to La Ribera and the East Cape.

Three km south of Santiago, a large painted cement sphere marks the **Tropic of Cancer** (latitude 23.5° N), south of which you are "in the tropics." As if to sanctify the crossing, an impressive Guadalupe shrine has been built next to the rather unattractive marker.

MIRAFLORES

A 2.5-km (1.5-mile) paved road to Miraflores branches west off Mexico 1 at Km 71 next to a Pemex station. This ranching and farming community is known for leatherwork; **Curtiduría Miraflores** (Miraflores Tannery), just off the access road between the highway and town (look for a small sign reading "Leather Shop" on the north side of the road), sells handmade leather saddles, bridles, whips, horsehair lariats, and other ranching gear, as well as a few souvenir items such as leather hats, belts, and bags, and the occasional bleached cow skull.

Owned and operated by the Beltrán family, the tannery is particularly known for its rustic ranch saddles. One saddle may use up to eight cowhides, each tanned in the traditional *sudcaliforniano* manner with local palo blanco bark and powdered *quebrache,* a reddish-brown, tannin-rich extract from a type of dogbane tree grown on the mainland. Saddle frames are fashioned out of local woods—*ciruelo, copal*—or *cardón* skeletons. Custom orders are accepted. The *curtiduría* also sells engraved knives made from salvaged car springs—a source of particularly strong metal for knife blades—and sheathed in handtooled leather.

Miraflores honors the Virgin of Guadalupe as its patron saint, so Fiesta Guadalupana (12 December), celebrated throughout Mexico, is especially fervent here.

Food
Restaurant Las Bugambilias, a small five-table *palapa* restaurant on the road into town, serves tasty *burritos de machaca,* fish, *cocteles,* and ice-cold beer. The house *salsa picante* is *maravillosa* and the jukebox is well-stocked. Open daily except Tuesday 10 a.m.-10 p.m.

Restaurant Miraflores, next to Mini Super El Nidito near the market and plaza, makes good tacos with shrimp, fish, or beef. Several *mercaditos* in town provide local produce and *machaca.*

Vicinity of Miraflores
A dirt road northwest of Miraflores leads to **Boca de la Sierra** (Mouth of the Sierra), a settlement at the mouth of Cañon San Bernardo—the second of the three canyons providing access deep into the Sierra de La Laguna (see below). *Ejido* farms in the Boca de la Sierra area cultivate vegetables and herbs—especially sweet basil—for Cape Region supermarkets and restaurants as well as for export to the United States.

Another dirt road southwest of town leads to the mouth of Cañon San Pablo, a third Laguna hiking route. Inquire at the tannery about guided trips into the sierra to view Indian rock-art sites.

SIERRA DE LA LAGUNA

The mountainous heart of the Cape Region extends southward from the Llano de La Paz (the plains just south of La Paz) to Cabo San Lucas, a distance of around 135 km (81 miles). Originally called Sierra de La Victoria by the Spanish, the interior mountains were renamed Sierra de La Laguna in the early Mexican era. These peaks are unique among sierras in the southern half of Baja California in that they're granitic rather than volcanic. And unlike the sierras to the north, the entire Laguna range is tilted eastward instead of westward, i.e., its steepest slopes are on the west side of the escarpment rather than the east.

Picacho de La Laguna (elevation 2,161 meters/7,090 feet), roughly in the sierra's center, is usually cited as the highest peak in the range, although according to some sources **Cerro las Casitas**—approximately 6.5 km (four miles) southeast of Picacho de La Laguna and measuring 2,083 meters (6,835 feet) by most accounts—may be higher. Between these two peaks is a large, flat meadow called **La Laguna** (elevation 1,707 meters/5,600 feet). This depression held a mountain lake until around 1870, when Cañon San Dionísio became sufficiently eroded to drain away accumulated water.

The sierra flora has been little researched; the most recent detailed studies were undertaken in the 1890s by botanist T.S. Brandegee for the California Academy of Sciences. The foothills and mesas below 500 meters are covered with dry *matorral*—low-growing cacti, succulents, thornscrub, and abundant herbs. Common species include barrel cactus, cholla, *palo verde,* ironwood, damiana, and oregano. Canyon walls may be draped with *zalate* (wild fig). At elevations of 500-750 meters, tropical-subtropical deciduous forest and columnar cacti are the dominant flora (e.g., *mauto,* palo blanco, prickly pear, *cardón, palo adán*). From 750 to 1,200 meters, live-oak woodlands (encino, madrone) dominate, and above 1,200 meters a mix of live oak and piñon pine prevails. At its highest elevations, the La Laguna qualifies as a cloud forest during the moist summer months, when the peaks are consistently shrouded in mist or rain.

Islands in the Sky

The range's highlands receive more annual precipitation—up to 89 cm (35 inches) per year in some microclimates—than any other place in Baja California. As a result, the meadow of La Laguna and other flats and high canyons in the sierra contain a number of "relic environments" preserving flora and fauna long ago lost on the arid plains below.

These "islands in the sky" support a mix of desert, tropical, and subalpine plant species that are found together nowhere else in North America. Among the unlikely combinations seen growing side by side: mosses and cacti, madrone and monkey flower, palm and willow. Of the 447 plant species known to grow in the sierra, at least 70 are reportedly indigenous. Undisturbed by human progress, deer, coyote, mountain lion, Pacific tree frog, and dozens of hummingbird species also thrive in the highland areas of the sierra.

For many years, naturalists and outdoor enthusiasts clamored for the upper sierra to be declared a national park or preserve, and in June 1994 the Mexican government finally granted the Sierra de La Laguna official recognition as a "biosphere reserve." Such status prohibits development within the reserve's 32,519-hectare

core zone; local ranchers are permitted to graze livestock in a buffer zone surrounding the protected core.

Hiking and Backpacking

The Sierra de La Laguna is a popular hiking area for Cape residents, as it offers the opportunity to leave behind the fig trees and palms of the arid-tropical environment for a walk among cottonwoods and subalpine meadows. Three lengthy east-west canyons—Cañon Dionísio, Cañon San Bernardo, and Cañon San Pablo—provide the principal access into the sierra. All three routes enable hikers to cross the sierra's spine from east to west or vice versa. Primitive campsites are available along each of the three routes.

The northernmost and most popular route, via Cañon San Dionísio, leads directly to La Laguna, the range's largest and highest meadow. La Laguna lies at an altitude of just under 1,800 meters (6,000 feet), between Picacho de La Laguna and Cerro las Casitas, the sierra's tallest peaks. The scenery on this hike is impressive. A straight traverse of this route, starting from either side, is possible in three days, although this would allow little time for taking it easy. Add at least a day to these estimates to allow some time to enjoy La Laguna once you've reached it.

Cañon San Dionísio:
Western (Todos Santos) Approach

Most hikers ascend to La Laguna from the west side, which is a steeper but more straightforward hike (and about two km shorter) than from Rancho San Dionísio. Unlike the network of cattle trails on the east side—which are best negotiated with local guides—the western ascent can be easily accomplished without a guide. From the west side a roundtrip can be completed in two days.

Near Todos Santos, the sandy road to La Burrera leaves Mexico 19 about 100 meters south of the Punta Lobos turnoff. Past an old water tower, take the first left and continue straight through several intersections till the road ends at a gate and parking area. From the gate, follow the dirt road till you reach La Burrera (about 25 minutes away), where you'll see a sign in English advising hikers to follow marked trails (ironic since we've never seen any marked trails in the sierra). Also known as San Juan del

Aserradero, this village on the sierra's western slopes lies around 17.5 km (11 miles) northeast of Todos Santos. Continue along this road another 20 minutes or so till you see a clearing on the right that has been used for camping; look for a sign reading "No tire basura" (Don't throw trash). Just past this sign, the road ascends to a small rise, at the top of which the main trail begins. After 30 meters or so of easy grade, the trail begins its long, steady climb straight up the mountain. Following this wide, established (rutted in places), 11-km (seven-mile) trail, you should reach La Laguna in five to eight hours, depending on your pace. Along the way the vegetation changes quickly from desert and thornforest into lush piñon-oak woodlands; about 20 minutes before you reach La Laguna the forest canopy opens up to magnificent views of the sierra and Pacific Ocean.

Follow the arroyo that drains La Laguna at its southeast corner, near where the trail comes in from Rancho San Dionísio, to reach a 20-meter (66-foot) cascade with deep pools suitable for swimming.

The return descent along the same trail takes about four hours to reach La Burrera.

If you need a ride to La Burrera from Todos Santos, your best bet is to inquire at Siempre Vive (at the corner of Calles Juárez and Márquez de León) in the late morning, when ranchers from the western sierra sometimes turn up for supplies and gossip. Fees for such a ride are negotiable—some ranchers will give you a lift for gas money and a six pack of Tecate, others ask up to US$30. You might also inquire at the Todos Santos taxi stand next to the town park.

Cañon San Dionísio:
Eastern (Santiago) Approach

From the east side of the sierra, count on three to four days to La Laguna and back with time to explore the area. The eastern mouth of the main canyon is reached via a dirt road to Rancho San Dionísio from Santiago (19 km/12 miles). From there it's a 13-km (eight-mile) hike west through the canyon mouth, then into a side arroyo and finally along the southern rim of the canyon to La Laguna. Piñon pine and Cape live oak began appearing about two-thirds of the way up. This trail is relatively difficult to follow and is intersected by potentially confusing animal paths; a guide, available at Rancho San Dionísio or in Santiago, is highly recommended. If you decide to go it alone, be sure to carry a topo map and compass, and watch out for cattle trails branching off the main trail in every direction. Scout ahead at questionable junctions, even if it means going slower. Once you're up on the ridgeline you should be able to spot La Laguna in the distance and then confidently follow any trail heading in that direction.

Those wishing to explore a bit can follow the canyon four km straight west of the ranch into a steep area of boulders; where the arroyo forks there's a 20-meter (66-foot) waterfall and deep pools suitable for swimming. Don't attempt to follow the canyon all the way to the meadow unless you're into some very serious bouldering and scrambling.

Near the northwest edge of the meadow itself are a couple of herder's shacks. Just past these the trail cuts into the forest and divides; the southern branch descends to La Burrera, while the north branch ascends Picacho de La Laguna, a 90-minute hike away. (A lesser third trail leads to an arroyo with fresh water.) Easy to climb, the peak is bare of trees and provides splendid views of the surrounding terrain. Closer to the meadow, a hill surmounted by radio towers also makes a good vantage point.

Those wishing to traverse the sierra can descend westward from La Laguna another 11 km (seven miles) to La Burrera; see Western (Todos Santos) Approach, above. About 20 minutes into the descent from the meadow, you'll come upon terrific views all the way to the Pacific Ocean. Roads from La Burrera meet Mexico 19 south and north of Todos Santos; the area east of these junctions is honeycombed with other dirt roads, but if you continue in a westerly direction you'll eventually come to the highway.

The **Asociación Nacional de Guías en Ecoturismo y Turismo de Aventura**, Calle Bravo y Rubio, La Paz, tel. (1) 125-2277, fax (1) 125-8599, offers a five-day camping trek across the sierra from Santiago via Cañon San Dionísio, with a side trip into scenic Cañon de las Zorras. The trip costs around US$800 pp, with a minimum of six participants; this does not include transportation to La Paz, and you must bring your own sleeping bag.

SIERRA DE LA LAGUNA HIKING TRAILS

Cañon San Bernardo

The next route to the south, via Cañon San Bernardo, is a relatively easy (from east to west) hike that crests at around 900 meters (3,000 feet). The canyon trailhead is accessible via an eight-km (five-mile) dirt road from Miraflores to Boca de la Sierra, where the trail skirts a dam and follows the canyon to the crest, 16 km (10 miles) northwest. Several pools along the way provide fresh water year-round. From the 900-meter crest, the trail continues over the sierra to the village of Santo Domingo on the western side, for a total traverse of 22.5 km (14 miles). The Cañon San Bernardo crossing makes a

good four- to five-day hike, although it's possible to make a quick overnight to the crest and back from the eastern approach.

Cañon San Pablo

Cañon San Pablo provides the southernmost route into the sierra, reaching an elevation of around 1,000 meters (3,250 feet). The canyon mouth is best approached by taking a 6.5-km (four-mile) dirt road west from Caduaño, a village four km (2.5 miles) south of Miraflores, to Rancho El Salto. From Rancho El Salto, it's approximately 10.5 km (6.5 miles) to the crest; the trail continues over the ridge and along a steeper 4.8-km (three-mile) westward descent to the village of El Güerigo on the other side, where a network of dirt roads leads west to Mexico 19. A leisurely El Salto-El Güerigo hike takes four to five days.

Seasons

The best backpacking season here is late fall, after the rainy season has passed and sierra streams and *tinajas* are full. Temperatures above 1,500 meters (5,000 feet) typically measure 12-22° C (54-72° F) during the day, 5-12° C (41-54° F) at night. In January and February, temperatures can dip below freezing at night, while daytime temps run around 10-20° C (50-68° F).

The warmest temperatures are usually encountered in May and June, when the mercury reaches around 25° C (77° F) during the day, 10-15° C (50-60° F) at night. Although the scenery isn't as spectacularly green this time of year, it's a fine time to beat the heat down on the coastal plains.

July-Oct. rains may wash out trails and flood the canyons. Rainfall peaks in August, averaging 7.5 cm (three inches) but sometimes reaching a drenching 20 cm (7.8 inches) for the month.

Supplies

A compass and good topographic map are musts for any trip into the Sierra de La Laguna. To cover all three routes, you should possess copies of Mexico's relevant 1:50,000-scale topos: El Rosario F12B23; Las Cuevas F12B24; Todos Santos F12B33; and Santiago F12B34. (See Hiking and Backpacking in the On the Road chapter for recommended map sources.) Bring warm clothing and sleeping bags for the summit; morning frost isn't uncommon even in fall and spring. Long pants and sturdy hiking shoes are

recommended as a defense against the abundant cactus and nettles.

On the Cañon San Dionísio trail, bring all the water you'll need to reach La Laguna, as there are no dependable sources on the way up, even in wet weather. An arroyo at La Laguna itself carries water year-round. On the Cañon San Bernardo trail, pools of water can be found along the way year-round. Water may be available from ranchos along the Cañon San Pablo trail, but bring your own to be safe. Be sure to use a water-purification system of some kind on all water sources in the mountains; although the water is generally uncontaminated, the presence of livestock precludes absolute safety.

Guides

For eastern ascents into the sierra, those unsure of their backpacking and orientation skills should consider hiring a local guide, since trails across the eastern escarpment are often obscured and junctions not always obvious. A guide can also prepare simple camp meals and point out items of natural interest—Amerindian rock art, flora and fauna—that first-timers might otherwise miss. Guides are available in Santiago and Miraflores; simply ask around. For the Cañon San Dionísio route, you can sometimes arrange a guide at Rancho San Dionísio, just before the eastern trailhead.

The going rate for guides in Santiago is US$20-25 per day pp, plus an extra US$10 per day per pack animal. Rancho San Dionísio charges US$20 for a guide without mules, no matter how many people are hiking.

Many hikers make the western approach to Cañon San Dionísio from Todos Santos without a guide; the main difficulty is finding your way (or arranging a ride) to the trailhead. If you

decide you want to hire a guide, inquire at the Sierra de La Laguna Water Co., just northeast of Todos Santos on the highway to La Paz. The water company should be able to arrange a trip with the very competent and personable Davíd Saisa, who lives near La Burrera at Rancho San Martín. Señor Saisa charges US$30 per day, more if you take along horses or burros as pack animals. Another guide in Todos Santos, Jesús Arballo, can be contacted at the corner of Calles Pedrajo and Villarino, tel. (1) 145-0180.

Driving Across the Sierra

Visitors with sturdy, high-clearance vehicles may be able traverse the Sierra de La Laguna in dry weather via a road that leaves Mexico 1 about 16 km (10 miles) south of Miraflores (about eight km, five miles north of Santa Anita) near Km 55. Among gringo road hogs this route is often called the "Naranjas road"; the correct name is Ramal Los Naranjos (*naranjo* means "orange tree," a probable reference to the many small citrus farms in the area). Because parts of it may suffer from washouts, this is not a road to tackle during the rainy season (July-Sept.), and any time of year you should make inquiries to determine whether the road is clear all the way.

From the Mexico 1 turnoff the road leads west-northwest 42 km (26 miles) to the village of **El Aguaje,** past the *ranchitos* of San Miguelito, Cieneguita, San Pedro de la Soledad, and El Remudadero. The ungraded road runs past a couple of 1,500- to 1,800-meter (5,000- to 6,000-foot) peaks before cresting at around 1,035 meters (3,400 feet) and descending into a challenging set of sharp curves and grades approaching 30%. At 27 km (17 miles) from Mexico 1 you'll get your first view of the Pacific Ocean, by which point the road begins hugging the edge of a rock mountain. Shortly thereafter the road may be washed out or blocked by rock slides and you may not be able to continue further. The track eventually widens to a graded, gravel road near El Aguaje, then continues another 12.8 km (eight miles) before terminating at Mexico 19 near Playa Los Cerritos south of Todos Santos. Two INEGI topo maps, San José del Cabo F12B44 and La Candelaria F12B43, would make helpful—though not required—companions on this cross-sierra road trip.

EAST CAPE

The Cabo del Este (East Cape) consists of a succession of scenic arid-tropical coves and beaches extending from the northern end of Bahía de Palmas south to San José del Cabo, at the tip of the cape.

Beach camping is available along almost the entire length of the coast, although the area is developing gradually and some of the prettiest beaches now bear small-scale housing developments. Coastal development, in fact, is ongoing from Buena Vista all the way around the Cape to Cabo San Lucas, with land prices skyrocketing in recent years. Fortunately, a few choice spots remain where the fishing (some of the best in the world) and camping are free. The coastline north of Los Barriles as far as Bahía de los Muertos remains relatively untouched.

BAHÍA DE PALMAS

The gently curving shore of Bahía de Palmas, stretching 32 km (20 miles) from Punta Pescadero south to Punta Arenas, began its commercial life in the 1960s as a fishing resort accessible only by yacht or private plane. Now that the Transpeninsular Highway swerves to within a couple of miles of the bay, it has become a full-fledged, drive-in fishing and windsurfing mecca.

In many places along the bay, anglers can reach the 100-fathom line less than a mile from shore, especially toward Punta Pescadero (Fisherman's Point) at the north end. Billfish frequent the area June-Dec., yellowtail Jan.-June, and roosterfish, wahoo, tuna, and dorado year-round (best in summer, however). Inshore catches include pargo, cabrilla, grouper, amberjack, wahoo, and pompano, plus the occasional yellowtail or rooster. The world-famous "Tuna Canyon," about 6.5 km (four miles) directly south of Punta Pescadero, reaches depths of 50 fathoms and has a year-round population of sizable yellowfin tuna; rocks along Tuna Canyon's submerged walls tend to cut the lines of all but the most skilled sportfishers. Guided fishing trips can be arranged at any of the hotels along the bay; the cost is generally US$80-150 a day for a *panga,* US$200-325 a day aboard a fishing cruiser. You can launch trailered or cartopped boats off sandy beaches or at the boat ramp just north of the Hotel Buena Vista Beach Resort (see Buena Vista, below).

Sailboarders flock to Los Barriles Nov.-April when sideshore winds—collectively called El Norte and aided by thermals from the Sierra de La Laguna—blow 18-30 knots for weeks at a time. The rest of the year, you'll have to settle for around 12-14 knots—not too shabby. During the high-wind season, inshore water temperatures average around 22-24° C (72-75° F), with air temperatures in the 25-29° C (78-85° F) range. The same basic conditions can be found all the way north to El Cardonal. Several hotels on the bay rent windsurfing equipment and provide basic instruction.

With such favorable recreational conditions, it's little wonder legions of *norteamericano* anglers, boaters, and sailboarders are buying up property along the bay to build vacation and retirement homes. The Barriles-Buena Vista area is starting to look like a San Diego suburb. Several roads branch east off Mexico 1 between Km 110 and 105 to hotels and trailer parks—most owned by foreigners—scattered along the central section of Bahía de Palmas. Because zoning regulations are virtually nonexistent, construction varies from flimsy *palapa* extensions to impressive beach homes. Construction trash is unfortunately a common sight; in some spots an unmistakable stench indicates improper installation of cesspools. Those seeking more solitude and less development can head north of Los Barriles to Punta Pescadero at the northern end of Bahía de Palmas or farther north to El Cardonal.

PUNTA PESCADERO AND EL CARDONAL

The sandy, washboard road to Punta Pescadero and El Cardonal heads north from Los Barriles—look for a turnoff from Mexico 1 signed "El Cardonal." The road crosses a couple of arroyos that could be problematic in heavy rains.

Punta Pescadero

At the extreme north end of Bahía de Palmas (13.6 km/8.5 miles north of Los Barriles), **Hotel Punta Pescadero,** Apdo. Postal 362, La Paz, BCS 23000, tel. (1) 141-0101, U.S. tel. (800) 426-BAJA, fax (949) 766-6471, e-mail: anaivett@aol.com, is a small fishing resort on 125 palm-studded acres overlooking a sandy beach. Each room comes with a sea view, private veranda, a/c, satellite TV, and refrigerator; some have fireplaces (quite nice on winter evenings). The resort features a restaurant and bar, dive shop with compressor, small pool, lighted tennis court, nine-hole golf course, landing strip (1,065 meters/3,500

feet, Unicom 122.8), and rental equipment for scuba and free diving, boating, and fishing. Petroglyphs are visible in nearby rock caves that once served as Amerindian burial sites. The unpaved side road out to the actual point is not recommended for RVs or trailers. A housing development is growing up around the resort, so the Punta Pescadero's once-secluded nature is changing. Hotel Punta Pescadero can also be contacted in the U.S. at 31 Calle Alamitos, Rancho Santa Margarita, CA 92688. Rates: US$140 s/d, children under 12 free in same room with parents, additional adult US$25. Add to this 12% tax and 15% gratuity. Baja Bush Pilot and AAA discounts are available.

A mile north of Punta Pescadero along this same road, the little-known **Restaurant Marimar** serves simple but well-prepared seafood.

El Cardonal

Past Punta Pescadero and technically at the south end of Bahía de los Muertos, you'll come to El Cardonal (23 km/14 miles from Los Barriles). Inshore coral heads here provide worthwhile underwater scenery, while nearby prehistoric cave paintings reportedly depict marlin, turtles, and human figures.

The Canadian-owned **El Cardonal's Hide-A-Way,** tel./fax (1) 141-0040, U.S. tel. (514) 467-4700, fax (514) 467-4668, e-mail: elcardonaleddy @hotmail.com, offers tidy apartments as well as spaces for RV and tent camping. Each of the large beachfront studios comes with two full-size beds, a sofa, a fully equipped kitchen, ironing board, and ceiling fan. Small campers and tent camping on large campsites costs US$5 d per day; full hookups cost US$8 d. A dump station is available, as are fishing boats (*pangas* and a 32-foot cruiser), hot-water showers, a 24-hour restaurant, laundromat, picnic tables, ice, and equipment for fishing, windsurfing, diving, kayaking, and snorkeling. El Cardonal also rents horses. Rates: US$39 d per night, US$254 per week, US$499 for two weeks, US$550 for three weeks, and US$599 per month. Discounts offered for long-term stays.

Beyond El Cardonal, the road continues northward along the coast, then west across the Sierra El Carrizalito to San Juan de los Planes (see Southeast of La Paz).

LOS BARRILES

During the high-wind season, Nov.-March, hotels in Los Barriles can arrange package deals that include windsurfing seminars, use of state-of-the-art equipment, air transportation, and accommodations. Keep in mind that although lessons are typically geared to your level, wind and surf conditions at Los Barriles are best enjoyed by experienced boardsailors rather than novices.

For five days during the second week of January, Vela Windsurf Resort and sailboard manufacturer Neil Pryde cohost the annual **Vela-Neil Pryde Baja Championships** sailboard race at Los Barriles. The week before the competition, the center offers a race clinic staffed by world-class instructors. Nonwindsurfing spectators are welcome to watch the event from shore and to join in on the beach barbecues and partying. For more information, contact Vela Windsurf Resort (see below).

Accommodations
Inexpensive: Martin Verdugo's Beach Resort, Apdo. Postal 17, Los Barriles, BCS 23501, tel. (1) 141-0054, e-mail: martinv@lapaz.cromwell.com.mx, an extension of the trailer park of the same name, features around 29 well-kept rooms in a two-story hotel next to the beach. Facilities include a small pool and boat launch. Rates: US$46 s/d (US$51 oceanfront) without kitchenette, US$56 with kitchenette s/d. Additional persons US$5.

Expensive (All-Inclusive): Hotel Playa del Sol, P.O. Box 9016, Calabasas, CA 91372, tel. (818) 591-9463 or (800) 368-4334 in the U.S. and Canada, fax (818) 591-1077, has 26 a/c rooms, an oceanfront pool, tennis and volleyball courts, an outdoor terrace restaurant, bar with satellite TV, rental gear (for fishing, kayaking, mountain biking, and windsurfing), charter boats for sportfishing (US$220-300 per day, not including fishing permits), and a full-service Vela windsurfing center. Rates of US$65 s, US$100 d, US$135 t, and US$170 q include meals. Tax and service are extra. The hotel is closed in September.

Vela Windsurf Resort, tel. (831) 461-0820 or (800) 223-5443 in the U.S./Canada, fax (831) 461-0821, e-mail: info@velawindsurf.com, is based at the Hotel Playa del Sol. Seven-night packages start at US$887 and include all windsurfing equipment, instruction at every level except novice, accommodations, meals, tax, and service. Guests also have free use of kayaks and mountain bikes for days they don't feel like windsurfing or when the wind's not blowing; the staff provides good maps and descriptions of nearby kayaking/biking routes. Snorkeling, tennis, and volleyball are also available through the center at no cost to package guests. Scuba diving and horseback riding can be arranged at additional cost.

Vela opens just before Thanksgiving and closes the first week in March. Outside the center's peak period (20 Dec.-20 Jan.), nonpackage guests at Hotel Playa del Sol may be able to rent sailboards, kayaks, and bikes.

Los Barriles windsurfing

About 300 meters south of Hotel Playa del Sol and just a half mile off the highway, **Hotel Palmas de Cortez** (same contact information as the Playa del Sol) offers 50 standard a/c rooms with sea views, plus higher-priced suites and 10 premium-priced two-bedroom condos that sleep up to six. Rates: US$75 s, US$120 d, US$165 t, US$200 q, plus tax and service; rates include three meals daily. Facilities include a restaurant and bar, ping pong tables, a pool, tennis and racquetball courts, an 868-meter (2,850-foot) landing strip (Unicom 122.8), windsurfing gear, charter boats (US$220-350, not including fishing permits), and equipment for both fishing and hunting. Dove and quail hunting in the nearby Sierra de La Laguna is reportedly good.

Camping and RV Parks

North of Hotel Playa del Sol are **Martin Verdugo's Beach Resort,** Apdo. Postal 17, Los Barriles, BCS 23501, tel. (1) 141-0054, e-mail: martinv@lapaz.cromwell.com.mex, a well-run and well-maintained park, and **Playa de Oro RV Resort,** 3106 Capa Dr., Hacienda Heights, CA 91745, U.S. tel. (818) 336-7494. Both have beach frontage, dump stations, flush toilets, showers, boat ramps, laundry facilities, and full hookups for US$14 for two people, plus US$2 for each additional person. Tent sites cost US$11 a night at Verdugo's, US$10 at Playa de Oro. Verdugo's has a small pool and also operates a restaurant and is a short walk from the beach. Playa de Oro is next to the beach and offers bonded boat storage. Both parks can arrange fishing trips. Both tend to stay completely full during the windsurfing season, so be sure to arrange advance reservations Jan.-March.

On the west side of the dirt road heading north, the smaller **Juanito's Garden RV Park,** Apdo. Postal 50, Los Barriles, BCS 23501, tel./fax (1) 141-0024, has trailer and RV spaces without hookups for US$6-8 a night and offers bonded storage. Camping spaces are also available.

Free primitive camping is available in the area north of these three parks, usually referred to by gringos as the "North Shore."

Property Management

East Cape Vacation Rentals, tel./fax (1) 141-0381, handles rental properties in Los Barriles, Buena Vista, Punta Pescadero, and Los Frailes.

Food

Tío Pablo's, on the main north-south road through Los Barriles, is a large, smartly designed *palapa*-style structure with ceiling fans, a well-stocked bar, sports TV, and a menu of salads, sandwiches, and burgers. It's open daily 11:30 a.m.-10 p.m. **Tío's Tienda** next door stocks grocery items as well as office supplies. **Mañanas Pizza,** just past Juanito's Garden in a modern strip mall, tel./fax (1) 141-0344, specializes in wood-fired pizza, burgers, homemade lasagna, sausage, and chicken parmigiana. It's open Mon.-Sat. 4:30-9:30 p.m.; delivery is available.

Nearby **Otra Vez Restaurant and Cantina,** tel. (1) 141-0249, occupies a long, low white-washed building with a colorful arch out front. The restaurant features Thai and Chinese cuisine on Wednesday nights, Italian on Saturday nights, and a mix of American and Mexican the rest of the week.

In a strip mall just off Mexico 1 on the access road to Los Barriles, **Sunrise Café** serves gringo favorites like blueberry pancakes, omelettes, cinnamon rolls, and bagels; open daily 6 a.m.-2 p.m. **Buzzard Bay Sports Cantina,** in the same shopping center, offers a menu of burgers, sandwiches, appetizers, and Mexican food, and has both outdoor and indoor seating. Farther toward Los Barriles on this same access road, **Supermercado Chapito's** stocks basic food supplies. **Supermercado Fayla,** just past Juanito's Garden RV Park, is more American-oriented.

BUENA VISTA

Accommodations

Moderate: Off the highway near Km 109, opposite the Pemex station, **Casa Miramar Bed & Breakfast,** tel. (1) 141-0271, U.S. tel. (800) 533-8452, e-mail: mrbill@windriders.com, offers six beachfront rooms with a/c and breakfast. A full kitchen is available for guest use, and a variety of water-sports equipment can be rented. Rates: US$40 s, US$70 d, including tax. Casa Miramar also offers package deals including five days' accommodation, breakfast daily, and three days of diving for US$425 pp. A deluxe package includes a week of accommodations, breakfast daily, four days of diving, plus unlimited use of windsurfing equipment, kayaks, snorkeling gear, mountain bikes, and Hobie cats; cost is US$750 pp. Miramar is popular with windsurfers and kite-skiiers in winter and scuba divers in summer. All sports equipment is sold off at the end of each season, to be replaced with the latest state-of-the-art gear.

Expensive-Premium (All-Inclusive): Hotel Buenavista Beach Resort, 130 27th St., Chula Vista, CA 91911, tel. (1) 141-0033, U.S. tel. (619) 429-8079 or (800) 752-3555, fax (619) 429-7924, e-mail: spabna@1cabonet.com.mx, offers 60 a/c Mediterranean-style bungalows with private baths, sitting areas, and private terraces. Facilities include a garden, two pools, a swim-up bar, cocktail lounge, beachfront dining, water aerobics center, tennis courts, hot springs mineral spa, kayaks, horseback riding, and equipment for diving, snorkeling, fishing, and hunting. The resort organizes various outings, such as tours of cave-paintings and waterfalls, as well as birdwatching, hiking, and snorkel tours. All meals, snacks, nonalcoholic beverages, beer, and domestic well drinks are included. (You may also choose to stay on the European plan—rooms only, no meals.) All-inclusive rates: US$85-115 s, US$135-165 d, US$185-215 t, children 12 years and under sharing a room US$20 each. European plan rates: US$60-75 s/d Nov.-March, US$80-100 s/d April-October. Each extra adult is charged US$20, each extra child 12 and under US$10. Tax and service extra. Fishing and diving packages are also available.

The sportfishing fleet at the resort features a 23-foot *panga* (US$220), a 28-foot cruiser (US$330), a luxury 29-foot twin-engine cruiser (US$385), and a 31-foot twin-engine cruiser (US$440). Tax, tips, tackle, bait and fishing licenses are extra.

Roundtrip or one-way transportation from the airport can be arranged in advance by the U.S. reservations office.

Premium (All-Inclusive): Old-timer **Rancho Buena Vista,** P.O. Box 1408, Santa Maria, CA 93456, reservations tel. (805) 928-1719 or (800) 258-8200, fax (805) 925-2990, features a nice restaurant and bar facing the sea, as well as a pool, whirlpool, tennis and volleyball courts, a weight room, fitness programs, fishing tackle (including fly-fishing equipment), cruisers, windsurfing gear, a boat ramp, boat storage, unpaved airstrip, and 57 a/c cottages. All meals are included. Rates: US$80 s, US$140 d, US$180 t, US$35 each for children 6-14, plus 20% for tax

and service. It's easy to miss the entrance to the Rancho Buena Vista if you're coming south on Mexico 1. The left turn comes just after a small mountain pass that obscures it; watch for a blue highway sign on the right that says "hotel."

Trailer Park: About two km south of Hotel Buenavista Beach Resort is the modest **La Capilla Trailer Park,** with flush toilets, showers, and full hookups for US$7 a day.

Food

The modest but popular **Restaurant La Gaviota,** out on the highway, offers a standard list of fresh seafood (including fish tacos), *antojitos, carne a la tampiqueña,* and breakfasts. It's open daily 8 a.m.-9 p.m. The Gaviota also sports a jukebox stocked with *norteña* tunes. **Restaurant Calafia,** on Mexico 1 near the Buena Vista police station, offers good shrimp tacos and tables with views of Bahía de Palmas. It's usually open for lunch and early dinner only.

Diving

Although there's little to interest divers in Bahía de Palmas, **Vista Sea Sport,** tel./fax (1) 141-0031, VHF channel 71, offers snorkel tours from US$25 and dive trips to Cabo Pulmo and Los Frailes (US$100), Gorda Banks (US$140), and Punta Pescadero (US$75), as well as airfills and diving-gear rentals.

Casa Miramar, off the highway near Km 109, tel. (1) 141-0271, U.S. tel. (800) 533-8452, e-mail: mrbill@windriders.com, arranges two-tank scuba tours for US$75-130, including transportation to dive site, air, weight belt, boat, and divemaster. Airfills and diving-gear rentals are also available. Casa Miramar also offers multiday dive-and-room packages for US$425-750 through **Baja Adventures,** headquartered at Casa Miramar. Both Vista Sea Sport and Casa Miramar offer PADI scuba certification courses for US$350.

LA RIBERA

To reach the Coastal Road from the north, take the paved road signed "La Ribera" east at Km 93 off Mexico 1 (at Las Cuevas). This 20-km (12-mile) road passes through La Ribera (La Rivera), a small town of around 2,000 with a Pemex station, church, *tortillería,* cemetery, banana and mango trees, trailer shelters, and simple homes lining up along a network of sandy roads overlooking a sand beach. Worn *palapa* shelters at the south end of the beach can be used for camping when not occupied by fishermen. Several *mercaditos* in the village offer local produce and other supplies for long-term visitors.

Just north of La Ribera, in a large mango orchard near the beach, the tidy and well-run **La Ribera Trailer Park (Correcamino Trailer Park)** (no phone, CB channel 66) offers shady tent/camper/RV spaces with full hookups for US$8 per day. Facilities include hot showers, flush toilets, propane, bait, firewood, storage, and a boat ramp.

A sandy road just south of Trailer Park La Ribera leads 0.6 km (0.4 miles) to a casuarina-shaded beach where you can camp for free. A point at the north end of the small bay (also accessible from La Ribera) creates a surf break during heavy southwest swells.

AROUND PUNTA COLORADA

Punta Colorada lies at the south end of the bay, 16 km (10 miles) east of Mexico 1 via the La Ribera road.

Accommodations
Expensive (All-Inclusive): Hotel Punta Colorada, P.O. Box 9016, Calabasas, CA 91372, local tel. (1) 121-0044, U.S./Canada tel. (818) 591-9463 or (800) 368-4334, fax (818) 591-1077, is a favorite of roosterfish fanatics; the roosterfishing off nearby Punta Arena is usually the best in Baja. The hotel offers 29 large rooms with three meals daily included in the price. All tap water at the resort comes from a mountain well. The hotel also has an indoor/outdoor bar and its own airstrip (1,000 meters/3,200 feet, Unicom 122.8). Guided fishing trips are available starting at US$220 a day. The hotel is closed September and the first week of October. Rates: US$60 s, US$100 d, US$145 t, US$180 q.

Expensive-Premium (All-Inclusive): South of Buena Vista, just north of Punta Colorada, lies the secluded **Rancho Leonero Resort,** Apdo. Postal 7, Buena Vista, BCS 23501, tel./fax (1) 141-0216, or P.O. Box 698, Placentia, CA 92871, tel. (714) 692-6965 or (800) 646-2252 in the United States, e-mail: rancholeonero@worldnet. att.net. Perched on a low promontory overlooking the sea, this comfortable, quiet, and rustic resort features 30 spacious rock-walled, *palapa*-roofed rooms, suites, and bungalows. All have sea views, but to emphasize Rancho Leonero's sense of seclusion and retreat, none of the rooms contain phones or TVs. The expansive grounds hold a restaurant and bar, pool, jacuzzi, fully equipped dive center, sportfishing fleet, and 20 miles of running/hiking trails. A rock reef in front of the hotel is suitable for snorkeling. Three meals a day are included in the room price. Fishing charters start at US$160 a day for a regular *pangas,* US$220 for a super *panga,* US$300 and up for

cabins at
Rancho Leonero

cruisers. Snorkeling equipment is available for US$5 per day, and a snorkel tour costs US$25-50 pp. Horseback riding, kayaking, scuba, and hiking trips can also be arranged.

In the past Rancho Leonero was almost strictly a fishing holiday resort, which meant it filled up during summer and stood almost empty in winter, but now the resort has added a few fitness services, including massage therapy and use of an outdoor gym.

Rates: US$110-170 s, US$140-200 d, depending on size of the units and proximity to the beach. Additional adult guests in the same unit are charged $40 a night, and children five and under stay free. Tax and service are extra. A US$25 discount is offered August and September and Nov.-March.

Surfing
One of Baja's least-known surfing spots—simply because no one expects surf this far up the Sea of Cortez—can be found at **Punta Arena,** just below Punta Colorada. A left point break can crop up here anytime during the March-Nov. southwest swell, but the peak surf usually comes in late summer or early fall—*chubasco* season.

EL CAMINO RURAL COSTERO

La Ribera is the northern end of the notorious El Camino Rural Costero (The Rural Coastal Road), which runs all the way to Pueblo La Playa. About halfway along the route stands a brass plaque commemorating the road's May 1984 grading. For first-time drivers who have braved washouts and sandpits to read it, the sign never fails to elicit a few chuckles.

In general, driving conditions along the Coastal Road are suitable for passenger cars of average road clearance; even smaller RVs sometimes manage to make it all the way. Sand can be a problem in places, and shoulders are invariably soft. Weather plays an important role in day-to-day conditions; following late-summer or early-fall storms, parts of the Coastal Road can be impassable. Make inquiries before embarking on the trip and be prepared to turn back if necessary. The unpaved 77-km (48-mile) stretch between El Rincón and San José del Cabo can take up to four hours.

Eventually the Coastal Road is supposed to be paved all the way to San José del Cabo. Pavement is now slowly being laid along an interior track parallel to the current road; rumor says it will hit the coast again at Bahía de Los Frailes.

In spite of the rough access, certain areas along the route—e.g., Cabo Pulmo and Los Frailes—are filling up with small-scale housing/resort developments. Yet plenty of open space for beach camping is still available. Contrasting strongly with the budding resort developments toward the northern end of the route are several ranchos strung along the central and southern portions that raise cattle, goats, pigs, and sheep—mostly without fencing. If you substitute fiberglass *pangas* for dugout canoes, the ranchos today appear much as they must have in 1941, when John Steinbeck described Cabo Pulmo:

On the shore behind the white beach was one of those lonely little rancherías *we came to know later. Usually a palm or two are planted nearby, and by these trees sticking up out of the brush one can locate the houses. There is usually a small corral, a burro or two, a few pigs, and some scrawny chickens. The cattle range wide for food. A dugout canoe lies on the beach, for a good part of the food comes from the sea. Rarely do you see a light from the sea, for the people go to sleep at dusk and awaken with the first light.*

CABO PULMO

Heading south from La Ribera, the Coastal Road is paved for a short way, then turns to dirt. The unpaved portion of the 26.5-km (16.5-mile) stretch between La Ribera and Cabo Pulmo is usually in fair condition.

Bahía Pulmo
Noted for its reef-building corals, this tidy bay is bounded by Cabo Pulmo to the north and Corral de Los Frailes to the south. Coarse white-sand beaches ring the bay, most of them readily accessible from the parallel Coastal Road. Baja California pearling once reached its southernmost point here.

Playa Sirenita

A pristine, fine-sand beach known as **Playa La Sirenita** (Mermaid Beach, named for a rock formation whose silhouette resembles the head and bust of a female figure) lies against the north escarpment of Corral de Los Frailes at the bay's southeastern tip. Best reached by small boat or kayak from the village of Cabo Pulmo, the beach's crystal waters are protected from southerly winds in the summer and early fall; rock reefs close by offer snorkeling opportunities. There's just enough room above the tideline for undisturbed overnight camping.

Farther south around the wide headland of **Corral de Los Frailes** (named for a rock formation with a resemblance to hooded friars), a colony of sea lions lives among geometric boulder piles.

Take the first sand road that isn't barbwired north of Corral de Los Frailes to reach **Playa Corral de Los Frailes,** a secluded beach sheltered from most onshore winds.

Pulmo Reef System

The bay's reef system, the northernmost of only three coastal reefs in North America and the only coral reef in the Sea of Cortez, is rich with tropical marinelife and hence a favorite snorkeling and scuba-diving destination. Adding to its attraction is the fact that it's easily accessible from shore.

The reef consists of eight hard coral fingers scattered throughout the bay, from Cabo Pulmo at the north end to Corral de Los Frailes at the southern end. Four finger reefs extend from the center of bayshore: two solid lengths called **Las Navajas;** an unnamed broken length used by (harmless) nurse sharks as a breeding zone; and a solid, kilometer-long finger known as **El Cantil.** Water depths along these four reefs range 4.5-10.5 meters (15-35 feet).

Farther offshore (up to 3.2 km, two miles), running more or less parallel to the bayshore, are the reef fingers of **La Esperanza** (at depths of around 18 meters/60 feet), **El Bajo de los Meros** (15 meters/50 feet), and **Outer Pulmo** (30 meters/100 feet).

Soft coral heads can be found at **El Islote**—a rock island near La Esperanza—and at **Las Casitas,** rock caves just off Corral de Los Frailes at a depth of 13 meters (45 feet).

The reef system here is very delicate; reef corals can't tolerate temperatures lower than 21° C (70° F) and must have clear water since debris settling on their disks and tentacles will kill them. The reefs are important breeding grounds for several marine species, so if the corals die it will negatively impact all manner of fish in the area.

The Universidad de La Paz is currently surveying the bay for possible national-park status. Meanwhile, the Mexican government has declared Pulmo Reef an underwater nature preserve—no fishing or anchoring at the reef (or anywhere in Bahía Pulmo) is permitted. Shore development remains the reef's biggest ecological challenge, because the corals rely on unpolluted and unimpeded runoff. If resorts or housing developments further expand along Bahía Pulmo, the reef will probably perish.

Diving and Boating

Optimum visibility in the waters around Pulmo Reef occurs March-October. Aside from the natural reefs cited above, directly off Cabo Pulmo (the cape itself) lies the wreck of *El Vencedor,* a tuna boat that sank in 1981 and now forms an excellent artificial reef. Pilot whales are commonly seen in the vicinity in April, large jack crevalles Aug.-September.

Ask for personable José Luis Murrieta in Cabo Pulmo if you're interested in a guided dive or boat service. His **Pepe's Dive Center,** Cabo Pulmo-La Ribera, BCS, tel. (1) 141-0001, toll-free tel. (877) 733-2252, offers a complete diving service (including equipment rentals and airfills) to 14 dive sites in the area. Two other small dive centers—**Cabo Pulmo Divers** and **Pulmo Reef Dive Shop**—also operate out of Cabo Pulmo. Rates at the three run an economical US$45 pp for a one-tank dive tour, US$65 for a two-tank tour, US$35 for snorkeling tours, and US$50 for night dives. Pepe's English-speaking crew offers a PADI-approved scuba resort course for US$80 or full scuba certification for US$375. Rentals are available at US$10 per snorkel set, US$12 for a scuba tank, and US$10 per regulator or BCD. For US$50 a day you can rent full scuba gear and a kayak from Pepe's for self-guided beach diving.

The dive operators are also happy to arrange boat trips for nondivers interested in touring the bay, Playa La Sirenita, and the Corral de Los Frailes seal colony.

Fishing

Neither sport nor commercial fishing is permitted in Bahía Pulmo, but inshore north of Cabo Pulmo anglers can find giant seabass, snapper, pargo, ladyfish, and roosterfish. Offshore are grouper, sierra, skipjack, dorado, marlin, and tuna. The tuna are found closer in at Bahía de Los Frailes farther south, but anywhere along this coastal stretch the heavyweights can come within three km (two miles) of the shoreline. Peak months for most varieties are May-June and Oct.-November.

Accommodations and Camping

In the midst of Cabo Pulmo village, **Cabo Pulmo Beach Resort,** P.O. Box 774, Ketchum, ID 83340, local tel./fax (1) 141-0244, U.S. tel. (208) 726-9233 or (888) 99-PULMO, fax (208) 726-1306, e-mail: cpbr@primenet.com, offers 25 *palapa*-roofed, solar-powered cabañas by the day, week, or month. The bay is just a short walk from each. All accommodations come with kitchenettes or full kitchens, plus all bed and bath linens; some feature patios, decks, or barbecue grills. In addition, the resort now offers guided snorkeling (US$30—snorkel rental only is US$15), scuba diving (US$65), kayaking (US$30-45), tennis, fishing, hiking, and rock climbing. Rates: US$165 (Oct.-May), US$135 (June-Sept.) for a beach house that accommodates four to six persons; US$120/95 for *ca-*

Pepe's Dive Center,
Cabo Pulmo

sitas for up to four persons; US$60/45 s/d for basic bungalows; and US$85/65 s/d for deluxe bungalows. Additional guests over 12 years old pay US$15 per day each. Monthly rates available. Dive packages range US$95-148 pp double occupancy (US$75-125 June-September).

Just north of Cabo Pulmo Beach Resort stands **Villa and Casa del Mar,** P.O. Box 266, Ketchum, ID 83340, tel. (208) 726-4455 or (888) 225-2786, fax (208) 726-2529, a large, deluxe beachfront house with a full kitchen, spacious living areas, shaded terraces, and a rooftop sundeck. All rooms come with fan and a/c, which must be run sparingly since the house is solar-powered. The main part of the house rents for US$2,000 per week in peak season (Oct.-Nov., Dec. 20-Jan. 3, and Feb.-May), or US$285 per night the remainder of the year. These rates apply for up to four guests; additional guests are charged US$40 per night each. The smaller attached studio apartment costs US$600 per week in peak season, US$85 nightly off peak, plus US$30 pp beyond four guests.

You can camp for free on the beach at the south end of Bahía Pulmo, or for US$2 per night at the north end.

Food
Nancy's Restaurant and Bar, a rustic collection of tables beneath a *palapa* shelter (adjacent to the resort and near the road), provides a changing menu of fish (the café's own or bring your catch), pizza, tacos, vegetable enchiladas, soups, homemade breads, cinnamon rolls, and other delights prepared by an American cook. Popular with divers during the dive season, the simple restaurant has an especially cozy ambience at night when illuminated by hurricane lamps. Nancy appreciates two hours' notice for a full-course dinner (US$11); drop in anytime for breakfast or lunch.

Tito's, a casual *palapa* restaurant on the opposite side of the road, provides simple fish meals, beer, and drinking water—when you can find the proprietors. **Restaurant El Caballero,** on the opposite side of the road near Nancy's, is similar.

Getting There
Most visitors drive themselves to Cabo Pulmo via El Camino Rural Costero. With advance notice,

Cabo Pulmo Resort can arrange roundtrip transportation from Los Cabos airport for a fee; a stop at a grocery store near the airport on the way up can be included.

BAHÍA DE LOS FRAILES

About eight km (five miles) south of Cabo Pulmo village is a sandy spur road east to gently curving, white-sand Bahía de Los Frailes. With Bahía Pulmo just to the north serving as a protected nursery, onshore and inshore fishing is unusually good here. Surfcasters can land roosterfish, while boating anglers can hook yellowfin tuna, leopard grouper, skipjack, dorado, and marlin, all within a couple miles of shore.

The north end of the bay is protected from Nov.-April northern winds by Cabo Los Frailes, but windsurfers will find a steady cross-shore breeze at the bay's south end. The bay plummets here as deep as 210 meters (688 feet).

According to the owner of Hotel Bahía Los Frailes, Amerindian rock art can be found inland nearby.

Accommodations and Camping
Expensive (All-Inclusive): Hotel Bahía Los Frailes, Apdo. Postal 230, San Jose del Cabo, BCS, tel. (1) 141-0122, fax (1) 142-3578, offers well-constructed, nicely furnished cottages with high *palapa* roofs facing the south side of the bay. Three meals a day are included (beverages not included); suites are available. Deep-sea *panga* fishing, including boat and captain, runs US$195 per day (eight hours). Tackle is an additional US$15 per day and there's an extra charge for bait when available. Rates: single room, US$200 for two adults (extra adult US$75 each, children under 10 US$50, under five free); one-bedroom suite, US$250 for two adults (same rates for extra adults and children as in single rooms); two-bedroom suite (with four queen-size beds and two baths), US$450 for four guests (same rates for extra adults and children as in single rooms). Add 12% tax and 15% gratuity to all rates. For U.S. reservations, call (800) 934-0295, or e-mail: losfrailes@compuserve.com.

Beach camping is permitted along the north end of the bay—a nominal fee of US$2-3 per site may be collected to pay for trash collection.

SOUTH TO SAN JOSÉ DEL CABO

South of Los Frailes, the Coastal Road deteriorates rapidly, but those with sturdy vehicles and steady nerves will be rewarded by secluded arroyo campsites and vignettes of disappearing ranch life. About 12.5 km (7.5 miles) south of Los Frailes is **Rancho Tule,** followed after 5.5 km (3.5 miles) by **Rancho Boca de La Vinorama.** The coastal desert scenery along this stretch can be particularly impressive, with lots of green cacti and *torotes* (elephant trees). A late-summer beach break sometimes hits at Boca del Tule, sending a few clued-in surfers scurrying across the landscape in this direction.

Just south of Vinorama, a graded dirt road heads west across the lower Sierra La Trinidad to the ranching settlement of **Palo Escopeta.** From there it continues on to meet Mexico 1 near San José Viejo, a distance of 34 km (21.7 miles). Although roughly the same distance as the remainder of the Coastal Road to San José, the Palo Escopeta road often rides more smoothly and quickly. Hence, unless you're heading for a specific spot along the coast between Pueblo La Playa and La Vinorama, it's normally faster to cut across the hills here to Mexico 1 rather than follow the coast.

From La Vinorama along the coast, it's another five km (three miles) and 1.5 km (one mile) southwest, respectively, to **Rancho San Luis** and **Rancho Santa Elena.** This section of road is often the most rugged along El Camino Rural Costero, with lots of soft spots and washouts. Following another 5.5-km (3.5-mile) section is the small dairy farm of **La Fortuna,** after which the road improves a bit for 24 km (15 miles) before terminating at **Pueblo La Playa,** a fishing village on the eastern outskirts of San José del Cabo.

Jutting from the coast about 10.3 km (6.4 miles) before Pueblo La Playa is **Punta Gorda,** known for good onshore/inshore fishing and, in a south or southwest swell, surfing. Surfers know the breaks here as "Santa Cruz," the name of a small *ranchería* nearby (actually Santa Cruz de los Zacatitos). Beach campsites are free and plentiful in this area.

Around 10 km (six miles) offshore lie the world-famous **Gorda Banks,** a pair of seamounts that are a hot spot for marlin and wahoo fishing. *Pangeros* are sometimes available for guided fishing trips out to the Banks, but it's easiest to hire someone at La Playita, the beach behind Pueblo La Playa farther on. If you have your own boat, beach launching is generally easier at La Playita. Guided scuba trips to the Gorda Banks can be arranged through dive outfitters in Cabo San Lucas.

The last couple of kilometers between Pueblo La Playa and San José del Cabo are more tropical than the entire East Cape, offering up mango trees, huge banyan trees, and wild sugarcane.

SAN JOSÉ DEL CABO

Although closer to Los Cabos International Airport, San José del Cabo is a quieter, more traditional resort than neighboring Cabo San Lucas. A somewhat older tourist crowd frequents San José (pop. 25,000), leaving Cabo San Lucas to partying singles and young couples.

The Jesuit padres who founded a mission community here in the 18th century situated San José on a mesa a couple of kilometers north of the beach. Century-old brick and adobe buildings, many of them proudly restored, line the main streets radiating from the plaza and church. These are interspersed with Indian laurel trees and other greenery, making San José one of the most pleasant pedestrian towns in the Cape Region.

The architecture thins out and becomes more modern as you descend toward the beach, culminating in a golf course, condos, resort homes, and the *zona hotelera*. Because of the town's mesa geography, the beachfront hotels thankfully don't obscure the view from town. Areas to the north and east of town are dotted with irrigated orchards producing mangoes, avocados, bananas, and citrus.

As the *cabecera* (roughly equivalent to "county seat") of the Municipio de San José del Cabo, the town enjoys well-maintained streets and city services. Employment in the public as well as private sector has lured a variety of talented *bajacalifornianos* to establish residence here. A number of foreigners also have retirement or vacation homes in the area, although the overall gringo presence, whether resident or visiting, is much smaller than in Cabo San Lucas.

CLIMATE

San José del Cabo's climate, influenced by the city's tropical latitude, estuarine environment, and proximity to both sea and desert, belongs in the classic tropical-arid category. Average maximum temperatures run 30° C (86° F) in January up to 40° C (104° F) in June, the warmest month. Average minimum temperatures in the winter are around 18° C (64° F), though rare readings as low as 3° C (37° F) have been recorded.

Average annual rainfall amounts to just 32 cm (12 inches). September is typically the wettest month, while virtually no rainfall is usually recorded Feb.-July. Even "wet" September usually has just three or four rainy days, with total rainfall for the month under 10 cm (four inches). Like much of the Cape Region, San José is subject to occasional tropical storms called *chubascos* Aug.-October. On rare occasions a storm may bring torrential downpours, as in 1993 when a late-arriving November *chubasco* caused serious flood damage to beachside condos and hotels.

HISTORY

The Pericú who frequented the San José area before the Spanish *entrada* called the area "Añuiti," a name whose meaning has been lost. Spanish galleons first visited Estero San José—the mouth of the Río San José—to obtain fresh water near the end of their lengthy voyages from the Philippines to Acapulco in the late 17th and early 18th centuries. During this period the es-tuary was known among seamen as Aguada Segura (Sure Waters) and, less commonly, San Bernabe, a name left behind by Sebastián Vizcaíno during his coastal navigations. As pirate raids along the coast between Cabo San Lucas and La Paz became a problem, the need for a permanent Spanish settlement at the tip of the cape became increasingly urgent. The growing unrest among the Guaicura and Pericú south of Loreto also threatened to engulf mission communities to the north; the Spanish had to send

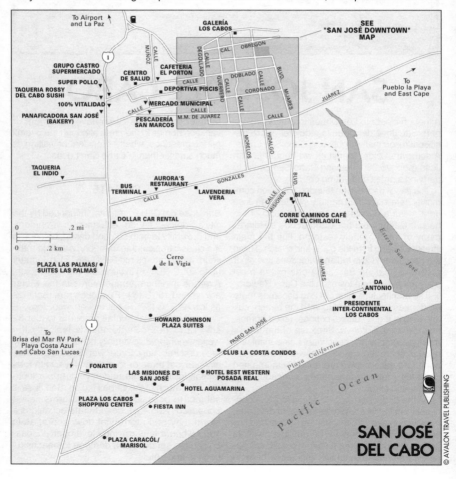

SAN JOSÉ
DEL CABO

© AVALON TRAVEL PUBLISHING

LEGEND OF THE FLAME

A little-known episode featuring a shipwrecked Irishman footnotes San José's colorful history. Fleeing political strife in 18th-century Ireland, John O'Brien and several of his countrymen sailed to the New World—along the same route followed by Sir Francis Drake and earlier English explorers—only to become stranded at Estero San José in 1795. After marrying a local Pericú woman, O'Brien refused rescue when his father and the rest of the Irish crew were later picked up by a ship on its way back to the British Isles.

From this point in the story onward, facts merge with fable as O'Brien gained legendary status among the *bajacalifornianos* as "La Flama" (The Flame), for his red hair and fiery disposition. Also known as Juan Colorado (Red John), or more prosaically as Juan Obregón, the Irishman set out on a lifetime adventure throughout the Californias as far north as San Francisco, working as a cowboy and singing the nostalgia-tinted praises of San José del Cabo everywhere he went. For O'Brien, San José replaced the Emerald Isle as his homeland, and one imagines him crying in a shot of tequila instead of ale as he expresses his longing for "San José del Arroyo," as imagined in Walter Nordhoff's book *The Journey of The Flame:*

On seeing our dear Valley of San José del Arroyo for the last time, with the cattle grazing everywhere, on both sides of the fertile land, on the hillsides, I remembered the violent stampedes of the wild bulls and the delicious sips of warm milk I stole, and I thought: If heaven is like this valley, I can only repeat after the Indians, "Father, lead us there!"

How many times, in subsequent years, someone galloping by my side in the desert has asked me, "Where are you from, countryman?" And when I answered him "From San José!," something crept into his voice that no other place is capable of evoking when he asked: "Would that be San José del Arroyo?" Then the horses could scatter, the cattle begin a stampede, the water be a thousand burning leagues away, or death lie close by in ambush for us, and nevertheless we had to stop. Because when two who love this Arroyo Valley meet and know each other, everything else loses importance.

armed troops to the Cape Region to quell Amerindian uprisings in 1723, 1725, and 1729.

In 1730 Jesuit padre Nicolás Tamaral traveled south from Misión La Purísima and founded Misión Estero de las Palmas de San José del Cabo Añuiti (or Misión San José del Cabo, for short) on a mesa overlooking the Río San José, some five km north of the current town site. Due to the overwhelming presence of mosquitoes at this site, Tamaral soon moved the mission to the mouth of the estuary, on a rise flanked by Cerro de la Vigía and Cerro de la Cruz. During the mission's first year, Jesuit records show the padre baptized 1,036 *salvajes* (savages), while at the same time establishing fruit orchards and irrigated farmlands.

Tamaral and the Pericú got along fine until he pronounced an injunction against polygamy, long a tradition in Pericú society. Wrote Tamaral about Pericú men:

It is highly difficult to induce them to leave the great number of women they have, because women are very numerous among them. Suffice it to say that the most ordinary men have at least two or three . . . because the larger the number of their women, the better served they are and better provided with everything necessary, as they lie in perpetual idleness in the shade of the trees, and their women work looking in the woods for wild roots and fruits to feed them with, and each one tries to bring her husband the best to be found in order to win his affection in preference to the others.

After Tamaral punished a Pericú shaman for violating the antipolygamy decree, the Indians rebelled and burned both the San José and Santiago missions in October 1734. Tamaral was killed in the attack. Shortly thereafter, the Spanish established a garrison to protect the community from insurgent natives and the estuary from English pirates.

By 1767, virtually all the Amerindians in the area had died either of European-borne diseases or in skirmishes with the Spanish. Surviving Pericú were moved to missions farther north, but San José del Cabo remained an important Spanish military outpost until the mid-19th century when the presidio was turned over to Mexican nationals.

During the Mexican-American War (1846-48), marines from the U.S. frigate *Portsmouth* briefly occupied the city. A bloody siege ensued, but the Mexicans prevailed under the leadership of Mexican naval officer José Antonio Mijares. Plaza Mijares, San José's town square, is named for him, as is Blvd. Mijares, the main avenue connecting town center and the hotel zone. As mining in the Cape Region gave out during the late 19th and early 20th centuries, the population of San

José and the rest of the region decreased. A few sugarcane farmers, cattle ranchers, and fishermen began trickling into the San José area in the 1930s, and in 1940 the church was rebuilt.

San José remained largely an agricultural backwater known for its avocados, mangoes, citrus, and other fruits until the Cape began attracting sportfishers and later the sun-and-sand set in the 1960s and '70s. Since the late '70s, Fonatur (the Mexican tourist bureau) has sponsored several tourist and residential development projects along San José's shoreline. Fortunately, the development has done little to change San José's Spanish colonial character, and local residents take pride in restoring the town's 18th-century architecture and preserving its quiet, laid-back ambience.

SIGHTS

Plaza Mijares

The shady town plaza at the intersection of Blvd. Mijares and Calle Zaragoza—San José's two main

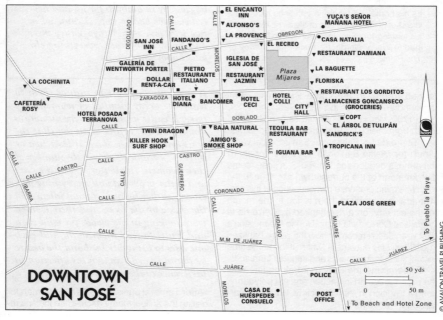

Estero San José

watching. The path begins at the Presidente and comes out on Blvd. Mijares near a modern water-treatment plant.

Zona Hotelera

Fonatur has developed 4,000 shoreline acres adjacent to San José into a hotel/recreation zone. Thus far, the zone contains five resort hotels, an 18-hole Campo de Golf, a shopping center, and several condo and housing developments. Some of the nicest homes are found along the north side of the golf course.

The wide, sandy beach here, known either as Playa Hotelera or Playa California, is perfect for sunbathing, but the undertow is very strong. For several years now, Fonatur has been discussing a proposal to develop a small marina on the shore between the Presidente Inter-Continental Los Cabos and Posada Real hotels.

La Playita and Pueblo La Playa

Just east of San José via Calle Juárez, adjacent to the village of Pueblo La Playa, is La Playita (Little Beach). An ocean beach away from the hotel zone, La Playita offers *pangas* for rent and free camping. This area can be reached by walk-

streets—is a well-tended expanse of brick with benches and a gazebo. At the plaza's west end is the twin-towered **Iglesia San José,** built in 1940 on the site of the original 1730 Misión San José del Cabo. A mosaic over the main entrance depicts a scene from the infamous 1734 Pericú uprising, with Indians shown dragging Padre Tamaral toward a fire, presumably to be burned alive.

Most town festivals are centered at Plaza Mijares.

Estero San José

The freshwater Río San José meets the Pacific Ocean at this 125-acre estuary just east of the Presidente Inter-Continental Los Cabos. A sandbar at the mouth of the river forms a scenic lagoon surrounded by tall palms and marsh grasses—habitat for over 200 species of birds including brown pelicans, ring-necked ducks, common egrets, and herons. You can rent canoes at Tío Sports next to the Presidente for paddling around the lagoon.

A public footpath, **Paseo del Estero,** follows the estuary and river through scenic fan palms, river cane, and tule—a perfect place for bird-

ing along the beach northeast of Presidente Inter-Continental Los Cabos about a kilometer, or by walking a similar distance east along Calle Juárez from downtown. Continue along a dirt road through the middle of the village, past a radio tower, to reach the most secluded spots.

Along the dirt road from here to Pueblo La Playa and beyond to the East Cape are a number of large banyan *(zalate)* and mango trees as well as wild sugarcane. Earlier this century much of the Río San José valley was planted in sugarcane.

Home development continues in the area. Fonatur has long been considering plans to develop a marina called "Puerto Los Cabos" at La Playita, a scheme that would involve building a huge semi-enclosed breakwater and completely dredging the beach to create a harbor.

ACCOMMODATIONS

Hotels in Town
Besides the major hotels and condotels in the *zona hotelera,* San José offers some smaller, reasonably priced inns in the town itself.

Shoestring: The very basic but clean **Hotel Ceci,** Calle Zaragoza 22 (opposite the church), contains 14 rooms with fans. At night, busy Calle Zaragoza might make this a noisy choice, but most of the noise subsides by 11 p.m. Rates: US$12.50 s, US$15 d, US$17 t. Even less expensive is **Hotel Diana,** at Calle Zaragoza 30, tel. (1) 142-0490, a bit west of the Hotel Ceci, which has spartan rooms with a/c, TV, and hot water. Rates: US$9 s/d. A little farther away from the heart of the tourist district but still very much downtown is **San José Inn (Youth Hostel),** on Calle Obregón between Degollado and Verde, tel. (1) 142-2464, fax (1) 142-3205. The two-story concrete building has 15 basic and slightly dank rooms with private baths. Rates: one bed US$11 s/d, two beds US$17, two beds plus TV US$21. Add US$2 for the key deposit. Weekly and monthly rates available.

Shoestring-Budget: Casa de Huéspedes Consuelo, Calle Morelos s/n, just south of María de Juárez on the west side of the street, tel. (1) 142-0643, is a long breeze-block building with two rows of about a dozen basic rooms. Although it's in a fairly quiet neighborhood, it's a 20-minute walk from the Zaragoza and Mijares restaurants. The rooms are nothing special, but all have attached toilets and showers. Rates: US$8/11.80 s with/without a/c, US$10.50/16.50 d, US$17/20 t, US$20/24 q.

Budget: Friendly and economical **Hotel Colli,** on Calle Hidalgo between Zaragoza and Doblado, tel. (1) 142-0725, offers 12 simple but clean and comfortable rooms. This is the best deal in town under US$30. Rates: US$16 s, US$19 d, US$21 t with fan and private bath, or US$19 s, US$21 d with a/c and private bath.

Budget-Inexpensive: Yuca's Señor Mañana Hotel (formerly Posada Señor Mañana), Calle Obregón 1, tel./fax (1) 142-0462, is a rambling affair behind the plaza at the northeast edge of town, overlooking some *huertas.* A small pool and open *palapa* sitting areas with hammocks are a bonus, as is the common kitchen area with individual locked pantry cabinets. Rollaway beds are available for an extra US$10. Rates: $30-45 s/d depending on the room—some have views, sizes vary, and some are newer than others.

Inexpensive: The hospitable **Hotel Posada Terranova,** on Calle Degollado just south of Zaragoza, tel. (1) 142-0534, fax (1) 142-0902, offers good value in this range. It's a converted home with 18 clean, a/c rooms, each with TV and two beds. Recently added direct-dial phones are a plus (but make sure not to use the multiple-digit prefix option that allows use of a credit card, as this accesses one of the infamous price-gouging American phone companies). The inn also features an intimate dining room with an outdoor eating section and a bar. Rates: US$45 s/d.

Moderate: Behind the Tropicana Bar and Grill, **Tropicana Inn,** Blvd. Mijares 30, tel. (1) 142-0907, fax (1) 142-1590, U.S. fax (510) 939-2725, features 40 attractively decorated rooms around a tile-and-cobblestone fountain courtyard. Each room comes with a/c, color satellite TV, coffeemaker, minibar, and direct-dial telephone; other amenities include a swimming pool and complimentary transportation to La Playita and Playa Palmilla. Complimentary continental breakfast is served in a gardenlike pool area. Rates: US$79 s/d.

The quiet, Mexican colonial-style **Hotel El Encanto,** Morelos 133, tel. (1) 142-0388, fax (1) 142-4620, e-mail: elencato@bcs1.telmex.net.mx, is a nicely landscaped oasis offering 19 clean, comfortable rooms, all with phones, a/c, and satellite TV. Alfonso's restaurant is next door. Rates: US$59 s/d standard, US$65 s/d junior suite, US$79 s/d large suite. Add 12% tax to all rates. May 1-Oct. 3 prices run US$53-69, including tax.

Expensive: Suites Las Palmas, Mexico 1, Km 31, tel. (1) 142-2131 or toll-free in Mexico (800) 714-2536, fax (1) 142-4442, e-mail: reservations@suiteslaspalmas.com, is in Plaza Las Palmas out on the highway through town. One- and two-bedroom suites come with fully equipped kitchens, a/c, satellite TV, and direct-dial phones with Internet access. Guests may use the outdoor heated pool on the second floor. The surrounding plaza offers several restaurants, boutiques, shops, a minimarket, and a movie theater. Free daily beach shuttle service is available. Rates: one-bedroom suites US$79-110 d (US$65-85 d low season), two-bedroom suites US$140 d (US$110 d low season). Additional persons US$10 each; add 12% tax to all rates.

Premium: Another new hotel in town is the posh **Casa Natalia,** Blvd. Mijares 4, tel. (1) 142-5100, toll-free (888) 277-3814, fax (1) 142-5110, e-mail: casa.natalia@1cabonet.com.mx. This contemporary Mexican-style hotel is right off the plaza and consists of 14 deluxe rooms, two jacuzzi suites, and two connecting rooms, all individually decorated with authentic artwork from San Miguel de Allende, Oaxaca, and Puebla. Besides the usual amenities found at accommodations in this price range, all rooms have private bougainvillea-covered terraces hung with hammocks. Other features include a heated pool, outdoor palapa bar, and in-room spa services. The attached Mi Cocina restaurant is open for breakfast, lunch, and dinner. Rates: US$220-350 plus tax and service high season, US$180-310 plus tax and service low season.

Beach Hotels

Five hotels widely spaced along Playa Hotelera are seldom full except in the peak months of December through mid-April. Friendly negotiation can often net a savings of as much as 40% off the usual rack rate. Rates given below do not include 12% tax and 10% service unless otherwise noted.

Moderate: The new **Marisol,** Plaza Caracol, tel. (1) 142-3846, U.S. tel. (800) 244-9317, fax (1) 142-3670, e-mail: marisol@caboline.com.mx, is a small eight-suite hotel attached to a shopping center/office complex. All suites come with a/c, TV, two beds, and private bath. Two larger suites at the end of the hall have separate sitting areas and an ocean view. A swimming pool and other facilities at the adjacent Fiesta Inn are available for guest use, and beach towels are provided. A central walkway through the middle of the shopping plaza leads to the beach. Rates: US$67 s/d.

Expensive: The 153-room **Fiesta Inn,** tel. (1) 142-0701, fax (1) 142-0480, U.S. tel. (800) 343-7821, offers a restaurant, pool, and remodeled rooms with a/c, TVs, and phones. Meals are included in the room rates. Rates: from US$80.

The three-story, 99-room **Hotel Aguamarina,** tel. (1) 142-0110 or 142-0077, fax (1) 142-0287, U.S. tel. (800) 897-5700, features clean, standard two-bed rooms with direct-dial phones and TV, a pool, and a restaurant. Rates: US$87-119 s/d, depending on occupancy level, lower in off season.

Expensive-Premium: The well-maintained **Hotel Best Western Posada Real,** tel. (1) 142-0155, fax (1) 142-0460, U.S. tel. (800) 528-1234, e-mail: posadareal@iserve.net.mx, features 150 recently renovated rooms and suites with a/c, telephone, and satellite TV. Hotel facilities include a heated pool, swim-up pool bar, tennis courts, two seaside jacuzzis, and restaurant. Most rooms offer ocean views. Rates: US$84 s/d in the low season; US$128 s/d in the high season. All rates include tax.

Premium (All-Inclusive): At the far northeastern end of the *zona hotelera* is the 236-room, four-suite **Presidente Inter-Continental Los Cabos,** tel. (1) 142-0211, fax (1) 142-0232, U.S./Canada tel. (800) 327-0200, e-mail: loscabos@interconti.com, a well-designed resort next to the Estero San José. Each spacious room comes with a/c, satellite TV, minibar, and telephone. Amenities include a large pool, tennis courts, jacuzzis, a fitness center, beach *palapas,* restaurants, a coffee shop, and auto/ATV rental. Rates of over US$300 a day cover accommodations, three meals a day (including buffets and à la carte dinners), open bar, service charges, all entertainment and recreational activities, and two nighttime theme parties weekly. The resort also maintains a playground and offers special children's activities. Tío Sports next to the hotel rents ATVs and sit-on-top kayaks. An additional 150 rooms, four suites, tennis courts, and a new restaurant were under construction when we stopped by. Although the hotel has a beautiful setting and has great potential for a high-end resort, we have received consistent complaints about the room quality, food quality, and overall service in this hotel. Rates: from US$320.

Condominiums and Condotels

Several condominium complexes in the golf course and beach area and on the hill west of Mexico 1 rent vacant units to visitors for anywhere from around US$65 a night for a studio or one-bedroom unit to around US$300 for a deluxe two- or three-bedroom unit. Discounted weekly and monthly rates are usually available. Local companies that help arrange condo rentals include: **Baja Properties,** Doblado and Morelos, tel. (1) 142-0988, fax (1) 142-0987; **Sunshine Services,** Doblado and Hidalgo, tel./fax (1) 142-2211; and **Dynasty Real Estate,** Apdo. Postal 66, San José del Cabo, BCS, tel./fax (1) 142-0523. Listed below are several complexes that take reservations directly.

Expensive: Along the south edge of the Campo de Golf, **Las Misiones de San José,** tel./fax (1) 142-1401, offers 82 one- and two-bedroom condos—with choice of ocean, pool, or golf-course views. All have a/c, full kitchen, and private terrace. Rates: US$110-120 a night. Southwest of San José del Cabo proper, near Playa Costa Azul, **Mira Vista Beachfront Condos,** tel./fax (1) 142-0523, rents one-bedroom condos by the week (only). Rates: US$600-800 plus tax. **Howard Johnson Plaza Suites,** Paseo Finisterra 1, tel. (1) 142-0999, fax (1) 142-0806, U.S. toll-free tel. (888) 844-4565, e-mail: hojo-cabo@cabonet.net.mx, is a Mediterranean-style resort next to the Campo de Golf. Deluxe a/c rooms and one-, two-, and three-bedroom suites all have satellite TV; each suite comes with private balcony, dining and living room, and phone. The resort boasts two restaurants, a large swimming pool, fitness center, travel agency, car rental agency, and minimarket. Rates: US$90-130.

At the southwestern end of the zone, a sprawling new condo complex called **Las Mañanitas** is under construction and will most likely be renting units by the night, week, and month after opening. Contact Baja Properties, tel. (1) 142-0986 for information.

Premium: Next to Playa Costa Azul, at Km 29, **La Jolla de Los Cabos,** tel. (1) 142-3000, fax (1) 142-0546, U.S. tel. (800) 455-CABO, e-mail: lajolla@1cabonet.com.mx, features 193 one- and two-bedroom suites and condos, each with private living room, balcony with ocean view, a/c, ceiling fans, satellite TV, phone, refrigerator, and coffeemaker. The one- and two-bedroom suites contain full kitchens, while studios feature wet bars. On the premises are four pools, a swim-up bar, fitness center, sauna, minimarket, and restaurant/lounge. Rates: from US$145 plus tax and service. Next door to La Jolla, white-and-blue, Mediterranean-style **Mykonos Bay Resort,** tel. (1) 142-0716, fax (1) 142-0270, rents 69 one- and two-bedroom condos, each with a/c, satellite TV, full kitchen, and washer/dryer. Amenities include a snack bar, gym, and lighted tennis courts. Rates: US$950 (one bedroom) or US$1,200 (two bedroom) per week, plus tax and service.

Bed and Breakfasts

Moderate: Perched on a bluff overlooking Playa Costa Azul and the Sea of Cortez (but across the highway from the beach), **Casa Terra Cotta,** Km 29, Mexico 1, tel./fax (1) 142-4250, e-mail: info@terracotta-mex.com, boasts a collection of four small, private *casitas* and a trailer in a quiet garden setting. Each has a ceiling fan, private bath, and a hammock-slung veranda; from one of the cottages, "Casita Azul," you can spot all three surf breaks—perfect for surfers who want to be able to check conditions without taking a long, steep walk down to the beach. Breakfast is complimentary, and healthy à la carte meals are available for lunch and dinner. A fully equipped kitchen is available for guest use for a fee of US$8 per day. Rates: US$75-95 per *casita* 1 Nov.-19 Dec. and 10 Jan.-31 May; US$50-70 1 June-31 October. Add 12% tax to all rates.

Expensive: Next to the public golf course, **Casa del Jardín,** Paseo Finisterra 107, tel. (1) 142-1964, e-mail: casa@casajardin.com, offers four rooms in a renovated former residence. Each room is named and decorated according to a different nature theme. All room have ceiling fans, a/c, and private balconies. The property is lushly planted with citrus trees, flowers, palms, and a large herb and vegetable garden. Guests have free run of the house (including an upstairs sitting room and downstairs living room, both equipped with TVs) as well as access to a telephone, fax, and computer. A full breakfast is served on a covered terrace overlooking the garden and swimming pool or in the formal dining room. Smoking is not permitted in the house. Rates: US$80-90 d; 15 Dec.-1 Jan. rates increase to US$100-110 d.

Expensive-Premium: About three km north of San José, east of the hamlet of Santa Rosa and across the Arroyo del San José, lies secluded **Huerta Verde Bed & Breakfast Inn,** tel./fax (1) 148-0511, U.S. tel. (303) 431-5162, U.S. fax (303) 431-4455, e-mail: jbruen2254@aol.com, an old ranch converted to a full-service bed and breakfast. Well-furnished suites are available in either a brick-and-tile building or separate cottages. Four of the suites overlook the pool and orchards. No two units are decorated the same. All have a/c and ceiling fans; the separate cottage units also contain kitchenettes. Two large Mexican breakfasts are included with each unit, and light lunches and fixed-price dinners are available upon request. A small pool is on the premises. The proprietors are happy to arrange fishing, biking, or hiking trips. Call or write for directions; Huerta Verde's U.S. mailing address is 7674 Reed St., Arvada, CO 80003. Rates: US$115-140.

La Playita
Moderate: Northeast of San José in the village of La Playita, **La Playita Inn,** Apdo. Postal 437, San José, BCS 23400, tel. (1) 142-4156, U.S. tel. (818) 962-2805 or toll-free (888) 242-4166, offers well-tended rooms each with a/c, ceiling fan, TV, and large shower. The inn is just a short walk from the sportfishing *pangas* on the beach. Rates run US$75 s/d 15 Nov.-15 May, US$50 the rest of the year, including tax.

Camping and RV Parks
Brisa del Mar RV Park, 3.2 km (two miles) southwest of San José off Mexico 1 at Km 28 (Apdo. Postal 45, San José del Cabo, BCS), tel. (1) 142-3999, e-mail: mortimer@brisadelmar.com, is the only beachfront RV park in Los Cabos. As such, it's often full Dec.-Feb., the high snowbird season. For two people/one vehicle, full-hookup RV slots range from US$18.50 for spaces in the back row up to US$30 for beachfront spots (US$25 March-Nov.). Tent spaces cost US$12 when available (US$11 March-Nov.), plus US$2 per additional guest. Weekly and monthly discounts are available. Facilities include flush toilets, showers, a laundry, pool, restaurant, and bar. Some full-timers have built studio apartments on the grounds, and these may occasionally become available as rentals. Brisa del Mar is easy to miss; watch carefully for the small sign.

You can camp free on the beach at La Playita between San José and Pueblo La Playa and between Brisa del Mar RV Park and the water. Within walking distance of the beach in Pueblo La Playa itself, cozy **El Delfín Blanco RV Park,** Apdo. Postal 147, San José del Cabo, BCS 23400, tel. (1) 142-1212, tel./fax (1) 142-1199, e-mail: eldelfinblanco@1cabonet.com.mx, rents

Calle Zaragoza, San José del Cabo

tent sites for two people for $10; if you don't have a tent you can rent one for $15. Campers can use the showers for a steep US$2.50. Cabañas are also available for US$30 s, US$36 d, US$43 t, and *casitas* for US$45 d, US$52 t, US$59 q. All rates include tax. El Delfín Blanco also rents bicycles for US$10 per day.

FOOD

Most of San José's fashionable restaurants are along Blvd. Mijares and Calle Zaragoza near the plaza. These eateries are for the most part geared to Mexican diners as well as foreigners—so far the town harbors no equivalents to Cabo San Lucas's Giggling Marlin or Squid Roe.

As a general rule, the closer a restaurant to the plaza, the more expensive the menu. To save money and experience local flavor, seek out the spots where San José residents eat—most are in the western part of town toward Mexico 1.

Alta Cocina

Restaurants specializing in Mexican foods prepared in the *alta cocina* ("high cuisine" or gourmet) style seem to have proliferated almost overnight in San José. **Tequila Bar Restaurante,** in a restored classic adobe just west of Blvd. Mijares on the south side of Doblado, tel. (1) 142-1155, was the first of the high-class eateries to open. It looks small from the entryway but opens onto a sizable open-air, tree-shaded courtyard in back. The tasteful, low-key Mexican decor is enhanced by candlelight after sunset. In addition to a prime list of tequilas, the restaurant specializes in traditional Mexican dishes such as *chile en nogada* (a fancier version of the *chile relleno*) and tequila shrimp served with grilled plantain and black beans, as well as innovative Pacific Rim/Mediterranean cuisine, including seafood ravioli, oriental spring rolls with orange ginger sauce, grapefruit and avocado salad, cold linguine salad, grilled fish with mango and ginger sauce, and grilled chicken breast sautéed in peanut sauce. Moderate to expensive; open daily for dinner only.

The new **Café Florentina,** tel. (1) 142-2799, is housed in an old colonial on Calle Zaragoza across from the church. Outdoor seating under trees strung with glowing lanterns creates a romantic ambience. The kitchen prepares delicious appetizers as well as all manner of Mexican-fusion entrées for around US$13-20. The restaurant offers a full bar, an extensive wine list, and friendly attentive service.

The upscale **Mi Cocina,** inside Casa Natalia, tel. (1) 142-5100, serves nouvelle Mexican-Euro cuisine in a beautiful contemporary outdoor setting. Open for breakfast, lunch, and dinner.

Antojitos and Fast Food

At the west end of Calle Doblado are several inexpensive taco stands and *fruterías*. The Mercado Municipal features a section of side-by-side, clean *loncherías* open 7 a.m. till around 4 or 5 p.m.

Restaurant El Descanso, an outdoor *palapa*-roofed place on Calle Castro, diagonally opposite the Mercado Municipal, serves inexpensive *menudo, pozole, birria, barbacoa,* tamales, and other Mexican soul food 24 hours a day. Look for large vats on a wood fire. **Cafetería El Portón,** on the north side of Doblado east of Calle Muñoz, tel. (1) 142-4115, offers good basic Mexican fare in clean surroundings. It's very inexpensive and very local; open Mon.-Sat. 8 a.m.-5:30 p.m.

Restaurant Las Hornillas, toward the west end of Calle Doblado, specializes in inexpensive mesquite-grilled chicken, steaks, and burgers for a mostly local clientele; open daily noon-9 p.m. **Super Tacos de Baja California Hermanos Gonzales,** on the north side of Calle Doblado, west of the Centro de Salud, is a branch of the famous taco stand of the same name in La Paz. Look for inexpensive fish, shrimp, and clam tacos, with a large selection of condiments.

Another good place for tacos is **Taquería Erika,** near Mexico 1 on the south side of the street. They serve *tacos de carne asada* and *tripa,* as well as quesadillas.

Taco stands come in and out of fashion—**Taquería Rossy,** next to Del Cabo Sushi off Mexico 1, happens to be the place of the moment in San José. It's popular with locals as well as tourists for delicious and inexpensive shrimp and fish tacos. Open daily 10:30 a.m.-10 p.m. **Tacos El Indio,** off the west side of Mexico 1 on Calle Malvarrosa (one street north of Calle González) in the Colina de los Maestros neighborhood, offers very good corn on the cob (*elotes*), *tacos de carne asada,* quesadillas, *frijoles charros, cebollas asadas,* and potatoes (*papas*), with choice of shrimp, mushrooms, steak, or corn. Lots of fresh condiments. Inexpensive; generally open 6 p.m.-midnight.

El Mesón del Ahorcado, on Calle Barlovento west of Mexico 1 almost across from Ferro Gases de Los Cabos, is a funky, rustic outdoor place with a full selection of quesadillas (including *huitlacoche,* mushrooms, squash-flower, and cactus fillings), tacos, *frijoles charros, champurrado,* and *café de olla.* Despite the fancy name, the restaurant's design can best be described as "flea-market junk decor." Look for a stuffed scarecrow-like effigy hanging outside. Open 6-11 p.m.

On the east side of Mexico 1 near Calle Doblado, **100% Vitalidad** serves *tortas,* enchiladas, tacos, and *chilaquiles.* Just south of that is **Lonchería y Cenaduría Jalisco.** It offers such Mexican favorites as *chiles rellenos, birria,* and *menudo,* as well as egg dishes. Open in the evening.

Aurora's Restaurant, just east of the bus terminal on Calle González, serves good, basic *antojitos* at low prices in a pleasant outdoor *palapa* atmosphere. It's popular with the locals; open Mon.-Sat. for breakfast, lunch, and dinner.

Cafetería Rosy, a small, humble Mexican café on Calle Zaragoza, is nicer on the inside than it looks on the outside. In addition to tacos (choice of beef, shrimp, fish, or chicken), the friendly family-run kitchen serves all sorts of well-prepared Mexican breakfasts, including *machaca, chilaquiles, molletes,* hotcakes, and French toast, along with fresh-brewed coffee. Inexpensive; open Mon.-Sat. 8 a.m.-10 p.m.

Super Pollo, perched on a rise overlooking the west side of the highway just north of Supermercado Castro, is a branch of Mexico's widespread chicken chain. This one outdoes itself with tasty roast chicken and out-of-this-world roasted banana chiles. Inexpensive; open daily 11 a.m.-11 p.m.

Baja Natural, on the south side of Calle Doblado between Hidalgo and Morelos, tel. (1) 142-3105, serves delicious fresh juices, malts, green salads, hot dogs, gardenburgers, *tortas,* fruit salads, and other fruit and vegetable concoctions with interesting names. The "chupacabra" is a made with blended pineapple, oranges, carrots, beets, and celery; the one-liter servings cost about US$3. Open Mon.-Sat. 7 a.m.-8 p.m.

Good fish and shrimp tacos are available at **El Recreo,** a small stand with a few tables just north of the church on the plaza. Open for breakfast at 7 a.m., then again in the middle of the day for tacos. Inexpensive.

Sandrick's, Blvd. Mijares, tel. (1) 142-1270, an informal late-lunch, après-beach kind of place, specializes in fajitas, fish or shrimp tacos, ribs, burgers, and chimichangas. Happy hour is 4-7 p.m., when you can get a bucket of five beers for US$4.25. Inexpensive to moderate; open 2-9 p.m. daily except Tuesday.

International

El Arbol del Tulipán (The Tulip Tree), on Manuel Doblado just off Mijares, is a casual place open for lunch and dinner. The menu features such gringo favorites as hamburgers, rib-eye steak, veggie burgers, salads, stir-fries, and pastas.

Corre Caminos Café and Bakery is a small a/c place with a few outdoor tables attached to a small shopping plaza on Blvd. Mijares. The café offers sandwiches (smoked turkey on a croissant with jack cheese, Cabo garden sandwich), subs, coffee drinks, lemonade, iced tea, smoothies, pastries, and fresh-baked breads. Open 7 a.m.-9 p.m.

In the Plaza Los Cabos shopping center in the *zona hotelera* are **Pizzería Tropicana,** tel. (1) 142-0922, offering free delivery to homes and hotels, and **Rusty Putter Bar and Grille,** a sports bar with some outdoor tables—the *palapa*-covered area is a good spot to catch a nice ocean breeze. The bar features live music on weekends.

Right off the plaza, **Floriska,** Blvd. Mijares 16-1, tel. (1) 142-4600, is an elegantly decorated place with three separate indoor eating areas and a patio dining area in the back. The ambience is upscale and the international menu is creative, with prices to match—US$17.50-28 for an entrée. Open 6-10:30 p.m.

Pietro Ristorante Italiano, tel. (1) 142-0558, is a tastefully decorated restaurant/bar serving Italian food for lunch (11:45 a.m.-3:45 p.m.) and dinner (5:45-11:15 p.m.). Moderate to expensive. The upscale **Da Antonio,** on the Estero San José, tel. (1) 142-0211, next to the El Presidente Inter-Continental Los Cabos, claims to be an authentic Italian trattoría. The outdoor tables have a view of the scenic estuary. Expensive. Open Tues.-Sun. for dinner only, 6-11 p.m.

Twin Dragon, on the south side of Calle Doblado between Guerrero and Morelos, is the better of San José's two Chinese restaurants. Look for inexpensive Cantonese dishes for lunch and dinner Mon.-Saturday.

In a building that was once a part of San José's original colonial hotel, **Fandango,** Obregon west of Morelos, tel. (1) 142-2226, uses Mexican colors and original accessories to create a fun, bohemian ambience in both indoor and outdoor dining areas. The ever-changing menu has featured Cuban coconut prawns, Moroccan chicken, sesame-seared tuna, and blue crab cakes. Prices are moderate. Open Mon.-Sat. 8-11:30 a.m. for breakfast, 11:30 a.m.-4:30 p.m. for lunch, and 6-10 p.m. for dinner. It stays open Friday and Saturday till 11:30 p.m. for appetizers and drinks; closed Sunday.

La Provence Garden Restaurant/Bar, in a historic building at the corner of Morelos and Obregón, tel. (1) 142-3373, specializes in Mediterranean cuisine prepared by French chef Jean Pierre Rivault and served on a pretty garden patio or at indoor tables. Rivault formerly worked as executive chef for the Westin Regina Los Cabos, in the Corridor between San José and San Lucas, and at the Hotel Inter-Continental in Istanbul. Expensive but worth it. Open daily except Tuesday, 5:30-11 p.m.

Next door to the El Encanto Inn, **Alfonso's,** Morelos 133, tel. (1) 142-0388, ext. 302, serves international cuisine in an ambience of floral tablecloths, oil paintings, and elevator music. The restaurant's signature dish is grilled lobster (US$21). The changing menu features such interesting creations as green corn tamales with caviar, chicken breast with mango chutney, and lamb chops with mint jelly. The restaurant offers a full bar and wine list. Open Mon.-Sat. 8 a.m.-10:20 p.m., closed Sunday.

A half block west of the TelMex tower, the new **Ché Gaucho,** Margarita de Juárez, tel. (1) 142-1244, is an Argentine steakhouse specializing in fresh pastas, barbecued meats, and grilled steaks.

Brisa Lighthouse, the simple restaurant/bar at Brisa del Mar RV Park, serves good, reason-

ably priced American and Mexican food for breakfast, lunch, and dinner.

Mexican
La Cenaduría, opposite the plaza on the south side of Calle Zaragoza, is a friendly eatery housed in an old thick-walled adobe. Inside are two high-ceilinged dining rooms, while up on the roof are a few more tables under a *palapa.* The varied menu covers a range of mainland-style *antojitos,* including tostadas, *gorditas, pozole, flautas,* enchiladas, quesadillas, tamales, tacos, *carne asada, pollo a la plaza,* and *pollo en mole.* The *pescado siete mares* or "seven seas fish" is a personal favorite. Inexpensive to moderate; open daily 11 a.m.-9 p.m.

Restaurant Bar Jazmín, just off Zaragoza on Morelos, opposite the *nevería,* is a once-casual local eatery now gone a/c and upscale. The menu offers fresh juices and *licuados,* Mexican breakfasts, French toast and pancakes, *chilaquiles,* burgers, tortilla soup, *tortas,* tacos, tostadas, fajitas, *carne asada,* and seafood. Moderately priced; open daily for breakfast, lunch, and dinner.

On the northwestern stretch of Calle Zaragoza, where tourists are rarely seen, **La Conchita** offers simple, inexpensive Mexican food daily 8 a.m.-4 p.m.

The new **El Chilaquil,** at Mijares and Paseo Finisterra, tel. (1) 142-3755, in a small shopping plaza toward the south end of Blvd. Mijares, specializes in authentic Mexican cuisine from various regions. Featured are four types of *chilaquiles, panuchos* (bean-stuffed tortillas topped with marinated chicken strips, red onions, sour orange, and a tart radish-and-cilantro mix) from the Yucatán, salads, *enfrijoladas,* enchiladas, and lobster. The namesake *chilaquiles* dishes all cost around US$5, while seafood entrées run US$12.50-25.50. Open 6-10:30 p.m.

Damiana, on the plaza, tel. (1) 142-0499, named for the Cape Region's legendary herbal aphrodisiac, is housed in a restored 18th-century townhouse and is one of the original romantic courtyard restaurants in Los Cabos. Rooms include a tastefully decorated bar, an indoor dining area, and a patio dining area—candlelit in the evening—surrounded by lush foliage. House specialties include cheese soup, shrimp, lobster, abalone, and steak. A complimentary taste of *damiana* liqueur is served to guests upon request. Expensive. Open daily 10:30 a.m.-midnight, serving *almuerzo,* lunch, and dinner.

Los Gorditos, just south of the plaza on Blvd. Mijares, tel. (1) 142-3733, is an upstairs restaurant overlooking the street. The moderately priced menu features well-prepared seafood and Mexican dishes. Open for breakfast, lunch, and dinner.

In a rustic decor emphasized by a worn brick facade and old doors, **Restaurant Xochimilco,** on the north side of Zaragoza near Guerrero, offers appetizers such as seafood *toritos* with plantain and black bean sauce, crepes, *brochettas,* and *chalupas,* along with other Mexican entrées prepared with fish, chicken, or lobster. Soups and salads round out the menu. Most dishes are moderately priced. Open daily noon-11 p.m.

Tropicana Bar & Grill, tel. (1) 142-1580, is a large, touristy restaurant/bar with outdoor patio, big-screen sports TV, and live music and dancing at night. The menu is basic Tourist Mex/Fake Caribbean, but the drinks are strong. Moderately priced; open daily for lunch and dinner.

The family-run **Posada Terranova,** on Calle Degollado just south of Zaragoza, tel. (1) 142-0534, features a small dining room and bar, and outdoor seating. In addition to standard Mexican dishes, the menu offers a good variety of high-quality Mexican and American breakfasts. Inexpensive to moderate; open daily 7 a.m.-10 p.m.

Though more of a bar than a restaurant, **Iguana Bar,** Blvd. Mijares, tel. (1) 142-0266, serves well-prepared seafood, ribs, chicken, and Mexican dishes. In the evenings, the restaurant transforms into a nightclub with live music. Moderately priced. Open daily 11 a.m.-1 a.m.

Between the golf course and the *zona hotelera* in the Plaza Los Cabos shopping center, **Restaurant El Sinaloense,** tel. (1) 142-3218, is a sparkling little Mexican restaurant popular with the business-lunch crowd. It serves well-prepared seafood, fish tacos, and burritos. Inexpensive to moderate; open Mon.-Sat. 11 a.m.-9 p.m.

La Playita and Pueblo La Playa

Just east of San José via Calle Juárez, **Los Dos Ricardos,** tel. (1) 142-3068, is a typical but out-of-the-way, open-air seafood *palapa* on the road through Pueblo La Playa. Inexpensive to moderate; open 9:30 a.m.-10:30 p.m. daily except Thursday.

Palapa-roofed **La Playita,** in Pueblo La Playa near the beach, has long held a good reputation for serving fresh seafood in a laid-back, beachy atmosphere. It changes management from time to time so it unfortunately lacks consistency, but it's worth a try in case it's going through a good phase. Open nightly for dinner only; occasional live music.

Going inland, just up from La Playita is **Restaurant/Bar El Gringo Viejo,** a very rustic place, then right next to that is **Lonchería La Pasadita,** serving *antojitos,* tamales, *tortas,* and tostadas.

Playa Costa Azul

Surfers, surfer wannabes, and tourists head to **Zipper's,** a round, *palapa*-topped beach restaurant at the southwest end of Playa Costa Azul. The menu offers tasty mesquite-grilled hamburgers, fish burgers, chili, *chiles rellenos,* and quesadillas. Indoor seating areas feature a/c, while the large outdoor patio offers an ocean view. Moderately priced. Open Mon.-Sat. 11 a.m.-11 p.m., Sunday 8:30 a.m.-11 p.m.; live music on weekends during the tourist season.

Groceries

The **Mercado Municipal,** between Calles Castro and Coronado in the west part of town, provides fresh fruits and vegetables, fish, meats, a *licuado* stand, and a cluster of *loncherías;* it's open daily from dawn to dusk. **Mini Super Gabrielle,** across from La Provence on Obregón, carries typical Mexican grocery items.

More expensive canned and imported foods, plus beer and liquor, are available at decades-old **Almacenes Goncanseco,** Blvd. Mijares 14-18 (opposite city hall); this supermarket accepts credit cards. Near the Hotel Diana on Calle Zaragoza, the **Supermercado Zaragoza** carries canned and bottled goods but very little produce. A couple of smaller grocery stores lie along the west end of Calle Zaragoza. Across from Piso 1, **Aramburo** on Zaragoza at Degollado is a basic medium-sized grocery store.

On the east side of Mexico 1, just north of the west end of Calle Doblado, **Supermercado Grupo Castro** is larger and more well-stocked than Almacenes Goncanseco. Better yet is the large and modern **Supermercado Plaza,** a half kilometer north of town on the east side of Mexico 1. Both of these supermarkets can supply just about any food/liquor/ice needs.

Mini Super, in Plaza Los Cabos opposite the Fiesta Inn, carries a few imported food items along with standard Mexican fare.

Toward the west end of Calle Zaragoza is **Pastelería y Panadería La Princesa,** with a good selection of Mexican cakes, pastries, and bread. Pricier European-style baked items are available at **La Baguette,** Blvd. Mijares 10, on the east side of the plaza. Open 8 a.m.-8 p.m.

Tortillería Perla, diagonally opposite the Centro de Salud health center on Calle Doblado, sells corn tortillas by the kilo Mon.-Sat. 6 a.m.-3 p.m., Sunday 6 a.m.-noon. On the west side of Mexico 1, almost opposite the west end of Calle Doblado, **Tortillería de Harina** supplies flour tortillas during roughly the same hours. Along the same side of the highway, just south of Calle Doblado, **Panaficadora San José** has the usual tongs-and-tray baked goods. On the north side of Calle Zaragoza near Guerrero, **Pastelería las Tres Leches** is similar.

The most convenient place to buy fresh seafood in town is **Pescadería San Marcos,** a

loncherías *in the Mercado Municipal*

small fish market near the Mercado Municipal on Calle Coronado.

Sweets
For Mexican-style ice cream or fresh-fruit popsicles, try **Paletería y Nevería La Michoacana** on Calle Morelos near Zaragoza across from Restaurant Jazmín. Their refreshing *paletas de mango* (mango popsicles) are good. For American-style ice cream, **Helados Bing,** on Blvd. Mijares, next to Sandrick's Bar and Grill, has a nice selection.

Dulcería Arco Iris, on the north side of Calle Doblado, west of Green, and **La Bonita del Señor San José,** on the south side of Doblado east of Morelos, both feature all types of Mexican candies.

ENTERTAINMENT AND EVENTS

Bars and Discos
While San José doesn't offer as much of a nighttime party scene as Cabo San Lucas, neither does the town close down at sunset—although in low season it may seem that way. One of the most relaxed spots is the **Iguana Bar,** on Blvd. Mijares, tel. (1) 142-0266, where live bands play a mix of Latino and international pop. The Iguana also hosts the occasional *travesti* (transvestite) performance troupe, an entertaining lineup of drag queens performing popular music in near-camp style.

Piso 1 (formerly Piso 2), directly across from Supermercado Aramburo on Calle Zaragoza, is a casual rooftop bar sheltered by a combination tent and *palapa,* with a view of the street below. A downstairs section contains a few pool tables.

On Mijares, the popular **Tropicana Bar & Grill,** tel. (1) 142-1580, features lounge-lizard folk music in the front room and canned music in the back. Both bars host a two-drinks-for-the-price-of-one happy hour in the late afternoon.

La Habana, perched on a rise overlooking Mexico 1 and Playa Costa Azul, hosts live music Thurs.-Sun.; at least one night a week, an excellent local combo plays Cuban and salsa.

Cinema
In Plaza Las Palmas, on the west side of Mexico 1 at Km 31, is **Cinemas Los Cabos,** a two-screen theater showing first-run movies.

Miniature Golf
Near the Rusty Putter Bar and Grille in the Plaza Los Cabos shopping center is **Caddy Shak,** an 18-hole miniature golf course.

Events
On most Saturday evenings during the Dec.-March high tourist season San José hosts a fiesta in Plaza Mijares. Although mostly held for the benefit of tourists, lots of locals attend as well. Typical events include folk dances, mariachi performances, cockfight demonstrations, and piñata breaking. Numerous vendors sell arts and crafts and food; profits from food and beverage sales go to local charities and service clubs.

San José's biggest annual festival is held 19 March, the feast day of its patron saint. In addition to music, dancing, and food, celebratory activities include horse races and parades.

SHOPPING

Arts, Crafts, and Souvenirs
Near the intersection of Blvd. Mijares and the road to Pueblo La Playa, about halfway between the *zona hotelera* and the plaza, is a large open-air market selling inexpensive Mexican handicrafts; it's generally open 11 a.m.-9 p.m. Higher-quality, higher-priced arts and crafts are offered in shops along the east end of Calle Zaragoza and the north end of Blvd. Mijares. These include **Antigua Los Cabos** (handmade furniture, antiques, rugs, folk art, and ceramics), **Bye-Bye** (T-shirts and souvenirs), **Sol Dorado** (*artesanía* and jewelry), **Veryka** (Mexican crafts), **Copal** (Mexican crafts), and **La Mina** (silver jewelry).

Galería de Wentworth Porter, Calle Obregón 20 near Morelos, tel. (1) 142-3141, features large colorful oil paintings of Mexican landscapes and people by Dennis Wentworth Porter, as well as works by other artists. Prints and art cards are also on sale. Open Mon.-Sat. 10 a.m.-5 p.m., other times by appointment only. Closed 15 Aug.-15 October.

Organización Sierra Madre, on Blvd. Mijares near Sandrick's, tel. (1) 142-4151, sells nature-oriented books, T-shirts emblazoned with endangered species, and other ecologically conscious souvenirs. Proceeds from the sale of these items support a variety of conservation efforts in Baja California and northwestern Mexico, including cleanups of Estero San José. Unfortunately, the staff also seems to have some kind of association with time-share sales.

Cigars
Amigos Smoke Shop and Cigar Bar, Calle Doblado and Morelos, tel. (1) 142-1138, features a walk-in cigar humidor and offers good Italian espresso, premium wines, and spirits.

Interior Design
In recent years San José has amassed quite a collection of shops dealing in interior design products of all kinds. **Galería Los Cabos,** on Calle Hidalgo north of Obregón, sells a unique assortment of antique and rattan furniture, stoneware, crafts, decorator items, and locally made barrel-back chairs. Also on Calle Hidalgo, **La Hormiga** and **Arte Contemporaneo and Antiques** specialize in original designs as well as antiques.

Casa Paulina, more or less opposite Bancomer on Calle Zaragoza, sells high-quality, original home accessories and furniture—perfect for anyone looking to furnish a vacation home.

Rattan Bamboo, near La Mina on Blvd. Mijares, purveys uniquely designed sculpture and furniture fashioned from giant bamboo.

Surf Shop
Killer Hook Surf Shop, on the east side of Calle Guerrero at Doblado, tel. (1) 142-2430, stocks surfing, snorkeling, and other water-sports equipment, as well as T-shirts and stickers. Killer Hook also has a branch opposite Playa Costa Azul, southwest of town, where you can rent surf gear.

Clothing
On Calle Hidalgo between Zaragoza and Doblado is **Clio,** a small boutique featuring fashions for young women. **La Sangría,** just north of Restaurant Damiana, specializes in women's clothing of original design.

Reading Material
Publicaciones May, on the north side of Calle Doblado near the street's west end, carries a

large collection of books, magazines, and newspapers—though mostly in Spanish. A new branch of **Libros Libros,** on the west side Blvd. Mijares, just north of Plaza José Green, carries a good selection of English-language paperbacks, magazines, maps, books on Baja, children's books, and U.S. newspapers. Open daily 9 a.m.-9 p.m.

SPORTS AND RECREATION

Fishing
All hotels in the *zona hotelera* can arrange guided fishing trips. Since San José has no harbor or marina, all trips are in *pangas*. One of the more reputable outfits is **Victor's Sportfishing,** headquartered at Hotel Posada Real, tel. (1) 142-1092 or (800) 521-2281 in the U.S., fax (1) 142-1093. A six-hour *panga* trip for two or three persons costs US$150; bring your own food and drinks. An eight-hour trip aboard a 28- to 32-foot cabin cruiser can accommodate up to six anglers for US$395. You can also hire *pangas* directly from the *pangeros* at the beach next to Pueblo La Playa. For example, **Gordo Banks Pangas,** tel./fax (1) 142-1147, U.S. reservations (800) 408-1199, rents 22-foot *pangas* for US$170 (six hours, one to three anglers) or 23-foot *super pangas* for US$200 (six hours, one to three anglers). Whether using a guide arranged through one of the hotels or at La Playita, it's best to bring your own rods and tackle as the quality of local guide-supplied gear is low.

roosterfish

Onshore and inshore catches include cabrilla, grouper, roosterfish, sierra, snapper, jack crevalle, pompano, and the occasional yellowtail. Farther offshore you might catch tuna, dorado, and sailfish. One of Baja's best marlin and wahoo grounds is Bancos Gorda (Gorda Banks), two seamounts about 16 km (10 miles) southeast of San José. Striped marlin are seen year-round in Cape Region waters; angling for dorado, roosterfish, and sailfish is best in the late summer and early fall.

Just north of Plaza José Green, **Punta Gorda Sportfishing,** Blvd. Mijares, tel. (1) 142-1154,

also organizes fishing trips.

Killer Hook Surf Shop, on Calle Guerrero in town, tel. (1) 142-2430, rents rod-and-tackle sets for US$6 a day. **Deportiva Piscis,** on the south side of Calle Castro, tel. (1) 142-0332, sells fishing tackle as well as bait. Open 9 a.m.-7 p.m.

Golf and Tennis
Though not a world-class course, the **Campo de San José** (San José Country Club, also known simply as "Campo de Golf") is an attractive, nine-hole, par-35, 2,900-yard course designed for intermediate and beginning golfers. Built and well maintained by Fonatur, it's surrounded by nicely landscaped residential properties and has a sea view. This is a popular course with the locals; it does not take reservations. There are plans to add another nine holes in the near future. Greens fees are US$30 for nine holes, US$55 for 18. Golf carts rent for US$25 (nine holes) or US$50 (18 holes). Bottled water and other services may be purchased at the caddy shack. The club also features tennis courts, a pool, clubhouse, pro shop, restaurants, and a bar. Call (1) 142-0905 for more information.

Kayaking
Los Lobos del Mar Kayak Ventures, based at Brisa del Mar RV Park, tel. (1) 142-2983, offers several different sea kayaking itineraries, including a US$55 sunset paddle that includes a beach picnic by lantern light. A full-day Cabo Pulmo trip costs US$104 pp, including kayak and snorkeling gear, breakfast, lunch, and roundtrip transportation between San José and Cabo Pulmo.

Surfing
Nearby **Playa Costa Azul** (Blue Coast Beach) boasts two good summer breaks: a short fast inside known as "Zippers" and a middle right point break called "The Rock." At the next little bay south, almost invisible from the highway, **Playa Acapulquito** (Little Acapulco Beach) gets an outside break that sometimes connects with the Costa Azul waves in larger summer swells.

Killer Hook Surf Shop on Guerrero at Doblado, tel. (1) 142-2430, rents surfboards with leash and wax for US$15 per 24 hours. Rentals of four days or more earn a discount. A bodyboard and fins can be rented for US$10 (or bodyboard alone for US$8).

Organized Tours
Nómadas de Baja, P.O. Box 254, San José del Cabo, BCS 23400, tel./fax (1) 142-4388, e-mail: nomadas@1cabonet.com.mx, organizes a full range of guided expeditions throughout southern Baja. You can choose from mountain hiking (nine hours, US$60), historic walking tours, kayak adventures around Cabo Pulmo (nine hours, US$105), snorkeling and diving (nine hours, US$125), and mountain-bike tours (two and a half to five hours, US$25-35). Rates include a bilingual guide, all related gear, lunch and/or snacks, and beverages.

INFORMATION AND SERVICES

Tourist Office
The city maintains a tourist information office on the plaza near the intersection of Calle Zaragoza and Blvd. Mijares. The stock of brochures and maps on hand includes nothing unusually informative, but staff are helpful and friendly. It's open Mon.-Sat. 8 a.m.-5 p.m.

Changing Money
Four banks in town offer foreign-currency exchange services Mon.-Fri. 8:30-11:30 a.m. The lines at Bancomer, one block west of the plaza at Calles Zaragoza and Morelos, are generally the longest; during high tourist season if you're not in line by 11 a.m., you might not make it to the foreign-exchange window before it closes.

Serfín, two blocks west of Bancomer on Calle Zaragoza, usually has shorter lines, and its ATM cuts the queue even further. Bital, in a small relatively new shopping center on Blvd. Mijares, just south of Calle Misiones, also offers exchange services. The new Banamex, in Plaza José Green on Blvd. Mijares, south of Coronado, has an ATM.

Baja Money Exchange, on Blvd. Mijares just north of Sandricks, will change cash and traveler's checks at a low exchange rate. The major hotels will also gladly take your dollars at a low exchange rate. Stick to the banks if you want the most pesos for your dollar.

USEFUL SAN JOSÉ DEL CABO TELEPHONE NUMBERS

San José del Cabo area code: 1
Police: 142-3937
Red Cross: 142-0316
Fire: 142-2466
General Hospital: 142-0013
IMSS Hospital: 142-0076
Tourism Office: 142-2960, ext. 150

Post and Telephone
San José's post and telegraph office, on Blvd. Mijares, is open Mon.-Fri. 8 a.m.-5 p.m. Next to the post office, the Telecomm office sends and receives Western Union telegrams.

Mail Boxes Etc. maintains an outlet at Plaza Las Palmas, tel. (1) 142-4355, fax (1) 142-4360. MBE carries mailing supplies, postage stamps, and magazines and rents mailboxes.

The telephone office on Calle Doblado, opposite the hospital, offers direct-dial long-distance phone service. LADATEL booths, the most convenient public phones for making international calls, are at Calles Doblado and Muñoz and on Calle Hidalgo between Obregón and Comonfort.

E-mail and Internet Services
Cabo Cafe.com, in Plaza José Green on the east side of Blvd. Mijares toward the *zona hotelera,* charges US$7.50 per hour, US$4.25 per half hour for computer use.

Canadian Consulate
The office of the Canadian consulate is on the second floor of Plaza José Green, Blvd. Mijares, tel. (1) 142-4333, fax (1) 142-4262, emergency toll-free tel. (800) 706-2900. Open Mon.-Fri. 9 a.m.-1 p.m.

RV Service and Supplies
Wahoo RV Center, near the CFE electric utility office in Col. Chula Vista, off Mexico 1 (turn west between the Super Pollo and the turnoff for the Pemex station), tel./fax (1) 142-3792, sells RV parts and accessories, does maintenance and repairs—including a/c and refrigeration—for trailers and motorhomes, and offers the use of a dump station. It's open Mon.-Fri. 8 a.m.-1 p.m.

COTP
Although it's unlikely any international boaters will be needing a Captain of the Port since there are as yet no marinas or harbors in San José del Cabo, the town does have its own Capitanía del Puerto, tel. (1) 142-0722. The office sits at the east end of Calle Doblado after it crosses Blvd. Mijares.

SEMARNAP
A *subdelegación* office of the Secretaría de Medio Ambiente, Recursos Naturales y Pesca (SEMARNAP), the government organ responsible for ecological protection, can be found at the southwest corner of Calle Obregón at Morelos.

Storage
Los Cabos Mini & RV Storage, tel. (1) 142-0976, U.S. tel. (310) 924-5853, offers locked, garage-style storage units within a fenced and lighted complex with 24-hour security. One of the few services of its kind anywhere in southern Baja, the storage facility can be found at Km 37 on Mexico 1 (about five km south of Los Cabos International Airport).

Laundry
Lavandería Vera and **Lavamatica San José,** both on Calle González east of the bus terminal, offer washing, drying, and folding services Mon.-Sat. 8 a.m.-8 p.m.

TRANSPORTATION

Air
Los Cabos International Airport (SJD), 12.8 km (eight miles) north of San José del Cabo via a speedy four-lane section of Mexico 1 at Km 44, tel. (1) 142-0341, serves both San José and Cabo San Lucas. An official port of entry, Los Cabos' paved, 2,195-meter (7,200-foot) runway is tower-controlled (Unicom 118.9) and can receive DC-10s and 747s. Aviation fuel is available.

Two terminals now serve this airport. The old terminal holds several snack bars, souvenir shops, a money-exchange service, and an upstairs restaurant but has no seats in the waiting area for arriving flights—a minor inconvenience for those meeting incoming passengers. This terminal is served by seven airlines: Aero California, Aeroméxico, Aerolitoral, American Air-

lines, America West, Continental, and Mexicana.

Mexicana maintains a ticket office at Plaza Los Cabos on Paseo San José in the *zona hotelera;* Aero California's offices are in the Centro Comercial Plaza and in Plaza Naútica in Cabo San Lucas. Mexicana and Aero California also have ticket counters at Los Cabos airport; Continental handles ticket sales only at the airport.

Aero California, tel. (1) 142-0943, 143-0848 or (800) 9-0314, offers daily flights to Los Cabos from Los Angeles, Guadalajara, and Monterrey.

Mexicana, tel. (1) 142-2722, 142-0600, or (800) 5-0220, fields daily flights to Mexico City, Guadalajara, Mazatlán, and Los Angeles.

Aeroméxico, tel. (1) 142-0397 or (800) 9-0999, has flights from San Diego and Mexico City, while **Aerolitoral** flies to Los Mochis, La Paz, Loreto, and Chihuahua on one route and to Culiacán, Ciudad Obregón, and Hermosillo on another.

American Airlines, tel. (1) 142-2492, flies from Dallas/Ft. Worth daily, while **Continental,** tel. (1) 142-3840, fax (1) 142-3890, offers non-stops between Houston and Los Cabos daily. **America West,** tel. (1) 142-2880, offers daily nonstop flights from Phoenix and connecting flights from Seattle and many other U.S. cities.

Operating out of the new terminal, **Alaska Airlines,** tel. (1) 142-1015 or (800) 426-0333, schedules nonstop flights to Los Cabos from Los Angeles, San Francisco, and Phoenix, with connecting flights from Seattle/Tacoma. Alaska only sells tickets in the Los Cabos area at the airport. The second level of the new terminal has a couple of snack bars as well as several relatively upscale shops.

Airport Transportation: A *colectivo* (shared) van into town runs US$11 pp. A private taxi from the airport to any destination in San José del Cabo costs US$30, or US$65 to Cabo San Lucas—a huge increase over prices in the last edition.

Auto rental agencies with airport booths include Alamo, Budget, National, Avis, Hertz, Dollar, and Thrifty. National, Thrifty, and Budget rent their cars from offices opposite the old terminal.

Bus
From San José's main bus station on Calle González, tel. (1) 142-1100, Águila/ABC runs 11 buses a day to La Paz (US$10) and nine buses to Cabo San Lucas (US$2). The last bus to Cabo San Lucas leaves around 10 p.m. Each day at

4:30 p.m. a first-class bus also leaves for the 24-hour trip to Tijuana (US$78), with stops in Ciudad Constitución (US$17.50), Mulegé (US$27), Loreto (US$22), Guerrero Negro (US$42.75), and Ensenada (US$62). The bus station contains a small cafeteria and a *licuado* stand.

Vehicle Rental
Auto rental agencies with desks at Los Cabos International Airport as well as offices in or near town include: **Avis,** tel. (1) 142-1180, U.S. tel. (800) 331-1212; **Budget,** tel. (1) 142-0100, U.S. tel. (800) 472-3325; **Dollar,** tel. (1) 142-0663 or 142-0100, U.S. tel. (800) 800-4000; **Hertz,** tel. (1) 142-0930, U.S. tel. (800) 654-3001; **National,** tel. (1) 143-1818, U.S. tel. (800) 227-7368; and **Thrifty,** tel. (1) 142-3380, U.S. tel. (800) 367-2277.

Most agencies allow you to pay rental plus a per-kilometer charge, or pay a higher price with free kilometers. All the companies appear to charge roughly the same rates, from US$20/day plus 17 cents/km for a subcompact up to US$45/day plus 26 cents/km for a Jeep, or US$45/day with free miles for the same subcompact up to US$78/day with free miles for the Jeep. Some companies also offer a "topless" or open-air VW bug for US$25 a day (US$150 per week), including unlimited free kilometers.

In town, Budget has an office on Blvd. Castro, while Dollar runs an office at the corner of Mexico 1 and González, and National has an office on Zaragoza next to La Cenaduría. Thrifty has an office at the southeast corner of Mijares and Doblado, while Hertz has a lot a little north of town on the east side of highway. In general the best place to cut a deal on a rental car is at the airport booths, where you can look at price lists and compare one agency with another. Often you can negotiate the rental price downward.

Taxi
Visitors staying in town or at the beach are able to see most of what San José has to offer on foot. If you tire of walking, cabs are available; typical taxi fares are US$2 from the *zona hotelera* to the plaza downtown, US$3 from downtown to Pueblo La Playa, US$15 from town to Los Cabos airport, and US$30 all the way to Cabo San Lucas. Taxis congregate in front of the bus station, the beach hotels, and along Blvd. Mijares toward the plaza. A taxi stand signed "Sitio San José" can be found on Blvd. Mijares, just south of Plaza José Green.

THE CORRIDOR

The Transpeninsular Highway's 29-km (18-mile), four-lane stretch between San José del Cabo and Cabo San Lucas provides access to numerous beaches, coves, points, and tidal pools along the Pacific Ocean/Sea of Cortez. It's known officially as the Corredor Náutico (Nautical Corridor), or more commonly in English simply "the Corridor." The whole strip is sometimes referred to as Costa Azul or "Blue Coast," although this is also the name of a single beach near San José.

Private companies have begun stringing utility poles all along the Corridor. Already the highway is well-lit along its northeast end between San José del Cabo and the Westin Regina Los Cabos. Most of the roads branching south of the highway are unpaved. Almost all can be negotiated by ordinary passenger vehicles, though the overall number of public access roads continues to decline due to private development. In some cases it's necessary to park along the highway or in a nearby hotel parking lot and walk down to the beach. It is illegal for any hotel or other private development to block all access to any beach along the corridor.

Near Km 17 Mexico's ruling party constructed a monolith inscribed "Construido en Solidaridad" to mark the highway's 1993 completion. In November of the same year, a rainstorm heavily damaged the just-completed highway, destroying the three bridges spanning major arroyos along the route. Repairs and/or alternate routes were completed within weeks, and today this roadway represents one of Mexico's finest non-toll routes.

BEACHES ALONG THE CORRIDOR

BEACH	NEAREST KM MARKER	DISTANCE WEST OF KM MARKER IN METERS
Costa Azul	29	500
Acapulquito	27	800
Arroyo Seco/ Punta Palmilla	26	400
Punta Bella	24	400
Buenos Aires	22	400
El Mirador	20	—
San Carlos	19	—
El Zalate	17	500
Costa Brava	17	100
Cantamar	16	700
Del Tule	15	400
Punta Chileno	14	—
Santa María	12	200
Twin Dolphin (Las Viudas)	11	500
Barco Varado (Shipwreck)	9-10	—
Cabo Bello	6	200
Cemeterio	4	

BEACHES AND ACTIVITIES

One after another, beautiful beaches and coves hug the coastline between San José and Cabo San Lucas. Some are hidden from highway view by bluffs, others are marked by resort development.

To find these beaches, follow the blue-and-white signs along Mexico 1, sometimes labeled "Acceso a Playa" but more often than not simply bearing a simple outline of a snorkel mask or swimmer. The accompanying key lists all those beaches accessible from the highway.

Swimming
Not all the Corridor beaches are suitable for year-round swimming. Starting from the San José end, one of the best is **Playa Costa Azul,** where a long strip of sand next to the

Bahía Chileno

Mykonos and La Jolla condo developments is gently washed by low breakers (except during the *chubasco* season—see Surfing, below). A restaurant/bar called **Zipper's** serves food and booze.

Playa Palmilla at Km 26 is a decent swimming beach—local kids dive here for golf balls that have dropped into Neptune's realm from the Palmilla Golf Club Ocean Course links. **Restaurant-Bar Pepe's** will cook your catch for US$4, or you can rely on the restaurant's own dependable source of seafood. **Victor's Sportfishing** can be booked at Pepe's as well.

Farther southwest, a new breakwater has tamed the waters along **Playa El Mirador,** a lengthy stretch of beach north of the Hotel Meliá Cabo Real and part of Bahía El Bledito. Look for an access road just north of Km 20. As the huge Cabo Real development expands, public access may change though hopefully access won't be (illegally) denied.

A little more than halfway to Cabo San Lucas, the wide crescents of sand rimming Bahía Chileno and Bahía Santa María constitute two of the Corridor's most popular and accessible swimming beaches. **Playa Chileno** is larger and more well-endowed with public facilities. Visitors walk through a gate in the chain-link fence protecting the beach from vehicles and follow a path through a grove of fan palms to reach the beach itself. The palms provide natural shade, a component lacking at most other Corridor beaches. Free public restrooms and showers are available, while Cabo Acuadeportes rents water-

sports equipment from a booth at the south end of the beach. Beneath the houses perched on headlands at either end of the bay are rocky areas with good snorkeling. Though very picturesque and suitable for swimming, **Playa Santa María** offers a smaller beach and is short on facilities and shade; it's a beach best enjoyed by snorkelers and divers rather than swimmers. Both Chileno and Santa María enjoy an extraordinary abundance of marinelife.

Playa Las Viudas (Widows Beach), more commonly known as Twin Dolphins Beach, is reached via a rough sand turnoff at Km 12 next to the private entrance to the Hotel Twin Dolphins. Vehicles with high road clearance will fare better than ordinary sedans. The tan-colored beach—actually several scalloped beaches separated by small rocky points—tends to be on the pebbly side, though the swimming is usually excellent.

Northeast of Cabo San Lucas at Km 4, little-known and uncrowded **Playa Cemeterio** offers calm swimming and white sands.

Just northeast of the Meliá Cabo Real at Km 19.5 is the upscale **La Concha Beach Club and Restaurant,** tel. (1) 144-0102. This beautiful secluded spot consists of three small, curving, sand-fringed bays. The club offers a splash pool, showers, beach umbrellas, and beach chairs and rents towels (US$2) and snorkeling equipment (US$5). The restaurant serves international cuisine and is open for lunch and dinner 11 a.m.-10 p.m. daily. Instead of an entrance fee, there's a US$11 food-and-drink minimum pur-

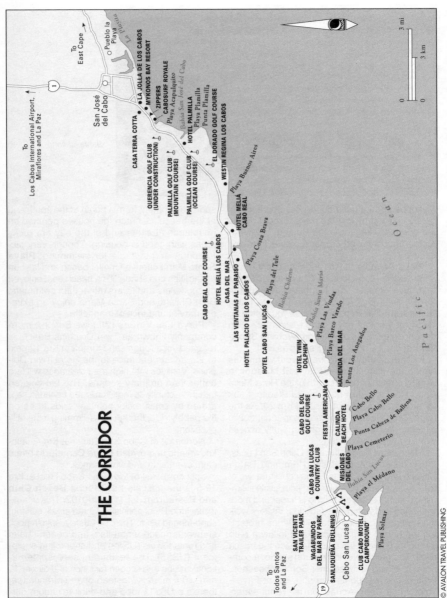

THE CORRIDOR

To East Cape

Pueblo la Playa

La Playita

San José del Cabo

To Los Cabos International Airport, Miraflores and La Paz

CASA TERRA COTTA

LA JOLLA DE LOS CABOS
MYKONOS BAY RESORT
ZIPPERS
CABOSURF ROYALE
Playa Acapulquito
HOTEL PALMILLA
Playa Palmilla
Punta Palmilla
EL DORADO GOLF COURSE
WESTIN REGINA LOS CABOS

QUERENCIA GOLF CLUB
(UNDER CONSTRUCTION)
PALMILLA GOLF CLUB
(MOUNTAIN COURSE)
PALMILLA GOLF CLUB
(OCEAN COURSE)

Bahía San José del Cabo

Playa Buenos Aires

HOTEL MELIÁ
CABO REAL

CABO REAL GOLF COURSE

HOTEL MELIÁ LOS CABOS
CASA DEL MAR

Playa Costa Brava

LAS VENTANAS AL PARAÍSO

Playa del Tule

HOTEL PALACIO DE LOS CABOS

Bahía Chileno

HOTEL CABO SAN LUCAS

HOTEL TWIN
DOLPHIN

Bahía Santa María

Playa Las Viudas
Playa Barco Varado
Punta Los Arenados

CABO DEL SOL
GOLF COURSE

FIESTA AMERICANA

CALINDA
BEACH HOTEL

HACIENDA DEL MAR

Cabo Bello
Playa Cabo Bello
Punta Cabeza de Ballena

Playa Cemeterio

MISIONES
DEL CABO

CABO SAN LUCAS
COUNTRY CLUB

Bahía San Lucas

Playa el Médano

SAN VICENTE
TRAILER PARK

VAGABUNDOS
DEL MAR RV PARK

SANLUQUEÑA BULLRING

CLUB CABO MOTEL/
CAMPGROUND

Cabo San Lucas

To Todos Santos and La Paz

Playa Solmar

Ocean

Pacific

3 mi

3 km

© AVALON TRAVEL PUBLISHING

chase requirement (easily achieved in the club's well-run open-air dining areas). It's forbidden to bring in pets, ice chests, or food from the outside. Open daily 10 a.m.-10 p.m.

Surfing

Although Los Cabos is less famous than Baja's northern and central Pacific coast for surf, the summer southwest swell brings consistent wave action to the tip of the peninsula, when most of the west coast points are flat. The surf reaches peak height during the *chubasco* season, late summer to early fall. The most dependable surfing area between San José and Cabo San Lucas is **Playa Costa Azul,** at Km 29-28, where a grinding shore-breaker called "Zippers" is sometimes backed by Hawaii-style outside breaks in heavy swell. See Surfing under the San José del Cabo section for further detail.

Punta Palmilla, below the Hotel Palmilla at Km 28-27, whips out a sometimes large right point break, while the bay to the point's immediate north, **Playa Acapulquito,** between Costa Azul and Palmilla, offers a good reef break in heavy swell.

Reef breaks sometimes occur at **Playa Buenos Aires,** Km 22 (beware strong rips), and at **Playa Cabo Real,** Km 20; then there's a gap until **Playa Cantamar** at Km 16 and **Punta Chileno** at Km 14, both offering workable point breaks. To reach Cantamar—which is often confused with **Playa El Tule** (also known as Puente del Tule)—you need eagle eyes. Coming from Cabo San Lucas in your own vehicle (the turnoff is only accessible from this side of the highway), cross Arroyo El Tule and then immediately turn right off the highway as the road begins to rise toward the Solidaridad monument. Here look for a small dirt road through a gate in a barbed-wire fence (usually open), after which a sand road leads around to the northeast end of Puente El Tule, a good spot to park and camp.

In summer, a good-sized, well-shaped, right point break sometimes forms off **Playa Barco Varado,** Km 9—access comes just northeast of the turnoff for the Cabo del Sol golf course/hotel complex. This site seems to have missed the attention of the Baja surf reports and west coast surfing magazines.

Playa Cabo Bello, between Km 6 and 5 (near the Hotel Cabo San Lucas), is known for a con-

sistent left point break nicknamed "Monuments" for the H-shaped concrete monument that used to stand next to the highway near here. This break is fueled by northwest swell refracted off Cabo San Lucas and is the easternmost break for winter surfing. During heavier swell it may be joined by an outer reef break.

Most of these beaches now feature some sort of condo or resort development in progress, but there's always a way to drive through or around them: it's illegal to restrict public beach access.

Diving

Several beaches along the Corridor feature rock reefs suitable for snorkeling and scuba diving, particularly **Playa Santa María** (Km 12), **Playa Chileno** (Km 14), and **Playa Barco Varado** (Shipwreck Beach, Km 9-10). Santa María offers rock reefs at either end of a protected cove at depths of 13 meters (40 feet) or less. The north point displays sea fans and gorgonians, along with the usual assortment of tropical fish. The south end has sea caves, coral outcroppings, and large rocky areas inhabited by reef fish and lobster.

The remains of the Japanese tuna boat *Inari Maru No. 10,* stranded on rocky shoals in 1966, is the main diving destination at Shipwreck Beach. A local story says that when Cabo *pescadores* noticed the Japanese vessel fishing illegally, they extinguished the nearest lighthouse beacon and rigged a light of their own that lured the boat onto the shoals after nightfall. The hull and other wreckage lie 2-26 meters (6.5-85 feet) underwater; nearby are scenic rock reefs. Tidal pools along Shipwreck Beach support starfish and sea urchins.

HOTELS

The priciest and best-situated hotels in Los Cabos grace the coast along the Corridor. Designed to appeal to the well-heeled hedonist seeking a degree of privacy and seclusion not found in Mexican beach resorts like Puerto Vallarta, Cancún, Mazatlán, or Acapulco (and avoiding the hot, rainy summers elsewhere in coastal Mexico), these resorts take full advantage of their desert remoteness. Don't forget to pack your irons and woods; golf is quickly becoming as big an attraction as beachgoing and fishing now that the area boasts six world-class golf courses, with more under construction. Major resort developments are so far centered around four courses: Cabo Real, El Dorado, Palmilla, and Cabo del Sol. Welcome to Palm Springs, Mexico.

All of the resorts listed below fall in this book's premium price category except the Hotel Palacio de Los Cabos and the Calinda Beach Hotel, both of which are in the expensive category. Even if you have no plans to stay in the area, the hotel restaurants or bars are well worth a visit for a meal or drink and the ocean view.

Cabo Surf Royale

Hidden away below Mexico 1, just two km southwest of San José at Km 28, Cabo Surf Royale, tel./fax (1) 148-6563, fax (1) 148-8563, U.S. tel. (800) 896-8196, offers a small cluster of eight comfortable apartments and villas overlooking Playa Acapulquito. All units come with terraces, and continental breakfast is included in the price. Kitchenettes and full kitchens are available. On the grounds are a large barbecue area, jacuzzi, and plunge pool. Rates: US$125-250.

Hotel Palmilla Resort

Covering 384 hectares (950 acres) of Punta Palmilla near Km 27, the 114-room Hotel Palmilla, tel. (1) 144-5000, is the Cape's first major resort; it was built in 1956 by "Rod" Rodríguez, son of former Mexican president Abelardo Luis Rodríguez. Coconut palms, clouds of hibiscus, and sweeping sea views dominate the grounds. Facilities include an oceanfront pool with a swim-up bar; fitness center; tennis, croquet, paddleball, and volleyball courts; a giant outdoor chessboard; stables; two restaurants and a bar; a chapel used for weddings; and a 1,370-meter (4,500-foot) illuminated airstrip (Unicom 122.8). All rooms and suites feature TV, VCR, voice mail, and dataport-equipped telephones. The Hotel Palmilla maintains its own sportfishing fleet, offering *panga* trips (one to three anglers) for US$250 per day or long-range cruises (one to four anglers) for US$395 per day. Scuba-diving programs cost US$40-60 for guided beach dives, US$50-75 for boat dives.

Palmilla also boasts a world-class golf course (see Golf Courses, below). For U.S. reserva-

tions, contact Hotel Palmilla Reservations, 4343 Von Karman Ave., Newport Beach, CA 92660-2083, tel. (714) 833-3033 or (800) 637-2226.

Rates: from US$375 d for rooms to US$1,100 d for suites, not including 10% tax and 15% service; lower prices are available on weekdays and in low season (6 July-19 Dec.).

If even the Hotel Palmilla's Bar Neptuno (open daily till midnight) seems beyond your budget, you might at least enjoy the beach below by stopping in at **Restaurant-Bar Pepe's** on Playa Palmilla, where the first drink is on Pepe; if he's not in attendance, the first *two* drinks are on the house.

Westin Regina Resort Los Cabos

Hidden from the highway by brick-hued Cerro Colorado, just past Km 22 on the Transpeninsular Highway (10 minutes' drive from San José del Cabo), the *gran turismo*-class Westin Regina Los Cabos, tel. (1) 142-9000, fax (1) 142-9011, U.S. tel. (800) WESTIN-1, e-mail: relos@westin.com, opened in 1994 at a cost of US$200 million, making it the most expensive hotel ever built in Mexico. Renowned Mexican architect Javier Sordo Magdaleno endowed the bold curvilinear design with a bright palette of colors abstracted from the surrounding geological, floral, and marine environment. A Zen-like rock-and-cactus garden on a hillside overlooks a dramatic seaside pool fed by a sophisticated water-recycling system. On the opposite hillside to the immediate north of the hotel stand numerous pastel-colored time-share and residential units managed by the hotel.

All 243 rooms and suites come with sea views, large marble bathrooms, ceiling fans, a/c, in-room safes, refreshment bars, furnished balconies, satellite TVs, and IDD phones. Rates: US$275-630 nightly for the resort section, up to US$2,520 a night for the 2,000-square-foot presidential suite. These rates do not include 12% tax and 10% service charge.

The resort's **Restaurant Arrecifes** commands a view of the wave-battered beach below and offers an eclectic menu emphasizing Mediterranean, sushi, and seafood. A restaurant on the ground floor, **La Cascada,** specializes in Mexican and seafood. Guests have golf privileges at the Cabo Real golf course, about 2.5 km southwest.

Cabo Real

A bit farther down the highway at Km 19.5, the Cabo Real complex presides over scenic Bahía El Bledito and comprises the Hotel Meliá Cabo Real, Hotel Casa del Mar, and Casa del Mar Condos, as well as the renowned Cabo Real Golf Course and the new Jack Nicklaus-designed El Dorado Golf Course (see Golf Courses, below).

Rated a *gran turismo* resort, the **Meliá Cabo Real,** tel. (1) 144-0000, fax (1) 144-0192 or 144-0101, U.S. tel. (800) 336-3542, e-mail: caboreal@1cabonet.com.mx, offers 302 well-appointed rooms and suites—recently refurbished and almost all with ocean view—laid out like a squared-off horseshoe around a huge glass-and-onyx, pyramid-topped open-air lobby. Guests can swim at the beach (tamed by the addition of a rock jetty) or in the hotel's free-form pool, which is billed as the largest in Los Cabos. A new spa and shopping gallery are recent additions to the list of amenities. On the beach, Tío Sports rents sports equipment and organizes scuba tours/instruction. Three restaurants, including the *alta cocina* Ailem and Cafetería El Quetzal, offer complete food service in the high style required by Sol Meliá, a hotel management group based in Spain. Rates: from US$202 1 May-13 Oct., from US$250 the rest of the year. Tax and service extra.

The **Casa del Mar Golf Resort,** tel. (1) 144-0030, fax (1) 144-0034, U.S. tel. (800) 221-8808, e-mail: casamar@cabonet.net.mx, is a smaller place containing 25 ocean-view rooms plus 31 deluxe one-bedroom suites with spacious bathrooms, a/c, complete kitchenettes, direct-dial phones, fax machines, minibars, and in-room safes. Also on the premises are a full-service European-style spa, a pool, four tennis courts, the adjacent Cabo Real Golf Club, three bars, and a restaurant. Guests receive a US$30 daily food and beverage credit and a 25% discount on golf fees. Rates: from US$325-375 d per night, plus tax and service.

The newest Meliá property in Cabo is the **Meliá Los Cabos All Suites Beach and Golf Resort,** tel. (1) 144-0202, fax (1) 144-0085, e-mail: mlcvtas@1cabonet.com.mx. Opened in 1998, it consists of 136 deluxe ocean-view suites with a/c, phone, satellite TV, kitchenette, and minibar. Near the Robert Trent Jones II-designed Cabo Real Golf Course and the new Jack Nicklaus-designed El Dorado Golf Course, the resort offers two restaurants, a bar, a gym with spa facilities, two tennis courts, and an outdoor swimming pool with a swim-up bar. Rates: starting at US$240-280 depending on the season.

Las Ventanas al Paraíso

One of the most talked-about newer resorts in Los Cabos, if not all of Mexico, Las Ventanas, just northeast of Km 20, tel. (1) 144-0300, brings a new level of luxury and service to the Corridor's already distinguished market. Under the auspices of Rosewood Hotels and Resorts (which also manages the prestigious Mansion on Turtle Creek and Hotel Crescent Court in Dallas, The Lanesborough in London, and Little Dix Bay in the

Meliá Cabo Real

British Virgin Islands), Las Ventanas was designed using an innovative combination of Mexican-Mediterranean architecture and interior design. Unlike the bright primary colors favored by many Mexican beach resorts, here pastels and earth tones are emphasized. Underground tunnels hide many of the day-to-day guest service activities to keep aboveground architecture to a minimum, adding to the overall sense of intimacy.

Guest suites average 90 square meters (960 square feet), and each features custom-made furniture, inlaid stone-and-tile floors, an adobe fireplace, private furnished patio with individual splash pool/hot tub, computerized telescope aimed at the sea, dual telephone lines for modem/phone use, satellite TV/VCR, in-room CD/stereo equipment, freshly cut blooms, and a huge bathroom. Each room also comes with a complimentary bottle of high-end tequila.

Garden view junior suites cost US$475 d a night, while ocean view junior suites and rooftop-terrace junior suites are US$525 and US$575. One-bedroom luxury suites are available for US$1,800 a night, and if that won't accommodate the family trust, there's a three-bedroom presidential suite for a paltry US$3,000. One-, two-, and three-bedroom residences are also available. Add 15% gratuity and 12% tax to these rates.

Guests have free use of a full-service spa and fitness center. The beach in front of the resort, Playa Costa Brava, is a little too *brava* for most swimmers, but overlooking the beach is a large free-form horizon pool with swim-up bar. The resort's restaurant—simply called The Restaurant and managed by a chef with nine years experience at the Mansion on Turtle Creek—offers one of the most adventurous cuisines in all of Baja. The menu changes seasonally, but at last pass we saw such dishes as grilled shrimp hash with poached eggs, sliced tomatoes, and roast chile sauce for breakfast; Baja shellfish and fettuccine in saffron broth for lunch; and habanero- and merlot-glazed tuna mignon with pinto beans for dinner, among many other interesting offerings.

The concierge can arrange play at any golf course in the Corridor.

For further information or reservations, contact Las Ventanas al Paraíso, c/o Rosewood Hotels & Resorts, 500 Crescent Court, Suite 300, Dallas, TX 75201, tel. (888) 525-0485.

Hotel Palacio de Los Cabos

The Palacio de Los Cabos, Apdo. Postal 2-57, La Paz, BCS 23040, tel. (1) 143-3377, fax (1) 143-3388, overlooks Playa Cantamar near Km 17. Though not in the same class as the Corridor's *gran turismo* resorts, each of the hotel's 40 one- and two-bedroom suites comes with full kitchen, sitting room, satellite TV, and a/c. The nicely landscaped premises feature a pool, restaurant, bar, and health center. Rates start at a bargain (in this neighborhood) US$90 per night, not including tax and service. A three-night package is available for US$157 through Baja Motion Tours, including airport transfers and tax. Call (619) 474-1991 or toll-free (877) 246-2252 in the U.S. for more information.

Hotel Cabo San Lucas

Farther southwest between Km 15 and 14, the Hotel Cabo San Lucas, tel. (1) 144-0014, fax (1) 144-0015, sits on Punta Chileno, facing Playa del Tule. Another heavy hitter in the colonial-luxury league, the Cabo San Lucas came along early in the game in 1958. Almost more Hawaiian than Mexican in style, the resort features 77 rooms, suites, and studios and eight beachfront villas, plus its own hunting ranch, sportfishing excursions, horseback riding, a three-level swimming pool, dive center, restaurant, bar, 1,200-meter (3,950-foot) airstrip, and Asian art gallery. The reef below the hotel, on the Playa Chileno side of the point, is suitable for snorkeling and surfing.

Rates: Standard rooms are US$195 in season. One- and two-bedroom apartments that sleep up to four and three- to seven-room villas are also available for up to US$545. Add 27% tax and service to these rates. For U.S. reservations, call (323) 655-2323 or (800) 733-2226, fax (323) 655-3243, or e-mail: cabotravel@earthlink.net.

Hotel Twin Dolphin

One of the Corridor's original 1950s' triumvirate, the Twin Dolphin, at Km 11.5, tel. (1) 143-0256, fax (1) 143-0496, U.S. tel. (800) 421-8925, U.S. fax (213) 380-1302, offers splendid ocean views. Playa Santa María, to the immediate north, is one of Los Cabos' best snorkeling/diving beaches. The hotel has its own fishing fleet, 18-hole putting green, dive center, pool, tennis courts, horseback riding, restaurant, and quiet, wood-paneled bar reminiscent of Cabo's more macho past. Each of the 50 oceanfront rooms has a private terrace. Rates: from US$275 Nov.-May, from US$195 off season (plus 12% tax and service). Modified American plan (two meals per day) and American plan (three meals per day) rates are available for an additional US$51 pp and US$70 pp respectively.

Cabo del Sol

On the drawing board at Cabo del Sol are the usual housing sites, a tennis center, and two exclusive hotels, tentatively including Grand Hyatt and Ritz-Carlton. (Fiesta Americana Grand Cabo del Sol will open soon—see below). One hotel already up and running on the beach side of Cabo del Sol is **Hotel Hacienda del Mar,** tel. (1) 145-8000, reservations (1) 145-8020, fax (1) 145-8008, a plush Mediterranean-style spot with 124 suites, all equipped with a/c, satellite TV, and kitchenettes. Some rooms also contain jacuzzis. Other amenities include a three-tier pool and tropical gardens. In season rates run US$280-1,620 nightly, plus tax and service charge.

Next to the hotel is **Pitahayas,** tel. (1) 145-8010, a large open-air restaurant with an impressive underground wine cellar and an innovative menu of Pacific Rim cuisine focusing on fresh seafood and a mesquite grill. Pitahayas is open daily for breakfast, lunch, and dinner. Formal resort attire required.

The main access road for Cabo del Sol leaves Mexico 1 near Km 10.

Fiesta Americana Grand Cabo del Sol

Scheduled to open soon, this US$70 million resort will consist of 250 guest rooms and 50 time-share villas, with 300 more planned. Facilities will include four pools, two championship tennis courts, and a full-service spa. The Jack Nicklaus-designed Cabo del Sol Golf Course is adjacent to the resort.

Calinda Beach Hotel

Off Mexico 1 at Km 6, this is the nearest of the Corridor hotels to Cabo San Lucas and also one of the least expensive. Calinda Beach, tel. (1) 143-0034, fax (1) 143-0077, U.S. tel. (800) 4-CHOICE, features 125 rooms with balcony or patio, ocean or garden view, all with a/c, phone, and satellite TV. The grounds encompass landscaped gardens,

a restaurant, lobby bar, two pools, three jacuzzis, and two lighted tennis courts. Rates: US$176-198 per night in season plus tax and service charge; lower in the off season.

Misiones del Cabo

At Km 5.5 near Cabo San Lucas, Misiones del Cabo, tel. (1) 145-8091, fax (1) 145-8097, U.S. toll-free (888) 377-8762, U.S. fax (831) 460-2653, e-mail: tina@caboresort.com, is a resort offering dramatic views, safe swimming beaches, lighted tennis courts, pool and swim-up bar, a cliffside restaurant, and a complimentary daily shuttle to/from Cabo San Lucas. The 120 one- and two-bedroom condominium suites have full kitchens, satellite TV, a/c, and spacious private balconies. Rates: US$200-350.

GOLF COURSES

Golf is king in the Corridor, which is home to three Nicklaus-designed golf courses—the 27-hole Palmilla, the new 18-hole El Dorado at Cabo Real, and the 18-hole Cabo del Sol—and the Robert Trent Jones II-designed Cabo Real course. A new Tom Weiskopf 18-hole course has broken ground and will be added to Cabo del Sol, and the Corridor's first private course, Querencia, will soon appear near the Palmilla.

These courses boast landscapes and playing terrain comparable to that found in many Arizona and California desert courses, the main difference being the visual addition of the sparkling Sea of Cortez. Despite the professional status of the four main courses, which have attracted the PGA Grand Slam Tournament annually since 1995, all are eminently playable. As a local golf guide put it, "Low handicap players will find them challenging and will appreciate the genius and skill that went into their designs, while less experienced players will be rewarded with a good day's combat."

Palmilla

Opened in 1992, the Jack Nicklaus-designed 27-hole golf course at the Palmilla is divided into an arroyo course, a mountain course, and an ocean course, splendid by all accounts. Nearly every hole has a view of the Sea of Cortez in the distance. This course hosted the 1997 PGA

Senior Slam, 1997 Taylor Made Pro-Am, and 1998 World Pro-Am tournaments. Nicklaus himself, though admitting his bias as the designer (this was his first course in Latin America), claims the 17th and 18th holes are the best finishing holes in the world. The course's signature hole is the 440-yard, par four "Mountain Five," which necessitates a long drive across two desert arroyos. Gray water is used to irrigate the fairways and greens, easing the strain on the Los Cabos water supply. The public is charged a greens fee of US$127-198 per 18 holes, depending on the day of the week and time of year. Fees include golf cart, practice balls, bottled water, and use of the driving range. Clubs may be rented for US$39. The golf course serves as the centerpiece of a 384-hectare (950-acre) development surrounding the original hotel with fairway homes, a network of paved roads, a clubhouse, and a tennis complex. Call (1) 144-5250 for more information.

Cabo Real

The Cabo Real complex now boasts two world-class golf courses. The 18-hole, par-72 **Cabo Real Golf Course** stretches over more than 7,000 yards of verdant landscape. The first six holes are in mountainous terrain, while others lie along the shore. The course is open to the general public for a greens fee of US$176 for 18 holes, including tax, golf cart, practice facilities, club service, and bottled water. These are high season rates that run 15 Oct.-15 June; the rest of the year the fee drops to US$115.50. Hotel guests staying at the Westin Regina Los Cabos, Meliá Cabo Real, and Casa del Mar are entitled to special rates. Club rentals are available for US$25. Call (1) 144-0040 or e-mail: caborealgolf@cabonet.net.mx for course information.

The recently completed Jack Nicklaus-designed **El Dorado Golf Course** is the second championship course in the Cabo Real development. The 18-hole, par-72 course features six oceanfront holes; the rest are carved out of two picturesque canyons surrounded by trees, cacti, and rock formations. Six holes come into play beside four lakes. This 7,050-yard course has been called the finest course in Mexico and

one of the best in the world. Greens fees run US$137.50-198, depending on the season, and include tax, golf cart, practice facilities, club service, and bottled water. The clubhouse and restaurant afford views of the Sea of Cortez and the ninth and 18th holes. Call (1) 144-5440 for more information.

Cabo del Sol

Jack Nicklaus designed his second set of Mexican fairways on 730 hectares (1,800 acres) of land between Playa Barco Varado and Cabo Bello. This is Los Cabos' highest-rated golf course so far. *Golf Digest* has rated it as one of the top 10 public golf courses in the world. Seven of the course's holes feature dramatic oceanfront play along the shore of Bahía de Ballenas. The front nine is 3,597 yards, par 36, while the back nine extends 3,440 yards, also par 36. A greens fee of US$138-209 (depending on time of year) for 18 holes includes tax, a golf cart, practice facilities, club service, and bottled water. "Big Bertha" clubs can be rented for US$40 plus tax. For information on the golf course, call (1) 145-8200 or (800) 386-2465 in the U.S.

A total of three 18-hole golf courses are planned for the Cabo del Sol development. Construction has begun on a Tom Weiskopf-designed 18-hole course, his first in Mexico. The signature course will have desert and ocean views and will spread across 57 hectares (140 acres) of desert landscape. A third 18-hole course for Cabo del Sol is still in the planning stages.

Querencia

Under construction when we visited, Querencia will be the first completely private course in Los Cabos. The course will cover 341 hectares (840 acres) of hills between Palmilla and Costa Azul, near San José del Cabo. Querencia will include an 18-hole Tom Fazio-designed course (his first outside the U.S.), a nine-hole short course (also designed by Fazio), a modern practice facility, and a spacious clubhouse with sea views. The Querencia development will also feature home sites, villas, and condos. Call (1) 142-4435 in Mexico or (888) 346-6188 in the U.S. for more information.

CABO SAN LUCAS

Cabo San Lucas and San José del Cabo enjoy equal access to the great beaches along the Corridor between the two towns, but because the San Lucas harbor provides shelter for a sizable sportfishing and recreational fleet, the preponderance of the 300,000-plus yearly Los Cabos visitors station themselves here rather than in San José or along the Corridor. Several cruise lines also feature Cabo San Lucas on their itineraries. With a permanent population of only 25,000, many of them retirees, the city has a tourist-to-resident ratio higher than elsewhere in the Cape Region, especially during the peak Nov.-March tourist season.

Yet in spite of all the tourists—most of whom confine themselves to the waterfront—Cabo manages to retain something of a funky, small-town feel. Away from Blvd. Marina, many of the unpaved, sand streets are lined with the *tortillerías,* hardware shops, and markets typically found in any small coastal Mexican town. The city only recently installed its second traffic light.

Named for the slender cape extending eastward from Baja California's southernmost tip, Cabo San Lucas is the only city in Mexico with a marine preserve within its city limits. Created in 1973, the protected 36-square-km (14-square-mile) patch of sea and shore designates special boat lanes, boating speed limits, and restricted fishing and recreation craft areas, all

under the watchful eye of Grupo Ecológico de Cabo San Lucas. Nowhere else among Mexico's top-drawing seaside resorts will you find such pristine beaches within so short a distance (5-10 minutes by boat taxi) of the town center.

Outside this area, however, hotel and condo development marches ahead full steam. Pedregal—a fashionable hillside district to the west—the marina, and Playa El Médano to the east are all chockablock with condos and villas. Next to undergo development will probably be the large section of unused harborfront property near the inner harbor entrance, where an old cannery and ferry pier sit abandoned.

While yachting and sportfishing bring an older, early-to-bed crowd to Cabo, the town's nightlife attracts an energetic youth market, creating a more vibrant ambience than at relatively staid San José del Cabo, 29 km (18 miles) northeast. As the last stop on the 1,700-km (thousand-mile) transpeninsular Baja road trip, Cabo also acts as a receptacle for old Baja hands looking for a few days or weeks of R&R before beginning the long return drive across relatively unpopulated desert landscapes.

Thus, as residents and repeat visitors will point out, you never know who you'll run into in Cabo; yachties on their way to and from exotic South Pacific ports, cops on a fishing vacation, Baja road warriors, honeymoon couples, Mexico

Playa El Médano, Cabo San Lucas

City denizens cleaning out their lead-filled lungs, rockers resting up after a continental tour, or Montana cowboys escaping the snow—they've all set themselves temporarily adrift in the Pacific, like the Cape itself as it inches westward from mainland Mexico.

CLIMATE

Cabo San Lucas lies below the Tropic of Cancer and is sunny and mild year-round. The town's location at the confluence of the Pacific Ocean and the Sea of Cortez means ocean currents and airstreams from both sides of the peninsula tend to moderate the general climatic influences of each; neither the cool Pacific nor the warm Cortez completely dominates in any given season. Hence summers aren't as hot as in La Paz (220 km north on the Cortez side), and winters aren't as cool as in Todos Santos (72 km north on the Pacific).

The average temperature in August is 27° C (81° F); in January it's 18° C (64° F). Maximum temperatures rarely exceed 33° C (92° F), and minimum readings seldom fall below 13° C (56° F). Since Cabo is completely protected from prevailing north winds, winters here are warmer than anywhere else in Baja, a distinct attraction for the snowbird market.

Cabo San Lucas boasts an average of 360 days of sunshine a year. Annual rainfall averages a scant 19 cm (7.5 inches), most falling Aug.-October. Brief showers are sometimes encountered as late as November or early December.

HISTORY

The Pericú and the English

In pre-Cortesian times the only humans enjoying Cabo San Lucas were the Pericú, one of the nomadic Guaycura Amerindian groups that inhabited the Cape Region for hundreds if not thousands of years. Standard anthropology says that, like other Amerindians in North and South America, the Pericú were descendants of Asian groups who traversed the prehistoric land bridge between the Eurasian and American continents. One fringe theory, however, suggests the Pericú may have descended from Tahitian mariners blown off course on their way to Hawaii. English accounts from the 17th and early 18th centuries lend at least partial credence to this theory by pointing out how much the physical and social characteristics of the Pericú differed from that of other Amerindians of the same era.

Spaniard Juan Rodríguez Cabrillo made first contact with the Pericú here in 1542 while exploring the coastline. Sir Francis Drake stopped off in 1578, followed by privateer Thomas Cavendish in 1587. English pirating exploits inspired the Spanish to gain a stronger foothold on the Cape. Spanish explorer Sebastián Vizcaíno spent a week here in 1596, then returned in 1602 to map the region with cartographer Gerónimo Martín Palacios. Vizcaíno strongly recommended the establishment of a colony at Cabo San Lucas; Loreto, farther north on the Sea of Cortez, was selected instead, leaving Cabo to the English for another hundred years.

Until the mid-18th century, English pirates used the harbor as a hiding place for attacks on Manila galleons. Woodes Rogers anchored here in 1709, when he and his crew captured the

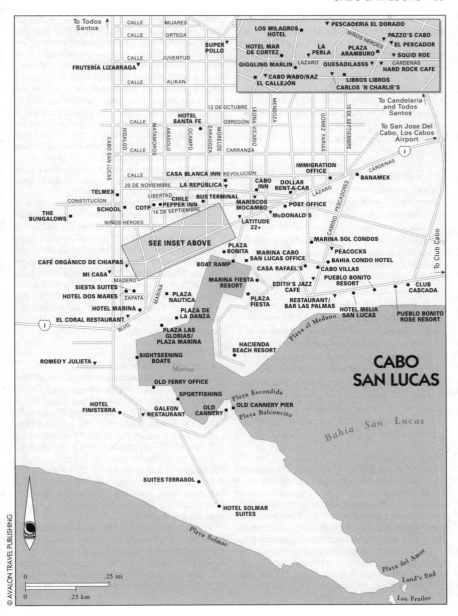

INSET:

LOS MILAGROS HOTEL ▼ PESCADERÍA EL DORADO ▼
PAZZO'S CABO ▼
HOTEL MAR DE CORTEZ ■ LA PERLA ▼ PLAZA ARAMBURO ■ NIÑOS HÉROES EL PESCADOR ▼ SQUID ROE ▼
GIGGLING MARLIN ■ LAZARO QUESADILASSS ▼ CARDENAS HARD ROCK CAFE ▼
■ CABO WABO/KAZ EL CALLEJÓN LIBROS LIBROS ■
CARLOS 'N CHARLIE'S ■

MAIN MAP:

To Todos Santos
CALLE MIJARES
CALLE ORTEGA
SUPER POLLO ▼
CALLE JUVENTUD
FRUTERÍA LIZARRAGA ▼
CALLE ALIKAN

12 DE OCTUBRE
HOTEL SANTA FE ■
OBREGÓN
CALLE
HIDALGO
MATAMOROS
ABASOLO
OCAMPO
MORELOS
ZARAGOZA
LEONA VICARIO
MENDOZA
GOMEZ FARIAS
16 DE SEPTIEMBRE
CARRANZA

CABO SAN LUCAS

To Candelaria and Todos Santos
To San Jose Del Cabo, Los Cabos Airport
CARDENAS

CALLE
CASA BLANCA INN ■ REVOLUCIÓN
IMMIGRATION OFFICE ■
BANAMEX ■
20 DE NOVIEMBRE LA REPÚBLICA ■
CABO INN ■
DOLLAR RENT-A-CAR ■
TELMEX ■
CONSTITUCIÓN
LIBERTAD
CHILE PEPPER INN ■
BUS TERMINAL ■
MARISCOS MOCAMBO ■
POST OFFICE ■
THE BUNGALOWS ■
SCHOOL ■ COTP ■
16 DE SEPTIEMBRE
McDONALD'S ■
NIÑOS HÉROES
LATITUDE 22+ ■

SEE INSET ABOVE

MARINA SOL CONDOS ■
CAFÉ ORGÁNICO DE CHIAPAS ■
PLAZA BONITA ■
MARINA CABO SAN LUCAS OFFICE ■
PEACOCKS ■
BAHIA CONDO HOTEL ■
MI CASA ▼
BOAT RAMP
CASA RAFAEL'S ■
CABO VILLAS ■
SIESTA SUITES ■
HOTEL DOS MARES ■
ZAPATA
MARINA FIESTA RESORT ■
EDITH'S JAZZ CAFE ■
PUEBLO BONITO RESORT ■
CLUB CASCADA ■
HOTEL MARINA ■
PLAZA NAUTICA ■
PLAZA FIESTA ■
RESTAURANT/ BAR LAS PALMAS ■
EL CORAL RESTAURANT ■
BLVD.
PLAZA DE LA DANZA ■
HOTEL MELIA SAN LUCAS ■
To Club Cabo
ROMEO Y JULIETA ▼
PLAZA LAS GLORIAS/ PLAZA MARINA ■
PUEBLO BONITO ROSE RESORT ■
MARINA
HACIENDA BEACH RESORT ■
Playa el Medano
SIGHTSEEING BOATS ■
OLD FERRY OFFICE ■
SPORTFISHING ■
Playa Escondida

CABO SAN LUCAS

HOTEL FINISTERRA ■
GALEON RESTAURANT ■
OLD CANNERY ■
OLD CANNERY PIER
Playa Balconcito

Bahia San Lucas

SUITES TERRASOL ■

HOTEL SOLMAR SUITES ■

Playa del Amor
Land's End
Los Frailes

Playa Solmar

0 ___ .25 mi
0 ___ .25 km

© AVALON TRAVEL PUBLISHING

Spanish galleon *Encarnación*. Another English corsair, George Shelcocke, landed in 1721 and carried out a regional survey that included extensive drawings of the Pericú. In his descriptions, Shelcocke wrote:

The men are tall, straight, and well formed; they have very large arms and black, thick, poorly cared for hair, which does not reach the thighs, as a previous sailor reported on his voyage [apparently a rebuke to Woodes Rogers's earlier descriptions], nor even barely to the shoulders. The women are smaller; their hair is longer than the men's and sometimes almost covers their faces, Some of both sexes have a good appearance, although of a darker color than other Indians I have seen in these seas, as they have a dark copper color. The reader may reasonably conclude that they cannot be more savage, but there is much difference between what one would think on first sight of them, and what they truly are: because from everything I could observe of their behavior with each other and us, they are endowed with all imaginable humanity, and might shame some other nations . . . because during our entire stay there, constantly among so many hundreds of them, we observed only perfect harmony; when one of us gave something edible to one of them in particular, he always divided it into as many parts as there were people around, and normally reserved the smallest part for himself.

The First Settlers

During the remainder of the Spanish colonial era, Cabo's natural harbor was periodically used by passing galleons, but since it offered no source of fresh water and scant protection from late-summer *chubascos* rolling in from the southeast, it was largely ignored in favor of San José del Cabo, where fresh water was abundant.

The Mexican independence movement largely bypassed San Lucas, although the Chilean ship *Independence* visited Cabo in 1822 in support of the Mexican struggle. The visit accomplished little as a military exercise since Mexico had gained independence from Spain the previous year, but it may have sparked renewed interest in San Lucas as a convenient harbor in this part of the world. By the end of the 19th century, an enterprising group of *bajacalifornianos* began processing and shipping bark from the local *palo blanco* tree, a key ingredient in leather tanning. The principal route for the bark trade ran between Cabo San Lucas and San Francisco. Shipping traffic gradually increased, and port authorities built the lighthouse now known as Faro Viejo at nearby Cabo Falso in 1890.

In 1917 an American company floated a tuna cannery from San Diego to San Lucas to take advantage of the abundance of tuna in the area. As San Lucas gathered a small population, a roadbed to San José del Cabo, the nearest federal government seat, was laid in the 1920s. By the 1930s, a cannery and a small fishing village inhabited by around 400 hardy souls occupied the north end of the Cabo San Lucas harbor. Fish-canning remained the backbone of the local economy until the cannery was heavily damaged by a hurricane in 1941. During WW II the area was all but abandoned as Japanese submarines cruised the Pacific coast; Cabo seemed destined for obscurity.

Marlin Alley and
La Carretera Transpeninsular

Fortunately for *sanluqueños* (residents of San Lucas), post-WW II leisure travel brought fly-in anglers, who spread the word that Cabo was a gamefish paradise. The Cape sportfishing craze of the 1950s and '60s—when the waters off the peninsula's southern tip earned the nickname "Marlin Alley"—expanded the population to around 1,500 by the time the Transpeninsular Highway was completed in 1973. Following the establishment of the highway link between the U.S. and Cabo San Lucas, the town was transformed from a fly-in/sail-in resort into an auto-and-RV destination.

When Baja California Sur received statehood in 1974, a ferry route from Puerto Vallarta on the mainland was established, thus opening the area to increased Mexican migration. The construction of Los Cabos International Airport near San José del Cabo in the '80s brought Cabo within reach of vacationers who didn't have the time for a six-day drive from border to Cape and back. The establishment of a water pipeline between San José and San Lucas further loosened the limits on development.

Today the local economy rests on the provision of tourism services—hotels, restaurants, fishing, diving, and other water sports—and on the construction industry, which supplies the growing need for leisure, residential, and business structures throughout the lower Cape Region. At the moment Cabo San Lucas's population is roughly equal to that of San José del Cabo, the *cabecera* or *municipio* seat—but the San Lucas population may soon exceed its older twin's. A vocal group of *sanluqueños* is campaigning for the Cabo area to separate from San José's jurisdiction and become the state's sixth *municipio*.

LAND'S END

A large cluster of granitic batholiths, carved by wind and sea into fantastic shapes, tumbles into the sea at the Cape's southernmost point. Forming the coccyx of a rocky spine that reaches northward all the way to Alaska's Aleutian Islands, the formations are collectively known as **Finisterra**, or Land's End.

El Arco, a rock outcropping at the tip of Land's End, has become Cabo San Lucas's most immediately recognizable symbol. During low tide you can walk along Playa del Amor to the 62-meter (200-foot) rock formation, which features an eroded passage through the middle. El Arco is also known as the "Arch of Poseidon" since it marks the "entrance" to a precipitous submarine canyon—the perfect throne room for the King of the Seas—just offshore. Running northwest from El Arco and Playa del Amor are several more unnamed rock formations, including two large granite clusters as tall or taller than El Arco. These should be of interest to rock climbers.

Just offshore stand **Los Frailes** (The Friars), two rock islets shaped like clusters of hooded monks and frequented by sea lions. A smaller, bird-limed rock pinnacle off the northeast side of the cape, **Roca Pelicanos** (Pelican Rock), serves as a crowded pelican roost. The base of the pinnacle, about six meters (20 feet) down, is richly endowed with marinelife, in-

rock formations, Land's End

cluding coral, sea fans, gorgonians, sea urchins, and numerous tropical fish. Recent reports from divers say visibility at the rock is declining, however, due to discharge from cruise ships moored in the outer harbor.

Cerro La Vigía, rising 150 meters (500 feet) above the harbor, once served as lookout point for English pirates awaiting Manila galleons to plunder. Today it's still an excellent vantage point for viewing Land's End, the town, the marina, Playa Solmar (the beach next to the Hotel Solmar), and Cabo Falso. A steep trail begins just behind the old cannery on the harbor and leads to La Vigía's summit, which is marked by a crucifix.

BEACHES

Beachgoers can choose among five beaches close to the downtown area and a string of beaches and coves along the San José del Cabo to Cabo San Lucas Corridor.

Playa El Médano

The most popular and easily accessible local beach, Playa El Médano (Dune Beach) extends several kilometers along Bahía San Lucas northeast from the inner harbor's entrance channel. This is Baja's most heavily used beach—it's packed with swimmers and sunbathers during peak vacation periods—and is one of the few local beaches where swimming is safe year-round. Besides swimming and lying on the sand, a variety of other activities here entertain beachgoers. Beach vendors rent *pangas,* jet skis, inflatable rafts, sailboards, snorkeling equipment, volleyball equipment, *palapas,* and beach furniture. Several *palapa* bars and restaurants scattered along the beach—Billygan's Island, The Office, El Delfín, and Las Palmas—offer cold beverages and seafood.

Minor annoyances at Playa El Médano include the many vendors who plod up and down the beach hawking jewelry, rugs, hammocks, hand-painted plates, and the like (they won't persist if you show no interest) and the condo developments in the background that mar the view of the Sierra de La Laguna foothills.

Playa del Amor

Cabo's next most popular beach can only be reached by boat or by a difficult climb over two rock headlands along the ocean. Named one of Mexico's 10 best beaches by *Condé Nast Traveler* magazine, Playa del Amor (Love Beach), also known as Playa del Amante (Lover's Beach), lies near the tip of Cabo San Lucas—the cape itself, not the town—just northwest of the famous arch-shaped rock formation featured in virtually every Los Cabos advertisement. The wide, sandy, pristine beach actually extends across the cape behind the arch to the other side, forming two beachfronts—one on Bahía San Lucas and one on the Pacific. The latter is sometimes whimsically called "Divorce Beach."

Only the beachfront facing the bay is generally safe for swimming. Bring along a cooler full of beverages, as the entire area is free of vendors and commercial enterprises. Unless you have a portable beach umbrella, go early in the day to command one of the shady rock overhangs. The southeast end of the bay features a series of coral-encrusted rocks suitable for snorkeling; a deep submarine canyon lying

only 50 meters (164 feet) offshore is a popular scuba-diving site.

You can reach Playa del Amor by water taxi from the marina for US$5 or take a Dos Mares glass-bottom boat tour (US$7) and arrange a drop-off at the beach. Any tour boat in the vicinity will give you a ride back to the marina upon presentation of your ticket stub; the last tour boat leaves the marina around 3 p.m. In calm seas, you can also rent a kayak on Playa El Médano and paddle across the inner harbor entrance to the beach.

Those skilled at bouldering can reach the south side of the beach by climbing from the east end of Playa Solmar (in front of the Hotel Solmar) over two rocky points that separate the two beaches. The climb is best attempted during low tide, when the cove between the rock formations reveals a sandy beach useful as a midway rest stop. The second set of rocks, to the east, is more difficult than those to the west; turn back after the first set if you've reached the limit of your climbing skills.

Playa Solmar

This very wide, very long beach running along the southwestern edge of the cape is accessible via the road to Hotel Solmar. The strong undertow and heavy surf make it suitable for sunbathing and wading only. Solmar's biggest advantage is its lack of people, even during peak tourist seasons.

Cannery Beaches

Next to the abandoned Planta Empacadora (the old tuna cannery on the south side of the inner harbor entrance) are two small public beaches virtually ignored by most Cabo visitors. The first, **Playa Escondida** (Hidden Beach), lies next to the cannery pier and is easily reached by walking along the west bank of the marina and alongside the main cannery building. The sand extends only around 50 meters (164 feet), less in high tide, but it's popular with local Mexican families because Dad can fish from the pier while the kids play in the calm water. I once watched a local resident haul in a 4.5-kg (10-pound) tuna with a handline here.

Playa Balconcito (Little Balcony Beach), a bit larger than Playa Escondida, lies beyond the pier on the other side of the cannery toward the

Playa del Amor, Cabo San Lucas

sea. You must walk along a stone ledge—part of the cannery foundation—to get there.

Corridor Beaches

Northeast of Cabo San Lucas—on the way to San José del Cabo—are a number of uncrowded, relatively pristine beaches suitable for swimming, fishing, camping, snorkeling, and scuba diving. See the special topic Beaches along the Corridor for names and locations.

ACCOMMODATIONS

Cabo San Lucas offers a greater number and variety of hotels than neighboring San José. Most are in the US$50-110 range although two hotels charge under US$35 a night and several cost well over US$110 in winter and early spring.

Unless otherwise noted, rates quoted below are for peak season, usually Nov.-May. Some hotels may offer a 15-20% discount March-October. Add 12% tax to all rates; some hotels may charge an additional 10-15% service charge.

Downtown Hotels

Although Cabo's beaches are the average visitor's preferred address, you can save considerably by staying downtown and walking or driving to the beach.

Budget: A bit off the beaten track, on Calle Revolución a half block east of Morelos (and close to the bus terminal), **Casa Blanca Inn,** tel. (1) 143-0260 or 143-1033, offers 15 basic rooms with ceiling fans. Although lacking in atmosphere, the Casa Blanca has the advantage of being relatively quiet. Rates: US$17 s, US$20 d.

The economical, two-story **Hotel Marina,** Blvd. Marina at Guerrero, tel./fax (1) 143-2484, has 16 clean and tidy a/c rooms and seven large a/c suites with refrigerators and TVs. On the premises are a modest pool and jacuzzi. Rooms fill up fast. One drawback is that it can get a bit noisy during peak season (Dec.-March), when the hotel is jam-packed and there's lots of pedestrian traffic on Blvd. Marina. Rates: standard rooms US$30, suites US$50.

Inexpensive: One of the best values downtown is the friendly and efficient **Siesta Suites Hotel,** Calle Zapata between Guerrero and Hidalgo, tel./fax (1) 143-2773, U.S. tel./fax (909) 945-5940, e-mail: siesta@cabonet.net.mx, near the better downtown restaurants and one block from the marina. All 15 rooms are immaculate and quiet, and most come with kitchenettes. Four of the rooms have ceiling fans but no a/c, the rest have a/c. Because of price and location, Siesta Suites is a popular spot; advance reservations are recommended, even in summer (when fishing's high season lures droves of North American anglers). Rates: US$45 s/d without a/c; US$55 s/d with a/c. Add US$10 for each additional guest beyond two.

Nearby, the friendly **Hotel Dos Mares,** Calle Zapata s/n, tel. (1) 143-0330, fax (1) 143-4727, rents adequate, non-a/c rooms for US$40.

In the same vicinity as Casa Blanca Inn, **Olas Hotel,** Calle Revolución at Gómez Farías, tel. (1) 143-1780, fax (1) 143-1380, has 24 rooms, each with TV, fan, and patio. Rates: US$38 plus tax and service.

Cabo Inn Hotel, 20 de Noviembre between Leona Vicario and Mendoza, tel. (1) 143-0819, is a cash-only place with nice courtyard areas downstairs and small, clean rooms with a/c, ceiling fans, and tiny bathrooms. A shared TV is usually on in the downstairs lobby, though it's turned off at a reasonable hour. The roof patio has a seating area furnished with a sofa, chairs, and a cabinet full of books, as well as a "social pool." Rates: US$45.

Three blocks back from the marina, old gringo standby **Hotel Mar de Cortez,** Blvd. Lázaro Cárdenas at Guerrero, tel. (1) 143-1432, U.S. tel. (800) 347-8821, U.S. fax (831) 663-1904, e-mail: info@mardecortez.com, stays full virtually all season. Its clean a/c rooms surround a small pool and patio area planted with date palms; some of the rooms have their own small patios attached. Facilities include a restaurant and outdoor bar area. Rates: US$37-47 s, US$41-51 d, US$55 t, suites US$51 s, US$58 d, US$62 t, US$66 q.

Moderate: A large arched metal door leads to the attractive walled courtyard of the new **Los Milagros Hotel,** Matamoros 116, tel. (1) 143-4566, U.S. tel. (800) 524-5104, e-mail: fish@cabonet.com.mex. The 13 spacious rooms—some with kitchenettes—are well decorated and well maintained. An inviting splash pool/jacuzzi is available. Rates: US$55-65 s/d, plus US$10 for each additional person.

Another new place in this price category is the friendly **Chile Pepper Inn,** on 16 de Septiembre, tel./fax (1) 143-0510 or 143-4780, e-mail: chilepepper@cabonet.net.mx, next to the Capitanía del Puerto. The one-story mustard-colored building holds nicely furnished fair-sized rooms, all with a/c and satellite TV. Guests may use the office phone for free local calls. Rates: US$48 low season, up to US$60 high season.

Hotel Santa Fe, at the southwest corner of Zaragoza and Obregón, tel. (1) 143-4402, fax (1) 143-4401, e-mail: santafe@cabonet.net.mx, is a tidy, Mexican-style compound containing 46 studios, each with kitchenette, a/c, satellite TV, and phone. Amenities include off-street parking, 24-hour security, a restaurant, pool, and laundry. Rates: US$75.

Expensive-Premium: One block off the marina on the second floor of Plaza de la Danza, **Viva Cabo Hotel and Cantina,** Blvd. Marina, tel./fax (1) 143-5810, e-mail: vivacabo@cabonet.net.mx, is a small luxury hotel featuring eight studios with fully equipped kitchens, a/c, satellite TV, and sitting areas. Amenities include a restaurant and bar, with a pool and fitness center next door. Rates: US$99-125 d.

Playa El Médano Hotels

The preponderance of Cabo's beach hotels are along this long strip of sand southeast of the town center.

Inexpensive-Moderate: East along Playa El Médano, behind San Vicente and Vagabundos RV Parks, **Club Cabo Motel and Campground Resort,** Apdo. Postal 463, Cabo San Lucas, BCS, tel./fax (1) 143-3348, e-mail: clubcabo@cabonet.net.mx, rents eight one- and two-bedroom suites with TVs, verandas, and king-size beds, some with a/c and full kitchens. Other amenities

Hotel Meliá San Lucas

include laundry facilities, Internet access, ping pong tables, a trampoline, pool, jacuzzi, a large refrigerator for storing your catch, and a shuttle to town. English, Spanish, and Dutch are spoken. Club Cabo is primarily an RV park; see Camping and RV Parks for further information. It's a 15-20 minute walk from the park to the marina/downtown, and a short walk to the beach, which is separated from the park by a dirt road and one of the last stands of natural thornforest in the Cabo area—a good birding site. Rates: US$40 s, US$50-80 d, each extra person US$10-20.

Premium: Surrounded by coconut palms, the stately mission-style **Hacienda Beach Resort,** tel. (1) 143-0122 or 143-0663, fax (1) 143-0666, U.S. tel. (800) 733-2226, e-mail: hhbrcabo@ cabonet.net.mx, has presided over the south end of the beach since 1960. The resort has recently undergone an extensive renovation. Some of its 115 spacious a/c rooms have ocean views, and some are two-story affairs with sleeping lofts and full kitchens. On the grounds are a pool, tennis court, water-sports center, full-service dive shop, small-boat anchorage, and five restaurants and bars. The hotel provides free shuttle service to San José del Cabo. Rates: garden patio rooms US$135-192, deluxe and honeymoon suites US$231-330, colonial rooms and deluxe studios US$173-251, cabaña rooms US$194-298, one-bedroom townhouses US$252-363, two-bedroom townhouses US$299-385.

Moving northeast along the beach, next up is the **Hotel Meliá San Lucas,** tel. (1) 143-4444, fax (1) 143-0420, U.S. tel. (800) 336-3542, U.S. fax (305) 530-1626, a multistory resort built in a horseshoe shape around a large pool and patio area. The first phase of a US$1 million renovation program has recently been completed. Facilities include IDD telephones, a/c, satellite TV, in-room safes, minibar, in-room coffeemakers, two heated pools, two lighted tennis courts, three restaurants, two bars, live nightly entertainment, a water-sports center, horseback riding, a shopping arcade, and a beauty salon. Most of the Meliá's 142 spacious rooms and suites have ocean views. Rates: from US$216 d 1 May-26 Sept. to US$231 d during peak weeks. More expensive deluxe suites are available.

A couple of hundred meters northeast along the beach is the striking **Pueblo Bonito Resort,** tel. (1) 143-2500, fax (1) 143-1995, U.S. tel.

(800) 252-8008 or (800) 442-5300, U.S. fax (619) 456-8005, a white, five-story Mediterranean-style building topped by blue-tiled domes and arrayed in a horseshoe around gardens and a free-form pool with a waterfall, similar in conception to its immediate neighbor. One of the hotel's finest features is its lavish lobby, which is decorated with velvet draperies, a 17th-century Flemish tapestry, and fountains surrounded by 16th-century Italian baroque cherubs. The 146 junior and luxury suites come with IDD telephones, satellite TV, fully equipped kitchenettes, and ocean views. In addition to its large pool, the hotel offers two restaurants, two bars, and a full-service health spa and fitness center. Rates: US$180-220 (rates are higher in peak times).

Farther northeast is the sister resort of the Pueblo Bonito, the **Pueblo Bonito Rose Resort,** tel. (1) 143-5500, fax (1) 143-5523. The 260 suites are situated on 2.2 hectares (5.5 acres). Rooms feature private balconies, ocean views, hand-painted terra-cotta floors, full kitchens, and original artwork. Amenities include a fitness center, a free-form pool, a European health spa, and various sports activities. Rates: US$160-1,200 s/d.

Yet another Mediterranean-inspired structure, **Villa del Palmar Cabo Beach Resort & Spa,** Mexico 1, Km 0.5, tel. (1) 143-2694, fax (1) 143-2664, U.S. reservations tel. (800) 795-1809, e-mail: reserv.vdp@1cabonet.com.mx, stands along a more secluded area of El Médano and offers 204 studios and one- to three-bedroom ocean-view suites with full kitchens, marble bathrooms, and furnished balconies. A new addition with 132 suites is scheduled to open soon. Other amenities include two pools (one with poolside bar), two lighted tennis courts, a large European-style health spa, a fitness center, a water-sports facility, and rooftop and beachside restaurants. Rates: US$222-850 per night; some units are only available by the week. These rates are valid for up to four persons per unit, above which each extra person pays US$10.

Not on the beach, but close to it, is the 10-room **Casa Rafael's,** tel. (1) 143-0739, fax (1) 143-1679, e-mail: casarafa@caboland.com, tastefully decorated in Mexican-colonial style. Rooms with handicapped access are available; some rooms have jacuzzis and some have ocean views. The premises are generously planted in banana and papaya and feature exotic caged birds, a pool, jacuzzi, small gym, piano bar, cigar lounge, and a restaurant with a good wine collection. Rates: US$125 d.

Playa Solmar Hotels

Two of Cabo's most distinguished hotels are secluded from the rest of town by the rocky ridge leading to Land's End.

Expensive-Premium: Impressively constructed high on the ridge itself, overlooking the beach and Pacific Ocean, is the 1971-vintage, 247-room **Hotel Finisterra,** tel. (1) 143-3333, fax (1) 143-0590, e-mail: finister@cabonet.net.mx. A newer tower wing, known as the Palapa Beach Club, offers spacious suites with ocean views and extends from the beach below all the way to the original hotel and lobby area, to which it is connected by a bridge. A 1,040-square-meter (11,200-square-foot) swimming pool with whirlpools and swim-up bar sits on the beach at the foot of the Palapa Beach Club. Some of the rooms and suites in the original Finisterra section feature city, marina, or garden views rather than bay views. Amenities include lighted tennis courts, a travel agency, wedding chapel, restaurant, and bar. Rates: Finisterra section, marina- or garden-view rooms US$99-125, marina- or city-view rooms US$130-160; Palapa Beach Club US$150-185. For U.S. reservations, call (714) 476-5555 or (800) 347-2252.

Premium: The sleek V-shaped **Hotel Solmar Suites,** tel. (1) 143-3535, fax (1) 143-0410, U.S.

tel. (213) 459-9861 or (800) 878-4115, features 90 one-bedroom and two-bedroom suites built right on the beach, directly into the rocks that form Land's End, plus 35 time-share/condo units overlooking the beach. Some of the suites have a private jacuzzi on the terrace. The suites have ocean views and kitchenettes, and all rooms have a/c, satellite TV, in-room safes, coffeemakers and direct-dial phones. Down at the original beach wing are tennis courts, an aquatic center, an indoor-outdoor restaurant, and two heated pools with swim-up *palapa* bars and jacuzzis. The Solmar is renowned for its fishing fleet; special all-inclusive fishing packages are popular during the late-summer fishing season. The hotel's dive boat, the *Solmar V,* is one of the finest in Baja. Rates: US$165-285 in season.

Marina Hotels

Moderate-Expensive: Overlooking the east side of the marina, the **Marina Cabo Plaza,** tel. (1) 143-2076, fax (1) 143-2077, U.S. tel. (510) 652-6051 or (800) 524-5104, U.S. fax (510) 652-9039, has a pool and is adjacent to a new shopping center with restaurants, stores, and a private mail center. Playa El Médano is a 10-minute walk away. Kitchenettes available. Rates: US$75-85 s/d, US$90-100 with kitchenette.

Premium: Next to Plaza Fiesta, near the Marina Cabo San Lucas office, stands **Marina Fiesta Resort & Hotel,** tel. (1) 143-2690, fax (1) 143-1998, U.S. tel. (800) 332-2252. The hotel's well-designed, comfortable suites come with

Hotel Finisterra

kitchenettes. Among the facilities are a sundeck and solarium (both with jacuzzis), a massage and therapy room, 24-hour supermarket, drugstore, children's playground, and a free-form heated pool with a swim-up *palapa* bar. Rates: US$145-224 depending on size.

Largest of the marina hotels is **Plaza Las Glorias,** tel. (1) 143-1220, fax (1) 143-1238, U.S. tel. (713) 448-2829 or (800) 342-2644, a pseudo-Pueblo-style pink structure on the marina's west side. The sprawling, 287-room hotel is nicknamed "Cabo Jail" because it takes so long to walk from one end to the other. All rooms come with a/c, telephones, refrigerators, and in-room safety box. Facilities include a pool, restaurants, bars, a shopping center, travel agency, and a beach club at Playa El Médano. Rates: US$120-220.

Condominiums, Time Shares, and Beach Homes

Some of the best deals for families or small groups are rental condos, which usually sleep up to four for US$75-180 per night. The following condo sites take reservations directly (rates do not include tax and service).

Near Casa Rafael's off Camino de los Pescadores, a short walk from Playa El Médano, stand the two round, whitewashed towers of **Cabo Villas,** tel./fax (1) 143-2558, U.S. tel. (253) 845-3210, e-mail: cabovillas@cabonet.net.mx. One-bedroom, one-bath units and two-bedroom, two-bath units are available. Rates: US$95-275 plus tax.

Well-managed, four-story **Bahía Condo Hotel,** just off Camino de los Pescadores above Playa El Médano, tel. (1) 143-1888, fax (1) 143-1891, U.S. tel. (408) 776-1806 or (800) 932-5599, U.S. fax (408) 932-5599, rents clean, comfortable a/c units, some with ocean views, all with fully equipped kitchenettes, satellite TV, and direct-dial phones. Other amenities include laundry facilities, a good restaurant, and a pool with jacuzzi and swim-up *palapa* bar. Rates: studio (pool view) US$87 low season/US$117 high season; studio (ocean view) US$107/137; studio double US$97/127; master suite US$200/260; penthouse US$240/300. All rates include tax.

Close to downtown but also within easy walking distance of El Médano, **Marina Sol Condominiums,** Apdo. Postal 177, Cabo San Lucas, BCS 23410, tel./fax (1) 143-1653, e-mail: clicha@cabonet.net.mex, features simple but good-sized and well-kept one- and two-bedroom condos built around a garden courtyard with a pool. A handicapped-accessible room is also available. The complex also has a jacuzzi, swim-up bar, and a small gym. An independently operated grocery store and laundry service can be found in the lobby. Rates: US$80-175 per night, plus tax and service charge. Discounts are usually available June-October.

Club Cascada, at the east end of El Médano next to Pueblo Bonito Resort, tel. (1) 143-0738, fax (1) 143-1881, is a nicely designed time-share complex with one- to three-bedroom interconnected villas, two pools, and tennis courts. Rates: US$185-1,050 in season.

The **Hotel Solmar Suites** (see Playa Solmar Hotels, above) rents a number of time-share/condo units on the hill overlooking Playa Solmar. Rates: US$220-280 in season.

Next door, the **Suites Terrasol,** tel. (1) 143-2751, fax (1) 143-1804, U.S. toll-free tel. (800) 524-5104, e-mail: terrasol@1cabonet.com.mx, rents studios, one-bedroom units, and two-bedroom units, all with full kitchens and ocean views. On the premises are two pools, a sauna, health club, restaurant, and bar. You can walk to the beach from both the Solmar and Terrasol. Rates: US$250-480; rates valid for up to four people.

In the exclusive Pedregal hill zone, **Pedregal Villas** consists of a variety of ocean-view vacation homes ranging from two to four bedrooms and up to 6,000 square feet. Some villas feature private pools, jacuzzis, and sunken baths; cook, maid service, and car rental are available. In season rates run a heady US$200-1,200 per day plus tax. Contact Los Cabos Properties, Apdo. Postal 244, Cabo San Lucas, BCS 23410, tel. (1) 143-1164, fax (1) 143-1162.

Property Management Companies

Many real-estate and property-management companies rent units in condo complexes not mentioned above. Some of these companies also handle time-share and beach-home rentals.

Companies with a broad variety of rental units in the Los Cabos area include: **Earth, Sea, and Sky Tours,** U.S. tel. (800) 745-2226, fax (831) 662-8426, e-mail: cabovillas@aol.com; **A-1 Cabo Vacation Properties,** tel. (1) 144-5089; **SeaSide Vacations,** tel./fax (1) 142-3789; **Accommodations Los Cabos,** U.S. tel. (800) 655-

CABO, fax (206) 440-9905; and **Los Cabos Vacation Rentals & Real Estate,** tel./fax (1) 142-2100, e-mail: aviani@1cabonet.com.mx.

Bed and Breakfast Inns
Expensive: Off Calle Constitución in the residential western part of town, **The Bungalows,** tel./fax (1) 143-5035, e-mail: bungalow@cabonet.net.mx, offers eight well-decorated one-bedroom suites, each with ceiling fan, a/c, fridge, stove, and TV; one larger, deluxe one-bedroom suite; one "honeymoon suite" with a private veranda and view of town; and six two-bedroom bungalows, each sleeping four to six guests. Smoking isn't permitted anywhere on the premises, inside or out. The small but well-landscaped grounds also contain a swimming pool, jacuzzi, and outdoor barbecue, plus a small gift shop selling many of the Mexican decor accessories seen in the guest rooms. A Mexican cook and pastry chef prepare the complimentary full breakfast.

Rates: standard suite US$85, deluxe suite US$95, honeymoon suite US$105, bungalow US$105. Extra persons in any of the units pay US$15, while children under 12 stay free of charge. For reservations, write The Bungalows, 9051-C Siempre Viva Rd., Suite 40-497, San Diego, CA 92173.

Camping and RV Parks
In the northwestern section of town on the way to Todos Santos, shady and well-kept **El Faro Viejo Trailer Park,** Matamoros at Mijares, Apdo. Postal 64, Cabo San Lucas, BCS, tel. (1) 143-4211 or 143-1927, offers 20 spaces with full hookups for US$12 d. Facilities include flush toilets, showers, a laundromat, public phone, security guard, and a reputable restaurant/bar. Add US$3 for each additional person per site. Monthly rates of US$290 are available. This park tends to fill up Nov.-May but is more likely to have a spot than Vagabundos or San Vicente (see below).

Three km northeast of Cabo San Lucas off Mexico 1, the **Vagabundos del Mar RV Park,** tel. (1) 143-0209, U.S. tel. (707) 374-5511 or (800) 474-2252, has 95 well-serviced slots with full hookups for US$15 for two plus US$3 per additional guest; discounts are available for members of the Vagabundos del Mar travel club. From November to June this park is usually booked up for weeks or months at a time, so be sure to make contact well in advance if you want to park here. Caravans are not accepted. Facilities include a restaurant, bar, flush toilets, *palapas,* showers, a pool, and laundry.

The nearby **San Vicente Trailer Park,** Apdo. Postal 463, Cabo San Lucas, BCS, tel. (1) 143-0712, is lushly planted, and all spots are ramada-shaded. Full hookups (when available) cost US$10-12, and on the premises are hot showers, a recreation room, bar, and restaurant. This park is also fully occupied much of the time, as evidenced by the many semipermanent, nicely constructed RV shelters and bungalows within.

Behind San Vicente and Vagabundos RV Parks and Playa El Médano is tidy **Club Cabo Motel and Campground Resort,** tel./fax (1) 143-3348; to get there, turn east off Mexico 1 onto the road to Club Cascada, then turn onto the first dirt road on your left and follow the signs. This small campground offers 10 tent sites and 10 RV slots—some shaded, some not. Tent sites cost US$7 pp, RV spots US$15 for two persons. Facilities include well-kept toilets, hot showers, a jacuzzi, hammock lounge area, ping-pong table, trampoline, and pool. Club Cabo also rents eight suites with full kitchens for US$40-80 a night—see Accommodations, above for further information.

Nowadays Club Cabo is more likely to have a vacancy than El Faro, Vagabundos, or San Vicente; it is also closer to the beach than the others. The proprietor, an accomplished pilot, can arrange ultralight flights and instruction in the area. Visiting pilots may receive discounts on accommodations. Other activities that can be arranged through Club Cabo include kayaking, sailing, horseback riding, and mountain biking. The adjacent natural thornforest is a habitat for many resident and migratory bird species.

On a rise at Km 5.5 on Mexico 1, **El Arco Trailer Park,** tel. (1) 143-0613, commands a view of town and Bahía San Lucas even though it's on the north side of the highway. El Arco has many permanent shelters and few vacancies; when available, full hookups cost US$12, tent sites US$6. The park features flush toilets, a pool, and a large *palapa* restaurant with distant bay views.

You can camp on the beaches farther northeast along Mexico 1 (see The Corridor, above) or northwest along Mexico 19.

FOOD

Downtown Cabo San Lucas is riddled with restaurants and bars, most of open-air design. Menus usually attempt to cover the bases demanded by any Mexican resort area—seafood, Italian, Mexican, and steak. Because Cabo is Baja's number-one resort town, prices are above what you'd find in La Paz, Ensenada, Tijuana, or other tourist areas. Quality is also generally high since Cabo attracts chefs from all over Mexico and beyond. One complaint: Cabo restaurants sometimes hold back on the chiles in Mexican dishes and table salsas, hence picante-lovers may be forced to request extra chiles or fresh *salsa cruda* to bring things up to the proper level of heat.

American and Eclectic

Latitude 22+, Blvd. Lázaro Cárdenas between Morelos and Leona Vicario, opposite the boat ramp, serves American fare throughout the day, but it's more of a bar than a restaurant. Daily specials include roast chicken, pork chops, chicken-fried steak, meat loaf, and roast beef. Inexpensive to moderate. Open 7 a.m.-midnight daily.

Francisco's Café, Plaza Bonita, Blvd. Marina, offers gourmet coffees, pastries, and sandwiches. Seating is available indoors or out on the terrace facing the marina. Open daily 7:30 a.m.-9 p.m.

Magnolia, Blvd. Marina, across from Plaza Las Glorias, tel. (1) 143-4977, prepares decent homemade pasta, designer pizzas, homemade bread, breakfast, and seafood. Happy hour runs daily 1 a.m.-6 p.m. Occasional live music. Inexpensive to moderate. Open daily 8 a.m.-midnight.

Olé Olé, tel. (1) 143-0633, faces the marina at Plaza Bonita. The large outdoor tapa bar features paella, brochettes, and tapas dinner combos such as *gazpacho andaluz, tortilla española,* and *jamón serrano* (Spanish-style cured ham). Try the *gambas a la ajo,* a plate of shrimp in garlic sauce, also available in an octopus version. Moderate to expensive. Open daily 11 a.m.-11 p.m.; paella is served only on Fridays from 7 p.m. and on Sundays from 1 p.m.

Cozy **Sancho Panza,** Locales D19-22, Plaza Las Glorias, tel. (1) 143-3212, is one of the best restaurant/bars in the Cape Region. To find it, walk under the pedestrian bridge that connects the wings of Plaza Las Glorias and look for it on your right, before Seafood Mama's. Aided by an artistic and colorful Miró-esque decor, the proprietors have created a first-class wine bar that stocks such hard-to-find, top-of-the-line Baja labels as Monte Xanic and Chateau de Camou along with over 150 other wines. The short menu offers delicious "new world tapas" that mix New American, Mediterranean, and Latin American influences with positive results—try the mushroom-brie fondue, smoked salmon cakes, vegetarian lasagna, or Cuban sandwich. Best salads in town, also espresso and live jazz. Expensive. Open Mon.-Sat. 1-11 p.m.

Pazzo's Cabo, corner of Niños Héroes and Morelos, tel. (112) 3-4313, is a Cabo branch of the Vail, Colorado, pizza place of the same name. Look for fresh pasta, pizza, calzones *mariscos,* and a TV tuned nonstop to sports channels. Live music is featured in the evening. The kitchen is open daily 10 a.m.-1 p.m.; the cantina stays open till midnight; free pizza delivery.

Peacocks, Camino de los Pescadores, tel. (1) 143-1858, next to the driveway of Hotel Meliá San Lucas, is a highly regarded continental kitchen presided over by a German chef. The changing menu at this large, *palapa*-roofed, open-air restaurant is diverse and creative, and the wine list is extensive. Moderate to expensive. Open daily 6-10 p.m.

Asian

Nick-San Sushi Bar, Plaza de la Danza, Blvd. Lázaro Cárdenas, is centrally located along the main strip and serves reliable Japanese barbecue and sushi. Moderately priced; open 3-10:30 p.m.

Kaz, a Japanese restaurant/sushi bar on Calle Guerrero just south of the Cabo Wabo entrance, tel. (1) 143-2396, features a *palapa*-roofed eating area upstairs and an air-conditioned section below. The cooks will prepare your catch if you bring it to them in advance. Open daily 4-11 p.m.

Restaurant Pacífico, also centrally located on the northwest corner of Lázaro Cárdenas and Leona Vicario, offers inexpensive Cantonese-style food. Open daily 11:30 a.m.-10 p.m.

Italian

Capo San Giovanni, Calle Guerrero at Madero, tel. (1) 143-0593, just across the road and south of Cabo Wabo, is a relatively new restaurant/bar with a pleasant ambience, a spacious courtyard out back, and an inventive southern Italian menu. Open Tues.-Sun. 5-1 p.m. Closed Monday.

Da Giorgio's II, Km 5.5 on the Corridor, part of the Misiones del Cabo complex, tel. (1) 145-8160, is a well-designed *palapa* restaurant with long-distance views of Land's End. Food quality varies; at times the pasta and seafood entrées upstage all the other local Italian venues, while at other times they can be disappointing. Very expensive. Open daily 8 a.m.-11 p.m.

Ristorante Italiano Galeón, Blvd. Marina just south of the Hotel Finisterra entrance, tel. (1) 143-0022, is an elegant restaurant with harbor views. Specialties include Neapolitan cuisine and pizzas baked in wood-fired ovens. Live piano music nightly. Expensive. Open 4-11 p.m.

Romeo y Julieta, on Blvd. Marina near Hotel Finisterra, tel. (1) 143-0225, offers an Italian menu featuring fresh pasta and wood-fired pizzas. Moderate to expensive. Open daily 4 p.m.-midnight.

Mexican

Mi Casa, on Calle Cabo San Lucas opposite the plaza, tel. (1) 143-1933, is often cited as the most authentic Mexican restaurant in Cabo. The tastefully designed, half-*palapa,* half-open-air dining room is encircled by pastel murals intended to look like a small Central Mexican village. The menu lists dishes from all over Mexico, including fajitas, *mole verde, mole poblano, pipián, carne asada a la tampiqueña, pollo barracho,* and *cochinita pibil.* The food is good but doesn't always match menu descriptions. Moderate to expensive. Open daily for dinner 5-10 p.m., open for lunch Mon.-Sat. noon-4 p.m.

Just to the northeast of Plaza Naútica, in Plaza del Sol, **O Mole Mío Restaurant & Bar,** tel. (1) 143-7577, features original Mexican recipes such as El Solo Mío (grilled red snapper seasoned with Cajun spices and served with mango salsa) or Camarones Frida y Omar (shrimp baked in a tequila sauce and topped with julienned potatoes). The interior, decorated with unusual custom-designed wicker-and-iron furniture, is as interesting as the menu. The bar section is a fun place for drinks and *botanas.* Open noon-1 a.m.

Those seeking *alta cocina* should check the new **La República,** Morelos and 20 de Noviembre, tel. (1) 143-3400. Served in an attractively

asadero, *Blvd. Marina*

landscaped, candlelit courtyard, the menu features a wide selection of regional Mexican dishes, such as *crema de calabaza fría* (cold cream of squash soup), along with such innovations as vegetarian enchiladas in peanut sauce. Steak and grilled red snapper are also house specialties, and fine wines are available. Prices average US$11.30-15 per entrée. Open daily from 6 p.m.

About one block behind Banamex south of Lázaro Cárdenas, **La Diligencia,** tel. (1) 143-6898, is a relatively new upscale restaurant offering Mexican *alta cocina* from various regions, as well as steak and seafood dishes. Diners are serenaded by live piano music. Open noon-10 p.m. (the attached sports bar, **La Carreta,** is open 2 p.m.-3 a.m.).

For authentic Mexican dishes that won't cost a lot, two places off the main tourist track can be recommended. **La Perla,** Blvd. Lázaro Cárdenas at Guerrero, is a simple Mexican eatery supported by a mainly local clientele. The menu features inexpensive *desayuno, tortas, molletes, tingas,* tacos, burritos, quesadillas, and *licuados;* the daily *comida del dia* costs only US$3.20. Open Mon.-Sat. 7:30 a.m.-4:30 p.m. **El Restau-**

rant de Doña Lolita, opposite Pescadería El Dorado on Niños Héroes near Matamoros, serves inexpensive, authentic *antojitos mexicanos*, plus *champurrado* (hot chocolate made with cornstarch). Open daily 6:30-10:30 p.m.

Back in gringolandia, **Pancho's,** Calle Hidalgo off Blvd. Marina, tel. (1) 143-0973, serves huge Mexican platters at reasonable prices, good Mexican breakfasts, and over 190 varieties of tequila. All the waiters speak English. Mexican beer costs US$1 a bottle, cheap house tequila shots 30 cents. Pleasant outdoor seating. Open daily 6 a.m.-11 p.m.

La Bamba, in the courtyard of Plaza Naútica, on Blvd. Marina, tel. (1) 143-1051, offers an extensive menu featuring several types of enchiladas, burritos, quesadillas, California-style nachos, soups, salads, Mexican *platillos,* fajitas, and Mexican breakfasts. For bigger pocketbooks, lobster, shrimp, and certified Angus beef are also available. Good service. Moderate to expensive. Open daily noon-11 p.m.

Carlos'n Charlie's, Blvd. Marina, tel. (1) 143-1280, functions primarily as a place for tourists to drink themselves silly. But this Grupo Anderson restaurant serves good Mexican food. Volleyball court on the premises. Moderately priced. Open daily 11:30 a.m.-midnight.

Casa Rafael's, tel. (1) 143-0739, is a small hotel with an elegant dining room specializing in *nacional novelle,* or nouvelle Mexican cuisine—served à la carte or as a seven-course, fixed-price meal. The changing menu also features international dishes and seafood. Expensive. Open Mon.-Sat. 6-10:30 p.m.; reservations suggested.

Cilantro's Bar & Grill, at the Pueblo Bonito Resort on Playa El Médano, tel. (1) 143-2900, is one of Cabo's better hotel-oriented Mexican restaurants, featuring mesquite-grilled seafood and homemade tortillas. Moderate to expensive. Open daily 11 a.m.-11 p.m.

Salsitas, in Plaza Bonita on Blvd. Marina, tel. (1) 143-1740, is mostly a tourist scene, serving Mexican food adapted for gringo palates. But the terrace tables with marina views make it worth trying. Moderate to expensive. Open daily 6:30 a.m.-11 p.m.

Seafood
El Coral, opposite Plaza Las Glorias on Blvd. Marina, is a rambling outdoor restaurant serving inexpensively priced Mexican and seafood meals; nowhere else in town can you consume a lobster dinner for US$10. Open daily 11 a.m.-11 p.m.

El Pescador, Zaragoza at Niños Héroes, serves very good Baja-style seafood—oysters, shrimp, and red snapper are specialties—at low prices. The humble *palapa* restaurant is a piece of the old Cabo, and still patronized by locals. Open daily 8 a.m.-9 p.m.

The Fish Company, Guerrero at Zapata (next to the Río Grill), tel. (1) 143-1405, is a small eatery with a simple but very well-prepared menu of fresh fish *empanizada* (breaded) or *al mojo de ajo* (in garlic butter), plus grilled shrimp, *carne a la tampiqueña,* fajitas, *chiles rellenos,* and enchiladas. Ice-cold beers cost US$1 apiece; good, inexpensive breakfasts are also available. Open daily 8 a.m.-10 p.m.

Mariscos Mocambo, on the west side of Calle Morelos between Calles 16 de Septiembre and Niños Héroes (just south of Almacenes Grupo Castro), tel. (1) 143-2122, is a very casual, local-style place with a huge seafood menu and low to moderate prices. Open daily 11 a.m.-10 p.m.

Río Grill, on Blvd. Marina near Calle Zapata, tel. (1) 143-1335, serves well-prepared steak, lobster, shishkebab, and Mexican combos, and offers live music nightly. It's one of the nicer outdoor restaurant/bar combinations in the central marina area. Moderate to expensive, except for breakfast, which is economically priced compared to breakfasts at local hotel restaurants. Open daily 7 a.m.-midnight.

El Shrimp Bucket, in the Plaza Fiesta shopping center on the marina, near Marina Fiesta Resort, tel. (1) 143-2599, is a transplant from Mazatlán and the best of the several restaurants in town with the word "Shrimp" in the name. The pink crustaceans are served in every conceivable fashion, including the ever-popular fried shrimp served in a terra-cotta bucket. Breakfasts are also good here. Moderately priced. Open daily 6 a.m.-midnight.

The Shrimp Factory, Blvd. Marina at Guerrero, tel. (1) 143-5066, serves shrimp only by the half kilo or kilo; each order comes with salad, bread, and crackers. It's a no-frills, open-air place. Inexpensive to moderate. Open daily noon-11 p.m.

Las Palmas, on Playa El Médano, tel. (1) 143-0447, was the first *palapa* restaurant on

Médano, and most residents agree it's still the best, in spite of the ugly concrete addition. The grilled seafood is always a good choice. Moderately priced. Open daily 11 a.m.-11 p.m.

Squid Roe, Blvd. Lázaro Cárdenas at Zaragoza, tel. (1) 143-0655, is one of the many Grupo Anderson restaurant/bars in Mexico that combine zany, tourist-on-the-loose fun with tried-and-true menus based on regional cuisine. House specialties at this one include seafood, barbecued ribs, and Mexican combos; the kitchen will cook fish you bring in. Moderately priced. Open daily noon-3 a.m.

Giggling Marlin, on Calle Matamoros near Blvd. Marina, tel. (1) 143-0608, is better for appetizers and booze than entrées. Most tourists come here to snap photos of themselves hanging upside down—like landed marlins—from the restaurant's block-and-tackle rig. Others come for the big-screen satellite TV. Moderately priced. Open daily 7 a.m.-1 a.m.

Tacos and Fast Food
The local fast-food scene is concentrated along Calle Morelos, where a string of stands offer tacos, *carne asada,* and *mariscos* at the lowest prices in town. The *taquerías* seem to change owners and names every other year or so but rarely close down completely. You'll also find a cluster of inexpensive restaurants serving seafood cocktails, chicken, and *tortas* at the south end of Calle Ocampo where it meets Blvd. Lázaro Cárdenas.

From December to March a trolley cart at the corner of Blvd. Lázaro Cárdenas and Guerrero assembles delicious custom fruit salads for US$1 a cup, including your choice of sliced papaya, watermelon, cucumber, mango, orange, cantaloupe, and jicama, with a squeeze of lime. Salt and chile powder optional.

Seven American fast-food chains have crept into Cabo: **KFC** and **Dairy Queen,** next to Plaza Las Glorias on Blvd. Marina; **Domino's Pizza** (complete with a fleet of delivery motorcycles), tel. (1) 143-0592; **Baskin-Robbins,** at Plaza Naútica; **Pizza Hut,** directly across from Giggling Marlin, tel. (1) 143-4600; **Burger King,** right next to Libros Libros behind the Hard Rock Café; and the most recent import (it was only a matter of time), **McDonald's,** on Lázaro Cárdenas just east of the post office.

Restaurant San Lucas (Broken Surfboard), on Calle Hidalgo opposite the east extension of Calle Zapata, has been a local institution for over 20 years. The casual, open-air spot serves reasonably priced Mexican and American breakfasts, Mexican sandwiches (try the marlin *torta*), seafood, and *licuados.* Surfers are invited to scribble something on the wave mural. Open daily 7 a.m.-9 p.m.

Ali's Burger, Calle Morelos at 16 de Septiembre, is an old standby for quick American breakfasts, omelettes, burgers, and fish tacos. French is spoken, and North African couscous is available by special order. Inexpensive; open daily 7 a.m.-11 p.m.

Felix's, almost across from Pancho's on Hidalgo, specializes in fresh fish tacos served with 19 handmade salsas. Note for the sanitation-oriented: here they keep their slaw and *crema* in the refrigerator. As Mexican fish taco places go it's not cheap—shrimp tacos cost US$1.60 each, fish tacos US$1.20 each—and the tacos are ordinary. The *licuados* are more like American smoothies, full of crushed ice. Only the tremendous salsas compel a return visit. Open daily 11 a.m.-10 p.m.

Las Quesadillasss, opposite Plaza Aramburo on the corner of Blvd. Marina and Lázaro Cárdenas, is a little two-story outdoor spot under a *palapa* roof near the marina serving dependable tacos, quesadillas, grilled lobster, and beer. Inexpensive and good. Open daily 8 a.m.-10 p.m.

El Pollo de Oro, on Morelos just north of Niños Héroes, is a longtime favorite for Sinaloa-style barbecued chicken, as well as grilled shrimp, lobster, and ribs. Good breakfasts. Inexpensive. Open daily 7 a.m.-11 p.m.

El Pollo Sinaloense, Calle Zaragoza at 20 de Noviembre, is similar to El Pollo de Oro. Open 11 a.m.-10 p.m.

Super Pollo, Morelos at Ortega, tel. (1) 143-0788, is part of the Sinaloa-style chicken chain found throughout Baja. Very reliable and inexpensive. Open daily 11 a.m.-10 p.m.

Tacos El Chilorio, Blvd. Lázaro Cárdenas at Ocampo, opposite La Perla, offers good, quick, inexpensive *tacos de carne asada* and no-frills atmosphere. Open Mon.-Sat. 10 a.m.-10 p.m.

There is a string of inexpensive Mexican restaurants along Calle Leona Vicario, north of Revolución, including **Taquería los Paisas** (tacos and stuffed potatoes), **El Encanto Jarocho** (open evenings, inexpensive seafood and ceviche), and, a bit farther north past Carranza, **Carnitas El Michoacano.** A good spot to cool off with a fresh fruit shake is **El Dengue,** a *licuado* and *aguas frescas* stand next to Panaficadora la Moderna on Calle Leona Vicario.

Wabo Grill, on Calle Guerrero between Madero and Lázaro Cárdenas, is part of Cabo Wabo, the Sammy Hagar–owned nightclub. The menu offers excellent taco platters, *tortas,* tortilla soup, burgers, and breakfasts, served inside or out on the patio. Moderately priced. Open daily 7 a.m.-11 p.m.

Groceries

Cabo's several supermarkets stock a variety of Mexican and U.S. foodstuffs—from fresh Mexican cheeses to Sara Lee frozen cheesecake—plus cooking and cleaning supplies, and even auto parts. Ranging from small to huge, they include **Almacenes Grupo Castro** (southwest corner of Calle Morelos and Revolución), **Supermercado Sánliz** (three locations: Blvd. Marina at Madero; Calle Ocampo at Matamoros; and Calle Leona Vicario at López Mateos), and **Supermercado Plaza** (at Plaza Aramburo, Calle Lázaro Cárdenas at Zaragoza). Supermercado Plaza stocks the largest selection of both domestic and imported foods.

Pescadería El Dorado, in a new location on the south side of 5 de Febrero, between Abasolo and Ocampo, stocks a large selection of fresh finfish and shellfish. The most convenient place to buy fresh tortillas is **Tortillería Perla,** on the west side of Calle Abasolo just south of Calle 16 de Septiembre, tel. (1) 143-0121.

Panaficadora la Moderna, on Calle Leona Vicario across from Maricos Mocambo, is a small bakery with a decent selection of Mexican baked goods.

La Baguette, on Blvd. Lázaro Cárdenas next to the entrance for Pedregal, carries European and American-style baked goods including pastries, bagels, and breads; it's open Mon.-Sat. 8:30 a.m.-7:30 p.m. **Swiss Pastry,** Hidalgo at Lázaro Cárdenas (across from the plaza), tel. (1) 143-3494, serves chicken pot pie, sandwiches, fresh bagels, and other pastries as well as coffee. It's open Mon.-Sat. 7 a.m.-4 p.m. and has a few tables in front as well as inside.

Frutería Lizarraga, Calle Matamoros at Av. de la Juventud, tel. (1) 143-1215, stocks a very good selection of fruits and vegetables; several local hotel and restaurant chefs shop here. **Frutas Selectas Santa Barbara,** on the south side of 20 de Noviembre a little bit west Morelos, is also good.

The best shopping area for beer and liquor is the string of *subagencias* and *licores* along Calle Matamoros.

ENTERTAINMENT AND EVENTS

Bars

Nightlife in Cabo starts in the bars downtown near the marina and after midnight moves to the discos, which stay open till 3 or 4 a.m. Tourists bent on getting well-primed for the evening pack **Río Grill** (Blvd. Marina at Zapata), **Magnolia** (farther east along Blvd. Marina), or **Giggling Marlin** (Calle Matamoros at Blvd. Marina).

The **Whale Watcher Bar** at the Hotel Finisterra has a more sedate but well-attended 3:30-5:30 p.m. happy hour that features two drinks for the price of one. The bar hosts an excellent mariachi group Thurs.-Sun. and offers great Pacific views every day of the week.

One of the oldest and funkiest bars in town is **Latitude 22+** ("Lat 22"), on Blvd. Lázaro Cárdenas between Morelos and Leona Vicario, opposite the boat ramp. This is a yachties' hangout with authentic marine decor assembled from salvaged boats. There's a pool table in back. Prices for drinks (very good Bloody Marys) and food are very reasonable; the bar is open Wed.-Mon. 7 a.m.-11 p.m. and offers a happy hour 4-6 p.m.

If wine is your beverage, head to **Sancho Panza,** in Plaza Las Glorias off Blvd. Marina, which offers the best wine list in southern Baja. Although there's no dress code, you'll fit into the artsy decor better if you wear something other than beachwear. This is the perfect place for a quiet drink, and the tapas menu is tops.

The lively bar at **Hacienda Beach Resort,** south end of Playa El Médano, doubles as a weekend social center for older resident gringos. **Edith's,** near Playa El Médano, on the west side of the Camino de los Pescadores, presents live and recorded jazz (mostly 1940s and '50s vintage) nightly 6 p.m.-1 a.m.; enjoy views of

Bahía Cabo San Lucas and Land's End as long as the sun's up.

Hard Rock Café, Blvd. Marina, Plaza Bonito, tel. (1) 143-3779, marked by a pink vintage Cadillac protruding from the front of the building at Plaza Bonita, is a lively place featuring sports-oriented TV rather than music videos, the entertainment staple of HRCs elsewhere. The Hard Rock hosts occasional live rock bands from La Paz and the mainland. Open 11 a.m.-2 a.m.

Cabo has recently become a minor Mexican capital for "exotic dancing"—the international English euphemism for women dancing barebreasted or nude on a stage. The audience consists mostly of young American males, although there are plenty of Mexican voyeurs as well. Major venues include **Lord Black,** tucked away behind Plaza Naútica and advertising "sushi and showgirls"; **Showgirls,** Zaragoza at Blvd. Lázaro Cárdenas, opposite Plaza Aramburo; and **Splash,** Guerrero at Lázaro Cárdenas. It's ironic that Mexican laws forbidding topless dancing in nightclubs are strictly enforced these days in

A beach band rocks the afternoon.

Tijuana and Juárez, yet the practice thrives in Cabo. In the local clubs' favor, it should be mentioned that they appear to be clean, well-run, and safe—possibly inspired by the growing crop of "gentlemen's clubs" in the United States.

Dance Clubs/Discos

Cabo's discos begin filling up around 11 p.m. but the crowd doesn't really break a sweat till around midnight or later. A perennial favorite is the two-story dance floor at **Squid Roe,** Blvd. Lázaro Cárdenas at Zaragoza, where bleacher-balconies offer a bird's-eye view of the swirling masses below. The Squid may stay open as late as 3 a.m., depending on the crowd.

Californians are partial to **Cabo Wabo** on Calle Guerrero between Madero and Lázaro Cárdenas, tel. (1) 143-1188, a dance club/restaurant owned by California rock 'n' roller Sammy Hagar; the music here alternates between a recorded mix (with video) and live bands. Cabo Wabo was built in 1989 and named for a Van Halen song describing the "wobble" exhibited by tourists walking around town after a night of club-hopping. Sammy and his band play at the club at least twice a year (on the club's April anniversary and again for the Red Rocker's birthday in October) and occasionally more often—Christmas or New Year's is often a good bet. The atmosphere is loose, though not beachy.

After 10 p.m., **Kokomo,** opposite the northwest corner of the marina on Blvd. Marina, transforms from a Giggling Marlin-style bar/restaurant into a beachy tourist disco à la Squid Roe. It's still relatively new; time will tell whether it becomes as steady as the Squid.

If you're more adventurous than the average Cabo visitor, dip into **Hey!** a newer, more sophisticated disco and salsa club on Blvd. Lázaro Cárdenas east of the Banamex. In keeping with Latin tastes, people dress a little more for this one.

Charreada

Despite the name, **La Sanluqueña Bullring,** a small wooden stadium at the northeast corner of Mexico 19 and Mexico 1, actually hosts horseback-riding shows rather than bullfights. One of the performances, here billed as "Ladies on Horseback Ballet"—is *escaramuza,* a female equestrian event from the traditional *charreada.* The facility also rents horses (see Other

Sports and Recreation, below). Call (1) 147-8675 for reservations and information.

Events

Cabo San Lucas hosts several sportfishing tournaments throughout the year. The largest is the **Bisbee's Black and Blue Marlin Jackpot Tournament,** held for three days each October. The purse for the contest has exceeded US$850,000, making it the world's richest marlin tournament. Proceeds go to local charities. For information call the tournament organization, tel. (1) 143-1622, or the Hotel Finisterra in Cabo San Lucas, tel. (1) 143-0100, fax (1) 143-0590, U.S. tel. (714) 476-5555 or (800) 347-2252.

Another notable yearly event falls around the Festival of San Lucas on 18 October; look for a week of music, dancing, and feasting in the Mexican tradition.

SHOPPING

The streets of Cabo are filled with souvenir shops, street vendors, clothing boutiques, and galleries—probably more shops of this type per capita than anywhere else in Baja.

Arts, Crafts, and Souvenirs

For inexpensive handicrafts—rugs, blankets, baskets, leatherwork—from all over Mexico, try the outdoor **Mercado Mexicano** on Calle Hidalgo at Obregón; for the best prices you'll have to bargain. Another place where bargaining is useful is the **Tianguis Marina,** an outdoor souvenir market on the southwest side of the inner harbor toward the old ferry pier. Typical items here include "Baja-style" hooded cotton pullovers, wood sculptures, straw hats, T-shirts, and costume jewelry.

Among the more interesting craft shops in town are **Gaby's Huaraches,** on Lázaro Cárdenas just east of Matamoros, offering all types and sizes of Mexican-made leather sandals as well as cloned sport sandals; **Faces of Mexico,** Calle Hidalgo off Blvd. Marina (next door to Pancho's Restaurant), selling Mexican masks and other ethnic art; **Taxco Silver,** on Calle Hidalgo opposite Capitán Lucas Restaurant, with the best selection of silver jewelry in town; and **Joyería Albert,** on Calle Matamoros between

local pottery

Niños Héroes and Lázaro Cárdenas, a branch of the reputable Puerto Vallarta jeweler.

The newer shopping centers are all along the marina side of Blvd. Marina. Modern **Plaza Bonita** faces the marina and holds shops offering tourist-oriented sportswear, jewelry, and souvenirs. Two of the more interesting shops are **Dos Lunas** (handpainted clothing) and **Cartes** (rustic colonial furniture, Talavera pottery, arts and crafts, and classy home-decor accessories).

The arrival of a **Sergio Bustamante** gallery in Plaza Bonita shows that Cabo San Lucas has attained a market rank similar to Cancún and Puerto Vallarta. People tend either to love or to hate Bustamante's whimsical but costly ceramic sculptures, with their angelic faces and otherworldly, Peter Max-like themes.

Books and Magazines

Libros Libros/Books Books, in Plaza Bonita, tel. (1) 143-3171, stocks an excellent selection of English-language paperbacks, magazines, maps, books on Baja, children's books, and U.S.

newspapers. A second, larger branch recently opened on Blvd. Marina, near Carlos'n Charlie's. Open daily 9 a.m.-9 p.m.

Home Decor
El Callejón, on Calle Guerrero between Blvd. Lázaro Cárdenas and Blvd. Marina, stocks a good collection of Talavera ceramics, religious art, pewter, wood and wrought-iron furniture.
    Decor America Interiors, Mendoza and Obregón, tel./fax (1) 143-0575, is a full-service interior design shop, offering a wide selection of furniture, custom upholstery, and accessories.
    Northeast of town, at Km 4 on Mexico 1, **Artesanos** is a large shop selling handpainted Mexican tiles, colorful ceramic sinks, terra-cotta wall sconces, and many other ceramic and iron decorating accessories, all at low prices (for Cabo). Next door, **Marmol y Granito** stocks marble and granite materials for floors, kitchens, and bars.

Leather, Coffee, and Cigars
Plaza Marina, attached to the Hotel Plaza Las Glorias on the marina, contains a string of small shops; good buys in leather are available at **Navarro's,** tel. (1) 143-4101.
    In a kiosk on Blvd. Lázaro Cárdenas, a short distance east of Hotel Mar de Cortez, **Café Organico de Chiapas** sells ground or whole-bean organic coffee for US$10.60 per kilo. Freshly brewed coffee is available by the cup.
    Cuban cigars have really taken off in Cabo. One of the nicest Cuban cigar stores is **J & J Habanos** on Blvd. Marina near Madero. **Pazzo's Cigars,** at Morelos and Niños Héroes (next to Pazzo's Cabo), tel. (1) 143-4313, has a walk-in humidor and sells Cuban cigars, tequilas and liquors. You'll also find Cuban *puros* in several shops along Blvd. Marina. Be sure you know your *habanos,* as fakes aren't unknown.

Sporting Goods
Another shopping center near the marina, **Plaza Naútica,** contains the useful **Cabo Sports Center,** which sells beach supplies (coolers, umbrellas, etc.), sports sandals, and varied equipment for golf, swimming, surfing, snorkeling, boogie-boarding, and mountain-biking.

FISHING

Other than swimming and lying on the beach, sportfishing is Cabo's number-one outdoor activity. An average of 50,000 billfish a year—marlin, sailfish, and swordfish—are hooked off the cape, more than anywhere else in the world. The biggest trophy of all, the *marlín azul* (blue marlin), can reach five meters (16 feet) in length and weigh close to a ton. In the Cape area, it's not unusual to hook 200- to 400-kg (440- to 880-pound) blues. A smaller species, the *marlín rayado* (striped marlin), grows to over 270 kg (600 pounds), while the *marlín negro* (black marlin) is almost as big as the blue.
    To catch a glimpse of these huge gamefish, stop by the sportfishing dock on the marina's west side around 3-4 p.m., when sportfishing boats return with their catches. Note the flags flown over the boats; a triangular blue flag means a billfish has been bagged while a red flag with a T means one has been tagged and released. All Cabo sportfishing outfits request that anglers release billfish to fight another day; some even require it. Instead of skinning and mounting these beautiful fish, they recommend bringing a video camera along to record the catch from start to finish. Even where customers demand to keep a billfish, the Sportfishing Association of Los Cabos stipulates that only one billfish per boat may be killed (you can catch and release as many as you like).
    Good marlin-fishing spots include **Banco San Jaime,** 29 km (18 miles) southwest of Cabo Falso, and **Banco Golden Gate,** 31 km (19 miles) west of Cabo Falso. Dorado and wahoo are also

---

TIME-SHARE AND "ACTIVITIES" VENDORS

Because Blvd. Marina is such a popular shopping and strolling area, several time-share vendors (the kind that provoke local T-shirts reading "What part of 'No' don't you understand?") have set up booths along the street. So far every booth sits on the north side of Blvd. Marina; walk along the south side of this road (the side with the shopping malls) to avoid the worst of the come-ons.

common in those areas. Sportfishing cruisers—powerboats equipped with electronic fish-finders, sophisticated tackle, fighting chairs and harnesses, and wells for keeping live bait—are the angler's best chance for landing large gamefish.

Almost unbelievably, marlin are also somewhat common just beyond the steep dropoffs between Los Frailes and Cabo Falso, an area easily reached by *panga* or skiff. Without the technology of a fishing cruiser, *panga* marlin-fishing becomes the most macho hook-and-line challenge of all—the resulting fish stories reach *Old Man and the Sea* proportions. For anglers with more humble ambitions, black seabass, cabrilla, sierra, and grouper are found in inshore waters; surfcasters can take corvina, ladyfish, sierra, and pargo.

Guided Sportfishing

Guided cruiser trips are easy to arrange through any major Cabo hotel. Solmar, Finisterra, and Meliá Cabo Real each have their own fleets.

yellowfin tuna, Cabo San Lucas

Solmar Fleet, next to the harbor near the old cannery on Blvd. Marina, tel. (1) 143-0646, fax (1) 143-0410, U.S. tel. (310) 459-9861 or (800) 344-3340, U.S. fax (310) 454-1686 (U.S. mailing address: P.O. Box 383, Pacific Palisades, CA 90272), operates custom-built 23- to 26-foot in-board-diesel-powered *pangas.* Boats depart at 7 a.m. and return about 2:30 p.m. Fishing trips aboard the smallest *panga* start at US$30 pp, while a 26-footer costs US$260 for three people, a 29-footer US$350 for four people, and a 42-foot sportfishing cruiser US$650 for eight people. Solmar Fleet also offers more expensive long-range fishing cruises aboard the luxurious 110-foot *Solmar V.* Rates include the services of a skipper, deckhands, and fishing guide, plus fishing tackle, licenses, and permits; they do not include bait, food, beverages, tips paid directly to the skipper, or the 10% tax.

Several outfitters unaffiliated with local hotels also arrange sportfishing trips. Rates average US$250 a day (or around US$150 per half-day) on a four-angler, 26-foot custom *panga,* US$450-500 a day for a six-person, 36-foot fishing cruiser, US$330-350 on a 28-foot cruiser, or US$180 per couple on a 31-foot party boat. Charter boats generally hold up to six anglers; rates usually include tax, license, gear, and ice. **Pisces Fleet,** Blvd. Marina at Madero (opposite Supermercado Sán-liz), tel. (1) 143-1288, fax (1) 143-0588, is one of the more reliable independent outfitters; others can be found along the west side of the harbor.

Whomever you go with, be sure to get a breakdown of exactly what to expect on any guided trip. One reader wrote to us and complained he paid for eight hours of marlin fishing but got two hours of marlin fishing, three hours of bottom fishing, one hour waiting to buy bait, and two hours of idle boating. If you know that you're expected to provide your own bait, shop ahead. And expect that the farther out you go, the more time you'll spend in transit to and from your intended fishing destination.

Panga Trips

The least expensive fishing trips of all are those arranged directly with local *pangeros,* the men who own and operate single fishing *pangas.* Such *pangas* are sometimes available in Cabo San Lucas, but most *panga*-fishing trips operate out of La Playita near San José del Cabo. The typical *panga* trip costs US$125-130 in a three-person, 22-foot boat. Off Playa El Médano you can sometimes find *pangeros* willing to go out for just US$65 a day. *Panga* rates usually don't include rental gear or fishing licenses. When inquiring about rates—panga or cruiser—ask whether the quote includes filleting of edible gamefish. The better outfits include fish preparation and packing among their services at no extra charge.

Surfcasting

Cheaper yet is to forgo boating altogether and drop a line from the beach. The best surfcasting in the immediate area is at **Playa Solmar,** but watch the surf closely, as very large waves sometimes seem to arrive out of nowhere. You can also fish from the old pier extending from the abandoned tuna cannery at the entrance to the harbor, where the water is relatively calm. On **Playa El Médano,** you can fish only at the far northeastern end of the beach.

Bait, Tackle, and Fish Processing

Minerva's Baja Tackle, Blvd. Marina at Madero, next door to Pisces Fleet, tel. (1) 143-1282, is well stocked with lures and other tackle designed specifically for Cabo sportfishing. Minerva's is also the area's official IGFA representative.

Fresh bait can be purchased at the San Lucas harbor docks for about US$2 cash. Locals here will also clean and fillet your catch on the spot for tips. You can arrange to have fish cleaned, processed, vacuum-packed, and frozen through **Rocky's Smoke House,** Plaza Las Glorias, tel. (1) 143-2566.

DIVING AND SNORKELING

Cabo is a unique diving destination because it's in the middle of a transition zone between tropical and temperate waters. Strikingly large fish like amberjack, hammerheads, and manta rays—which are partial to temperate waters—mix with the smaller, more colorful species typical of tropical waters.

It's also unique in that several snorkeling and scuba sites are only a 15- to 25-minute boat ride from the marina. Snorkelers find the base of the cliffs on each side of **Playa del Amor,** about three meters (10 feet) deep, worth exploring for coral and tropical fish. Nearby **Roca Pelicanos,** some six meters (20 feet) deep, is a bit more challenging. Strong divers, on calm days, can swim south around the arch to the seal colony at Los Frailes and frolic with the creatures.

Divers with experience below 30 meters (100 feet) can visit a vast **submarine canyon** that begins just 50 meters (164 feet) off Playa del Amor. Part of a national marine preserve, the canyon is famous for its "sandfalls,"—streams of sand tumbling over the canyon rim at a depth of around 30 meters and forming sand rivers between rock outcroppings. At a depth of around 40 meters (130 feet), the outcroppings give way to sheer granite walls, where the sand rivers drop vertically for over two kilometers (to a depth of around 2,750 meters/9,000 feet). The size of the sandfalls and sand rivers depends to a large extent on climatic conditions; during long spells of very calm weather they may even come to a halt.

The phenomenon was first documented by a Scripps Institute of Oceanography expedition in 1960 and later made famous in one of Jacques Cousteau's television documentaries. The edges of the canyon walls are also layered with colorful coral, sea fans, and other marinelife. These in turn attract schools of tropical fish, including many open-ocean species not ordinarily seen this close to shore.

Several spots along the Corridor between San Lucas and San José feature good diving and snorkeling, including **Playa Chileno** and **Playa Santa María** (for details, see The Corridor section, above).

Dives further afield to **Cabo Pulmo** (for details, see East Cape, above) and the **Gorda Banks** (sometimes incorrectly called "Gordo Banks") can also be arranged from Cabo San Lucas. The Gorda seamounts, at a depth of around 41 meters (135 feet), are famous for sightings of whale sharks (the world's largest fish), huge tuna, amberjacks, groupers, and manta rays.

Vigilantes Marinos, Apdo. Postal 13, Cabo San Lucas, BCS 23410, a local divers group, has taken up the cause of protecting Cabo's marine environment from illegal fishing, head dumping, and other ecologically harmful practices. In addition to supporting the enforcement of existing laws, the group's Mexican, English, and American members educate local diving guides in safe dive tactics and undertake periodic beach- and bottom-cleaning sessions.

Dive/Snorkel Guides and Outfitters

As with sportfishing, many Cabo hotels can arrange guided dive trips and equipment rentals. Independent outfitters include: **Amigos del Mar,** next to Solmar Fleet on the west side of the harbor, tel. (1) 143-0505, fax (1) 143-0887, U.S./ Canada tel. (800) 344-3349; **Cabo Acuadeportes,** Playa El Médano or Playa Chileno, tel./fax (1) 143-0117, VHF channel 82; **Cabo Diving Services,** Blvd. Marina at Hidalgo, tel. (1) 143-1109, fax (1) 143-1110, VHF radio 10; **Tío Watersports,** at the Meliá San Lucas, Meliá Cabo Real, and Marina Fiesta hotels; **Underwater Diversions,** Plaza Marina, attached to Plaza Las Glorias facing the marina, tel. (1) 143-4004, VHF radio 65; **Baja Watersports,** tel. (1) 143-2050; **Pacific Coast Adventures,** tel. (1) 143-1070; **Los Lobos del Mar,** tel. (1) 142-3999; and **Pisces Watersport Center,** tel. (1) 148-7530.

Typical rates run US$25-45 pp for snorkeling tours (the more expensive tours go to Playa Santa María), US$35-45 pp for a guided local, one-tank scuba dive, US$55-70 for a two-tank dive (to Shipwreck Beach or the sandfalls), US$110 for a Gorda Banks or Cabo Pulmo dive (including two tanks), US$350-400 for full PADI certification. Each of the foregoing outfitters also offers dive equipment sales and rental. During the summer months, some dive ops offer certification courses for just US$200; since summer is the best time to dive in Baja with regard to underwater visibility, this is a real bargain.

Solmar Fleet, c/o Cabo Resort Reservations, Inc., Blvd. Marina (P.O. Box 383, Pacific Palisades, CA 90272), tel. (1) 143-0646, fax (1) 143-0410, U.S./Canada tel. (310) 459-9861 or (800) 344-3349, U.S./Canada fax (310) 454-1686, offers luxury dive trips to the Gorda Banks, Los Frailes, El Bajo, Cabo Pulmo, and other more remote sites aboard the 110-foot Solmar V. The wood-and-brass-fitted boat features two onboard air compressors and a dive platform for easy exits. Prices run around US$1,000 for four-day trips and around US$1,500-2,400 for six- and seven-day trips, including all land transfers, food and beverages (including wine and beer), accommodations in a/c staterooms (each with TV and VCR), and up to three guided dives per day.

The **Pez Gato,** tel. (1) 143-3797, a large catamaran moored at Playa El Médano, offers a four-hour snorkeling tour to scenic Bahía Santa María along the Corridor, where divers will find rocky reefs, sea caves, coral outcroppings, and abundant tropical marinelife. The tour costs US$35 per adult (kids half price) and includes two hours of swimming and snorkeling at Santa María, plus ceviche, tuna salad, guacamole, salsa and chips, open bar, bottled water, sodas, and cold beer on the way back. The boat departs Sat.-Thurs. at 10 a.m. and returns around 2 p.m.; departure and return times are an hour later on Friday. Another cat, the **Sunrider,** tel. (1) 143-2252, leaves from the pier near Plaza Las Glorias and does a Santa María snorkel-and-lunch for only US$38 (children US$19), Tues.-Sun. 5:30-8 p.m. In this case the lunch consists of an open bar and full Mexican buffet.

Equipment

Divers seeking equipment rentals only can expect the following daily rates from outfitters in Cabo: wetsuit US$4-6; mask and snorkel US$5; fins US$3-5; wetsuit, fins, and mask US$10; weight belt and weights US$3-5; regulator US$8; tanks US$6 each; BCD US$4-6; underwater camera and film US$12; airfills US$3-4.

Cabo Sports Center in Plaza Naútica carries a limited selection of snorkeling gear. Some dive ops also dabble in sales.

Recompression

Servicios de Seguridad Subacuatica (Underwater Safety Services), tel. (1) 143-3666, maintains a hyperbaric recompression chamber at Plaza Las Glorias. **Cabo Diving Services,** Blvd. Marina at Hidalgo, tel. (1) 143-1109, fax (1) 143-1110, VHF radio 10, plans to establish its own chamber in the near future.

OTHER SPORTS AND RECREATION

ATV Trail Rides

The sandy beaches and dunes in the Cabo San Lucas area are open to ATVs (all-terrain vehicles) as long as they're kept away from swimming areas (Playa El Médano) or turtle-nesting areas (Cabo Falso). Any of the hotels in town can arrange ATV tours for US$40-45 pp per half-day (four hours), US$80 pp all day (six hours). The basic route visits sand dunes, the ruins of El Faro Viejo, and a 1912 shipwreck; the six-hour tour adds La Candelaria, an inland village known for its pottery and *curanderos* (traditional healers). On all-day trips rates include a box lunch and refreshments. Vendors along Blvd. Marina also book these trips.

Cabo's Moto Rent, on Blvd. Lázaro Cárdenas next to Latitude 22+, tel. (1) 143-0808, will allow two riders per ATV at a discounted rate. A single rider to El Faro Viejo, for example, pays US$45, while two riders on the same machine pay US$60. For the Candelaria tour one rider pays US$80, two US$100.

Boat Cruises

Dos Mares, tel. (1) 143-3266, VHF radio 05, operates a fleet of glass-bottom tour boats that depart frequently from the marina and from Playa El Médano between 8 a.m. and 3 p.m. each day. The standard 45-minute tour costs US$7 pp and covers Roca Pelicanos (Pelican Rock), the famous Land's End arch, and the sea lion colony. For no extra charge, the crew will let passengers off at Playa del Amor near the arch; you can flag down any passing Dos Mares boat and catch a ride back to the marina later in the day. Simpler launches without glass bottoms will do the same trip, including beach dropoff and pickup, for US$5.

Sunset Cruises: Bay trips with all the beer and margaritas you can drink are also popular and usually last around two hours and 15 minutes. You can make reservations at the marina or at most hotels; tickets cost US$20-40 pp depending on whether dinner is included.

The 42-foot Hawaiian-style catamaran **Pez Gato,** tel. (1) 143-3797, VHF channel 18, offers a US$30 pp sunset all-the-margaritas-you-can-drink cruise that leaves from the Hacienda Beach Resort dock at 6 p.m. and returns at 8 p.m. (the cruise can be booked through any hotel). **Kaleidoscope Sunset Cruise** does an adults-only catamaran cruise that leaves from the marina at 4 p.m. and returns at 6 p.m.; US$37 pp. A couple of similar boats operate sunset cruises from the west side of the harbor near Plaza Las Glorias. During high season these companies may offer sunset cruises on two separate boats simultaneously—a "romantic" cruise oriented toward couples, and a "booze cruise" for young singles.

Boating

With an average of 1,200 yacht arrivals per year, Cabo San Lucas is a major Baja California boating center. Even though harbor size and marine-repair facilities don't match those of La Paz, the greater variety of other services, nightlife, shopping, and dining venues more than compensates.

The outer harbor anchorages are mostly occupied by sportfishing cruisers; recreational boaters can moor off Playa El Médano to the northeast. Ringing the inner harbor, first dredged in the early 1970s, is **Marina Cabo San Lucas,** tel. (1) 143-1251, fax (1) 143-1253, U.S. tel. (310)

El Arco,
Cabo San Lucas

541-3830, e-mail: cabomarina@cabonet.net.mx, VHF 88A. Facilities include hot showers, restrooms, a pool, snack bar, laundry, dry storage and personal storage facilities, a chandlery, fuel (both diesel and gas), water, and 390 slips complete with electricity, telephone hookups, and satellite TV. Also available are a 70-ton lift and full-service boatyard. The marina can accommodate boats up to 180 feet. Permanent and monthly renters at Marina Cabo San Lucas have priority over short-term visiting boaters; daily rentals are available on a first-come, first-served basis. Guest boaters pay US$1.15-2.60 per foot per day, plus tax, minimum US$28.75 per day. Rates for permanent boaters start at US$266 per month for 20-foot boats; the slip-rate for a 43-foot boat would be US$792 per month, US$2,562 for a 120-foot boat. Visiting boaters should call the marina 15 days before arrival to check on the availability of slips. The Marina Cabo San Lucas office is open Mon.-Sat. 9 a.m.-5 p.m., Sunday 10 a.m.-3 p.m. The marina's condos are occasionally available as rentals, and the adjacent Marina Fiesta Resort & Hotel usually has vacant rooms.

Also in the inner harbor are two boat ramps, one near the old ferry pier and one at the northeast end of the harbor near Plaza Las Glorias. A fuel dock is between the old ferry pier and the abandoned cannery, just inside the entrance to the inner harbor. Cabo San Lucas is an official Mexican port of entry; the **COTP** office is on Calle Matamoros at 16 de Septiembre.

AMCSA Accesorios Marinos stocks basic marine supplies. It's next to Amigos del Mar and Solmar Fishing Fleet, on the west side of the harbor just past the turnoff for Solmar Suites.

Golf

Lining the highway between Cabo San Lucas and San José del Cabo are three world-class golf resorts: **Cabo del Sol,** tel. (1) 145-8200 or (800) 386-2465 in the U.S.; **Palmilla Golf Club,** tel. (1) 144-5250 or (800) 386-2465 in the U.S.; and **Cabo Real,** tel. (1) 144-0040 or (800) 393-0400 in the U.S. A second Jack Nicklaus-designed 18-hole course—the **El Dorado,** tel. (1) 144-5440—has recently opened at Cabo Real. For details on these courses, see The Corridor, above.

About one km north of the Cabo city limits, the 300-hectare (746-acre) **Cabo San Lucas Country Club,** tel. (1) 143-4653 or (800) 280-6998 in the U.S., offers a Roy Dye-designed course with views of Land's End and Bahía San Lucas from each fairway, and five tee-offs for each hole (back, championship, member, forward, and front). At 600 yards (par five), the seventh hole is said to be the longest in Mexico. The front nine is 3,651 yards (par 36), the back nine is 3,569 yards (par 36). Green fees are US$176 for 18 holes for non-members, including cart. In summer, fees are discounted to US$80 per 18, US$44 after 4 p.m. Clubs may be rented for US$35. Construction on a second Roy Dye-designed course is scheduled to begin soon. To avoid drawing excessively from the Cape's precious aquifer, gray water from the resort spends a month cycling through a series of duckweed ponds until the fast-growing plant renders the water safe for irrigation. Along with fairway homes, the resort features tennis, swimming, and fitness clubs.

Gyms

Most of the larger hotels contain fitness centers with free weights, weight machines, and exercise equipment. **Papito's Gym,** on the third floor of Plaza Bonita (above Salsita's), Blvd. Marina, offers exercise bikes, stair-step machines, and other equipment; some of the machines are on an outdoor terrace overlooking the marina. **Club Fit,** upstairs in Plaza Náutica (also on Blvd. Marina near the marina), adds pool aerobics to the usual gym array. More oriented toward weight-training alone is **Powerhouse Gym,** at the northwest corner of Cárdenas and Guerrero.

Horseback Riding

Red Rose (La Rosa) Riding Stables, at Km 4 on Mexico 1 (across from Cabo San Lucas Country Club), tel. (1) 143-4826, appears to be the area's most serious saddle outfit. A choice of Western or English tack is offered. A one-hour ride along Playa El Médano costs US$25; a two-hour mountain ride is US$40. Custom horseback trips and riding lessons are available.

Reyes Collins, behind the Hotel Meliá San Lucas, tel. (1) 143-3652, offers horseback riding either by the hour or on scheduled trail rides. The hourly rate is a relatively high US$20; better value is the three-and-a-half-hour trail ride to dune-encircled El Faro Viejo (The Old Lighthouse), built in 1890 for US$45. Take this ride in the morning or at sunset for maximum scenic effect. A 90-minute beach ride is also available for US$35.

La Sanluqueña Bullring, at the junction of Mexico 1 and Mexico 19, tel. (1) 147-8675, offers well-fed, well-trained horses for private trail rides or for rides along Playa Médano. Horses available for beginners as well as experts. A 75-minute ride runs US$30.

Paddling, Sailing, and Windsurfing
The onshore surf at Playa El Médano is mild enough for launching wind-and paddle-powered craft easily. You can rent kayaks, canoes, Hobie Cats, sailboards, and Sunfish sailboats from **Cabo Acuadeportes** at the Hacienda Beach Resort, tel./fax (1) 143-0117, VHF radio 82.

In stormy conditions it's not a good idea to try paddling or sailing across the harbor entrance. Be sure to inform the vendors where you plan to take the craft; they'll know the conditions and advise accordingly. Watch out for power-boats, yachts, and cruise ships; larger craft have the de facto right of way. Novices should stick close to Playa El Médano no matter what the conditions.

Race and Sports Book
Caliente Race and Sports Book, in Plaza Naútica near the marina, features a full-service bar and restaurant, a bank of closed-circuit television screens tuned to various sporting events, and the opportunity to place bets based on Las Vegas odds on thoroughbred and greyhound races, as well as on American football, basketball, baseball, and other games. In the afternoons and evenings Caliente also screens American films on video. You don't have to gamble to watch the TVs or use the facilities as long as you patronize the bar/restaurant. Hours are Mon.-Fri. 9 a.m.-midnight, Sat.-Sun. 8 a.m.-midnight.

Surfing
The nearest surfable waves occur well outside the city limits at **Playa Cabo Bello,** between Km 6 and 5, near the Hotel Cabo San Lucas. See The Corridor for details on this and other surf breaks northeast of town. Most good surf occurs here only during summer/early fall (Cabo Bello, recipient of a winter northwestern swell, is

the one exception). If you need equipment or ding repair in Cabo San Lucas, try **Cadillac Surf and Skate,** on Zaragoza near 16 de Septiembre.

Whalewatching
Whales pass within a few hundred meters of Cabo San Lucas throughout the year, but the most activity occurs during gray whale migration season, Jan.-March. The Dos Mares tour-boat fleet operates whalewatching trips from the marina during the migration season for US$30 pp. With binoculars you can also see passing whales from the Hotel Finisterra's Whale Watcher's Bar.

INFORMATION AND SERVICES

Tourist Information
Cabo San Lucas has no government tourism offices or information booths, although Fonatur maintains an office on the marina. Its representatives are always interested in speaking with potential investors, but they don't distribute general tourist information. Information on Los Cabos—maps and hotel lists—can be obtained from the state tourism office in La Paz, between Km 5 and 6 on Mexico 1, tel. (1) 142-1199, fax (1) 142-7722.

Magazines and Newspapers
The annual magazine **Los Cabos Guide** contains a number of features, ads, annotated lists, and announcements concerning hotels, restaurants, clubs, and recreational events as well as local social and business news. It's offered for sale at some local newsstands, but free copies can be collected at real estate offices. The local Spanish-language newspaper is **El Heraldo de Los Cabos. Gringo Gazette,** a tourist newspaper written and edited locally but printed in the U.S., carries whimsical local news stories and events listings. Another tourist rag, **Cabo Life,** contains less news and more ads.

USA Today and **The News** (from Mexico City) are usually available at **Supermercado Sánliz,** Blvd. Marina at Madero, as well as at other larger grocery stores catering to gringos. **Libros Libros/Books Books** in Plaza Bonita and on Blvd. Marina carries The News, USA Today, and the **Los Angeles Times.**

Post, Telephone, and Internet

Cabo's post office, on Blvd. Lázaro Cárdenas, is open Mon.-Fri. 8-11 a.m. and 3-6 p.m. Public telephone booths are found at various locations throughout town, including the main plaza and Plaza Aramburo.

Mail Boxes Etc., Blvd. Marina 39-F in the Plaza Fiesta shopping center (next to the marina and Marina Fiesta Resort), tel. (1) 143-3033, fax (1) 143-3031, carries mailing supplies, postage stamps, and magazines and rents mailboxes.

Dr. Z's Internet Café and Bar (NetZone), behind BajaTech on Blvd. Lázaro Cárdenas (across from the Pemex), tel. (1) 143-5390, fax (1) 143-3944, sells computer time for e-mail and web-surfing. AOL and CompuServe access is available. Fifteen minutes of terminal use runs US$4.23 (US$5.30 if you use your own laptop), 30 minutes about US$6.40 (US$8 for laptops), and an hour will cost US$8 (US$10.65 for laptops). Prepaid membership cards bring the cost down to as low as US$4.25 per hour (not available for use with laptops). The small, a/c facility features a full bar (advertising "fabulous martinis") and light food menu. The only drawback is the lack of ventilation, a problem that can become acute when smokers are in the room. Free parking.

You can also check your e-mail at **Caffé On Line,** Ave. Cabo San Lucas, tel. (1) 143-7283, one block from the main drag. Open Mon.-Sat. 9 a.m.-8 p.m. Closed Sunday. There's also **Internet Café Cabomail** in the Aramburo Super Plaza.

Immigration

Cabo's *migración* office is on Blvd. Lázaro Cárdenas between Gómez Farías and 16 de Septiembre.

USEFUL CABO SAN LUCAS TELEPHONE NUMBERS

Cabo San Lucas area code: 1
Police: 143-3977
Red Cross: 143-3300
Fire: 143-3577
IMSS Hospital: 143-1594
COTP: 143-0814
Immigration: 143-4001
U.S. Consulate: 143-3566

Changing Money

American dollars are readily accepted throughout Cabo, although in smaller shops and restaurants you'll save money if you pay in pesos. Foreign-currency exchange service is available 8:30 a.m.-noon at: Bancomer, Hidalgo at Guerrero; Banamex, Hidalgo at Lázaro Cárdenas; and Serfín, in Plaza Aramburo. All three banks now offer ATMs; the machine at Serfín appears to be more reliable than the other two. Hotel cashiers will also gladly change dollars for pesos, albeit at a lower rate than at the banks.

There's now a full-service American Express office (tel. 1-143-2787) in town near the marina on the east side of Plaza Fiesta. It offers emergency check-cashing, cardmember services, foreign exchange, and tours. Open Mon.-Fri. 9 a.m.-6 p.m., Saturday 9 a.m.-1 p.m.

Except in emergencies, stay away from Cabo's moneychangers, which charge high commissions or sell currency at low exchange rates. **Baja Money Exchange** (at Plaza Naútica and several other locations around town), for example, lists an exchange rate that's lower per U.S. dollar than the going bank rate, on top of which it charges five percent commission on personal checks and five percent plus bank fees for wire transfer or cash advances. Although this is expensive, many visiting foreigners—too timid to try a Mexican bank—line up for such services.

U.S. Consular Agent

A U.S. consular agent in Cabo, under the auspices of the U.S. consul general in Tijuana, maintains a small office on Blvd. Marina. The office, tel. (1) 143-3536, is open Mon.-Fri. 10 a.m.-1 p.m. The consular agent can assist U.S. citizens with lost or stolen passports and other emergency situations.

Laundry

Lavamática Cristy, tel. (1) 143-2959, and **Lavandería Evelyn,** both opposite El Faro Viejo Trailer Park on Calle Matamoros, offer banks of washing machines for self-service laundry; ask the attendants to start the machines for you. Or you can pay (by weight) to have the washing, drying, and ironing done by the staff—one-day service is the norm. Cristy is open Mon.-Sat. 7 a.m.-10 p.m., Sunday 7 a.m.-2 p.m., while Evelyn is open daily 7 a.m.-7 p.m. Several other *la-*

vanderías are scattered around town, including **Nela's Laundry** on the corner of Alikan and Zaragoza.

Tintorería Supernova, in the Plaza Aramburo shopping center off Blvd. Marina, does dry cleaning.

Travel Agencies
Cabo's major hotels—Solmar, Finisterra, Hacienda, Plaza Las Glorias—have their own travel agencies for making air reservations and flight changes or arranging local tours. In town, the most reliable and longest-running independent is **Los Delfines,** on Calle Morelos at Niños Heroes, tel. (1) 143-1396 or 143-1397; it's open Mon.-Fri. 8:30 a.m.-6 p.m., Saturday 8:30 a.m.-3 p.m.

GETTING THERE

Air
See the San José del Cabo Transportation section for details on domestic and international service to **Los Cabos International Airport.** The airport is 12.8 km (eight miles) north of San José del Cabo. **Mexicana** has a Cabo San Lucas office at Calles Niños Héroes and Zaragoza, tel. (1) 143-0411 or (800) 3-6654; **Aero California** is in Plaza Naútica, Blvd. Marina, tel. (1) 143-3700 or (800) 6-8555.

Private pilots will find a 1,550-meter (5,100-foot) paved airstrip just north of town; fuel is not available.

Sea
The SCT Cabo San Lucas-Puerto Vallarta ferry service was discontinued in 1989; SEMATUR, the private corporation that took control of the formerly government-owned ferry line, has no plans to reinstate service. The nearest ferry service to the mainland operates between La Paz and Mazatlán (see the La Paz section).

Marina Cabo San Lucas is the main docking facility for transient recreational boats; bow-stern anchorages are also permitted in the outer bay. See Boating for details on services and rates.

Land
Buses to/from La Paz: Autotransportes Águila operates 14 buses a day (6 a.m.-7 p.m.) to La Paz from Cabo's main intercity bus depot at Calle 16 de Septiembre at Zaragoza. Fare is US$9. Eight of the departures go via Todos Santos, which is the quickest route (about three and a half hours total), while the other six go via San José del Cabo (four to four and a half hours) for the same fare.

Buses to/from San José: Águila runs around five buses a day (7:15 a.m.-6:15 p.m.) to San José del Cabo; the trip takes 30-45 minutes and costs US$2 pp. Aside from the main depot, you can also catch buses to San José from a bus shelter on the south side of Blvd. Lázaro Cárdenas across from the Calle Leona Vicario intersection.

Buses to/from Todos Santos: Eight buses a day run to Todos Santos (about two hours from Cabo San Lucas) for US$3.25 pp. For northbound

*water taxi at
Playa del Amor*

passengers to Todos Santos and La Paz, Águila maintains a small bus office on the north side of town right where the highway to Todos Santos meets the city bypass, just south of a Pemex station. Or you can board the bus at the main depot.

Farther North: Águila operates one bus per day to Loreto (10:30 a.m., US$23) and Tijuana (4:30 p.m., US$78).

Driving: If you've driven down from the U.S. border, congratulations—you've reached "Land's End." If you've arrived via the La Paz ferry terminal and plan to drive north to the U.S., count on three eight-hour days (Mulegé first night, Cataviña second night) or 2.5 dawn-to-dusk days (Santa Rosalía first night, San Quintín second night). If you stretch your itinerary to include a week's driving time, you'll have a safer trip and more of an opportunity to enjoy the sights along the way.

GETTING AROUND

Airport Transport
Taxis from Los Cabos International Airport cost US$65 per vehicle for up to four persons. In the reverse direction, from San Lucas to the airport, you can usually get a taxi for US$30 for up to four persons. The less expensive airport shuttle bus from Plaza Las Glorias, tel. (1) 143-1220, is US$10 pp and departs from the hotel at 9 a.m., 11 a.m., noon, 1 p.m., and 3 p.m.

Taxi and Pedicab
In Cabo itself, you can easily get around on foot, bicycle, or scooter, though car taxis are available for US$2-4 a trip.

Checker Cabo is a fleet of mountain bikes welded to two-wheeled carts to produce Asian-style pedicabs. A pedicab trip anywhere in Cabo costs US$1 pp, maximum of two passengers per vehicle.

Water Taxi: You can hire harbor skiffs from the marina in front of Plaza Las Glorias to Playa El Médano (US$2.50 pp one-way) and Playa del Amor (US$5 roundtrip only). In the reverse direction, skiffs are plentiful at El Médano, but for Playa del Amor, advance arrangements for a pickup are necessary.

Vehicle Rental
You can rent VW sedans, VW combis (vans), and Chevy Cavaliers at Los Cabos International Airport (see Transportation in the San José del Cabo section, above). In Cabo, they can also be rented—albeit more expensively than at the airport—at **Dollar,** Blvd. Lázaro Cárdenas at Mendoza, tel. (1) 143-1250 or 143-1260, airport (1) 142-0671; **Avis,** downtown on Lázaro Cárdenas, tel. (1) 143-4607; and **Thrifty,** Westin Regina Hotel, tel. (1) 142-9000, Cabo San Lucas Hotel, tel. (1) 143-1666, and Hotel Finisterra, tel. (1) 143-3333. Rates vary from around US$20 a day plus 20 cents per kilometer for a no-frills Chevy Pop to US$45/day plus 26 cents/km for a VW Jetta. You can arrange kilometer-free rentals for these vehicles for higher day rates of around US$45 and US$78 per day, respectively. It's usually cheaper to rent at Los Cabos International Airport rather than in Cabo San Lucas, but it's always worth shopping around and, if necessary, bargaining.

Vendors along Blvd. Marina rent mopeds, ATVs, and motorcycles for US$5 an hour or US$20 per day.

Tours
Several local travel agencies and hotels offer land tours of the area, typically US$45 for the city and El Faro Viejo, US$80 for La Candelaria and Todos Santos.

For information on bay tours, see Other Sports and Recreation, above.

WEST CAPE

Although a paved, two-lane highway (Mexico 19) extends the full 76 km (47 miles) between Cabo San Lucas and Todos Santos (and beyond all the way to La Paz), this is still the least developed coastal stretch on the lower Cape. Some say it's only a matter of time before this area is dotted with resorts; housing developments are already slowly appearing along the southern end of the highway outside Cabo San Lucas. Local resistance to development—especially in the Todos Santos area—is growing, so perhaps the area farther north will remain preserved and relatively pristine.

Mexico 19 heads west out of Cabo San Lucas toward Cabo Falso before making a long lazy arc to the north. An alternate route heads due north out of San Lucas, following unpaved ranch roads to the picturesque foothills village of La Candelaria. From there, those with 4WD can follow a sandy arroyo road west, rejoining Mexico 19 near Playa Migriño. Those without 4WD will find a visit to La Candelaria worthwhile but will have to return to Cabo San Lucas the way they came, then head north up Mexico 19. Both routes are covered in detail below.

CABO FALSO TO PLAYA MIGRIÑO

About three km west of the Cabo San Lucas city limits is Cabo Falso, once incorrectly thought to be Baja California's southernmost point. Because the wide beach along Cabo Falso is protected as a nesting ground for sea turtles, visitors aren't permitted within 50 meters (165 feet) of the surf line. The dunes behind the beach, however, are a popular destination for rented ATVs from Cabo San Lucas. The abandoned lighthouse, **El Faro Viejo,** signaled ships from 1895 to 1961; the original lens is now installed in a newer lighthouse higher on the beach. Surrounded by loose sand for at least a half mile, the old lighthouse can only be approached on foot, ATV, or horse.

Past Cabo Falso the highway begins climbing over the southwestern foothills and coastal plateaus of the Sierra de La Laguna to reach the small ranching settlement of Migriño after about 21 km (13 miles). Playa Migriño, accessed at Km 94 or 97, is a long section of beach next to Estero Migriño, a small estuary linked with Río Candelaria. In winter, surfers can catch a point

break at the north end of the beach. Different sections of Playa Migriño are accessible via a network of sandy roads; several spots are suitable for camping.

Simple **Restaurant Migriño**, on the sea side of Mexico 19, just south of Km 102, serves *antojitos* and cold beer.

LA CANDELARIA

Palapa-roofed adobe and block homes, a small church, a school, split-rail and *carrizal* fences, and saddled burros tethered to paloverde and mesquite trees set the scene at this small village in the foothills of the lower Sierra de La Laguna. A palm oasis in a shallow canyon on the northwest edge of the quiet village holds an underground stream, which has been dammed to irrigate mangoes, citrus, guavas, avocados, papayas, corn, and bamboo. Pigs wander in and out of the canyon, seeking cool mud around the pumphouse. Around 80 people live in the village full time; the population swells during school sessions when children from ranchos deeper in the sierra board here to attend the local school.

The area's hilly, tropical-arid thornforest makes for good hiking. Bring plenty of water, even in winter, as the sun bakes everything unprotected by shade. At the edge of town near an old cane mill is a hill surmounted by a cemetery that can be reached on foot. Look for the headstone of Rafael Salvatierra, whose engraved dates of birth and death indicate he lived to the age of 130; opinions are divided as to whether the dates are accurate, although several generations ago residents in this area often passed the century mark.

Curanderos
La Candelaria is known throughout the Cape Region for its *curanderos* (healers). Tourism flacks in Los Cabos call the *curandero* culture "white magic," but in reality the local villagers simply have a way with medicinal herbs, which grow in the sierra in some abundance. Considering Candelaria's relative remoteness from modern pharmacies and lack of economic resources, it's not surprising that some knowledge of herbal treatments has been preserved by necessity.

Arts and Crafts
Local artisans produce rustic ranchware pots, cane baskets, and rustic *palo escopeta* chairs with palm-fiber bottoms. Look for a sign reading "Pottery" in the village if you're interested in purchasing these crafts. Candelaria resident Lorena Hankins sometimes leads pottery workshops; check with Lorena in La Candelaria or with Cuco in El Pescadero (see below), or ask around in Todos Santos.

Getting There
From Playa Migriño: The quickest way to La Candelaria is via a 9.1-km (5.6-mile) sandy arroyo road that turns inland off Mexico 19 near Playa Migriño (just on the north side of Río Candelaria). The unsigned turnoff lies three km (1.9 miles) south of the Km 94 marker, or about a half kilometer (0.3 miles) north of the main Playa Migriño turnoff. This road, suitable for 4WD vehicles only, parallels the deep, wide Río Candelaria arroyo. It's sandy and narrow in spots, so drivers must take care not to stray off the track into sand traps. And since the road runs across the bottom of the arroyo at one point, it would be risky during or after a hard rain. If you're two-wheeling it, stick to the San Lucas road both ways.

From Cabo San Lucas: This route is longer and more scenic than the road from Playa Migriño. From downtown Cabo San Lucas, begin driving toward San José along Blvd. Lázaro Cárdenas, then turn left at a sign marked "La Paz Via Corta" directly opposite the entrance to Club Cascada. You are now heading northwest toward Todos Santos and La Paz. After passing a soccer field on the left, look for a power plant on your right and turn onto the wide dirt road near the plant (1.7 km/1.1 miles from the Via Corta intersection); this turnoff lies opposite the entrance to Minisuper Luly's and a *llantera* at Calle Morelos.

From this intersection, La Candelaria is 27.7 km (17.2 miles) away according to my odometer (the highway sign says 23 km). Make another right 4.3 km (2.7 miles) from the highway at a road signed "La Candelaria" and "Los Pozos"; you'll pass through a fence and cattle guard here. A military checkpoint has on occasion been set up near this gate.

As you ascend the sierra foothills into relatively dense thornforest (very green in early fall)

CLAYWARE OF CANDELARIA

Candelaria is widely known in the Cape Region for its rustic clay pottery, known as *trastes de barro* locally or, among foreign collectors, as "ranchware." No one's sure how or when the pottery tradition arrived here, but one theory speculates that when the southern Baja missions were secularized in the 19th century, many mestizos who had worked for the mission system chose to establish ranches farther into the sierra, where water was more abundant and the land more fertile. They may have brought with them the simple pottery techniques that were eventually lost to the cities that grew up along the coast.

Earth for Candelaria ranchware is dug from local hillsides, traditionally during the two weeks between the full and new moons (due to a belief that earth collected during this time will make better potting material). After grinding and sifting the earth by hand, potters add water and knead it into clay, which is then pinched, pulled, and punched into the desired pot shape. Some coiling techniques—rolling clay into ropelike lengths, then coiling them in layers along the rim—may be used near the tops of the vessels.

When the basic shape is finished, the potter will smooth the vessel's surfaces using a cow's rib, a thick piece of leather, or a dried corncob. The pot is left to dry for 12 hours, then polished by troweling the surface with stones and water. Cycles of drying and polishing will continue until the artisan is satisfied with the overall aesthetic result. Then, after a final drying, the pots will be taken out of the sun in late afternoon and warmed on a stove until they are too hot to touch. Pots are then placed on a grate and individually covered with "cowchips" (dried cow dung), which are carefully ignited.

The burning fuel functions as a natural kiln, firing the pots without benefit of an oven or other exterior structure. Potters tend the fire to make sure it burns evenly and steadily, all the while checking between layers of chips to see how the pot is progressing; when the entire pot glows red (usually this takes about one hour), it is fired. Pots created this way will have a smooth, burnished terra-cotta appearance. Chips that may have touched the pot's surface dur-ing firing will have created blurred black "fire clouds," considered an error in the world of refined kiln techniques but valued by ranchware collectors.

Trastes de barro come in all shapes and sizes, from teacups to frijoles bowls to the rare *porrón,* a very large jar used for grain or water storage. The larger the piece, the more difficult it is to make and the more expensive it will be to buy. *Tinajas,* medium-size water jars, are easier to find and very functional. The slightly porous surfaces allow a little water to leak out and evaporate, thus keeping the vessel and its contents cooler than the ambient air temperature—call it ranch refrigeration.

American expatriate Lorena Hankins has helped to create a revival of traditional pottery in Candelaria.

and stands of *cardón* and pitahaya, it's not unusual to see cattle or burros in the road, so drive slowly. The road forks about 12 km (7.5 miles) from the highway; don't take the right fork signed for San Felipe and El Sauzal but rather the left one, which leads to the charming *ranchitos* and adobe ruins of Los Pozos. Pass a small chapel at 14 km (8.9 miles) and follow signs for La Candelaria and La Trinidad. Stay with the main road and ignore any smaller forks from this point.

The road begins climbing, and 18.5 km (11.5 miles) from the highway you'll see the Pacific Ocean to the west. Around 21 km (13 miles) from the highway you'll pass a signed turnoff for Rancho San Ramón, and at 24 km (15 miles) you'll come to a relatively major fork. The right branch is more direct to La Candelaria, though the left curves around to a *ranchito* and eventually cuts back onto the same road. About 0.8 km (0.5 miles) farther (following the right branch), the road crosses an arroyo that could be problematic in heavy rain. Ignore a right turn to La Trinidad at 26.4 km (16.4 miles). Less than 1.6 km (one mile) later you'll arrive at La Candelaria.

Note: Almost any type of vehicle can safely navigate the Cabo San Lucas-Candelaria road in dry weather. Low-lying Los Pozos—almost halfway to La Candelaria—may flood in heavy rains, so if it begins raining during the first half of the drive, turn back. Once you're past Los Pozos, keep going! Becoming stranded in La Candelaria would beat getting mired in Los Pozos.

EL PESCADERO AND VICINITY

Beaches South of El Pescadero

Of the many deserted beaches strung out along the Pacific coast between Playa Migriño and Todos Santos, one of the easiest to reach is **Playa Las Cabrillas,** south of El Pescadero (turnoff at Km 81). Flat and sandy, the beach was named for the plentiful seabass that can be caught from shore. Grass-tufted dunes provide partial windscreens for beach camping, which is free.

Other free beach campsites along this stretch of highway can be found at the ends of dirt roads branching off Mexico 19 at Km 89-90, Km 86, Km 75, and Km 70-71.

Cuco's

A sandy road near Km 73 leads to a trailer homestead where La Paz native Cuco makes customfitted *bajacaliforniano*-style leather sandals with recycled tire-rubber soles; US$20 a pair. He can take your measurements one day and have the sandals ready the next. An amateur naturalist, Cuco can also arrange mule trips into the Sierra de La Laguna and is a good source of information about sierra flora. He'll need about a week to make the arrangements. Cuco helps Lorena Hankins with Candelaria pottery workshops from time to time as well. To find Cuco's place, follow the dirt road off Mexico 19 all the way till it ends, then turn left and continue straight till you reach

Cuco Mayron custom-fits Baja-style huaraches *for a visitor.*

his gate; park outside the gate and walk in.

Surfer's Note: Punta Gaspareño, near Cuco's around Km 73, catches a right point break.

El Pescadero

At Km 62, El Pescadero (pop. 1,500) is little more than a plaza lined with *tiendas,* two *loncherías,* and a couple of small hotels and campgrounds, surrounded by farms and fishing shacks. But several pristine beaches lie along this stretch of the Pacific coast, and the town makes a good jump-off point for explorations of the western Sierra de La Laguna.

Accommodations: Hotel Bungalows Ziranda, tel. (1) 126-3850, sits on the northern edge of Pescadero on the east side of Mexico 19. The "bungalows" are actually four units in a cement block building, painted white with green trim. Rooms are basic but clean, and the rates fall within the shoestring category. Rates: US$12 s, US$15 d. A bit farther north on the opposite side of the road, **Hotel Las Auroras** is similar, but it's made of brick.

Pescadero Surf Camp, tel./fax (1) 145-0288, toll-free U.S./Canada tel. (800) 847-5921, e-mail: info@pescaderosurf.com, is on the west side of the highway near Km 63. Besides tent and *palapa* camping, you can rent a cabaña that sleeps six and is equipped with kitchen and bath. The camp rents surfboards and boogies boards by the hour. Rates: US$40 s, US$50 d a night, plus US$5 for each additional guest, or US$300 a week. Pescadero Surf Camp also offers campsites, some with shade palapas, for US$5 pp per night. Electrical and water hookups are available.

Food: Lonchería Rosita on the east side of Mexico 19, just north of the main Pescadero intersection, is a small *palapa*-roof place serving breakfast, lunch, and dinner. Specialties include *pescado empanizado, tamales de puerco,* quesadillas, enchiladas, chicken and *machaca* burritos, and soft drinks. BYOB. **Lonchería Choya,** nearby, is similar.

Los Arboles (The Trees), at Km 62 on the outskirts of Pescadero, serves American-style food, including pizza, breakfasts, and snacks, 7 a.m.-8 p.m. during the winter and spring, more erratically in summer and fall. Showers and laundry service are also available.

Rancho Nueva Villa, just before Km 60, is a well-known farm producing fruits and vegetables without chemical pesticides or fertilizers. You can sometimes purchase organic produce from the farm's roadside stand.

Playa Los Cerritos

Closer to El Pescadero at Km 64 (12.8 km/eight miles south of Todos Santos), a good dirt road branches 2.7 km (1.7 miles) southwest to Playa Los Cerritos, another fine beach for camping and fishing. Because the beach is sheltered by Punta Pescadero at its north end, swimming is usually safe. During the winter the northwest swell tips a surfable point break and during the summer a mushy beach break sometimes occurs. Because wave size rarely intimidates, Cerritos is popular with novice surfers.

Ejido-owned **Los Cerritos Trailer Park** is little more than a shell of what it once was, having ceased operations three or four years ago. You can still use the campround, but there are no functioning facilities to speak of. Someone from the *ejido* will probably visit your site and ask for US$3-4. If the trailer park gets up and running again, expect sewer hookups, toilet, and cold shower facilities to cost around US$6 a day or US$100 a month, possibly lower during the May-Oct. low season. Outside the park you may camp anywhere on the beach for US$4 a night in the winter or for free in the low season.

Playa San Pedro

Just south of Punta San Pedro begins the long Playa San Pedro (7.4 km/4.6 miles south of the Todos Santos town limits), which is stony at the north end but sandy for a long stretch south. The beach's south end, toward Punta Pescadero, is sometimes called Playa Pescadero. Surfing toward the north end can be good, and it's a lot easier to find than San Pedrito (see below); the 3.1-km (1.9-mile) access road west from Km 59 is clearly marked.

During the winter surfing season, the local *ejido* sometimes collects a nominal parking fee for vehicles parked in the small area at the end of the road near Punta San Pedro.

San Pedro has an RV/tent campground, **San Pedrito RV Park,** tel. (1) 145-0170 or 145-0147, which offers sites with full hookups for US$12.50 (negotiable to US$10 in the off season), tent sites with simple *palapa* shelters for US$3 pp a night, and 10 cabañas, each with private bath, for

US$35 d. Facilities include flush toilets, hot showers, a laundry, pool, bar, and *palapa* restaurant. The campground is popular all winter and is usually completely full around Christmas and New Year's. Its name, "San Pedrito," leads many people to mistakenly call this beach "Playa San Pedrito" (confusing it with the less frequented cove to the north).

Candylandia II, e-mail: ecobaja@cabotel. com.mx, on the beach between Playa San Pedro and Playa Los Cerritos, features five trailer/camper sites with water and sewer for US$7 a night or US$42 per week. A rustic two-bedroom apartment with one and half bathrooms is available for US$325 a week or US$700 a month.

Playa San Pedrito (Playa Las Palmas)

Just north of El Pescadero between Km 56 and 57 is an unsigned, 2.5-km (1.5-mile) dirt road west to Playa San Pedrito, called "Palm Beach" or Playa Las Palmas by local *norteamericanos*. Stretched between two rocky points and backed by Mexican fan palms and a saltmarsh, this scenic beach offers good fishing and the occasional mushy beach break for surfing or body-boarding. For swimming, the middle 200 meters or so in the center of the cove is usually the safest. Toward the north and south ends, the water looks deceptively shallow and inviting, but riptides have been known to carry swimmers out of the cove into open ocean or onto the rocks.

The best thing about Las Palmas/San Pedrito is that there is no easy vehicle access, so the sand isn't crisscrossed with vehicle tracks like many other beaches along the West Cape. However, the beach sand is often streaked with black volcanic sediments from Puerto Algodones a little farther north. If you arrive expecting "the most beautiful beach on the Pacific coast" (as one guidebook described Las Palmas), you may be disappointed, although the secluded nature of the beach and its visual completeness—framed by rocky headlands at each end and palms to the rear—lend a definite charm.

Trails lead across the headlands at either end of the cove to beach vistas. In back of Punta San Pedro, the slopes of **Cerro Los Viejos** offer a rough but scenic hike.

This beach is sometimes incorrectly called "Playa San Pedro." Mexican topographic surveys will confirm its original name as Playa San Pedrito or "Little San Pedro Beach"—since it's smaller than Playa San Pedro, immediately south of Punta San Pedro. Further proof can be found inside the Casa de la Cultura museum in Todos Santos, where a photo of this beach is clearly labeled "Playa de San Pedrito." This same museum contains a historical photo of the Hacienda de San Pedrito—the hacienda now standing in ruins at the back of Playa San Pedrito. Nonetheless most gringos and some locals confuse the names, chiefly because a campground on Playa San Pedro calls itself "San Pedrito."

Camping is no longer permitted in the palm grove or in the ruined hacienda behind it. Beach camping on the sand west of the palm grove is allowed, but don't leave any rubbish behind. The owner of the property behind the federal zone generously keeps the access road open so that people can visit the beach; if this privilege is abused by visitors who trash the beach, access could halt at any time. Water is available from a spring at the south end of the beach; treat before drinking.

Getting There: The more commonly used road to San Pedrito leaves Mexico 19 almost opposite the white buildings of the Campo Experimental on the east side of the highway between Km 56 and 57. A more direct road just a bit farther south is sometimes marked with a sign reading "Road Closed"; all the local residents use it anyway. Both roads intersect several other sandy tracks; when you see a ruined mansion just ahead, make sure you take the left fork that curves around to the south end of the palm orchard. If you head straight toward the middle or north end of the orchard you'll run into the saltmarsh and have to hike a couple of hundred yards through tall saltgrass and mud to reach the beach.

For information on beaches north of Playa San Pedrito, see Beaches in the Todos Santos section.

Exploring the Sierra

East of town, you can follow a network of dirt roads up into the sierra foothills to palm-filled arroyos, remote ranches, thick *cardonales* (*cardón* stands), and other delights whose existence most highway travelers aren't even slightly aware of. If you decide to explore the area,

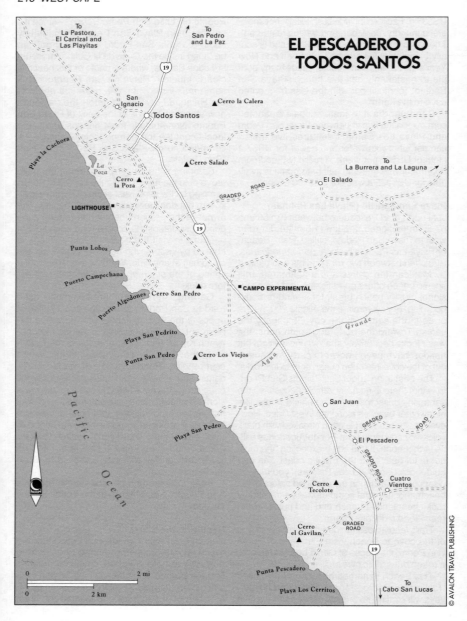

EL PESCADERO TO
TODOS SANTOS

To
La Pastora,
El Carrizal and
Las Playitas

To
San Pedro
and La Paz

19

San
Ignacio

Todos Santos

Cerro la Calera

Playa la Cachora

La
Poza

Cerro
la Poza

Cerro Salado

To
La Burrera and La Laguna

El Salado

GRADED ROAD

LIGHTHOUSE

19

Punta Lobos

Puerto Campechana

Puerto Algodones   Cerro San Pedro

CAMPO EXPERIMENTAL

Grande

Playa San Pedrito

Punta San Pedro   Cerro Los Viejos

Agua

Pacific

San Juan

GRADED   ROAD

Playa San Pedro

El Pescadero

GRADED ROAD

Ocean

Cuatro
Vientos

Cerro
Tecolote

GRADED
ROAD

Cerro
el Gavilan

19

0   2 mi

0   2 km

Punta Pescadero

Playa Los Cerritos

To
Cabo San Lucas

© AVALON TRAVEL PUBLISHING

you should do so only in a high-clearance vehicle, preferably with 4WD; better yet, park in the foothills and hike in. It's easy to become lost here, so you may be better off hiring a guide in Pescadero (the aforementioned Cuco may know someone willing to act as a guide) or in Todos Santos. Some of the best spots, such as **Cascada del Refugio,** a sparkling, palm-shaded waterfall, can only be reached by hiking across private land, for which you'll need permission—best arranged by someone local.

One road leading southeast from south of town near Playa Los Cerritos continues approximately 56 km (35 miles) across the Sierra de La Laguna to Mexico 1 between Santa Anita and Caduaño, about 16 km (10 miles) south of Miraflores; see Sierra de La Laguna in the Central Cape section for details. Parts of this road—properly called Ramal Los Naranjos but known by many Anglophone residents as the "Naranjas road"—are graded, but the middle section is passable only by sturdy 4WD.

TODOS SANTOS

One of the more lushly vegetated arroyo settlements in the Cape Region, Todos Santos (pop. 4,000) is a good midpoint stopover for travelers making their way between Cabo San Lucas and La Paz on Mexico 19. The town offers several restaurants, cafés, taco stands, and fruit stands; a few modest hotels, bed and breakfasts, and RV parks; and a Pemex station. Long-term visitors can wander miles of virgin, as-yet-undeveloped beaches stretching north and south from Todos Santos along the Pacific, explore the steep western escarpment of the Sierra de La Laguna, or simply hang out and soak up the small-town ambience.

The town sits on a *meseta* (low plateau) buttressing the sierra foothills. Looming over Todos Santos to the east, the sierra provides an underground stream that irrigates dozens of orchards laden with mangoes, avocados, guavas, papayas, citrus, coconuts, and other fruits. Most of these are cultivated along wide Arroyo de la Reforma to the town's immediate north, in an area commonly known as **La Huerta** or "The Orchard." At the west end toward the beach is **La Poza**, a small freshwater lagoon favored by resident and migrating waterfowl. North of town, amid a dense palm grove, is another natural pool where local children go swimming.

Beneath the town's sleepy surface, behind the century-old brick and adobe facades, lives a small, year-round colony of artists, surfers, and organic farmers who have found Todos Santos the ideal place to follow their independent pursuits. A number of La Paz residents maintain homes here as temporary escapes from the Cortez coast's intense summer heat; these are complemented by a seasonal community of California refugees from the high-stress film and media worlds who make the town their winter retreat. Several small farms in the area specialize in organic produce for the North American market.

Writeups in *Travel And Leisure* (". . . a new Mexican Oz in the making, destined to become the Carmel of Baja") and later the *Los Angeles Times* briefly stimulated outside interest, much of it focusing on real estate—the town's streets are now tacked with "For Sale" signs. With each passing year the town seems to move a little closer toward becoming, if not the next Carmel, then perhaps the next San José del Cabo.

CLIMATE

Straddling the Tropic of Cancer, Todos Santos has perhaps the coastal Cape Region's most comfortable climate. December through February nights are cool, days warm—warmer, in fact, than most areas along the Cortez coast, which is exposed to the prevailing north winds. Mulegé and Loreto, for example, can easily drop to 15° C (59° F) in Jan.-Feb. while Todos Santos remains in the 20s C (70s F). In March and April the air around Todos Santos begins warming up, but the ocean reaches its coldest annual temperatures (still comfortable for swimming).

Increasing air temperatures in June interact with the cooler seas to bring a marine fog in the evenings; visitors are often surprised how cool the nights are during this month. Although the air is relatively dry most of the year, the months of July, August, and September can become humid enough that the heat index may reach uncomfortable levels on days when there is no rain or cloud cover. At the same time, because of its location on a *meseta* facing the Pacific, the town receives the ocean's overall cooling effect, and hence summer temperatures are always lower than in Cabo San Lucas, San José, or La Paz, all of which are heated to greater or lesser degrees by the warmer Sea of Cortez. When it's 38° C (100° F) in La Paz or Cabo, for example, Todos Santos will register just 32° C (90° F).

July through September are peak rainfall months, although the Sierra de La Laguna partially blocks the heavier storms coming from the Mexican mainland that affect Los Cabos. The November 1993 storm that inundated San José and Cabo San Lucas and caused millions of dollars of damage, for example, barely touched Todos Santos. In September 1996, Todos Santos wasn't so lucky; a small hurricane came ashore and took down several roofs and utility poles. But few such storms ever reach the town.

The rain tapers off in October as temperatures descend a bit. November usually brings beautiful, sunny weather with an abundance of greenery.

HISTORY

The earliest traces of human habitation in the Todos Santos area date back 3,000 years to "Matancita Man," the defleshed and painted remains (thus indicating a second burial) of a tall male who lived to at least 75 years on a vegetable and animal-protein diet. The first Spaniard to sight the oasis, Jesuit padre Jaime Bravo, found nomadic Guaicura availing themselves of the inland water source and collecting shellfish along the coast.

Padre Bravo established a farm community and a *misión de visita* (visiting mission) called Todos Santos here in 1724, to supply the water-poor mission community at La Paz with fruits, vegetables, wine, and sugarcane. By 1731 Todos

remnants of a sugarcane mill

Santos was producing 200 burro-loads of *panocha*—raw brown sugar—annually, along with figs, pomegranates, citrus, and grapes. Two years later, deeming the local Guaicura amenable to missionization, Padre Sigismundo Taraval founded Misión Santa Rosa de las Palmas at the upper end of the arroyo about two km inland from the Pacific. Taraval fled to Isla Espíritu Santo near La Paz following a 1734 native rebellion, and the mission returned to visiting-chapel status the following year.

The local Guaicura population was soon wiped out by smallpox, and Pericú were brought in to work the fields. Reinstated as a *misión de visita* in 1735, Todos Santos outgrew La Paz by the mid-18th century; from 1737 until 1748, Padre Bernardo Zumziel actually spent more time in Todos Santos than at the mission in La Paz. Renamed Nuestra Señora del Pilar de Todos Santos in 1749, the town served as Spanish military headquarters for La Escuadra del Sur, the southern detachment of the Loreto presidio. This enabled the community to weather the Pericú rebellions to the southwest in Santiago and San Jose del Cabo, although 49 Todos Santos inhabitants were killed defending the town in one related skirmish. Polish Jesuit padre Carlos Neumayer presided over the mission from 1752 until his death in Todos Santos in 1764. Todos Santos remained an important mission settlement until secularization in 1840.

When Governor Luis del Castillo Negrete ordered the distribution of church lands to the local community in 1841, he was contested by Padre Gabriel González, a local priest and former president of the mission who had used mission property for his own farming and ranching, becoming a powerful local trader in the process. González's armed rebellion was put down in 1842; the priest and his followers fled to Mazatlán.

Anglo whalers visiting Todos Santos in 1849 praised the town as "an oasis" with "friendly and intelligent people." In the post-mission era, Todos Santos thrived as Baja's sugarcane capital, supporting eight sugar mills by the late 19th century. While carrying out a survey of Cape Region flora for the California Academy of Sciences in 1890, botanist T.S. Brandegee commented on the area's beauty and bounty. During this period handsome hotels, theaters, municipal offices, and homes for painters and sculptors were built.

Sugar prices dropped precipitously following WW II, and all but one mill closed when the most abundant freshwater spring dried up in 1950. The remaining mill closed in 1965, though smaller household operations continued into the early '70s. The town faded into near obscurity.

Around 1981 the spring came back to life, and the arroyo once again began producing a large variety and quantity of fruits and vegetables. Three years later, Mexico 19 was paved between San Pedro and Cabo San Lucas, opening Todos Santos to tourists and expatriates for the first time.

SIGHTS

Iglesia Nuestra Señora del Pilar
Although the structure itself is rather plain, this church facing the southwest edge of the main plaza contains an important orange- and blue-garbed figure of the Virgin of Pilar, the focus of the town's biggest festival each year in October. In August the famous Virgin of Loreto—considered the "mother" of all Baja churches founded by the Jesuits—is brought to the church from Loreto.

Casa de la Cultura
Housed in a restored U-shaped brick building on Av. Juárez at Obregón, the Casa displays a modest collection of artifacts evoking the anthropology, ethnography, history, and natural history of the region, along with small displays of modern art and handicrafts. The museum's pottery collection includes classic local ranchware, as well as older ceramics produced by the now-extinct Pericú. Some rare painted Indian skulls are also on display. One of the five exhibit rooms contains paintings by local artists, including a set of pastels of historic structures in Zacatecas. Open Mon.-Fri. 8 a.m.-5 p.m., Sat.-Sun. 9 a.m.-1 p.m.; free admission.

Architecture
Although Todos Santos has been inhabited continually since 1731, the oldest standing structures date back only 100-150 years. The town's most historic buildings—a mixture of one- and two-story affairs, all with courtyards—can be seen along the streets nearest the plaza, par-

ticularly along **Pilar, Centenario, Legaspi, Topete,** and **Obregón.** Most are constructed of fired Mexican brick laid in double or sometimes triple courses (some walls are plastered, some not) topped by flat parapet roofs. A few feature palm-thatched roofs. Large windows and doors bounded by *pilastres* in the classic Andalusian style (favored in provincial Mexico from the time of the Spanish until the middle of the 20th century) predominate in this area. The large building housing **Café Santa Fé** on Calle Centenario, facing the plaza, is one of the only substantial adobe structures downtown. Many of the buildings in this small, semihistoric district are owned or occupied by foreigners.

On the hill overlooking town (off Mexico 19 on the way out of town toward La Paz) stand a few older adobe ruins. In the newer eastern half of Todos Santos are many small residences built of adobe brick or *chiname*—mud plastered over woven *palo de arco* (trumpetbush) branches. Brick ruins of several of the old sugar mills can be seen around town.

BEACHES

The pueblo of Todos Santos sits a couple of kilometers inland from the beach, a fact that has probably helped to maintain tourism growth in the area at a slow, even pace. Added to this is the fact that none of the roads leading from Todos Santos to the beach are paved or even marked, and so far there hasn't been a single hotel or condo development along the Pacific shoreline for at least 65 km in either direction.

To enjoy nearby beaches, then, you'll need good directions and a little patience for those inevitable moments when you realize you've taken a wrong turn and need to retrace your steps. The following list starts south of Todos Santos and proceeds north.

Punta Lobos
About two km (1.2 miles) south of the town limits via Mexico 19, a signed, unpaved access road suitable for most vehicles leads 2.4 km (1.5 miles) to Punta Lobos, a rocky point at the south end of a sandy cove. The point is named for a resident colony of sea lions. The surf here is usually okay for swimming, but take a good look

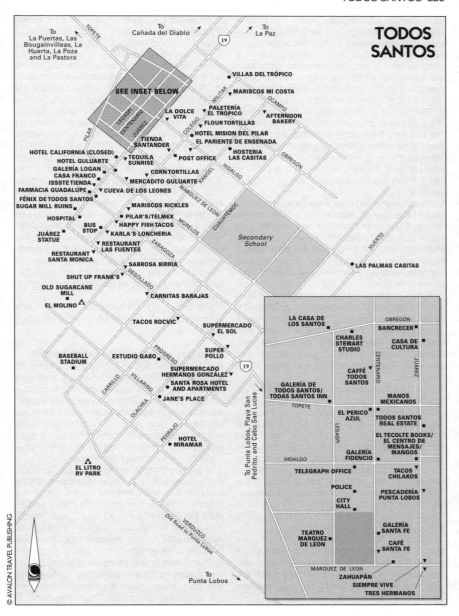

TODOS
SANTOS

To
La Puertas, Las
Bougainvilleas, La
Huerta, La Poza
and La Pastora

TOPETE

To
Cañada del Diablo

To
La Paz

19

VILLAS DEL TRÓPICO

MARISCOS MI COSTA

SEE INSET BELOW

MILITAR

OCAMPO

PALETERÍA
EL TRÓPICO

AFTERNOON
BAKERY

LA DOLCE
VITA

COLEGIO

FLOUR TORTILLAS

LEGASPI

CENTENARIO

JUÁREZ

PILAR

HOTEL MISION DEL PILAR

TIENDA
SANTANDER

EL PARIENTE DE ENSENADA

OBREGÓN

HOSTERIA
LAS CASITAS

HOTEL CALIFORNIA (CLOSED)

TEQUILA
SUNRISE

HIDALGO

POST OFFICE

HOTEL GULUARTE

GALERÍA LOGAN

CORN TORTILLAS

CASA FRANCO

RANGEL

ISSSTE TIENDA

MERCADITO GULUARTE

FARMACIA GUADALUPE

CUEVA DE LOS LEONES

FÉNIX DE TODOS SANTOS

MARQUEZ DE LEON

SUGAR MILL RUINS

MARISCOS RICKLES

HOSPITAL

PILAR'S/TELMEX

MORELOS

HAPPY FISH TACOS

CUAUHTEMOC

Secondary
School

HUERTO

BUS
STOP

KARLA'S LONCHERIA

JUÁREZ
STATUE

RESTAURANT
LAS FUENTES

ZARAGOZA

RESTAURANT
SANTA MONICA

SABROSA BIRRIA

LAS PALMAS CASITAS

DEGOLLADO

SHUT UP FRANK'S

OLD SUGARCANE
MILL

CARNITAS BARAJAS

EL MOLINO

TACOS ROCVIC

PROGRESO

SUPERMERCADO
EL SOL

BASEBALL
STADIUM

ESTUDIO GABO

SUPER
POLLO

19

CARRILLO

VILLARINO

SUPERMERCADO
HERMANOS GONZALEZ

SANTA ROSA HOTEL
AND APARTMENTS

To Punta Lobos, Playa San
Pedrito, and Cabo San Lucas

JANE'S PLACE

OLACHEA

PEDRAJO

HOTEL
MIRAMAR

EL LITRO
RV PARK

VERDUZCO

Old Road to Punta Lobos

© AVALON TRAVEL PUBLISHING

MOON

To
Punta Lobos

(Inset map)

OBREGÓN

LA CASA DE
LOS SANTOS

BANCRECER

CHARLES
STEWART
STUDIO

CENTENARIO

CASA DE
CULTURA

JUÁREZ

CAFFÉ
TODOS
SANTOS

GALERÍA DE
TODOS SANTOS/
TODAS SANTOS INN

TOPETE

MANOS
MEXICANOS

EL PERICO
AZUL

LEGASPI

TODOS SANTOS
REAL ESTATE

EL TECOLTE BOOKS/
EL CENTRO DE
MENSAJES/MANGOS

GALERÍA
FIDENCIO

HIDALGO

TACOS
CHILAKOS

TELEGRAPH OFFICE

POLICE

PESCADERÍA
PUNTA LOBOS

CITY
HALL

GALERÍA
SANTA FE

TEATRO
MARQUEZ
DE LEON

CAFÉ
SANTA FE

MARQUEZ DE LEON

ZAHUAPÁN

SIEMPRE VIVE

TRES HERMANOS

at the currents before leaping in. This cove is used as a launching point for the local fishermen, so there's always a small fleet of *pangas* toward the point. The *pangas* usually bring the catch in after 3 p.m.; watching the pilots time the waves so that they can safely run the boats onto the beach is a treat. Sometimes fresh fish can be bought directly from the *pangeros*.

The ruins of an old stone-walled cannery lie at the side of the access road toward the beach; north along the beach stands a lighthouse. Swimming in the lighthouse area is not recommended due to strong currents. If you continue walking past the lighthouse you'll eventually reach Playa Las Pocitas and Playa La Cachora (see below).

A small spring-fed lagoon lies behind the south end of the beach, marked by a large Virgin shrine. A narrow trail leads up and over the 215-meter (700-foot) headland to a panoramic view of the beach and sea below. On the other side of the headland you can see sandy **Puerto Campechano** and, farther south, Puerto Algodones (see below).

Punta Lobos can be reached on foot from town by following Calle Pedrajo southwest past Hotel Miramar one long block till you meet a wide dirt road. Turn left and follow the road until you can see the lighthouse on the right; take the next wide dirt road heading in that direction till you reach Punta Lobos. This walk takes 20-30 minutes each way.

Puerto Algodones: Hidden away two headlands south of Punta Lobos and almost surrounded by steep cliffs, this deep and secluded cove can be reached via a very rough, winding, and sometimes steep dirt and stone road that runs southwest off the Punta Lobos access road. According to local history, Algodones was used for the shipping of tomatoes, sugarcane, and canned fish from the 1930s through the '50s, when a stone-block road was laid between the cannery and the bay. How it got the name "Algodones" (cotton) is a mystery; no cotton was ever cultivated in the Cape Region.

Along the north side of the U-shaped cove stands a tall pier made of rough-hewn stone blocks. The sure-footed can hike along a narrow trail at the bottom of a cliff and reach the rock pier—worth the effort for the view back into the bay. Smaller animal paths lead up a steep

slope above the pier for more panoramic views. If you've got all day you could probably hike to Puerto Campechano and back from here.

A black-hued beach of rounded volcanic stones rims the middle reach of the bay, where the waves are sometimes suitable for bodysurfing. To reach the beach you can hike down a cliff or follow the old road. Snorkeling is good at the rocky headlands at each end of the bay, but currents and tidal surges can be too strong for some swimmers. Sea lions are sometimes seen along the rocks.

The old road to Algodones starts just east of the cannery ruins near Punta Lobos and climbs along the eastern rim of a large arroyo. You can hike to the bay from the cannery area in about 45 minutes at a steady pace, an hour if you take it slow. Start in the early morning and plan to spend the day there so that you can hike back in late afternoon, thus avoiding the hottest part of the day. If you have a sturdy off-highway vehicle that can take soft sand, you can drive about a fourth or a third of the way before the road becomes too rocky for anything but tractor tires.

For information on beaches south of Punta Lobos and Puerto Algodones, see El Pescadero and Vicinity.

Playa La Cachora and Playa Las Pocitas

Playa La Cachora is a very broad swath of sand backed by verbena-trimmed dunes, a good spot for strolling and sunset-watching. From the Galería de Todos Santos, follow Calle Topete across the palm-filled arroyo known as "La Huerta"; the first sand road on the other side leads west to the beach after curving through a quiet residential section perched on a *meseta* above the northwest corner of the arroyo.

If you walk south along Playa La Cachora, you'll come to Las Pocitas, also known as La Poza de Lobos. Along the back edge of the beach is a freshwater lagoon (La Poza), and toward the south end a rocky ridge heads inland. It's possible to walk back to town via a trail running along the base of the north side (the Huerta side) of this ridge.

The undertow and shore break along La Cachora and Las Pocitas are usually too heavy for swimming, except during the summer when there are occasional long periods of relative calm.

Playa La Pastora

A wider network of sand roads crosses the arroyo and runs north parallel to the beach for some 26 km (16 miles). The roads pass small coconut and papaya orchards and larger farms at Las Playitas and El Carrizal, then head inland to join Mexico 19. Several sandy tracks branch west off this road to a lengthy succession of dune-lined beaches perfect for secluded sunbathing and beachcombing.

For much of the year the surfline here is too precipitous for swimming, though surfers can ride the waves at a break called La Pastora, named for a meadow some distance away. In winter La Pastora offers a right point break in a northwest swell; in summer you'll find an occasional beach break in a southern swell, or a point break in southwestern swell.

La Pastora is about 5.6 km (3.5 miles) northwest of La Huerta via the only coastal road north; just past a wide arroyo that runs right up to the beach, look for a large, lone *palapa* next to a long, low stone wall.

Farther North

Beyond El Carrizal a rough dirt road snakes north along and away from the coast 57 km (36 miles) to a cluster of Ranchos—Los Inocentes, El Rosario, El Tepetate, and El Tomate—where another dirt road leads northeast 29 km (18 miles) to meet Mexico 1. Sand beach lines the entire coastline here all the way north to **Punta Marqués** (about 24 km/15 miles north of Rancho El Tomate) and **Punta Conejo** (18 km/11 miles north of Punta Marqués). Both points offer excellent surfing and windsurfing in the winter and

---

HEADS UP!

While walking close to the surf line along any of the beaches north of Punta Lobos, watch out for "sneaker" waves that rise up seemingly out of nowhere to engulf the beach. Though rare, accidental drownings have occurred on these beaches.

Also beware, during the late *chubasco* season, especially September, small blue jellyfish called *aguas malas* are commonly encountered in inshore waters.

---

early spring. And surfable reef and point breaks can form in many other spots along the 58-km (36-mile) stretch of sand extending south of Punta Marqués; check out **La Bocana**, an arroyo mouth near Los Inocentes. Self-contained beach camping is permitted anywhere along the shore.

ACCOMMODATIONS

Hotels

The town's several hotels come in a variety of price ranges, but overall Todos Santos is the second least expensive place to overnight in all of Baja California Sur, after La Paz.

Shoestring-Budget: Two family-run places provide similarly adequate rooms at similarly low prices. At Juárez and Morelos in the center of town, the two-story **Hotel Guluarte,** tel. (1) 145-0006, has clean rooms with hot-water showers. Upstairs is a common balcony with chairs; downstairs is a small pool. Rates: US$16 s/d with fan, US$26 s/d with a/c.

In a dusty but quiet neighborhood in the town's southwestern quarter stands **Hotel Miramar,** Mutualismo at Pedrajo, tel. (1) 145-0341. The two-story, L-shaped motel contains 10 clean, small rooms, each with two twin beds. On the premises are a pool, small restaurant, and laundry. Rates: US$13 s, US$18 d, US$24 t. The property was for sale when we last visited. The Guluarte is closer to local restaurants, but some visitors may prefer the Miramar's quieter location and the fact that it's about a 20-minute walk from the beach via the dirt road to Punta Lobos.

Budget: The friendly **Hotel Misión del Pilar,** Colegio Militar at Hidalgo, tel. (1) 145-0114, is a small, two-story modern place attached to a partially empty shopping center. The comfortable, nondescript rooms have a/c or fans, hot water, and TV. Discounts are available for long-term stays. Rates: US$21 for rooms with two beds and a fan, US$26 for larger rooms with king-size beds and fan, US$32 with a/c.

Occupying the top end of the budget category, **Santa Rosa Hotel and Apartments,** on Calle Olachea, tel. (1) 145-0394, near the south entrance to town, is a salmon-colored place offering eight large, fairly well-maintained studio units with kitchenettes. Facilities include a good pool, laundry, and enclosed parking. Small discounts

Hostería Las Casitas

are available for long-term stays. The signed turnoff for the Santa Rosa is three blocks south of the Pemex station, after which it's another two blocks west to the hotel. Rates: US$35 s/d, US$500 monthly.

Expensive-Premium: Todos Santos Inn, Calle Legaspi at Topete, tel./fax (1) 145-0040, occupies a well-restored, 1880-vintage brick building. The original owner was said to have thrown his cashbox down the hole of an outhouse to keep it from marauding revolutionaries in 1910. Since then the building has served as a school, cantina, and movie house; the faded mural in the foyer dates to the 1930s. Large rooms with high adobe-brick ceilings and private bath are simply but elegantly decorated with Mexican furniture, Saltillo tile, oriental rugs, mosquito nets, and ceiling fans. Two larger suites offer sitting areas, private patios, and a/c. Rates: Rooms in the main building cost US$85, suites US$125.

Before it closed in January 1999, the two-story, 16-room **Hotel California,** Av. Juárez be-

tween Morelos and Márquez de León, tel. (1) 145-0002, fax (1) 145-2333, was the most popular place to stay in Todos Santos for first-time visitors, some of whom mistakenly believed the hotel had some connection with The Eagles' song of the same name. So far there's been no word on when the hotel might open again.

Bed and Breakfast Inns
Inexpensive-Moderate: Hostería Las Casitas, on Calle Rangel between Obregón and Hidalgo (Apdo. Postal 73, Todos Santos, BCS 23300), tel./fax (1) 145-0255, offers a cluster of four charming, renovated *chiname* adobe cottages plus a new *casita* built of various desert woods, amid lush landscaping. Some rooms have private baths, others shared facilities. Room rates include a full breakfast for one person or continental breakfasts for two (additional breakfasts may be ordered from the kitchen), served on a shaded outdoor patio. Las Casitas also houses an art-glass studio specializing in architectural-quality art glass and kiln-worked dinnerware. Rates: US$45-65, depending on the room.

Guesthouses
Several homes in town, most of them owned by American or Canadian expatriates, offer lodgings in cottages adjacent to, in back of, or attached to the principal house. Often the owners are happy to supply information about things to see and do in Todos Santos and environs.

Inexpensive: In a residential section of unpaved streets south of Mexico 19, **Jane's Place,** at Villarino and Olachea, tel. (1) 145-0216, e-mail: bigdawgt@aol.com, offers four clean and comfortable apartments on a large, landscaped lot surrounded by a security wall. Three units come with kitchenettes and full-size refrigerators. Pleasant indoor and outdoor sitting areas are found throughout. Rates: US$45 daily, US$300 weekly with kitchenette; US$35 daily, US$225 weekly without kitchenette. Long-term stays are welcome.

In roughly the same neighborhood, **The Garden Casita,** at Olachea and Mutualismo, tel./fax (1) 145-0129, e-mail: hekman@writehere.com, is an owner-designed *palapa*-roofed guesthouse with a living area, dining area, fully equipped kitchenette with coffeemaker, bedroom, and patio surrounded by an enclosed courtyard.

Rates: US$45 nightly with a two-night minimum, US$295 weekly, US$595 monthly. Long-term rates include weekly maid service.

More in the center of town, a few blocks north of Mexico 19, **Las Palmas Casitas,** at Hidalgo and Huerto, tel./fax (1) 145-0213, e-mail: janeLB3@ aol.com, consists of two one-bedroom *casitas* and one two-bedroom, two-story *casita,* each with *palapa* roof, kitchen, covered patio, and modern amenities. Rates: US$80 per day (three-day minimum) or US$450 per week for one-bedroom units; US$700 per week (10-day minimum) for the two-bedroom unit.

Expensive-Premium: Across the wide arroyo north of town, on the south side of the road leading to Playa La Cachora, **Las Puertas,** tel./fax (1) 145-0373, e-mail: mwood75435@aol.com, features two large guesthouses with thick adobe walls, *palapa* roofs, and custom, Baja-style furniture. Surrounded by mango and other fruit trees, one unit comes with a separate, full kitchen while the other has an attached kitchenette. The beach is a five-minute walk away. The owners run an organic farm and can supply fresh produce on request. Rates: US$100 with attached kitchenette, US$125 with separate kitchen.

Premium: Farther down toward the beach on the opposite side of the road in La Cachora, **Las Bougainvilleas,** tel./fax (1) 145-0106, e-mail: omommag@aol.com, offers two semiluxurious guesthouses with kitchenettes and private patios inside a large, walled compound. The tall profile of one of the cottages encloses a sleeping loft overlooking a sitting room and kitchenette and affords a view of the beach and palms to the northwest, while the second *casita* features a round floor plan with a high, palapa roof. Guests may use a good-sized swimming pool and barbecue grill on the grounds. Rates: US$125 s/d.

Apartments and Houses

Monthly rentals in town range from around $350-450 a month for small, local-style cottages with few amenities to US$700-1,000 a month for larger, better-furnished houses.

Villas del Trópico, Calle Colegio Militar at Ocampo, tel. (1) 145-0019, consists of six simple, furnished apartments inside a shady, walled complex for US$100-125 a week, US$300-500 per month. Nightly stays can probably be

arranged in the off season, May-Oct., for US$30-40 a night. Outdoor washing machines may be used at no charge.

El Molino Trailer Park, tel. (1) 145-0140, near the baseball stadium in the southern part of town off Mexico 19, offers two comfortable studio apartments in a restored adobe that was once part of a large sugar mill complex on the site. Each unit has a ceiling fan, mosquito net, kitchenette, and private bath. Rentals are available by the week or month only. Rates: US$125 per week or US$400 per month.

A number of part-time Todos Santos residents rent their houses by the day, week, or month. For other current listings and availability, check with **El Centro de Mensajes** (The Message Center), Plaza de los Cardones, Av. Juárez (Apdo. Postal 48, Todos Santos, BCS 23300), tel. (1) 145-0003, fax (1) 145-0288, e-mail: message@cabonet.net.mx, or **Su Casa,** on Juárez between Obregón and Topete, tel. (1) 145-0219, fax (1) 145-0246, e-mail: heriberto@milagro.cc.

Hostels

Todos Santos Hostel, in a block house on the east side of Mexico 19 as you enter town coming from Cabo San Lucas, offers cheap lodging in a dormitory and one small private room. Shared facilities include an outdoor kitchen area, bathroom/shower, and wash tub and clothesline. The hostel runs a shuttle to Playa Los Cerritos daily, departing at 8 a.m. and returning at 3 p.m., for US$1.60 each way. Sports equipment, such as mountain bikes, surfboards, bodyboards, skim boards, wetsuits, and fishing poles, is available for rent. The management can arrange horseback-riding excursions as well as hiking trips to Sierra de La Laguna. Rates: dorm US$5, private room US$10.

Camping and RV Parks

Hostería Las Casitas (see Bed and Breakfasts, above) has some space for tent campers at US$5 per tent and one person, plus US$2.50 for each additional person.

El Litro RV Park, a big dirt lot surrounded by palm trees, south of Mexico 19 at the end of Calle Olachea, invites campers and RVers to park alongside full hookups for US$10 a night or US$135 a month. Tents are welcome here, too, for US$4 a night.

Three RV slots with *palapa* shelters and full hookups are available at **Villas del Trópico** (see Apartments and Houses, above) for US$12 per night.

El Molino Trailer Park, at the southeast edge of town off Mexico 19, tel. (1) 145-0140, has become a permanent RV community that doesn't rent spaces by the day anymore. RVers interested in long-term leases can try their luck. Facilities include flush toilets, showers, a laundry, and pool. Two rooms are available for rent by the week or by the month (see Apartments and Houses, above).

North of town a maze of sandy roads leads to a string of undeveloped beaches suitable for camping (see Beaches, above). La Pastora is popular with surfers. Camping, both free and fee, is also available at several of the beaches south of Todos Santos; see El Pescadero and Vicinity, above.

FOOD

For a small, relatively undiscovered town, Todos Santos has a surprising number of places to eat, though some seem to flourish and die with each successive tourist season.

Taquerías and Fast Food

Several vendors along the south end of Colegio Militar offer inexpensive but tasty fish tacos—usually either shark or dorado—and shrimp tacos. **Pilar's,** at the northeast corner of Colegio Militar and Zaragoza, is the most well known, but the **Happy Fish** vendor stand on the opposite corner, same side of the street, is even better. Open 11 a.m.-2 p.m.

Popular with locals for inexpensive seafood cocktails and ceviche is **Mariscos Rickles,** a simple unsigned vendor station on Calle Colegio Militar between Zaragoza and Morelos. **Karla's Lonchería,** on Calle Colegio Militar opposite the park, is a little outdoor place serving inexpensive Mexican breakfasts and *antojitos*.

Near the southwest corner of Juárez and Hidalgo in the center of town, **Tacos Chilakos** serves dependable *carne asada,* tacos, quesadillas, and coffee at a few outdoor tables on the sidewalk. Hours tend to fluctuate, but Tacos Chilakos is usually open Tues.-Sun. 8 a.m.-1

p.m., then closed for the afternoon, reopening 7-11:30 p.m. for the evening crowd. Nearby **Tres Hermanos,** Márquez de León at Juárez (opposite La Siempre Vive grocery), is a vendor stand selling especially good fish, shrimp, and clam tacos most days 8 a.m.-2 p.m., but sometimes open longer depending on the season. About a half block southeast is **Lonchería El Mariachi,** which serves *comida* (the menu varies) 9 a.m.-6 p.m. and then switches to *tacos de carne asada* and *papas rellenas* till 10 or 11 p.m. Open daily.

An unnamed vendor stand at the southwest corner of Morelos and Militar is a popular spot for *tacos de cabeza.*

On Degollado (Mexico 19) toward the south edge of town are several popular vendor stands, including **Sabrosa Birria** (goat stew), open during the day; **Carnitas Barajas,** serving *carnitas* during the day and *tacos de carne asada* at night; and **Taquería Rocvic,** featuring *tacos de carne asada,* quesadillas, and *champurrada* (a thick drink made from hot chocolate and cornmeal), open in the evening. **Super Pollo,** on Mexico 19 at Olachea, tel. (1) 145-0078, in the same small complex as Supermercado El Sol, is the only chain eatery in town. As usual Super Pollo serves inexpensive barbecued chicken and fries, with lots of tortillas and salsa. Beans and macaroni salad are offered as sides, all available either to go or at plastic tables on site. Open 10 a.m.-10 p.m.

At the northern outskirts of town on Mexico 19, amid the string of highway vendors selling fruit pastries and honey, a couple of simple *loncherías* offer a limited selection of burritos, tacos, and other *antojitos.* Very inexpensive.

At least three or four hot dog vendor carts roll out in the evening—usually one each on Juárez, Colegio Militar, and Degollado. Most sell only turkey dogs—often wrapped in bacon (ask for *sin tocino* if you don't want the bacon wrap).

Inexpensive Restaurants

The friendly **El Pariente de Ensenada** (also known as Carlos's), has moved to a new location on the southeast corner of Colegio Militar and Hidalgo. While waiting to dine on fresh seafood, you can chat with the English-speaking owner or leaf through his collection of books on Baja. House specialties include fish and shrimp tacos, *pescado frito* (fried fish), *camarones al mojo de* *ajo* (shrimp in garlic butter), and seafood *cocteles*. On request, Carlos is happy to prepare fish tacos with grilled fillets rather than in the usual breaded and fried manner, at no extra cost. A more casual taco stand is attached as an alternative to dining in the restaurant. Open Mon.-Sat. 9 a.m.-midnight.

Another good choice is sand-floor **Mariscos Mi Costa,** Colegio Militar at Ocampo. The *sopa de mariscos* and *camarón al ajo* are particularly recommended. Open daily 10 a.m.-8 p.m.

Old standby **Restaurant Santa Monica,** tel. (1) 145-0204, just north of the Pemex station on Mexico 19 (Calle Degollado), serves tasty shrimp, lobster, and *carne asada* dinners at reasonable prices. Service can be slow, but everything is made from scratch. One of the house specialties is *pollo estilo Santa Monica,* a quarter chicken braised in something akin to barbecue sauce. Open daily 7 a.m.-10 p.m.

If you're heading to La Paz along Mexico 19 and need a cup of java or a bite to eat, consider stopping off at **Lonchería La Garita** near Km 29, about 22.5 km (14 miles) northeast of Todos Santos. With its large *palapa* roof and open-front *carrizo* eating area, it looks much like any other Baja highway truck stop. But the family operating La Garita seems to have a special flair for preparing humble but high-quality fare. The fresh ranch cheese and the bean or *machaca* burritos with *panela* are superb here, as are *empanadas* filled with slightly sweet, cinnamon-spiced *frijolitos.* Yet another major draw is the coffee, made from fresh-roasted and fresh-ground Chiapas beans; many people buy bags of coffee beans from La Garita. Open daily 6 a.m.-6 p.m.

Moderate Restaurants

Popular among locals as well as visitors for fresh seafood, tasty Mexican dishes, and cold beer served in frosted mugs is **Restaurant Las Fuentes,** at Calles Degollado and Colegio Militar, tel. (1) 145-0257. The house specialty is *pescado empapelado,* fish baked in paper with tomatoes, mild chiles, and various other condiments, and it's one of the few restaurants in town with a full bar. You can dine in the well-lighted indoor seating area or out on the *palapa*-roofed patio, surrounded by three fountains, bougainvillea, and palms. Open daily 7 a.m.-9 p.m.

If you're in the mood for some gringo food, **Shut Up Frank's,** Degollado, tel. (1) 145-0146, is worth checking out. This sports bar and grill offers decent American-style dinners such as steak and lobster and a variety of burgers (even veggie), as well as burritos and other Mexican fare. Open Mon.-Sat. 10 a.m.-10 p.m., Sunday 10 a.m.-8 p.m.

At the well-run **Caffé Todos Santos,** tel. (1) 145-0300, housed in a historic building on Centenario between Topete and Obregón, you can choose between indoor seating, on chairs painted by local artists, or outdoor dining, either in the garden area out back or on the shaded veranda in front. The café offers excellent cappuccino and other coffee drinks, hot chocolate, fresh pastries, waffles, omelettes, deli sandwiches (smoked turkey is a specialty), vegetarian sandwiches, ice cream, bagels, granola, fruit shakes (made with produce from the owner's farm), fresh-baked bread, and other snacks. Delicious cheesy pizzas are available on Friday and Saturday evenings. Prices are a little high by local standards but so is the quality of the food, and portions are large. It's open Monday 7 a.m.-2 p.m., Tues.-Sun. 7 a.m.-8 p.m. most of the year, till 9 p.m. during high tourist season.

Relatively new **La Dolce Vita,** behind Land's End Realty on Calle Hidalgo, tel. (1) 145-0397, is a café/restaurant serving Italian cuisine in a pleasant walled brick patio setting. Open Mon.-Sat. 11:30 a.m.-9 p.m.

On Av. Juárez opposite the former Hotel California, **Tequila Sunrise Restaurant Bar** is a colorfully decorated, tourist-oriented restaurant featuring home-style Mexican food. Open daily 10 a.m.-9 p.m.

Fancier Fare

Housed in a 150-year-old *casona* with 46-cm-thick (18-inch-thick) adobe walls, the atmospheric **Café Santa Fé,** on Calle Centenario off Márquez de León facing the plaza, tel. (1) 145-0340, is still *the* place to eat and be seen during the Dec.-April high tourist season. The changing, mostly Italian menu emphasizes the use of fresh, local ingredients (including organic vegetables) to produce wood-fired pizza, ravioli (a shrimp and lobster version is the house specialty), *pasta primavera,* lasagna, fresh seafood, octopus salad, and the occasional rabbit. Complementing the menu are espresso drinks, a full wine list, tiramisu, and fresh fruits. Choose between interior tables or courtyard dining amid palm greenery. The service is crisp, and prices match the café's aristocratic flair. The Santa Fé is open Wed.-Mon. noon-9 p.m.; the restaurant closes each year in October during the town fiesta.

Groceries

The usual assortment of staples can be bought at any of several markets in town, which include: **Mercadito Guluarte** (next to Motel Guluarte), **ISSSTE Tienda** (Av. Juárez between Zaragoza and Morelos), **Tienda Disconsa** (Colegio Militar), and **Supermercado El Sol** (Calle Degollado). El Sol is the only market open on Sunday and the only one open late (till 10 p.m.).

La Siempre Vive, at Calles Juárez and Márquez de León, opens around 7 a.m., which is an hour or two earlier than the others. La Siempre Vive stocks household wares and a few ranch supplies as well as groceries; the meats, cheeses, produce, and honey sold here come from local farms and ranches.

Supermercado Hermanos González, off Mexico 19 at the south end of town on Calle Pedrajo, has the usual *tienda* items but also caters to the northern population by stocking such items as nonfat milk, bagels, yogurt, ricotta cheese, and balsamic vinegar, to name a few. Special orders are welcomed.

Panadería Todos Santos sells *bolillos, pan dulce, coyotes, arepas* and other Mexican-style baked goods cooked in the wood-fired oven, as well as *pan salado,* an Italian-style loaf. Open in the afternoon 2-8 p.m. or until sold out, closed Sunday, the bakery operates from an unsigned two-story brick building at the north end of Calle Rangel near Ocampo.

You can buy fresh and inexpensive corn tortillas for about 50 cents per kilo at the **Tortillería de Todos Santos** on Calle Colegio Militar between Morelos and Márquez de León. **Pescadería Punta Lobos,** a seafood market on Av. Juárez south of Calle Hidalgo, sells fresh fish and shellfish; hours are daily 8:30 a.m.-4 p.m. Even fresher seafood can often be purchased from the *pangeros* at Punta Lobos, south of town.

Agua Sierra de La Laguna (about one km north of town on Mexico 19) is the primary source of purified water for the town. All the various *tiendas* mentioned above sell this water in *garafónes,*

20-liter returnable containers, as well as the usual smaller-sized bottles. Beer is available from any market in town or from the *depositos:* on Calle Colegio Militar adjacent to the post office; on Calle Degollado near the gas station; and also on Calle Degollado next to Super Pollo. Ice is available at most *tiendas,* as well as at the purified-water plant and at beer *depositos.*

Fresh tropical fruits—mangoes, guavas, figs—are most abundantly available during the July-Sept. rainy season, although certain fruits, such as papaya, are available year-round. Fresh vegetables peak in January and February.

Homemade ice cream can be found at **Paletería El Trópico,** at Obregón and Militar, along with refreshing fresh-fruit *paletas* (popsicles). It's usually open 8 a.m.-9 p.m. You may see pushcart vendors selling El Trópico's *paletas* around town. Nearby **Nevería Andrea,** next to Hotel Misión del Pilar (look for the "Carnation" sign), has a good selection of ice cream as well and is open 10 a.m.-10 p.m.

Just north of town on the way to La Paz, along the east side of Mexico 19, vendors sell candies and pastries made from local produce. Among the goodies available: tasty *empanadas* (turnovers) made from mango, guava, and *cajete* (goat milk caramel); *panocha* (brown cane-sugar cakes); lemon peel and coconut candies; wild honey; and refreshing sugarcane juice.

ENTERTAINMENT AND EVENTS

Theater

The nicely restored **Teatro Márquez de León,** Calle Legaspi at Márquez de León, hosts musical and folkloric dance performances from time to time, especially during the annual October fiesta. Before the Teatro de la Ciudad in La Paz was built, this was the only proper theater in the state of Baja California Sur.

Simple outdoor cinemas—featuring grade-C Mexican films with the usual *ranchero/narcotraficante* themes—are sometimes set up next to the soccer field near La Huerta.

Bars and Dancing

The only real cantina in town is **Cañada del Diablo,** a large, round, *palapa*-roofed place a little out of town at the northeastern end of Calle Centenario. Cañada del Diablo offers a fully stocked

Teatro Marquéz de León on the plaza, Todos Santos

bar, including a few choice tequilas, and free popcorn. On occasion local residents will hire a live *norteña* ensemble to play for a party here. Women and families, as well as men, patronize this bar, whose management is good about not letting the rare *borracho* get out of hand.

Shut Up Frank's, on Degollado, is a popular expat bar featuring satellite broadcasts of sporting events. Happy hour is Mon.-Fri. 4-6 p.m. (see Food, above).

Las Palmas Beach Restaurant Video Bar, near Obregón and Militar, features live music on Friday and Saturday nights, music and sports videos at other times, depending on what's happening in the sports world. We haven't eaten there, and we've never seen anyone else eat there either. A very local scene.

Oasis, tucked away off Zaragoza next to the laundromat, is an open-air venue with a large dance floor. It usually opens on weekend nights at about 9:30 p.m., though things don't really get going until around midnight, and the crowd is predominantly local. A decent sound system pumps out dance tunes till the small hours.

The local **Cueva de los Leones** (Lion's Club) holds Saturday evening dances at their hall opposite the former Hotel California. A small cover charge is collected at the door; there's an additional fee to sit at a table.

Events

Fiesta Todos Santos is held around the feast day of the town's patron saint, Virgen del Pilar, on 12 October. For four days beginning the sec-

ond Saturday of the month, residents enjoy dances, soccer and basketball games, fishing tournaments, cockfights, horse races, theater performances, amusement-park rides, and other merriment centered around the church and town plaza.

For 12 days beginning **Día de Guadalupe** (12 December), Todos Santos Catholics participate in nightly candlelight processions to the plaza church. The celebrations culminate in a midnight mass on **Christmas Eve.**

In February the **Todos Santos Fiesta del Arte** is held at various venues around town. Sponsored by local galleries, the show features sculptures, paintings, ceramics, and other visual works by local artists as well as a few out-of-towners. If the town can unite behind it, the Fiesta del Arte could become an important Cape event.

SPORTS AND RECREATION

Much of the outdoor recreation enjoyed in the Todos Santos area—e.g., fishing, swimming, and surfing—focuses on the coast; see Beaches and El Pescadero and Vicinity, above, for beach descriptions.

Fishing

Many of the same gamefish commonly found from Cabo San Lucas to La Paz can be caught offshore here. *Pangas* and fishing guides can be hired at Punta Lobos for US$20-25 per hour with a three-hour minimum. One experienced guide is English-speaking *pangero* Marco Torres; he can be contacted in advance through El Centro de Mensajes.

Surfcasting, though possible at any of the Todos Santos area beaches, is safest and easiest at Playa San Pedrito (Palm Beach), Playa San Pedro, and Playa Los Cerritos (see West Cape Beaches).

Whether fishing onshore or inshore, you'll need to bring your own rods, tackle, and lures. Live bait can be purchased from the local fishermen at Punta Lobos.

Whalewatching

Although you won't see as many whales close to shore here as farther north in Bahía Magdalena (an important calving bay for the Pacific gray whale), newborn calves and their mothers do swim by on their "trial run" to the Sea of Cortez before beginning the long migration back to the Arctic Circle. The best months for spotting grays are Dec.-April.

With a pair of binoculars and some luck, you can stand on any beach in the vicinity and spot grays (and other whales) spouting offshore. One of the best places to see them is near the rocky ridge at Playa Las Pocitas. For a much better view from shore, climb Punta Lobos (see Beaches, above). *Pangeros* at Punta Lobos will take up to five passengers out to see the whales for US$25 an hour; inquire at the beach or at any of the hotels in town.

Surfing

Most of the Pacific breaks near Todos Santos hit their peak during the northwest swell, Dec.-March. See Beaches, above, and El Pescadero and Vicinity for beach locations. Experienced surfers who paddle around the larger points at Punta Lobos and Punta San Pedro during the late summer southern swell will sometimes turn up a nice break, although the usual summer custom is to head for the Corridor between Cabo San Lucas and San José del Cabo or to lesser known spots around the east side of the Cape (see the East Cape section).

You may see auto window stickers bearing the label "Todos Santos Surfboards," but don't go looking for them—they're a small made-in-California brand. The **Todos Santos Hostel** on Mexico 19, at the edge of town if you're coming from Cabo San Lucas, rents boards and wetsuits. Nearby, the new **Todos Santos Surf Shop** at Degollado (Mexico 19) and Rangel also rents surfing equipment.

Baseball

Todos Santos fields its own baseball team at the stadium on Calles Rangel and Villarino.

SHOPPING

Although Todos Santos hardly compares with Cabo San Lucas or San José del Cabo when it comes to variety and quantity, several interesting, high-quality shops have opened during the last few years.

Casa Franco, on Av. Juárez between Morelos and Zaragoza, tel.(1) 145-0356, carries a wide selection of rustic handmade furniture, as well as regional arts and crafts, most of it from mainland Mexico.

Nearby at Juárez and M. de León, in the Plaza de los Cardones commercial center, the recently expanded **El Tecolote Books/Libros,** tel. (1) 145-0295, fax (1) 145-0288, carries a good selection of foreign and Mexican magazines (including surf magazines), new and used paperbacks (trades welcome), maps, and a large number of hardcover and softcover books on Mexican arts, architecture, and culture, as well as over 150 books on tape for sale or rent. It also stocks art supplies such as paintbrushes and watercolor, acrylic, and oil paints. In the same building is **Mangos,** a new gift shop featuring a nice assortment of jewelry, rugs, accessories, textiles, clothing, and furniture from all over Mexico. Open 10 a.m.-5 p.m. Closed Sunday.

Another newcomer is **La Casa D Los Santos,** near the Todos Santos Inn in a historic building at Legaspi and Obregón (the site of the original Todos Santos Inn). The attractively displayed shop carries good-quality Mexican furniture and accessories. Open 9 a.m.-7 p.m.

On Calle Topete at Centenario, opposite Caffé Todos Santos, **El Perico Azul,** tel. (1) 145-0222, features women's clothing made from the best of Mexican textiles, handwoven and minimally processed. The shop also offers a few clothing items from Bali and India, local crafts, jewelry, and some leather pieces. On the opposite side of

Centenario, **Manos Mexicanas** carries rustic Mexican furniture and an interesting selection of decorative accessories and jewelry.

In a historic building, **Fénix de Todos Santos,** at Juárez and Zaragoza, tel./fax (1) 145-0028, is a shop specializing in handcrafted Mexican art. Jewelry, rugs, leather bags, handwoven fabrics, *equipal* furniture, rugs, and decorative tinware are on display, as well as resortwear from Puerto Vallarta.

Less upscale than the above, **Zahuapán,** a *palapa*-roofed *artesanía* on the northwest corner of Márquez de León and Juárez, sells Mexican crafts, T-shirts, quartz, and onyx. The craftspeople also weave *serapes* on site.

If you're looking for tropical plants—bougainvillea, hibiscus, jasmine, oleander, and more—to decorate your local villa, sooner or later you'll end up at **Vivero Heriberto** (formerly Vivero Tres Adelas), a plant nursery on Ocampo a few blocks southeast of Colegio Militar, or **Vivero Las Margaritas,** at Juárez and Ocampo.

Tienda Santander, on Calle Colegio Militar between Calles Márquez de León and Hidalgo, sells handcrafted ranching accoutrements collectively known as *talabartería*—saddles, lariats, bridles, *chaparreras,* and boots—as well as *huaraches* (leather sandals), engraved machetes, and other farm and ranch hardware.

Artist Studios and Galleries

Todos Santos has a small but growing colony of expat artists, most of whom live in or near the town year-round. At last count nine art galleries were in operation, remarkable for a town of less than 5,000 people. One of the first artist arrivals was Charles Stewart, who has a home gallery, the **Charles Stewart Gallery & Studio**—usually referred to as "Stewart House"—at Centenario and Obregón, tel./fax (1) 145-0265. You can't miss this 1810-vintage, French-designed house smothered in foliage and enlivened by caged singing birds. Formerly of Taos, New Mexico, Stewart produces watercolor and oil paintings, wooden sculptures, and handcarved doors; among his more recently conceived works are small *retablo*-style pieces that feature colorful *bajacaliforniano* pictograph motifs on salvaged wood. His home studio is open to the public daily 10 a.m.-4 p.m.

Galería de Todos Santos, at Topete and Legaspi, tel. (1) 145-0050, in the same building as the Todos Santos Inn, is owned by American artist Michael Cope and his wife Pat. The high-ceilinged gallery focuses on the work of artists who reside in Baja California. Look for pieces by Walker and Derek Buckner, Gloria Marie V., Gabo, Nanette Hayles, Robert Gordon, and Paulino Pérez. The works displayed are of high quality—many high-end hotels and restaurants in the Cape Region shop here—and the collection changes every six weeks or so.

A brightly hued house at Juárez and Morelos contains **Galería Logan,** tel. (1) 145-0151, focusing on the work of artist Jill Logan, who creates dramatically colored landscapes, still lifes,

artist Gloria Marie V. at Galería de Todos Santos

and portraits in oil and acrylic. Open Mon.-Sat. 11 a.m.-4 p.m. Logan's work is also featured at **Galería Fidencio,** Centenario and Hidalgo, along with fanciful wood carvings of saints and angels created by owner Fidencio Romero as well as sculptures, paintings, and furniture created by other artists. The historic building in which the gallery is housed was formerly the town billiards hall; it once appeared in a Chris Isaak music video. Hours are Mon.-Sat. 11 a.m.-4 p.m.

Galería/Studio de N.E. Hayles, Calle Cuauhtémoc, tel./fax (1) 145-0183, displays unique paper-tile mosaics, multimedia art, and tables fashioned by the artist/owner. Open Mon.-Sat. 11 a.m.-4 p.m. or by appointment. **Galería El Guayabate,** Zaragoza and Rangel, tel. (1) 145-0364, features watercolors by Margaret McGall-Boyles, Emilio Galindo, and others. Watercolor classes are also offered. Open Mon.-Sat. 10 a.m.-4 p.m.

Next door to the Café Santa Fe (on Calle Centenario facing the plaza), the **Galería Santa Fé,** tel./fax (1) 145-0340, offers a large variety of arts and crafts from all over Mexico, along with accessories of Mexican design and a few works of art by Italian owner Ezio Colombo and other local artists.

Many artists and galleries in town use the quality framing services of **Estudio Gabo,** Calle Progresso between Olachea and Carrillo, tel. (1) 142-3437. Gabo, a native of La Paz, is himself an accomplished artist whose work is inspired by Baja's colors and textures, and his work can be found at Estudio Gabo and at the small **Galería Orsay** on the northwest corner of Centenario and Topete, diagonally opposite Manos Mexicanas.

INFORMATION AND SERVICES

Tourist Information
Although Todos Santos has no tourist office as such, you can usually find someone to answer your questions at El Tecolote Libros, El Centro de Mensajes, or Caffé Todos Santos. If you speak Spanish and seek information on the sierra backcountry, try La Siempre Vive at Calles Juárez and Márquez de León; this is where sierra ranchers traditionally come to supplement foods they produce at home.

The locally produced *El Calendario de Todos Santos,* issued monthly, is an excellent source of current events and short articles on regional culture; it's distributed free at El Centro de Mensajes, El Tecolote Libros, and many other establishments in town.

The Todos Santos Book, written by local residents Lee Moore and Janet Howe and available at El Tecolote Books, contains lots of useful information on things to see and do in the area.

Money
Bancrecer, Calles Juárez at Obregón, is open Mon.-Fri. 8:30 a.m.-1 p.m. Although the bank changes money and cashes traveler's checks only for those who hold Bancrecer accounts, a 24-hour *cajero* (ATM) is available and usually functional.

Post Office
The post office is on Colegio Militar (Mexico 19) between Hidalgo and Márquez de León. It's supposed to open Mon.-Fri. 8 a.m.-1 p.m. and 3-5 p.m., but the hours can be erratic.

Telephone
Long-distance phone calls can be made from the rustic public telephone office at Pilar's, Colegio Militar at Zaragoza; it's open daily 7 a.m.-7 p.m. Be wary of the private phone services that charge outrageous rates for international calls; the phone office at Pilar's is hooked into the latest ripoff system from the United States. Ask to use TelMex or, if you have an access number for your long-distance carrier at home, use that; of course there will be a surcharge, but that's usually cheaper than using the fly-by-night long-distance services that charge as much as US$14 a minute.

El Centro de Mensajes Todos Santos (The Message Center), Juárez at Hidalgo (Apdo. Postal 48, Todos Santos, BCS 23300), tel. (1) 145-0003, fax (1) 145-0288, e-mail: message@ cabonet.net.mx, can give you a quick and honest rate comparison between TelMex, AT&T, MCI, and other telephone companies. The office charges a reasonable surcharge over whichever long-distance service you choose. In addition to long-distance calling, this office offers fax, copying, DHL courier, mail forwarding, reservations, travel agency, and answering services.

An Internet café is a new addition (see below). El Centro de Mensajes is open mid-October through May Mon.-Sat. 8 a.m.-5 p.m., the rest of the year Mon.-Fri. 8 a.m.-1 p.m. and 3-5 p.m., Saturday 8 a.m.-2 p.m.

E-mail and Internet Service
Internet service has recently become available at **El Centro de Mensajes.** Rates are US$4.25 per hour and the coffee is free.

Internet service at similar rates is also available at **Todos Santos Real Estate,** on Juárez between Topete and Hidalgo, tel./fax (1) 145-0269, e-mail: todoreal@todosantos.com.mx. Open Mon.-Sat. 9 a.m.-5 p.m.

Pharmacies
Farmacia Todos Santos, tel. (1) 145-0030, and **Farmacia Guadalupe,** tel. (1) 145-0300, both on Av. Juárez, can fill prescriptions any time of day or night.

Laundry
El Zopilote Lavamática, on Calle Zaragoza near Rangel, has one of the best do-it-yourself laundry facilities in town. It's open Mon.-Sat. 8:30 a.m.-5 p.m. Another choice is **Lavandería Gama,** at Miltar and Hidalgo, inside the Hotel Misión del Pilar. It offers wash-and-dry service and is open Mon.-Sat. 9 a.m.-6 p.m., Sunday 10 a.m.-3 p.m. Hot water is available at both laundries.

A *lavandería* attached to the Hotel Miramar is open Mon.-Sat. 8 a.m.-4 p.m., Sunday 8 a.m.-noon.

Transportation
Seven Águila buses a day run between Todos Santos and La Paz to the north and Cabo San Lucas to the south. The buses to La Paz are scheduled to leave at 8 a.m., 8:30 a.m., 11:30 a.m., 1:30 p.m., 4:30 p.m., 5:30 p.m., and 7 p.m. Buses to Cabo San Lucas and San José del Cabo depart at 10 a.m., 3 p.m., 7 p.m. and 9 p.m.; three buses to Cabo San Lucas only leave at noon, 1 p.m., and 5 p.m. In everyday practice, of course, these times are not strictly adhered to. The La Paz and Cabo San Lucas bus trips take about two hours and cost about US$3 pp; a bus through to San José del Cabo costs US$5. Tickets are sold on the buses, which arrive at and depart from Colegio Militar and Zaragoza, opposite Pilar's fish taco stand/phone office.

Taxis: A small fleet of blue vans parked next to the park opposite Pilar's can provide taxi service around town for US$2 a trip. A van all the way to Los Cabos International Airport will cost US$80; one van can hold 8-10 people with luggage.

RESOURCES
BOOKLIST

DESCRIPTION AND TRAVEL

Berger, Bruce. *Almost an Island: Travels in Baja California*. University of Arizona Press, 1998. Berger, a pianist, poet, desert aficionado, and keen observer of human behavior, surveys Baja's social landscape, with a special focus on La Paz.

Burleson, Bob, and David H. Riskind. *Backcountry Mexico: A Traveler's Guide and Phrase Book*. Austin, TX: University of Texas Press, 1986. Part guidebook, part anthropological study covering Northern Mexico, with some relevance to Baja California backcountry travel.

Cudahy, John. *Mañanaland: Adventuring with Camera and Rifle Through California in Mexico*. Duffie and Co., 1928. Provides an interesting glimpse of pre-WW II Baja, but no outstanding revelations.

Cummings, Joe. *Baja Handbook*. Emeryville, CA: Avalon Travel Publishing, 2000. If you like the Cape Region, you'll probably love the rest of Baja California Sur and Baja California to the north. Now in its fourth edition, this guide covers the entire peninsula from Tijuana to Cabo San Lucas.

Cummings, Joe. *Northern Mexico Handbook*, 2nd ed. Emeryville, CA: Avalon Travel Publishing, 1998. The first guidebook ever published in English to a largely undiscovered region that shares many geographical and cultural characteristics with Baja California. The book covers mainland Mexico's nine northernmost states—Sonora, Sinaloa, Chihuahua, Durango, Coahuila, Nuevo León, Tamaulipas, Zacatecas, and San Luis Potosí.

Mackintosh, Graham. *Into A Desert Place*. Graham Mackintosh Publications, P.O. Box 1196, Idyllwild, CA 92549. A thoroughly engaging report of Mackintosh's walk around the entire coastline of Baja California over the course of two years. Destined to become a classic of gringo-in-Baja travel literature for its refreshingly honest style and insights into Baja fish-camp and village life.

Miller, Max. *Land Where Time Stands Still*. Dodd, Mead, and Co., 1943. A classic travelogue that chronicles Baja life during WW II, when Mexicans alternately fell prey to German and American propaganda.

Salvadori, Clement. *Motorcycle Journeys Through Baja*. Whitehorse Press, 1997. The author, a senior editor for *American Rider* and *Rider*, does an admirable job of digesting the peninsula for other motorcyclists who might want to tackle the Holy Grail of North American road trips. Contains lots of invaluable tips.

Steinbeck, John. *The Log from the Sea of Cortez*. New York: Penguin USA, Viking, 1941. This chronicle of the author's Baja research voyage with marine biologist Ed Ricketts (the inspiration for *Cannery Row* protagonist "Doc") reveals Steinbeck as a bit of a scientist himself. Annotated with Latin, the book is full of insights into Pacific and Sea of Cortez marinelife as well as coastal *bajacaliforniano* society. Sprinkled throughout are expositions of Steinbeck's personal philosophy, implicit in his novels but fully articulated here. Also reveals the source for his novella *The Pearl*.

HISTORY AND CULTURE

Crosby, Harry. *Antigua California*. Albuquerque: University of New Mexico Press, 1996. This well-researched history covers the Jesuit period in Baja, from the mission planning stages in Sonora and Sinaloa through the expulsion from New Spain.

Frances, Padre James Donald. *The Lost Treasures of Baja California.* Black Forest Press, 1996. A slim, hardbound volume containing chronicles of 19 Jesuit missions, in Spanish and English. Notable for its identification of some of the more obscure saints and iconographic elements in the mission sanctuaries, and the inclusion of photos of models constructed by the author depicting missions—such as Comond—that no longer exist.

Paz, Octavio. *The Labyrinth of Solitude: Life and Thought in Mexico.* New York: Grove/Atlantic Inc., Grove Press, 1961. Paz has no peer when it comes to expositions of the Mexican psyche, and this is his best work.

Robertson, Tomás. *Baja California and its Missions.* La Siesta Press, 1978. Robertson was the patriarch of an old Baja California–Sinaloa family of northern European extraction as well as a patron of Baja mission restoration. His useful amateur work synthesizes Baja mission history from several sources; like its sources, the book contains a few minor contradictions and muddy areas.

NATURAL HISTORY

Case, T.J., and M.L. Cody, eds. *Island Biogeography in the Sea of Cortez.* Berkeley: University of California Press, 1983. A collection of essays on the geography and wildlife of various Cortez islands.

Krutch, Joseph Wood. *The Forgotten Peninsula: A Naturalist in Baja California.* Tucson: University of Arizona Press, 1986 (reprint from 1961). Combines natural history and a curmudgeonly travelogue style to paint a romantic portrait of pre-Transpeninsular-Highway Baja.

Leatherwood, S., and R.R. Reeves. *The Sierra Club Handbook of Whales and Dolphins.* San Francisco: Sierra Club Books, 1983. A very useful field guide for identifying cetaceans in Baja seas.

Nickerson, Roy. *The Friendly Whales: A Whale-watcher's Guide to the Gray Whales of Baja California.* San Francisco: Chronicle Books, 1987. A light study, with photographs, of the friendly whale phenomenon in Laguna San Ignacio, where gray whales often initiate contact with humans.

Peterson, R.T. and E. L. Chaliff. *A Field Guide to Mexican Birds.* Boston: Houghton Mifflin Co., 1973. Although it may be a little weak on birds found in Baja, this is still the best handbook for identifying Mexican birdlife.

Roberts, Norman C. *Baja California Plant Field Guide.* Natural History Publishing Co., 1989. Contains concise descriptions of over 550 species of Baja flora, more than half illustrated by color photos.

Scammon, Charles Melville. *The Marine Mammals of the Northwestern Coast of America.* Mineola, NY: Dover Publications reprint, 1968. Originally published in the 19th century by the whaler who almost brought about the gray whale's complete demise, this is *the* classic, pioneering work on Pacific cetaceans, including the gray whale.

Wiggins, Ira L. *Flora of Baja California.* Stanford, CA: Stanford University Press, 1980. This weighty work, with listings of over 2,700 species, is a must for the serious botanist. But for the average layperson interested in Baja vegetation, Norman Roberts's *Baja California Plant Field Guide* (see above) will more than suffice.

Zwinger, Ann Raymond. *A Desert Country near the Sea.* New York: Penguin USA, Truman Talley Books, 1983. A poetic collection of essays centered around Baja natural history (including a rare passage on the Sierra de La Laguna), with sketches by the author and an appendix with Latin names for flora and fauna.

SPORTS AND RECREATION

Fons, Valerie. *Keep It Moving: Baja by Canoe.* Seattle: The Mountaineers, 1986. Well-written account of a canoe trip along the Baja California coastline; recommended reading for sea kayakers as well as canoeists.

Kelly, Niel, and Gene Kira. *The Baja Catch*. Apples and Oranges, 1997. The latest version of this fishing guide pushes it firmly to the top of the heap. Contains extensive discussions of lures and tackle, expert fishing techniques, and detailed directions to productive fisheries, plus numerous maps.

Lehman, Charles. *Desert Survival Handbook*. Phoenix: Primer Publishers, 1990. A no-nonsense guide to desert survival skills; should be in every pilot's and coastal navigator's kits.

Romano-Lax, Andromeda. *Sea Kayaking in Baja*. Berkeley: Wilderness Press, 1993. This inspiring 153-page guide to Baja kayaking contains 15 one- to five-day paddling routes along the Baja coastline, plus many helpful hints on kayak camping. Each route is accompanied by a map; although these maps are too sketchy to be used for navigational purposes, a list of Mexican topographic map numbers is provided so that readers can go out and obtain more accurate material.

Tsegeletos, George. *Under the Sea of Cortez (Early Underwater Exploration and Spearfishing)*. Professional Press, 1998. Early in this case means starting in 1962, and the accounts make for fascinating, if a bit sorrowful (knowing how much marinelife has been lost in just 30 years), reading.

Williams, Jack. *Baja Boater's Guide, Vols. I and II*. H.J. Williams Publications, 1988 (Vol. I) and 1996 (Vol. II). These ambitious guides, one each on the Pacific Ocean and the Sea of Cortez, contain useful aerial photos and sketch maps of Baja's continental islands and coastline.

Wong, Bonnie. *Bicycling Baja*. El Cajon, CA: Sunbelt Publications, 1988. Written by an experienced leader of Baja cycling tours, this book includes helpful suggestions on trip preparation, equipment, and riding techniques as well as road logs for 17 different cycling routes throughout the peninsula.

Wyatt, Mike. *The Basic Essentials of Sea Kayaking*. San Francisco: ICS Books, 1990. A good introduction to sea kayaking, with tips on buying gear, paddling techniques, safety, and kayak loading.

REAL ESTATE

Combs-Ramirez, Ginger. *The Gringo's Investment Guide*. Monmex Publishing, 1994. Succinct but complete advice on buying and selling real estate in Mexico.

Peyton, Dennis John. *How to Buy Real Estate in Mexico*. Law Mexico Publishing, 1994. The most thorough and in-depth reference available in English on buying Mexican property. Anyone considering real estate investments in Mexico should read this book before making any decisions.

ON THE INTERNET

USEFUL WEB SITES

So far World Wide Web sites focusing on the Cape Region are sadly lacking in the quality and quantity of information. Most content is clearly tailored to selling a tourism product—hotel, condo, restaurant, sports activity—without offering related information of much use.

Amigos de Baja BajaNet
http://www.bajanet.com/
Lots of weather and fishing, some road info, good web links, and active discussion centers.

Baja.com
http://www.baja.com/
This newcomer is arguably the best-looking and hippest Baja site on the web. Although the content is still a little on the slim side, this is one to watch.

Baja Nomad
http://www.bajanomad.com
Still the best all-around Baja site for hard information that doesn't appear to have been paid for, with more nitty-gritty information than any rival. Great links page, copious information on hotels and restaurants, plus continually updated Baja news and essays.

Baja-Web
http://www.baja-web.com/
Lots of information on accommodations, transportation, and other practical detail in list form, but slanted toward larger cities.

CNN Weather
http://cnn.com/WEATHER/cities/mexico.html
One of the fastest loading and better all-round weather sites, with info listed by city.

Cruise the Sea of Cortez
http://www.cruisecortez.com/index.html
As the title indicates, this is a site for people who sail or who would like to sail the Cortez. Although it was a year out of date when we last visited, the site nonetheless carries valuable info and links to other sailing-oriented sites.

Eco Travels in Latin America
http://www.planeta.com
A rich site with information on officially protected areas in Mexico and elsewhere in Latin America, as well as regularly updated files on ecologically related news. News on Baja and the Cape Region is a little thin so far, but should improve as the site develops.

Information Pages on Baja California, Mexico
http://math.ucr.edu/~ftm/baja.html
A home-grown, one-man Web site with decent Baja links. The Road Conditions section would be useful if your upcoming Transpeninsular drive happens to coincide with one of the author's recent updates—reportedly every three or four months.

In Search of the Blue Agave
http://www.georgian.net/rally/tequila/index.html
An excellent website devoted to tequila connoisseurship.

Instituto Nacional de Estadística, Geografía e Informática
http://ags.inegi.gob.mx/
This Mexican government agency publishes statistics on population and economics for all of Mexico, as well as complete topographical maps. The maps aren't available online yet, but many statistics are.

Mexican Embassy in Washington, D.C.
www.embassyofmexico.org/english/main2.htm
Carries information posted by the Mexican foreign service regarding visas and other immigration matters, with links to other government sites.

Mexico Online
http://www.mexonline.com/baja.htm
Carries much general information on Mexico in many categories, plus hot links to other sites. Some Los Cabos information as well.

Moon Handbooks
http://www.moon.com
Moon's website contains occasional excerpts from this book and other Moon titles, ordering information, an online travel newsletter with articles on Mexico, and links to various related sites.

Mr.News.Mx
http://www.mrnewsmx.com/default.asp
A news digest for Mexico news in English from many sources.

NaftaNet
http://www.nafta.net
Information pertinent to the North American Free Trade Agreement.

Olsen Currency Converter
http://www.oanda.com/converter/travel
For fast quotes on exchange rates for all international currencies, including the Mexican peso. Print out a "cheat sheet" to make easy conversions without having to do any math.

Quick Aid
http://www.quickaid.com
International airport information and flight schedules.

Secretaría de Turismo (SECTUR)
http:// www.mexico-travel.com
Well-constructed home page for Mexico's Ministry of Tourism, organized by region and by state. Information on the Cape Region is sparse.

SEMATUR
http://www.ferrysematur.com.mx/
Ferry schedules, passenger fares, and reservation information.

U.S. Embassy
http://www.usembassy-mexico.gov/
Contains the home page for the U.S. Embassy in Mexico City, with information on consular services to U.S. citizens as well as State Department warnings.

INTERNET PROVIDERS IN THE CAPE REGION

Baja Net
http://www.baja.net.mx

Cabonet
http://www.cabonet.net.mx

Electrónica Cromwell
http://www.cromwell.com.mx

GLOSSARY

abarrotes—groceries

aduana—customs service

antojitos—literally "little whims," quick Mexican dishes like tacos and enchiladas

bahía—bay

basura—trash or rubbish; the sign No Tire Basura means "Don't throw trash."

boca—literally "mouth," a geographic term describing a break in a barrier island or peninsula where sea meets lagoon

calle—street

cañon—canyon

cardón—*Cereus pringelei,* the world's tallest cactus

carrizo—cane reed

casa de huéspedes—guesthouse

cerro—mountain peak

cerveza—beer

charreada—Mexican-style rodeo

charro/charra—horseman/horsewoman

colectivo—van or taxi that picks up several passengers at a time for a standard per-person fare, much like a bus

correo—post office

corrida de toros—"running of the bulls" or bullfight

COTP—Captain of the Port

curandero—traditional healer

Diconsa—Distribuidora Conasupo, S.A., a government-subsidized food distributor

efectivo—cash payment

ejido—collectively owned agricultural lands

ensenada—cove or small bay

FONATUR—Fondo Nacional de Fomento del Turismo (National Foundation for Tourism Development)

Gral.—abbreviation for "General" (rank)

hostería—hostelry, inn

IMSS—Instituto Mexicano del Seguro Social (Mexican Social Security Institute)

indios—Mexicans of predominantly Amerindian descent

INEGI—Instituto Nacional de Estadística, Geografía e Informática (National Institute of Statistics, Geography, and Information)

ISSSTE—Instituto de Seguridad y Servicios Sociales para Trabajadores del Estado (Security and Social Services Institute for Government Workers)

laguna—lagoon, lake, or bay

llano—plains

lleno—full

malecón—waterfront promenade

mariscos—literally "shellfish," but often used as a generic term for seafood

mercado—market

mescal/mezcal—alcoholic beverage distilled from maguey extract

mochila—knapsack or backpack (*mochilero:* backpacker)

nopalitos—strips of cooked or pickled prickly pear cactus

palacio municipal—literally "municipal palace," equivalent to city or county hall in the U.S.

palapa—thatched umbrella-like shade shelter or roof

PAN—Partido Acción Nacional, the main opposition party to the ruling Partido Revolucionario Institucional (PRI)

panadería—bakery

parrada—bus stop

Pemex—Petroleos Mexicanos (Mexican Petroleum)

pensión—boardinghouse

playa—beach

plazuela—smaller plaza

PRD—Partido Revolucionario Democrático, a close second behind PAN in effective electoral opposition to the PRI

pre-Cortesian—a reference to Mexican history before the arrival of the Spanish conquistador Hernán Cortés, i.e., before 1518; other terms with the same meaning include "pre-Columbian" and "pre-Hispanic"

presidio—military garrison

PRI—Partido Revolucionario Institucional

punta—point

ramal—branch road

rancheria—a collection of small ranching households, most often inhabited by *indios*

ranchito—small ranch

SECTUR—Secretaría de Turismo (Secretariat of Tourism)

SEDESOL—Secretaría de Desarrollo Social (Secretariat of Social Development)

SEMARNAP—Secretaría de Medio Ambiente, Recursos Naturales y Pesca (Secretariat of the Environment, Natural Resources, and Fishing)

tienda—store

tinaja—pool or spring

topes—speed bumps

ultramarinos—delicatessen/liquor store

SPANISH PHRASEBOOK

PRONUNCIATION GUIDE

Consonants

c   as c in cat, before a, o, or u; like s before e or i
d   as d in dog, except between vowels, then like th in that
g   before e or i, like the ch in Scottish loch; elsewhere like g in get
h   always silent
j   like the English h in hotel, but stronger
ll like the y in yellow
ñ   like the ni in onion
r   always pronounced as strong r
rr trilled r
v   similar to the b in boy (not as English v)
y   similar to English, but with a slight j sound. When y stands alone it is
    pronounced like the e in me.
z   like s in same
b, f, k, l, m, n, p, q, s, t, w, x as in English

Vowels

a   as in father, but shorter
e   as in hen
i   as in machine
o   as in phone
u   usually as in rule; when it follows a q the u is silent; when it follows an h or g
    its pronounced like w, except when it comes between g and e or i, when it's also
    silent

NUMBERS

0	cero	11	once	40	cuarenta
1	uno (masculine)	12	doce	50	cincuenta
1	una (feminine)	13	trece	60	sesenta
2	dos	14	catorce	70	setenta
3	tres	15	quince	80	ochenta
4	cuatro	16	diez y seis	90	noventa
5	cinco	17	diez y siete	100	cien
6	seis	18	diez y ocho	101	ciento y uno
7	siete	19	diez y nueve	200	doscientos
8	ocho	20	veinte	1,000	mil
9	nueve	21	viente y uno	10,000	diez mil
10	diez	30	treinta		

DAYS OF THE WEEK

Sunday — *domingo*
Monday — *lunes*
Tuesday — *martes*
Wednesday — *miércoles*

Thursday — *jueves*
Friday — *viernes*
Saturday — *sábado*

TIME

What time is it? — *¿Qué hora es?*
one o'clock — *la una*
two o'clock — *las dos*
at two o'clock — *a las dos*
ten past three — *las tres y diez*
six a.m. — *las seis de mañana*
six p.m. — *las seis de tarde*
today — *hoy*

tomorrow, morning
   — *mañana, la mañana*
yesterday — *ayer*
day — *día*
week — *semana*
month — *mes*
year — *año*
last night — *anoche*

USEFUL WORDS AND PHRASES

Hello. — *Hola.*
Good morning. — *Buenos días.*
Good afternoon. — *Buenas tardes.*
Good evening. — *Buenas noches.*
How are you? — *¿Cómo está?*
Fine. — *Muy bien.*
And you? — *¿Y usted?*
So-so. — *Más ó menos.*
Thank you. — *Gracias.*
Thank you very much. — *Muchas gracias.*
You're very kind. — *Muy amable.*
You're welcome; literally, "It's nothing."
   — *De nada.*
yes — *sí*
no — *no*
I don't know. — *Yo no sé.*
it's fine; okay — *está bien*
good; okay — *bueno*
please — *por favor*
Pleased to meet you. — *Mucho gusto.*
excuse me (physical) — *perdóneme*
excuse me (speech) — *discúlpeme*
I'm sorry. — *Lo siento.*
goodbye — *adiós*

see you later; literally, "until later"
   — *hasta luego*
more — *más*
less — *menos*
better — *mejor*
much — *mucho*
a little — *un poco*
large — *grande*
small — *pequeño*
quick — *rápido*
slowly — *despacio*
bad — *malo*
difficult — *difícil*
easy — *fácil*
He/She/It is gone; as in "She left," "He's
   gone" — *Ya se fue.*
I don't speak Spanish well.
   — *No hablo bien español.*
I don't understand. — *No entiendo.*
How do you say . . . in Spanish?
   — *¿Cómo se dice . . . en español?*
Do you understand English?
   — *¿Entiende el inglés?*
Is English spoken here? (Does anyone
   here speak English?)
   — *¿Se habla inglés aquí?*

TERMS OF ADDRESS

I — *yo*
you (formal) — *usted*
you (familiar) — *tú*
he/him — *él*
she/her — *ella*
we/us — *nosotros*
you (plural) — *vos*
they/them (all males or mixed gender)
   — *ellos*
they/them (all females) — *ellas*

Mr., sir — *señor*
Mrs., madam — *señora*
Miss, young lady — *señorita*
wife — *esposa*
husband — *marido* or *esposo*
friend — *amigo* (male), *amiga* (female)
sweetheart — *novio* (male), *novia* (female)
son, daughter — *hijo*, *hija*
brother, sister — *hermano*, *hermana*
father, mother — *padre*, *madre*

GETTING AROUND

Where is . . . ? — *¿Dónde está . . . ?*
How far is it to . . .?
   — *¿A cuánto queda . . . ?*
from . . . to . . . — *de . . . a . . .*
highway — *la carretera*
road — *el camino*
street — *la calle*
block — *la cuadra*
kilometer — *kilómetro*

mile (commonly used near the
   U.S. border) — *milla*
north — *el norte*
south — *el sur*
west — *el oeste*
east — *el este*
straight ahead — *al derecho* or *adelante*
to the right — *a la derecha*
to the left — *a la izquierda*

ACCOMMODATIONS

Can I (we) see a room?
   — *¿Puedo (podemos) ver un cuarto?*
What is the rate? — *¿Cuál es el precio?*
a single room — *un cuarto sencillo*
a double room — *un cuarto doble*
key — *llave*
bathroom — *lavabo* or *baño*
hot water — *agua caliente*

cold water — *agua fría*
towel — *toalla*
soap — *jabón*
toilet paper — *papel higiénico*
air conditioning — *aire acondicionado*
fan — *ventilador*
blanket — *frazada* or *manta*

PUBLIC TRANSPORT

bus stop — *la parada del autobús*
main bus terminal
   — *terminal de buses*
railway station
   — *la estación de ferrocarril*
airport — *el aeropuerto*
ferry terminal
   — *la terminal del transbordador*

I want a ticket to . . .
   — *Quiero un boleto a . . .*
I want to get off at . . .
   — *Quiero bajar en . . .*
Here, please. — *Aquí, por favor.*
Where is this bus going?
   — *¿Adónde va este autobús?*
roundtrip — *ida y vuelta*
What do I owe? — *¿Cuánto le debo?*

DRIVING

Full, please (at gasoline station).
— *Lleno, por favor.*
My car is broken down.
— *Se me ha descompuesto el carro.*
I need a tow. — *Necesito un remolque.*
Is there a garage nearby?
— *¿Hay un garage cerca?*
Is the road passable with this car (truck)?
— *¿Puedo pasar con este carro
(esta troca)?*

With four-wheel drive?
— *¿Con doble tracción?*
It's not passable — *No hay paso.*
traffic light — *el semáfora*
traffic sign — *el señal*
gasoline (petrol) — *gasolina*
gasoline station — *gasolinera*
oil — *aceite*
water — *agua*
flat tire — *llanta desinflada*
tire repair shop — *llantera*

AUTO PARTS

fan belt — *banda de ventilador*
battery — *batería*
fuel (water) pump —
bomba de gasolina (agua)
spark plug — *bujía*
carburetor — *carburador*
distributor — *distribuidor*
axle — *eje*
clutch — *embrague*

gasket — *empaque, junta*
filter — *filtro*
brakes — *frenos*
tire — *llanta*
hose — *manguera*
starter — *marcha, arranque*
radiator — *radiador*
voltage regulator — *regulado de voltaje*

MAKING PURCHASES

I need . . . — *Necesito . . .*
I want . . . — *Deseo . . .* or *Quiero . . .*
I would like . . . (more polite)
— *Quisiera . . .*
How much does it cost? — *¿Cuánto cuesta?*
What's the exchange rate?
— *¿Cuál es el tipo de cambio?*

Can I see . . . ? — *¿Puedo ver . . . ?*
this one — *ésta/ésto*
expensive — *caro*
cheap — *barato*
cheaper — *más barato*
too much — *demasiado*

HEALTH

Help me please. — *Ayúdeme por favor.*
I am ill. — *Estoy enfermo.*
pain — *dolor*
fever — *fiebre*
stomache ache — *dolor de estómago*
vomiting — *vomitar*
diarrhea — *diarrea*

drugstore — *farmacia*
medicine — *medicina, remedio*
pill, tablet — *pastilla*
birth control pills — *pastillas
anticonceptivas*
condoms — *preservativos*

FOOD

menu — *lista, menú*
glass — *vaso*
fork — *tenedor*
knife — *cuchillo*
spoon — *cuchara, cucharita*
napkin — *servilleta*
soft drink — *refresco*
coffee, cream — *café, crema*
tea — *té*
sugar — *azúcar*
purified water — *agua purificado*
bottled carbonated water — *agua mineral*
bottled uncarbonated water — *agua sin gas*
beer — *cerveza*
wine — *vino*
milk — *leche*
juice — *jugo*
eggs — *huevos*
bread — *pan*

watermelon — *sandía*
banana — *plátano*
apple — *manzana*
orange — *naranja*
meat (without) — *carne (sin)*
beef — *carne de res*
chicken — *pollo*
fish — *pescado*
shellfish — *mariscos*
fried — *a la plancha*
roasted — *asado*
barbecue, barbecued — *al carbón*
breakfast — *desayuno*
lunch — *almuerzo*
dinner (often eaten in late afternoon)
    — *comida*
dinner, or a late night snack — *cena*
the check — *la cuenta*

ACCOMMODATIONS INDEX

general discussion: 46-49
Spanish phrases: 245
Araiza Inn Palmira: 109
Bahía Condo Hotel: 193
Buenavista Beach Resort: 148
The Bungalows: 194
Cabañas de los Arcos: 109
Cabo Inn Hotel: 189-190
Cabo Pulmo Beach Resort: 152-153
Cabo Surf Royale: 178
Cabo Villas: 193
Calinda Beach Hotel: 181
Casa Blanca Inn: 189
Casa de Huéspedes Consuelo: 160
Casa de Huéspedes Palomar: 136
Casa de Huéspedes Sarita: 106
Casa del Jardín: 162-163
Casa del Mar Golf Resort: 179
Casa Miramar Bed & Breakfast: 147-148
Casa Natalia: 161
Casa Rafael's: 191-192
Casa Terra Cotta: 162
Chile Pepper Inn: 190
Club Cabo Motel and Campground Resort: 190-191
Club Cascada: 193
Club El Moro: 108
Club Hotel Cantamar Diver's Lodge: 109
Crowne Plaza Resort: 110
El Ángel Azul: 109
El Cardonal's Hide-A-Way: 145
El Centro de Mensajes: 227
El Molino Trailer Park: 227
Fiesta Americana Grand Cabo del Sol: 181
Fiesta Inn: 161
The Garden Casita: 226-227
Hacienda Beach Resort: 191
Hostería del Convento: 106
Hostería Las Casitas: 226
Hotel Aguamarina: 161
Hotel Bahía Los Frailes: 153
Hotel Best Western Posada Real: 161
Hotel Bungalows Ziranda: 216
Hotel Cabo San Lucas: 180
Hotel California: 226
Hotel Ceci: 160
Hotel Colli: 160

Hotel Diana: 160
Hotel Dos Mares: 189
Hotel El Encanto Inn: 160-161
Hotel Finisterra: 192
Hotel Gardenias: 107
Hotel Guluarte: 225
Hotel Hacienda del Mar: 181
Hotel La Posada de Engelbert: 109
Hotel La Purísima: 107
Hotel Las Auroras: 216
Hotel Lorimar: 107
Hotel Los Arcos: 109
Hotel Mar de Cortez: 190
Hotel Marina: 109, 189
Hotel Mediterrané: 108
Hotel Meliá San Lucas: 191
Hotel Miramar: 107, 225
Hotel Misión del Pilar: 225
Hotel Palacio de los Cabos: 180
Hotel Palmas de Cortez: 147
Hotel Palmilla Resort: 178
Hotel Pekin: 107
Hotel Peria: 108
Hotel Playa del Sol: 146
Hotel Plaza Real: 107
Hotel Posada Terranova: 160
Hotel Punta Colorada: 149
Hotel Punta Pescadero: 145
Hotel Revolución: 107
Hotel San Carlos: 106
Hotel Santa Fe: 190
Hotel Solmar Suites: 192-193
Hotel Twin Dolphin: 180-181
Hotel Yeneka: 107
Howard Johnson Plaza Suites: 162
Huerta Verde Bed & Breakfast Inn: 163
Instituto de la Juventud y el Deporte: 106-107
Jane's Place: 226
La Casa de Santa Brígida: 107
La Casa Mexicana Inn: 110
La Concha Beach Resort & Condos: 109-111
La Concha Hotel and Suites: 110
La Jolla de Los Cabos: 162
La Playita Inn: 163
Las Bougainvilleas: 227
Las Mañanitas: 162
Las Misiones de San José: 162
Las Palmas Casitas: 227
Las Puertas: 227

Las Ventanas al Paraíso: 179-180
Los Milagros Hotel: 190
Marina Cabo Plaza: 192
Marina Fiesta Resort & Hotel: 192-193
Marina Sol Condominiums: 193
Marisol: 161
Martin Verdugo's Beach Resort: 146
Meliá Cabo Real: 179
Meliá Los Cabos All Suites Beach and Golf Resort: 179
Mira Vista Beachfront Condos: 162
Misiones del Cabo: 181
Motel Calafía: 108
Motel Villa del Sol: 108
Mykonos Beach Resort: 162
Olas Hotel: 189
Palmas Suites: 110
Pedregal Villas: 193
Pensión California: 106
Pescadero Surf Camp: 216
Plaza Las Glorias: 193
Posada San Miguel: 106
Presidente Inter-Continental Los Cabos: 161-162
Pueblo Bonito Resort: 191
Pueblo Bonito Rose Resort: 191
Rancho Buena Vista: 148
Rancho Leonero Resort: 149-150
San José Inn: 160
Santa Rosa Hotel and Apartments: 225-226
Siesta Suites Hotel: 189
Su Casa: 227
Suites Las Palmas: 161
Suites Marina: 111
Suites Misión: 110
Suites Terrasol: 193
Todos Santos Hostel: 227
Todos Santos Inn: 226
Tropicana Inn: 160
Vela Windsurf Resort: 146
Villa and Casa del Mar: 153
Villa del Palmar Cabo Beach Resort & Spa: 191
Villas del Trópico: 227
Vista Coral: 110
Viva Cabo Hotel and Cantina: 190
Westin Regina Resort Los Cabos: 178
Yuca's Señor Mañana Hotel: 160
see also specific place

RESTAURANT INDEX

Alfonso's: 166
Ali's Burger: 198
Baja Natural: 165
Bismark II: 114
Bougainvillea Restaurant: 113
Brisa Lighthouse: 166
Burger King: 198
Buzzard Bay Sports Cantina: 147
Café Bar Capri: 113
Café del Trópico: 113
Cafe El Callejón: 114
Café Florentina: 164
Café San Francisco: 114
Café Santa Fé: 229-230
Cafetería El Portón: 164
Cafetería Rosy: 165
Caffé Gourmet: 112
Caffé Todos Santos: 229
California Grill: 113
Capo San Giovanni: 195-196
Carlos'n Charlie's: 114, 197
Carnitas Barajas: 228
Carnitas El Michoacano: 199
Carnitas y Chicharones San
    Pedro: 134
Casa Rafael's: 197
Ché Gaucho: 166
China Gourmet: 113
Cilantro's Bar & Grill: 197
Corre Caminos Café and Bakery:
    165
Da Antonio: 165-166
Da Giorgio's II: 196
Dairy Queen: 198
Damiana: 166-167
The Dock Café: 111-112
Domino's Pizza: 198
Dulcería El Oasis: 135
El Ángel Azul: 113
El Arbol del Tulipán: 165
El Cangrejo Loco: 115
El Chilaquil: 166
El Coral: 197
El Dengue: 199
El Encanto Jarocho: 199
El Mesón del Ahorcado: 165
El Oasis Restaurant and Bar: 113
El Paraíso de San Pedro: 134
El Pariente de Ensenada: 228-
    229
El Pescador: 197

El Pollo de Oro: 198
El Pollo Sinaloense: 198
El Quinto Sol: 115
El Restaurant de Doña Lolita:
    196-197
El Shrimp Bucket: 197
El Taste: 113
El Tecolote: 119
El Zarape: 114
Expresso Café: 113
Fandango: 166
Felix's: 198
The Fish Company: 197
Floriska: 165
Francisco's Café: 195
Giggling Marlin: 198
Happy Fish: 228
Iguana Bar: 167
Karla's Lonchería: 228
Kaz: 195
KFC: 198
Kiwi Restaurant Bar: 113
La Bamba: 197
La Caleta: 115
La Carreta: 196
La Casada: 178
La Cenaduría: 166
La Cochinita: 112
La Concha Beach Club and
    Restaurant: 175, 177
La Conchita: 166
La Diligencia: 196
La Dolce Vita: 229
La Fabula Pizza: 112
La Paz Gourmet: 114
La Pazta: 113
La Perla: 196
La Playita: 167
La Provence Garden
    Restaurant/Bar: 166
La República: 196
Las Palmas: 197-198
Las Quesadillasss: 198
La Terraza: 113
Latitude 22: 195
Le Bistro Français: 113
Lonchería Choya: 216
Lonchería El Mariachi: 228
Lonchería La Garita: 229
Lonchería La Pasadita: 167
Lonchería Rosita: 216

Los Arboles: 216
Los Dos Ricardos: 167
Los Gorditos: 167
McDonald's: 198
Magnolia: 195
Mañanas Pizza: 147
Mar de Cortéz: 115
Mariscos Mi Costa: 229
Mariscos Mocambo: 197
Mariscos Rickles: 228
Mercado Bravo: 112
Mercado Municipal Francisco E.
    Madero: 112
Mi Casa: 196
Mi Cocina: 164
Mi-Lien: 112
Nancy's Restaurant and Bar: 153
Nick-San Sushi Bar: 195
Olé Olé: 195
O Mole Mío Restaurant & Bar:
    196
100% Vitalidad: 165
Otra Vez Restaurant and Cantina:
    147
Palapa Azul: 119
Pancho's: 197
Pazzo's Cabo: 195
Peacocks: 195
Peña La Pitahaya de Janicua: 114
Penthouse Racing Club: 112
Pietro Ristorante Italiano: 165
Pilar's: 228
Pitahayas: 181
Pizza Hut: 198
Pizzería Tropicana: 165
Posada Terranova: 167
Recreo: 165
Restaurant Arrecifes: 178
Restaurant/Bar El Gringo Viejo: 167
Restaurant Bar Jazmín: 166
Restaurant Bar Mariscos Don
    Mares: 115
Restaurant-Bar Pepe's: 175, 178
Restaurant Bermejo: 115
Restaurant Calafia: 148
Restaurant Dragón: 112
Restaurant El Caballero: 152
Restaurant El Descanso: 164
Restaurant El Mexicano: 114
Restaurant El Paso: 135
Restaurant El Sinaloense: 167

Restaurant Grill Campestre: 112
Restaurant La Gaviota: 148
Restaurant La Mar y Peña: 114
Restaurant Las Bugambilias: 138
Restaurant Las Fuentes: 229
Restaurant Las Hornillas: 164
Restaurant Los Burritos: 135
Restaurant Marimar: 145
Restaurant Migriño: 213
Restaurant Miraflores: 138
Restaurant Pacífico: 195
Restaurant Plaza Real: 114
Restaurant San Lucas (Broken Surfboard): 198
Restaurant Santa Monica: 229
Restaurant Xochimilco: 167
Río Grill: 197
Ristorante Italiano Galeón: 196
Romeo's Pizza: 112
Romeo y Julieta: 196

Rosticería California: 114
Rusty Putter Bar and Grille: 165
Sabrosa Birria: 228
Salsitas: 197
Sancho Panza: 195
Sandrick's: 165
The Shrimp Factory: 197
Shut Up Frank's: 229
Squid Roe: 198
Sunrise Café: 147
Super Pollo: 114, 165, 198, 228
Super Tacos de Baja California Hermanos Gonzales: 164
Super Tacos de Baja California Hermanos González: 112
Sushi Express: 112
Tacos Chilakos: 228
Tacos el Chilorio: 198
Tacos El Indio: 164-165
Taquería Erika: 164

Taquería los Faroles: 112
Taquería los Paisas: 198-199
Taquería Los Superburros: 112
Taquería Rocvic: 228
Taquería Rossy: 164
Tequila Bar Restaurante: 164
Tequila Sunrise Restaurant Bar: 229
Teriyaki San: 112
Tío Pablo's: 147
Tío's Tienda: 147
Tito's: 153
Tonantzin: 115
Tres Hermanos: 228
Tropicana Bar & Grill: 167
Twin Dragon: 166
VAS: 113
Viejo Oeste: 112
Wabo Grill: 199
Zipper's: 167

INDEX

A

acacia: 11
agaves: 9-10
Agua Caliente: 136
air travel: general discussion 82-83, 88; airlines, list of 88; Cabo San Lucas 210; charter flights 88; La Paz 129-130; San José del Cabo 172; *see also specific place*
Alamo: 27
alcoholic beverages: 57-60; *see also* bars/cantinas; Restaurant Index; *specific place*
American Express: 129
Amerindians: general discussion 20-21; Cochimí people 20-21; Guaicura people 20, 100, 156-157, 221; Guaycuras 20-21, 184; Las Cuevitas petroglyphs 122; Museo de Antropología 103; Pericú people 25, 100, 156-158, 184, 186; *see also specific place*
Antigua Los Cabos: 169
antojitos: 51-52
apartment/condo/house rental: general discussion 48-49; Cabo San Lucas 193-194; La Paz 110-111; Los Barriles 147; San José del Cabo 162; Todos Santos 227; *see also specific place*
aphrodisiacs: 11
architecture/historic buildings: 222
Arrecife de la Foca: 133
Arte Contemporaneo and Antiques: 169
Artesanía Cuauhtémoc: 118
Artesanías La Antigua California: 118
Artesanos: 202
arts and crafts: Cabo San Lucas 201; La Candelaria 213-214; La Paz 118; Miraflores 138; San José del Cabo 169; Todos Santos 232-234; Todos Santos Fiesta del Arte 231
Asociación Nacional de Guías en Ecoturismo y Turismo de Aventura: 140

B

ATMs/debit cards: 75, 171, 209
ATV trail rides: 205-206

backpacking: *see* hiking/backpacking
Bahía de la Ventana: 132
Bahía de Los Frailes: 153
Bahía de los Muertos: 132
Bahía de Palmas: 144-145
Bahía Pulmo: 150-151
Bahía San Gabriel: 122
Baja Coast SeaFaris: 125-126
Baja Diving and Service: 126
Baja Expeditions: 126-127
Baja Quest: 126, 128
Banco Golden Gate: 202

Banco San Jaime: 202
banks/banking: general discussion 75-76; business hours 81; Cabo San Lucas 209; La Paz 128-129; San José del Cabo 171; *see also specific place*
barracuda: 16-17
barrel cactus: 8-9
bars/cantinas: general discussion 60-61; bar lingo phrases 60; Cabo San Lucas 199-200; La Paz 116; San José del Cabo 168; Todos Santos 230-231; *see also* discos/nightclubs; Restaurant Index; *specific place*

BEACHES

best beaches: 33
Cabo Pulmo: 151
Las Cruces: 120
Península El Mogote: 120
Playa Acapulquito: 170
Playa Baladra: 119
Playa Balconcito: 188-189
Playa Barco Varado: 177
Playa Buenos Aires: 177
Playa Cabo Bello: 177, 208
Playa Cabo Real: 177
Playa Caimancito: 118-119
Playa Cantamar: 177
Playa Capulquito: 177
Playa Cemeterio: 175
Playa Chileno: 175, 177, 204
Playa Corral de Los Frailes: 151
Playa Costa Azul: 167, 170, 174-175, 177
Playa Coyote: 120
Playa del Amor: 188, 204
Playa del Tesoro: 119
Playa El Coromuel: 118
Playa El Médano: 188, 190
Playa El Mirador: 175
Playa El Tecolote: 119
Playa El Tule: 177
Playa Escondida: 188

Playa La Cachora: 224
Playa La Pastora: 225
Playa Las Cabrillas: 215
Playa La Siernita: 151
Playa Las Pocitas: 224
Playa Las Viudas: 175
Playa Los Cerritos: 216
Playa Migriño: 212-213
Playa Palmilla: 175
Playa Palmira: 118
Playa Pichilingue: 119
Playa Punta Colorada: 119
Playa San Pedrito: 217
Playa San Pedro: 216-217
Playa Santa María: 175, 177, 204
Playa Solmar: 188, 192
Puerto Algodones: 224
Punta Arena: 150
Punta Chileno: 177
Punta Colorada: 149-150
Punta Conejo: 225
Punta Gorda: 154
Punta Lobos: 222, 224
Punta Marqués: 225
Punta Palmilla: 177
Punta Pescadero: 145
see also islands; *specific place*

bass: 16; *see also specific place*
Becerra, Capt. Diego: 21-22
bed and breakfasts: Buena Vista 147-148; Cabo San Lucas 194; La Paz 110; San José del Cabo 162-163; Todos Santos 226
beer: 57, 60; *see also* bars/cantinas; Restaurant Index; *specific place*
Biblioteca de Histórica de las Californías: 103, 105
Biblioteca Justo Sierra: 103
bicycling/mountain biking: general discussion 89-90; best off-highway cycling 33; La Paz 128; Los Barriles 146; tours 90, 171
billfish: 14; *see also specific place*
billiards: 117
birds/birdwatching: 17-18, 159; *see also specific place*
Bisbee's Black and Blue Marlin Jackpot Tournament: 201
bites/stings: 63-64
biznaga: 8-9
boating: general discussion 39-42; Cabo Pulmo 152; Cabo San Lucas 206-207; Captain of the Port 172; charters/excursions 41, 125-126, 206; fuel/supplies 42; La Paz 124-126; nautical charts 41; parts/repairs 125; permits/regulations 41-42, 131; shuttle service 123; tide tables 41; trailering 40; *see also* marinas; ocean cruises/yacht travel; skiffs/*pangas; specific place*
Boca de la Sierra: 138
bookshops: Cabo San Lucas 201-202; San José del Cabo 169-170; Todos Santos 232
border crossings: 68
Bravo, Jaime: 221
bribes: 72-73
Buena Vista: 147-148
bullfights: 117
business hours: 81
business travel: 67
bus service: general discussion 82-84, 88; Cabo San Lucas 210-211; La Paz 130-131; San José del Cabo 172-173; Spanish phrases 245; Todos

Santos 235; *see also specific place*

C
Cabo del Sol: 181-182, 207
Cabo Falso: 212-213
Cabo Pulmo: 150-153, 204
Cabo Real: 179, 182, 207
Cabo San Lucas: general discussion 183-185; accommodations 189-194; beaches 187-189; campgrounds/RV parks 190-191, 194; climate 184; entertainment 199-201; festivals/events 201; food/restaurants 195-199; history 184, 186-187; services 208-210; shopping 201-202; sports/recreation 202-208; tourist information 208; transportation 210-211; *see also* Accommodations Index; Restaurant Index; *specific place*
Cabo San Lucas Country Club: 207
Cabrillo, Juan Rodríguez: 184
cacti: 8-9, 139
Caliente Race and Sports Book: 117, 208
campgrounds/RV parks: general discussion 35, 49; Bahía de la Ventana 132; Buena Vista 148; Cabo San Lucas 190-191, 194; camping gear regulations 69; El Cardonal 145; El Pescadero 216; Isla Espírutu Santo 122-123; Isla Partida 122-123; La Paz 111; La Ribera 149; Los Barriles 147; San Antonio de la Sierra 136; San José del Cabo 163-164; San Pedro 216-217; Todos Santos 227-228; travel clubs/discounts 81; *see also specific place*
Canada/Canadians: Canadian Consulate 171; entry regulations for Canadians 66-68; overstay penalties 67; reentering Canada 72
candies: 55
canoes: 159; *see also* kayaking
Cañon San Bernardo: 142

Cañon San Dionísio: 139-140
Cañon San Pablo: 142
cantinas: *see* bars/cantinas
Cape Loop: 33-34
Cape Oak-Piñon Woodlands: 2-3
Captain of the Port: 172
Cárdenas, Lázaro: 29
cardón: 8
Carnaval: 117-118
Carranza, Venustiano: 28
car rental: *see* driving; roads/routes; *specific place*
Cartes: 201
Casa de la Cultura: 222
Casa Franco: 232
Casa María: 118
Cascada del Refugio: 219
Catedral de Nuestra Señora de La Paz: 103
Catholic church: general discussion 24-26; Catedral de Nuestra Señora de La Paz 103; Iglesia Nuestra Señora del Pilar 222; Iglesia San José 159; *see also* missions; *specific person; place*
Cavendish, Sir Thomas: 23, 101, 184
celebrities: 29, 120
Centro de Arte Regional: 118
Centro de Idiomas, Cultura y Comunicación (CICC): 129
ceramics: *see* pottery/ceramics
Cerro las Casitas: 138
Cerro La Vigía: 187
Cerro Los Viejos: 217
cerveza: 57, 60
charreadas: 117, 200-201
charter boats/fishing boats: *see* boating; fishing/fishing charters
charter flights: 88
children's library: 103
cholla: 9, 139
chubascos: 7, 100
chuckwalla: 18
churches: *see* Catholic church; missions; *specific place*
cigars: 71-72, 169, 202
climate: general discussion 5-8; Cabo San Lucas 184; La Paz 99-100; San José del Cabo 155; Todos Santos 220-221; *see also specific place*
climbing: 188

Cochimí people: 20-21
coconut palm: 11
coffee/coffeehouses: general
    discussion 57; Cabo San Lucas
    202; La Paz 112-113, 116;
    Todos Santos 229
condo rentals: see
    apartment/condo/house rental
cooking methods: 53
Copal: 169
cordonazos: 7
coromuels: 7, 100
The Corridor: general discussion
    174, 176; accommodations
    177-181; beaches 174-175,
    177; food/restaurants 175, 178;
    sports/recreation 177, 181-182
Cortés, Hernán: 4-5, 21-22, 100
corvinas: 14
cottonwood trees: 12
coyotes: 12
credit cards: 74-75, 129
croakers: 14
Cuban products/cigars: 71-72,
    202
Cuco's: 215-216
curanderos 213
currency exchange: general
    discussion 73-75; Cabo San
    Lucas 209; La Paz 128-129;
    San José del Cabo 171; Todos
    Santos 234; see also specific
    place
customs regulations: 69, 71-72

D
damiana: 3, 11, 139
date palm: 10-11
datura: 12
Decor America Interiors: 202
deer: 12
de Guzmán, Nuño: 21-22, 100
dehydration: 62
de Iturbi, Capt. Juan: 24
de Iturbide, Augustín: 26
desert iguana: 18
deserts: 3, 33; see also specific
    place
desserts: see sweets/desserts
de Ugarte, Padre Juan: 101
de Ulloa, Capt. Francisco: 4, 22
DHL: 129
Día de Guadalupe: 231
diarrhea: 61-62

DIVING/ SNORKELING

general discussion: 45-46
Bahía de la Ventana: 132
best diving/snorkeling
    areas: 33
Buena Vista: 148
Cabo Pulmo: 152
Cabo San Lucas: 188,
    204-205
Club Hotel Cantamar
    Diver's Lodge: 109
The Corridor: 177
Isla Cerralvo: 133
Isla Espíritu Santo: 122
La Paz: 126-128
Los Barriles: 146
Punta Arenas de la
    Ventana: 132-133
recompression chambers:
    46, 205
San José del Cabo: 170
tours/instruction: 46, 148,
    171
Vigilantes Marinos: 204-205
see also specific place

Díaz, Porfirio: 28
discos/nightclubs: best of Cape
    Region 33; Cabo San Lucas
    200; La Paz 116-117; San José
    del Cabo 168; Todos Santos
    231
diving/snorkeling: general
    discussion 45-46; Bahía de la
    Ventana 132; best dolphins: 13
Dominicans: 26-28
dorado: 14, 16
Dos Lunas: 201
Drake, Sir Francis: 22-24, 184
drinking water: 56-57, 61, 230
driving: general discussion 84-86,
    91-98; boat trailering 40; Cabo
    San Lucas 211; gas/oil 95-96;
    Green Angels 97; insurance
    requirements 69, 84-85;
    parts/repairs 96-97;
    precautions/hazards 92-94;
    rental cars 85-86, 97-98, 131,
    173, 211; roadblocks 72-73;
    road signs 94; Spanish phrases

94, 96, 246; traffic offenses 95;
    vehicle permits 69, 85-86, 130;
    see also roads/routes; specific
    place
drug offenses: 72
dulcerías: 55
Dye, Roy: 207

E
ecology: Bahía de Palmas 145;
    islands 4, 35; marine life 15;
    organizations 169, 172; reef
    system 151-152; Sierra de La
    Laguna 139
economy 186-187; see also
    specific place
El Aguaje: 143
El Arco: 187
El Bajito: 127
El Bajo: 127
El Bajo de los Meros: 151
El Camino Rural Costero: 150
El Cantil: 151
El Cardonal: 145
El Chorro: 136
El Dorado: 207; Golf Course 182
electrical current: 76
El Embudo: 122
El Faro Viejo: 212
El Islote: 151
El Perico Azul: 232
El Pescadero: 215-216
El Triunfo: 134-135
embassies/consulates: Canadian
    Consulate 171; Mexican
    Consulate in San Diego 68;
    U.S. Consular Agent 209
emergencies: emergency
    evacuation 64-65;
    recompression chambers 46,
    205; see also specific place
Ensenada de los Muertos: 132
entertainment: Cabo San Lucas
    199-201; La Paz 116-117; San
    José del Cabo 168-169; Todos
    Santos 230-231; see also
    specific place
epidemics: 25, 221
Estero San José: 159
Estudio Gabo: 234
explorers: 21-22; see also specific
    person; place
extended stays/residency visas:
    67-68

FISHING/FISHING CHARTERS

general discussion: 14-17, 35-39, 186-187
Bahía de la Ventana: 132
Bahía de Palmas: 144-145
Bahía Pulmo: 152
best fishing areas: 33
Bisbee's Black and Blue Marlin Jackpot Tournament: 201
Cabo San Lucas: 202-204
Gorda Banks: 154
Isla Cerralvo: 133
La Paz: 124
licenses/regulations: 38-39, 69
Los Barriles: 146
Punta Arenas de la Ventana: 132-133
San José del Cabo: 170
Spanish phrases: 38
tide tables: 38
Todos Santos: 231-232
world records/fish size: 36, 202
see also specific place

F

Faces of Mexico: 201
fauna: 12-19, 139; see also specific fauna; place
Fazio, Tom: 182
Fénix de Todos Santos: 233
ferry service: 86-87, 129-130, 210
festivals/events: 117-118, 169, 231; see also specific place
Fiesta de La Paz: 118
Fiesta Todos Santos: 231
film/cinema: 117, 168-169
Finisterra: 187
first aid: see health/first aid
fishing industry: 186; see also specific place
flatfish: 16
flora: 8-12, 139; see also specific flora; place
flying fish: 17
food/drink: 50-62; Spanish phrases 247; see also

bars/cantinas; Restaurant Index; specific place
fossils/minerals: 103
Franciscans: 26
furniture/home decor: 169, 201-202, 232-233; see also specific place

G

Gaby's Huaraches: 201
Galería de Todos Santos: 233
Galería de Wentworth Porter: 169
Galería El Guayabate: 234
Galería Fidencio: 234
Galería Logan: 233-234
Galería Los Cabos: 169
Galería Orsay: 234
Galería Santa Fé: 234
Galer/iáStudio de N.E. Hayles: 234
galloping cactus: 9
gambling: 117, 208
gardens: 103
gasoline/fuel/oil: boating fuel 42; La Paz 131; Pemex stations 95-96; see also specific place
geography: see land
golf courses: Cabo del Sol 182; Cabo Real 182; Cabo San Lucas 207; Casa del Mar Golf Resort 179; Meliá Los Cabos All Suites Beach and Golf Resort 179; San José del Cabo 170; see also specific place
González, Padre Gabriel: 221
Gorda Banks: 154, 204
Green Angels: 97
Green Tortoise: 84
Greyhound Bus Lines: 83
gringo defined: 32
grocery markets: general discussion 55-56; Cabo San Lucas 199; El Pescadero 216; La Paz 115-116; Los Barriles 147; San Jose del Cabo 167-168; Todos Santos 230; see also specific place
Guadalupe Island palm: 10
Guaicura people: 20, 100, 122, 156-157, 221
Guaycuras: 20-21, 184
guesthouses: 226-227
guides/tours: bicycling/mountain

biking 90, 171; city tours 128; diving/snorkeling 118, 126-128, 148, 171, 205; fishing 124, 170, 203-204; Green Tortoise 84; hiking 140, 143, 171; kayaking 43, 123, 126; walking 171; whalewatching 13, 152, 208; see also specific activity; place
Gulf Coast Desert: 3
guns: 72
gyms: 207

H

hallucinagens: 12
health/medical care: general discussion 61-65; curanderos/healers 213; emergency evacuation 64-65; hiking 34-35; medical assistance 64-65; pharmacies 235; recompression chambers 46, 205; Spanish phrases 246; see also specific place
herbs: general discussion 12; Biblioteca Justo Sierra 103; curanderos/healers 213; damiana 3, 11
Hidalgo y Costilla, Padre Miguel: 26
highlights: 33-34
hiking/backpacking: best hiking areas 33; Cerro Los Viejos 217; guides/tours 140, 143, 171; Isla Espíritu Santo 122; Playa San Pedrito 217; Sierra de La Laguna 139-143; supplies 34-35, 142-143; trails 34, 141
history: general discussion 20-30; Cabo San Lucas 184, 186-187; La Paz 100-103; San José del Cabo 156-158; Todos Santos 221-222; see also specific person; place
horseback riding: 207-208
hostels: 48, 106-107, 160, 227; see also specific place
hot chocolate: 57
hot springs: 136
house rentals: see apartment/condo/house rental
house-sitting: 49
huaraches: 201, 215-216

I

Iglesia Nuestra Señora del Pilar: 222
Iglesia San José: 159
immigration/customs: border crossings: 68; Cabo San Lucas 209; entry regulations 66-68; extended stays/residency visas 67-68; La Paz 129; tourist fee 66; travel with pets 67; vehicle permits/insurance requirements 69, 84-86, 130
inflatable boats: 40
inflation/devaluation: 74-75
insects: 63-64
Instituto de la Juventud y el Deporte: 106-107
Instituto Tecnológico de La Paz: 106
insurance requirements: 69, 84-85
internet/email access: general discussion 79-80; Cabo San Lucas 209; La Paz 129; providers 240; San José del Cabo 171; Todos Santos 235; useful web sites 239-240
Isla Cerralvo: 127, 133
Isla Espíritu Santo: 122-123, 127
Isla Espírutu Santo: 122-123
islands: general discussion 4, 120-122; best islands to visit 33; camping 35; El Bajito 127; El Bajo 127; Isla Cerralvo 127, 133; Isla Espíritu Santo 122, 127; island-hopping 4; Isla Partida 122, 127; Isla San Francisco 122; Isla San José 122; Isla Santa Cruz 127; Islas Las Animas 127; La Reinita 127; Los Islotes 122, 127
Isla Partida: 122-123, 127
Isla San Francisco: 122
Isla San José: 122
Isla Santa Cruz: 127
Islas Las Animas: 127

J

jack fish: 14
jejenes: 63
jellyfish: 64
Jesuits: 24-26, 134, 157-158, 221
jewelry: 118, 169, 201, 232; *see also specific place*

Jiménez, Fortún: 22, 100
jimsonweed: 12
Jones, Robert Trent: 181
Joyería Albert: 201
Juárez, Benito: 27-28

KL

kayaking: general discussion 42-43; best places for kayaking 33; Cabo San Lucas 188, 208; islands 120, 123; La Paz 126; Los Barriles 146; San José del Cabo 170
La Bocana: 225
La Candelaria: 213-215
La Casa D Los Santos: 232
La Esperanza: 151
La Fortuna: 154
La Hormiga: 169
La Laguna: 138-139
La Mina: 169
la mordida/ bribes: 72-73
land: 1-5; *see also specific place*
land mammals: 12-13
Land's End: 187
language: 31-32, 129; *see also* Spanish language/phrase translation
La Paz: general discussion 99, 104; accommodations 106-111; beaches 118-120; campgrounds/RV parks 111; city tours 128; climate 99-100; entertainment 116-117; festivals/events 117-118; food/restaurants 111-116; history 100-103; islands 120-123; services 128-129; shopping 118; sights 103, 105-106; sports/recreation 124-128; tourist information 128; transportation 129-131; *see also* Accommodations Index; Restaurant Index
La Playita: 163, 167
La Reina/La Reinita: 127, 133
La Ribera: 148-149
La Rotonda de los Sudcalifornianos Illustres: 105
La Saniuqueña Bullring: 200-201
La Sanluqueña Bullring: 208
Las Casitas: 151
Las Cruces: 120
Las Cuevas: 138

Las Cuevitas: 122
Las Navajas: 151
La Unidad Cultural Profesor Jesús Castro Agúndez: 105
leatherwork: 138, 201-202, 215-216, 233; *see also specific place*
legal matters/legal system: arrest, in case of 73; police/military 72-73; traffic offenses 95; *see also* immigration/customs; licenses/permits; *specific place*
libraries: Biblioteca de Histórica de las Californías 103, 105; Biblioteca Justo Sierra 103
licenses/permits/regulations: boats 41-42; fishing 38-39; tourist permits/visas 66-67; vehicle permits 69, 85-86, 130
lighthouses: 212, 224
liquified petroleum gas (LPG): 96
living in Baja: extended stays/residency visas 67-68; purchase/lease of property 70-71
lizards: 18
Los Barriles: 146-147
Los Cabos International Airport: 82
Los Frailes: 187
Los Islotes: 122, 127
Los Lobos del Mar Kayak Ventures: 170

M

Madero, Francisco: 28
madrone: 139
madroño: 3
maguey: 10
malecón: 105-106
Mangos: 232
mangroves: 3-4
Manila galleons: 22-23, 100-101, 184, 186-187
Manos Mexicanas: 233
maps: 34, 81-82; nautical charts 41; topographic 82, 142
marble: 202
Marina Cabo San Lucas: 206-207
marinas/marine supplies: 124-126; *see also specific place*
marine mammals: 13
marlin: 202-203
Marmol y Granito: 202

Márquez de León International Airport (LAP): 82, 129
marshes: see wetlands
Mar y Aventuras: 126
matorral: 139
Maximilian, Ferdinand: 28
May y Aventuras: 123
Mazatlán-La Paz ferry: 87
medical care: see health/medical care
Mercado Abastos: 115
Mercado Bravo: 112, 115
Mercado Mexicano 201
Mercado Municipal Francisco E. Madero: 112, 115, 118
mescal: 59
mesquite trees: 11
Mexican-American War: 26-28, 102, 158
Mexican Consulate: 68
Mexican fan palm: 10
Mexican needlefish: 17
Mexican piñon pine: 3, 11
Mexican Revolution: 28-29
México Lindo: 118
Migriño: 212-213
mimosa trees: 11-12
miniature golf: 169
mining industry: 28, 134-135
minors: 66
Miraflores: 137-138
missions: history of 24-26, 101, 157-158, 221; Misión de Santiago el Apóstol 136; Misión Santa Rosa de las Plamas: 221; see also Catholic church; specific person; place
money matters: see banks/banking; currency exchange
mosquitoes: 63
motion sickness: 62-63
motorcycles/motor scooters: 98, 131
motor oil: 96
mountain biking: see bicycling/mountain biking
mountain lions: 12
mountains: 2-3, 138-143, 217, 219; see also specific place
museums: Casa de la Cultura 222; La Unidad Cultural Profesor Jesús Castro Agúndez 105; Museo de Antropología 103

N
NAFTA (North American Free Trade Agreement): 67, 69, 72
nautical charts: 41
newspapers: 128, 208; see also specific place
Nicklaus, Jack: 181-182, 207
nightclubs/nightlife see bars/cantinas; discos/nightclubs
Nómadas de Beja: 171
nopal: 9

O
oak trees: 11
Obregón, Álvaro: 28-29
O'Brien, John: 157
ocean cruises/yacht travel: general discussion 41-42; La Paz 124-126, 130-131; marinas/marine supplies 124-126; permits/regulations 41-42, 131; see also marinas; specific place
off-highway/off-road travel: general discussion 91-92; ATV trail rides 205-206; Cabo Falso 212-213; Cascada del Refugio 219
oil industry: 29; see also motor oil
opuntia: 9
organized tours: see guides/tours
Outer Pulmo: 151
outfitters/sports equipment: Cabo Pulma 152; Cabo San Lucas 44, 202, 204-205, 208; La Paz 118, 126; Los Barriles 44; San José del Cabo 44, 169-171; Todos Santos 232; see also specific activity; place; sport
overseas visitors entering U.S. from Mexico: 68
overstay penalties: 67

P
Pacific bonito: 16
Palmilla: 181-182
Palmilla Golf Club: 207
palmita 3, 10
palo blanco: 11-12
Palo Escopeta: 154
panaderías: 56
pangas: see skiffs/pangas
Parque Zoológico: 136
pearls/oysters: 102, 120

people: 30-32; see also specific people; place
Pericú people: 25, 100, 156-158, 184, 186
petroglyphs: 122
pets: 67
pharmacies: see health/medical care
photography equipment: 69
Picacho de La Laguna: 138
Piedras Gordas: 133
piñon pine: 139
pipe cactus: 9
pirates/privateers: 22-23, 100-101, 184, 186-187
pitahaya: 9
Planta Empacadoro: 188-189
Playa Costa Azul: 167, 170, 177
playas: see beaches
Plaza Constitución: 103, 105
Plaza Mijares: 158-159
police procedures: 72-73
Polk, James: 27
population: 30; see also specific place
Portuguese men-of-war: 64
postal service: 80, 129, 171, 209, 234; see also specific place
pottery/ceramics: 118, 169, 213-214
prickly pear: 9, 139
private boats/yachts: see boating; ocean cruises/yacht travel
Prohibition in U.S.: 29, 65
property, purchase/lease of: 70-71
Pueblo La Playa: 154, 167
Puerto Algodones: 224
Puerto Campechano: 224
Punta Arena: 150
Punta Arenas de la Ventana: 132-133
Punta Colorada: 149-150
Punta Conejo: 225
Punta El Mechudo: 124
Punta Gaspereño: 216
Punta Gorda: 154
Punta Lobos: 222, 224
Punta Marqués: 225
Punta Pescadero: 145

QR
Querencia: 182
rabbits: 12-13

Race and Sports Book: *see* Caliente Race and Sports Book
rainfall: *see* climate
Rancho Boca de La Vinorama: 154
Rancho San Dionísio: 136, 138
Rancho San Luis: 154
Rancho Santa Elena: 154
Rancho Tule: 154
rays: 16
recompression chambers: 46, 205
Red Rose (La Rosa) Riding Stables: 207
reefs: 127, 133, 151-152, 177, 204, 225
rental cars: general discussion 85-86, 97-98; Cabo San Lucas 211; La Paz 131; San José del Cabo 173; *see also* driving; road/routes; *specific place*
Reyes Collins: 207-208
roadblocks: 72-73
roads/routes: general discussion 91-94; Bahía de Los Fraíles/San José Del Cabo 154; Bahía de los Muertos 133; Cape Loop 33-34; Cascada del Refugio 219; distances 91; El Camino Rural Costero 150; La Candelaria 213, 215; Playa San Pedrito 217; Punta Marqués 225; San Antonio 135; Sierra de La Laguna 143; Transpeninsular Highway 30, 174; West Cape 212-213; *see also specific place*
Roca Montaña: 133
Roca Pelícanos: 187, 204
rodents: 13
rodeos: 117, 200-201
Rogers, Woodes: 23, 101
RVs/trailers: general discussion 97; fuel/oil 95-96; service/supplies 171; *see also* campgrounds/RV parks; driving; roads/routes

S

safety/precautions: 65, 92-94; *see also* health/first aid
sailboarding: *see* windsurfing/sailboarding
Salvatierra: 126-127
Salvatierra, Padre Juan María: 24

San Antonio de la Sierra: 134-136
San Bartolo: 135-136
San Evaristo: 124
San José del Cabo: general discussion 155-156; accommodations 160-163; campgrounds/RV parks 163-164; climate 155; entertainment 168-169; festivals/events 169; food/restaurants 164-168; history 156-158; services 171-172; shopping 169-170; sights 158-160; sports/recreation 170-171; tourist information 171; transportation 172-173; *see also* Accommodations Index; Restaurant Index; *specific place*
San Juan de los Planes: 132
San Pedro: 134, 216-217
Santa Anna, Antonio López de: 26-27
Santander: 118
Santa Rita: 136
Santiago: 136-138
Santo Domingo: 136
schools/universities: Centro de Idiomas, Cultura y Comunicación (CICC) 129; Instituto Tecnológico de La Paz 106; La Unidad Cultural Profesor Jesús Castro Agúndez 105; Universidad Autonomía de Baja California Sur 106
scorpions: 19, 63-64
scuba diving: *see* diving/snorkeling
sea kayaking: *see* kayaking
sea lions: 13, 127, 151, 187, 222, 224
Sea of Cortez: general discussion 1-2, 4-5; climate 6-7; endangered marine life 15; *see also specific place*
sea urchins: 64
seawall promedade: 105-106
Selkirk, Alexander: 23
Sergio Bustamante: 201
sharks: 16, 127
shellfish: 17
shipwrecks: 126-127, 132-133, 152, 177
shopping: Cabo San Lucas 201-202; customs regulations 68-

69, 71-72; El Pescadero 215-216; La Candaleria 213-214; La Paz 118; San José del Cabo 169-170; Spanish phrases 246; Todos Santos 232-234; *see also specific place; product*
shuttle boats: 123
sierra: 16, 33, 217, 219
Sierra de La Laguna: 2-3, 138-143
skiffs/*pangas*: 122, 125, 132-133, 203-204, 231-232; *see also specific place*
snakes: 19
snapper: 16
snorkeling: *see* diving/snorkeling
soft drinks: 57
Sol Dorado: 169
sotol: 10
Spanish conquest/rule: 21-26, 100, 156-157, 184, 186; *see also specific person; place*
Spanish language/phrase translation: bar lingo 60; classes/courses 129; driving terms/auto parts 96; fish 38; foods 52-53; glossary 241-242; maps 34; phrasebook 243-247; road signs 94
spiny lobster: 17
sports equipment: *see* outfitters/sports equipment
sports/recreation: general discussion 34-46, 69;

SURFING

general discussion: 44-45
best surfing areas: 33
Cabo San Lucas: 208
The Corridor: 177
Pescadero Surf Camp: 216
Punta Arena: 150
Punta Conejo: 225
Punta Gaspereño: 216
Punta Gorda: 154
Punta Marqués: 225
Rancho Boca de La Vinorama: 154
San José del Cabo: 170-171
Todos Santos: 232

sports/recreation *(continued):*
Cabo San Lucas 202-208; The
Corridor 177, 181-182; La Paz
124-128; San José del Cabo
170-171; Todos Santos 231-
232; *see also specific
activity; place; sport*
squid: 16
statehood: 29-30
Stewart, Charles, Gallery &
Studio: 233
stingrays: 64
storage: 172
storms: 7, 100; *see also specific
place*
submarine canyon: 204
sugarcane: 221-222, 224
sunburn: 62
sunset cruises: 206
surfcasting: 204, 232

T
tackle: 37-38, 124, 204; *see also
specific place*
Tamaral, Nicolás: 157-158
Taraval, Padre Sigismundo: 221
Taxco Silver: 201
taxes/tipping: 75
taxi service: general discussion
88-89; Cabo San Lucas 211; La
Paz 131; San José del Cabo
173; Todos Santos 235; *see
also specific place*
tea: 57
teddy-bear cholla: 9
telephone/long distance service:
general discussion 76-80; area
codes 77; Cabo San Lucas
209; La Paz 129; San José del
Cabo 171; Todos Santos 234-
235; *see also specific place*
tennis: 170
tequila: 57-59
Texas Independence: 27
theater/performing arts: Teatro de
la Ciudad 105; Teatro Márquez
de León 230
Tianguis Marina 201
ticks: 63
tide tables: 38, 41, 45
Tienda Santander: 233
tiles: 118
time-shares: 71, 202

time zone: 76
Tlaco palm: 3, 10
Todos Santos: general discussion
220; accommodations 225-227;
beaches 222, 224-225;
campgrounds/RV parks 227-
228; climate 220-221;
entertainment 230-231;
festivals/events 231;
food/restaurants 228-230;
history 221-222; services 234-
235; shopping 232-234; sights
222; sports/recreation 231-232;
tourist information 234;
transportation 235; *see also
Accommodations Index;
Restaurant Index*
Todos Santos Fiesta del Arte: 231
topographical maps: 82, 142
Topolobambo-La Paz ferry: 87
tourista: 61-62
tourist information: 81, 239-240;
see also specific place
tours: *see* guides/tours
trails: 34, 141
Transpeninsular Highway: 30, 174
transportation: 82-98; Spanish
phrases 245-246; *see also
specific mode of transport;
place*
travel clubs/discounts: 81
travel seasons: 7-8, 37, 99-100,
142
trees: 3-4, 10-12
tropical forests: 3; *see also
specific place*
Tropic of Cancer: 6, 138, 220
tuna: 16; *see also specific place*
turtles: 18

UV
Uget: 118
United States: Consular Agent
209; customs/reentry
regulations 39, 68-69, 71-72;
import restrictions 71-72;
Mexican-American War 26-28,
102, 158; Mexican Consulate
68; overseas visitors entering
U.S. from Mexico 68;
Prohibition 29, 65; tourist
permits/visas for U.S. citizens
66-68

Universidad Autonomía de Baja
California Sur: 106
vegetarian/natural foods: 115-
116, 165, 216
vehicles: *see* driving
Vela-Neil Pryde Baja
Championships: 146
venomous snakes: 19
Veryka: 169
Vigilantes Marinos: 204-205
Villa, Pancho: 28
visas: 66-68
Vizcaíno, Sebastián: 23, 100,
156, 184

W
wahoo: 16
walking/nature trails: 159, 171
War of Reform: 27-28
wasps/bees/hornets: 63
water taxis: 211
weavers: 118
web sites: 239-240; *see also
specific place*
weights/measures: 76
Weiskopf, Tom: 181-182
wetlands: 3-4
whales/whalewatching: general
discussion 13; Cabo Pulmo
152; Cabo San Lucas 208; La
Paz 128; Todos Santos 232
what to bring: 34-35, 37
wild figs: 3, 12, 139
wild plums: 3
willows: 11
windsurfing/sailboarding: general
discussion 43-44; Bahía de la
Ventana 132; Bahía de Palmas
144; best windsurfing areas 33;
Cabo San Lucas 208; Los
Barriles 146-147; Vela-Neil
Pryde Baja Championships 146
wine: 60
Woodes, Rogers: 184, 186

XYZ
yachts: *see* boating; ocean
cruises/yacht travel
youth hostels: *see* hostels
yucca: 9-10
Zahuapán: 233
Zapata, Emiliano: 28
zoos: 136

ABOUT THE AUTHOR

Joe Cummings has written about travel and culture for many years. Attracted to geographical extremes, his first in-depth journeys involved the river deltas and rainforests of Southeast Asia, where he worked as a Peace Corps volunteer (Thailand) and university lecturer (Malaysia). He later contributed to popular guidebooks on Thailand, Malaysia, Singapore, Burma, Laos, Indonesia, and China.

Joe became infatuated with desert terrains while exploring the Sierra del Carmen and Chihuahuan Desert reaches of Texas's Big Bend Country for Moon's *Texas Handbook.* His love of South Texas border culture, including *norteña* music and food, eventually spilled over into Mexico. He has since clocked over 50,000 miles on peninsular roads and is now a full-time resident of Baja.

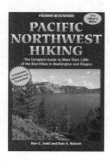

FOR TRAVELERS WITH
SPECIAL INTERESTS

GUIDES

The 100 Best Small Art Towns in America • Asia in New York City
The Big Book of Adventure Travel • Cities to Go
Cross-Country Ski Vacations • Gene Kilgore's Ranch Vacations
Great American Motorcycle Tours • Healing Centers and Retreats
Indian America • Into the Heart of Jerusalem
The People's Guide to Mexico • The Practical Nomad
Saddle Up! • Staying Healthy in Asia, Africa, and Latin America
Steppin' Out • Travel Unlimited • Understanding Europeans
Watch It Made in the U.S.A. • The Way of the Traveler
Work Worldwide • The World Awaits
The Top Retirement Havens • Yoga Vacations

SERIES

Adventures in Nature
The Dog Lover's Companion
Kidding Around
Live Well

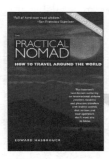
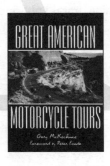

MOON HANDBOOKS

provide comprehensive coverage of a region's arts, history, land, people, and social issues in addition to detailed practical listings for accommodations, food, outdoor recreation, and entertainment. Moon Handbooks allow complete immersion in a region's culture—ideal for travelers who want to combine sightseeing with insight for an extraordinary travel experience.

USA

Alaska-Yukon • Arizona • Big Island of Hawaii • Boston
Coastal California • Colorado • Connecticut • Georgia
Grand Canyon • Hawaii • Honolulu-Waikiki • Idaho • Kauai
Los Angeles • Maine • Massachusetts • Maui • Michigan
Montana • Nevada • New Hampshire • New Mexico
New York City • New York State • North Carolina
Northern California • Ohio • Oregon • Pennsylvania
San Francisco • Santa Fe-Taos • Silicon Valley
South Carolina • Southern California • Tahoe • Tennessee
Texas • Utah • Virginia • Washington • Wisconsin
Wyoming • Yellowstone-Grand Teton

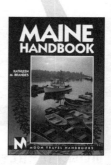

INTERNATIONAL

Alberta and the Northwest Territories • Archaeological Mexico
Atlantic Canada • Australia • Baja • Bangkok • Bali • Belize
British Columbia • Cabo • Canadian Rockies • Cancún
Caribbean Vacations • Colonial Mexico • Costa Rica • Cuba
Dominican Republic • Ecuador • Fiji • Havana • Honduras
Hong Kong • Indonesia • Jamaica • Mexico City • Mexico
Micronesia • The Moon • Nepal • New Zealand • Northern Mexico
Oaxaca • Pacific Mexico • Pakistan • Philippines • Puerto Vallarta
Singapore • South Korea • South Pacific • Southeast Asia • Tahiti
Thailand • Tonga-Samoa • Vancouver • Vietnam, Cambodia and Laos
Virgin Islands • Yucatán Peninsula

www.moon.com

www.travelmatters.com

User-friendly, informative, and fun:
Because travel *matters.*

Visit our newly launched web site and explore the variety of titles and travel information available online, featuring an interactive *Road Trip USA* exhibit.

also check out:

www.ricksteves.com

The Rick Steves web site is bursting with information to boost your travel I.Q. and liven up your European adventure.

www.foghorn.com

Visit the Foghorn Outdoors web site for more information on the premier source of U.S. outdoor recreation guides.

www.moon.com

The Moon Handbooks web site offers interesting information and practical advice that ensure an extraordinary travel experience.

U.S.~METRIC CONVERSION

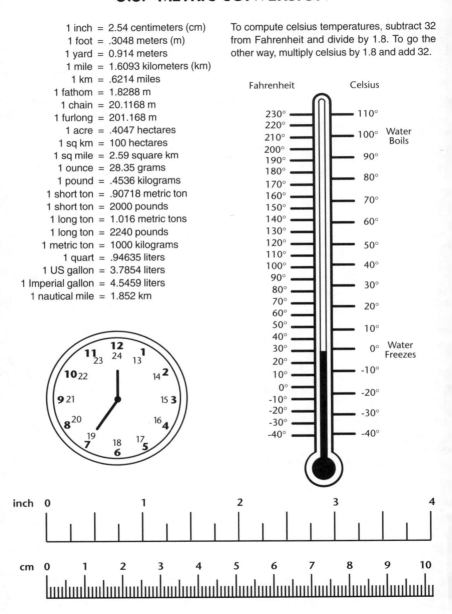

1 inch	= 2.54 centimeters (cm)
1 foot	= .3048 meters (m)
1 yard	= 0.914 meters
1 mile	= 1.6093 kilometers (km)
1 km	= .6214 miles
1 fathom	= 1.8288 m
1 chain	= 20.1168 m
1 furlong	= 201.168 m
1 acre	= .4047 hectares
1 sq km	= 100 hectares
1 sq mile	= 2.59 square km
1 ounce	= 28.35 grams
1 pound	= .4536 kilograms
1 short ton	= .90718 metric ton
1 short ton	= 2000 pounds
1 long ton	= 1.016 metric tons
1 long ton	= 2240 pounds
1 metric ton	= 1000 kilograms
1 quart	= .94635 liters
1 US gallon	= 3.7854 liters
1 Imperial gallon	= 4.5459 liters
1 nautical mile	= 1.852 km

To compute celsius temperatures, subtract 32 from Fahrenheit and divide by 1.8. To go the other way, multiply celsius by 1.8 and add 32.

Fahrenheit   Celsius

230° — 110°
220°
210° — 100° Water Boils
200°
190° — 90°
180°
170° — 80°
160° — 70°
150°
140° — 60°
130°
120° — 50°
110°
100° — 40°
90°
80° — 30°
70°
60° — 20°
50°
40° — 10°
30° — 0° Water Freezes
20°
10° — -10°
0°
-10° — -20°
-20° — -30°
-30°
-40° — -40°

inch 0   1   2   3   4

cm 0 1 2 3 4 5 6 7 8 9 10

Planning Your Vacation Just Got Easier

Next time, make your *own* hotel arrangements.

Yahoo! Travel

Do You YAHOO!?